D1261297

## ABOUT THE AUTHOR

J. M. C. TOYNBEE is Laurence Professor *Emerita* of Classical Archaeology at Cambridge University, and is a member of the Faculty of Archaeology, History, and Letters of the British School at Rome. She is a Fellow of the British Academy, the Society of Antiquaries of London, and the Royal Numismatic Society, and is also a Vice-President of the Society for the Promotion of Roman Studies. Professor Toynbee studied at Cambridge and Oxford Universities, and she is the author of *The Art of the Romans.*

ASPECTS OF GREEK AND ROMAN LIFE

*General Editor: H. H. Scullard*

* * *

# DEATH AND BURIAL IN THE ROMAN WORLD

*J. M. C. Toynbee*

# DEATH AND BURIAL IN THE ROMAN WORLD

J. M. C. Toynbee

CORNELL UNIVERSITY PRESS
ITHACA, NEW YORK

*First published 1971*

International Standard Book Number 0–8014–0593–9

Library of Congress Catalog Card Number 77–120603

PRINTED IN ENGLAND

# CONTENTS

# LIST OF ILLUSTRATIONS

PLATES

FIGURES

## CHAPTER I

# ETRUSCAN ANTECEDENTS

### (A) ETRURIA AND ROME

AMONG ALL THE SPHERES of social and religious life in which Rome was deeply and permanently indebted to Etruria, that of burial customs may justly claim pride of place. Hence it is self-evident that at least some general consideration of Etruscan afterlife ideas, and of the practices and monuments relating to the dead which those ideas inspired, must form the essential prelude to any understanding and discussion of their Roman counterparts. There are, indeed, certain marked features of Etruscan other-world beliefs and funerary art which find no place in Rome. Some ideas and customs inherited initially from the Etruscans developed very differently in the Roman world, where potent influences, other than Etruria's, were also at work. Roman tomb-art, in particular, was immeasurably wider in its range than was Etruria's, both in style and content. Nonetheless, there persisted, down to the end of the pagan Empire, at any rate, habits of thought and forms of architectural and artistic expression concerned with the cult of the departed that remained unmistakably Etruscan in their origins.

### (B) IDEAS ON DEATH AND THE AFTERLIFE

For the Etruscans' ideas on death and the afterlife, as for their funerary customs, all the evidence is archaeological, derived from the nature of their cemeteries and from the wall-paintings and the sculptures that adorned their tombs. No other people has displayed a greater preoccupation—not to say obsession—with man's fate at and after death. None has been more lavish in providing, in the terms of this life, for the soul's life beyond the grave, whether that life was conceived of as lived in the tomb itself or in some invisible, probably subterranean, realm of the deceased. For, wherever the dead dwelt, their condition was clearly believed to resemble that of the living very closely and to require the surroundings and amenities (food, vessels for cooking, eating, and drinking, toilet articles, arms, armour, and the like, either real or counterfeited in art) that had been familiar to them in their mundane existence.

In the tomb-paintings of the sixth and fifth centuries BC the prevailing theme may be said to be Elysium, with the dead imagined as enjoying, either as participants or as spectators, the jollities, sports, and pleasant pastimes of a well-to-do and cultured people—feasting,[1] fishing and fowling,[2] athletic games,[3] horsemanship,[4] dancing,[5] and music,[6] often portrayed in an idyllic setting of trees, plants, flitting birds, and dangling flower-garlands. Of all these motifs that of the *symposium* (drinking party), where the departed are seen reclining, in groups or singly, at other-world banquets,[7] was destined to enjoy the greatest vogue and the longest history, far on into the story of Roman art. Some such Etruscan scenes of later (fourth-century and Hellenistic) date depict, in painting, a husband reclining at the feast on a couch at the foot of which his wife is seated[8] or sculptural figures, single or paired, of banqueters.[9] Meanwhile, in the funerary art of the earlier centuries death itself, the actual passage from this life to the next, is relatively seldom portrayed; and little reference is made to those divinities and their agents whom a man or woman must encounter in the awesome process of the sundering of soul and body. One of the earliest known representations of such beings is a late-fifth-century bronze statuette from Campania of a Vanth, a kindly-faced, winged, female creature, who carries a snake, symbol of the dead, on either wrist.[10] An early-fourth-century sculptural group, worked in stone, shows a dead youth reclining at ease in the afterlife, with a gentle Vanth, who holds an open scroll of destiny, seated protectingly at his feet.[11] But in a similarly composed group of roughly the same date the banqueter, an elderly man, wears, most unusually, a troubled look and is accompanied by a grotesquely-featured goddess of the dead, who lays her hand upon his wrist.[12] From this time onwards, although the friendly Vanths do not vanish, there are sculptures in which less kindly ones make their appearance.[13] These, however, are mild in mien as compared with the hideous male demons that now repeatedly confront us, particularly in painting, and of whom Charun, beak-nosed, blue-fleshed, grasping or swinging a hammer or clutching a pair of menacing serpents, is by far the most grisly.[14] (*Pls.* 1, 2)

It does, in fact, seem to be the case that during the fourth century BC the Etruscans' attitude to death underwent a change that endured until late in the story of their culture. Not only are these terrifying demons virtually new at the beginning of this period to their funerary art, but concurrently, both in their tomb-paintings and in the reliefs on their ash-chests and sarcophagi, the choice of mythological themes evinces a prevailing taste for scenes of slaughter and violent destruction—the fratricidal ends of Eteocles and Polynices, the sacrifice of Polyxena, the murder of the Trojan captives at the tomb of Patroclus, the deaths of Agamemnon and Clytaemestra, the death of Amphiaraus, the fatal chariot race of Pelops and Oenomaus, and other episodes of the same character. There is likewise a partiality for battle-pieces, bloody beast-fights, and so forth. All this has been held to be accounted for by political and economic causes, by Etruria's loss of independence and wealth and by the impoverishment of her countryside, as Rome's control of the Italian peninsula spread and tightened.[15] Disasters such as these, it has been urged, produced a state of pessimism and despair in this life which was matched by a concept of the next world as a place of unrelieved horror and suffering.

It is not, however, very easy to reconcile this theory of widespread moral and material depression with the fact that a number of the most elaborate and ambitious tomb-paintings of Etruria date from the fourth and third centuries;[16] that the fourth, third, and second centuries witnessed a quite remarkably flourishing art of the decoration with reliefs (based on late-classical and Hellenistic models, or at any rate worked in late-classical and Hellenistic styles) of stone sarcophagi[17] and of alabaster and terracotta ash-chests;[18] and that the undiminished care bestowed on their cemeteries and on providing for their dead's necessities suggests no wish on the part of the Etruscans to keep reminders of the next world at a distance. Nor can we cavalierly dismiss as mere meaningless tradition[19] the large-scale figures of the dead on the lids of sarcophagi and ash-chests, now sleeping peacefully on their backs,[20] now reclining, well-groomed and contented, at the other-world banquet—figures, mainly in the round, which dominate the grim or melancholy scenes in relief below them. The change, whatever caused it, whether national misfortunes or a heightened sensitiveness to the tragic and pathetic elements in human destiny, would appear to have been less concerned with the life beyond death than with the process of death itself as the moment of the painful parting of relatives and friends,[21] of the violent and irrevocable separation of the soul from the body (hence the nails and the hammers that feature in this later funerary art),[22] of judgment passed on conduct in this life,[23] and of encounter with the fearsome beings thought to be the agents of these ordeals. The idea of death as a dread and dangerous experience is not incompatible with belief in happiness for the departed once its 'gloomy portals' had been left behind. The group of the worried-looking banqueter and his sinister companion (p. 12) would seem to be exceptional. Occasionally even in this latter-day Etruscan art a light-hearted episode from Elysium takes the place of the gruesome themes. A later stone sarcophagus, for example, shows the occupant in effigy fast asleep on the lid, while on one long side a cheerful game of kottabos is being played by two men, with some alert, but not unfriendly, serpents looking on to remind the spectator that the scene is laid in the world beyond the grave.[24] Death's inevitability and violence, the grief of parting, and the thought of judgment to come are, of course, recurring themes in Roman literature and tomb-art. But Etruria's horrifying demons as presiding at every death Rome rejected totally. She accepted the Greek Erinyes, but reserved their tortures for the damned in Hell. (*Pl.* 3)

## (c) FUNERARY RITES

There is no direct evidence that beliefs about death and the after-life had any special bearing on the methods used by the Etruscans for disposing of their dead. The two rites of cremation and inhumation (the term that is used loosely to cover all cases of non-cremation) existed contemporaneously in all regions and the choice of the one or the other would appear to have been determined mainly by family tradition and individual preference.[25] But burning and the burial of unburnt remains, if never mutually exclusive as regards place and period, were not practised everywhere and at all times in the same proportions. The former was, on the whole, less frequent than the latter in the early period, becoming commoner from the fourth to the second centuries, and it prevailed in the central and northern areas; whereas inhumation was chiefly in favour in the south and along the western coast. Any large pot or jar could be used for the ashes of cremated persons. But from the late-eighth to the early-sixth centuries such relics were sometimes put into terracotta vessels that resembled in shape a rudimentary human form ensconced in a high-backed chair—the so-called Canopic urns.[26] Other early receptacles were large terracotta vases and cinerary urns of bronze or terracotta imitating dwelling huts, rectangular or round.[27] There are also life-size stone human figures, dating from the second half of the fifth century, which contained cremated remains.[28] In the later period, from the early-fourth-century onwards, besides the more sophisticated imitations of houses in stone or terracotta,[29] rectangular ash-chests of alabaster or terracotta, elaborately decorated with reliefs and surmounted by effigies, were the normal fashion.[30] When the body was to be burnt, a pyre to receive the corpse and some of the dead person's goods, would have been prepared near the tomb in which the ashes were destined to be placed. (*Pl.* 4)

As regards inhumations, in the early Etruscan period plain sarcophagi of wood or stone were set in the earth or rock in trench-graves (the equivalent of Roman *fossae*). When chamber-tombs began to become general towards the end of the seventh and in the sixth century, sarcophagi made of various materials and artistically adorned were disposed in them, either free-standing or on benches along the walls.[31] In some early chamber-tombs, on the other hand, the unburnt bodies were not enclosed in sarcophagi, but left to corrupt on funerary beds. In the seventh century these beds were the real ones of wood or metal on which the dead had been laid out at home and carried to the grave; from the sixth to the fourth century they were stone ones cut from the sides of rock-hewn tombs. Such imitation beds were either plain, block-like benches along the walls of the chamber, occasionally painted to resemble true beds, or realistically sculptured copies of actual funerary beds, with matresses, pillows, carved legs, and so forth, the most elaborate examples being those in the Tomb of the Alcove and the Tomb of the Reliefs at Caere (Cerveteri).[32] There are also quite simple imitation beds in shelf-like recesses slit into the rock of the walls (resembling Roman *loculi*);[33] and beds in the form of a trough, hollowed out of the rock, into which the corpse was lowered, the later examples of this type having gables at head and feet, but no lids, thus forming as it were half-sarcophagi.

The stucco work in the Tomb of the Reliefs at Caere gives an exceptionally complete picture of the items of daily life, including pet animals and birds, that the departed were believed to need in their other-worldly abode, that is, of the grave-goods, real or simulated, with which the Etruscan dead, whether cremated or inhumed, were always richly furnished (*cf.* pp. 52–4, 142, 143).

A death-bed scene—one of the few direct allusions in early Etruscan art to death itself (*cf.* p. 12)—is vividly portrayed in a painting in archaic style in the Tomb of the Dying or Dead Man at Tarquinia.[34] On an elaborate bed, with carved legs, a thick, embroidered matress, and two stout pillows, there lies upon his back a man who is either on the point of death or has just expired. A woman, presumably his wife, with long, dishevelled hair, is mounted on a footstool beside the bed and adjusts on her husband's head the hood of a long, enveloping cape, which a man standing at the foot of the bed arranges round the legs of the prostrate form. This man raises his right hand to his head in an attitude of grief, as do also two other men who stand respectively to right and left of the central group.[35] Another archaic work, a stone funerary bed in the Camucia Tomb at Cortona, shows in relief on the front eight women mourners, most probably professionals, kneeling on the ground in two confronted groups of four: the leader of each group tears her cheeks, while the rest beat their breasts.[36]

It is not known precisely how long an interval of time was allowed to elapse in Etruria between death and the funeral, while the body lay exposed in the house and the lamentations of relatives, friends, and professional mourners continued around it. Persons of all these three categories, together with musicians, doubtless formed the procession from the home to the tomb, the body on its funerary bed being either borne by bearers or transported on a cart.[37] But in later Etruscan art, in which most of the known processional scenes relating to death are found, a symbolic journey of the dead from this life to the next is, as a rule, substituted for the real cortège. In reliefs on sarcophagi and ash-chests the dead appear as though alive, walking or riding on horseback or drawn along in chariots or carts, often accompanied by relatives and friends, to whom they sometimes bid a sorrowful farewell, and by demons of death.[38] Similar renderings occur in tomb-paintings of the later period.[39] A number of sarcophagus and ash-chest reliefs show a dead man in his capacity as magistrate riding in state in a chariot, with attendants bearing *fasces* and musicians walking on foot before or behind him.[40]

It could be that some of the idyllic scenes in early Etruscan funerary painting of feasting, athletic exercises, dancing, music, and so forth (*cf.* p. 12) carry a twofold meaning and refer partly to the jovialities enjoyed by the dead in Elysium and partly to the banquets, games, and other shows that were held on the occasion of a death, or to honour the departed's memory, by the survivors in this world. The second interpretation is suggested by the fact that there are instances of these performances shown as deployed on either side of a large, firmly-closed, and nail-studded door, presumably that of the tomb.[41] In a frieze in the Tomb of the Lionesses at Tarquinia there are dancers at either end and in the centre a lyre-player and a piper flanking an enormous two-handled wine jar, of clay or pale metal, that stands on the ground between them and is wreathed with leaves.[42] Perhaps this jar functioned as an ash-urn; alternatively, and more probably, it may be a symbol of the funeral feast.

## (D) TOMB-FORMS AND CEMETERIES

One of the earliest and simplest Etruscan tomb-forms used for cremated remains was the cylindrical well ('pozzo'), cut in the rock or dug in the earth to a depth of between 3 and 5 metres, at the bottom of which there was generally a second, smaller well closed by a stone slab and containing the pot that served as cinerary receptacle. If the well was a single one, the ashes were put in a pot which, together with the grave-goods, was enclosed in a large jar sealed by a flat stone. Above the burial the well was filled up to ground level with stones and earth.[43] The early trench-graves, already mentioned in connection with the rite of inhumation (*cf.* p. 13), were rectangular in shape and excavated in the earth or rock. Occasionally these *fossae* have been found to contain cremations; and the furniture placed around the human relics, whether burnt or inhumed, was, on the whole, richer than that in the well-tombs.[44] It was probably from the trench-tomb that developed the third and most characteristically Etruscan type of sepulchre, the chamber-tomb.[45]

The seventh-century Regolini-Galassi Tomb at Caere (Sorbo necropolis) might, indeed, almost be described as a colossal trench-grave.[46] It consists of a corridor, 40 metres long and about 2 metres wide. The lowest part of the walls of this corridor is rock-cut, but the rest of them is built up in large, squared blocks of tufa and at the top the walls bend inwards to form a truncated ogival vault fashioned of similar blocks. Roughly half-way along the corridor two oval compartments, cut in the tufa, open off it symmetrically to right and left. The whole was covered by a huge circular tumulus over 47 metres in diameter: this comprised a double ring-wall of masonry at the base, which was once surmounted by the conical, grass-grown mound that is typical of the great Etruscan cemeteries at Caere (Banditaccia necropolis), Tarquinia (where the mounds, formerly existing, have now largely disappeared), Volterra, and other sites. (*Cf. Pl.* 5)

The Regolini-Galassi burial-chamber represents the simplest type of chamber-tomb. The great majority of the Caeretan, partly rock-cut, partly masonry-built, tombs under tumuli are much more complex in plan.[47] They are multi-roomed, composed of anything up to seven rectangular compartments, of which the middle ones are generally the largest, with the smaller ones opening off them. All are symmetrically arranged about a central axis and they are approached from the outer edge of the tumulus by a corridor or *dromos*. Most of the smaller tumuli held one chamber-tomb only: one of the more complicated of these is the Tomb of the Capitals in Tumulus V, with its two rounded pillars upholding the flat ceiling of its central oblong room.[48] But of the colossal mounds, Tumulus I covers two, Tumulus II four, the Tumulus of the Nave five, the Tumulus of the Painted Animals four, and the Tumulus of the Shields and Chairs three chamber-tombs. These monumental round barrows, with their masonry ring-walls, neatly bevelled externally at their bases,[49] and their numerous lesser brethren,[50] together with the spacious and harmoniously proportioned chamber-tombs that all, both large and small, contain, were architecturally the Etruscans' most imposing sepulchral legacies to Rome (*cf.* pp. 143–4, 170–88).

By no means all the well-designed chamber-tombs at Caere are under tumuli. A large number of them, also partly cut in the rock and partly built of masonry, lacked that protection and had only a relatively slight earth covering above their roofs. These vary greatly in size; and most of them are, like those in the mounds, approached by corridors of differing lengths. Some are complex, multi-roomed chamber-tombs. Others consist of a single large compartment which is sometimes just a plain rectangle, sometimes a plain rectangle partially divided into two by short projecting cross-walls, sometimes a rectangle with alcoves in its sides. An outstanding instance of the last type is the Tomb of the Reliefs, which has thirteen alcoves and two square pilasters supporting its ceiling.[51]

Some of the tombs not surmounted by tumuli seem to have stood, either singly or in groups of three or four, within precinct walls; while large numbers of those not so confined are arranged either in compact blocks of confronted chambers or in long series of chambers that are almost identical with one another in shape and size, strung out in rows. In the central section (the 'Recinto') of the Banditaccia necropolis there are, for example, rows of this kind comprising five, eight, and thirteen tombs. Such blocks and rows have all the appearance of having been built as units; and it it is the regular and careful 'town-planning' of this cemetery area at Caere which is one of its most arresting and important features.

A long street (*via principalis*) runs east and west right through the 'Recinto' and with it are aligned, on the north side, the great Tumuli I and II and several lesser tumuli: on the south side are more small tumuli and the row of thirteen chamber-tombs, with their entrance-corridors leading from the street. At the western end of the 'Recinto' a minor street, lined with tombs set singly or in blocks along it, runs into the main street obliquely. Between Tumuli I and II is a street running north and south lined on the west by eight chamber-tombs and on the east by three. It is joined towards its northern end by another minor street lined on each side by tombs. The circumferences of Tumuli I and II are linked on the south by a street running parallel to the *via principalis* and lined on its southern side by a row of four tombs which face on to this lesser byway and turn their backs to the main thoroughfare. In the eastern sector of the 'Recinto' three more minor streets fork southwards from the *via principalis*, the angles between them being filled by small tumuli and rows or groups of other tombs more or less aligned with each street. Finally, right at the eastern end of the 'Recinto', a street running north and south between the *via principalis* and the easternmost of the three forking streets is bordered on the east by an even row of five rectangular tombs all of almost the same dimensions and form. The whole street-plan of the 'Recinto' is, in fact, not unreminiscent of that of the Roman city of Ostia.[52] Outside the 'Recinto' to the south-west there is a much more sporadic scatter of four big tumuli and various other chamber-tombs; but along the line of the *via principalis*, to east and west of the crowded nucleus of the necropolis, tumuli and tombs are strung out continuously.

The Tarquinia necropolis,[53] justly famed for the paintings in its rock-cut chamber-tombs, offers today nothing in the way of the systematic planning of streets and tomb-groups that marks the 'Recinto' at Caere. But at Vulci the rock-cut, multi-roomed chamber-tombs in the Mandrione di Cavalupo necropolis are in

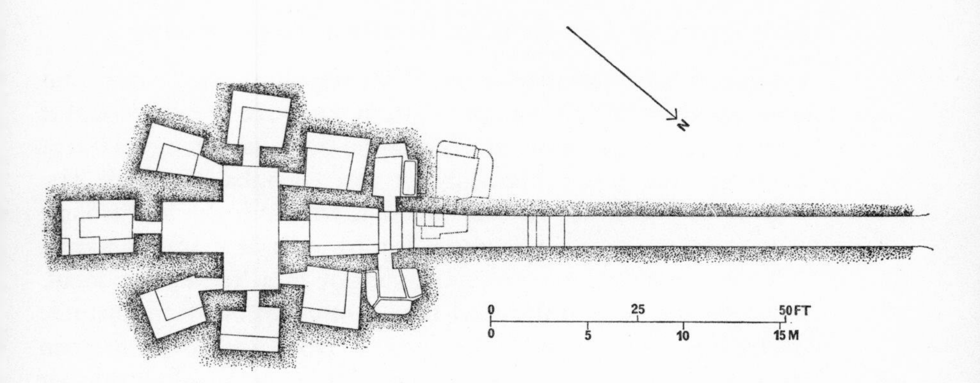


*Fig. 1 The François Tomb, Vulci*

regular rows and more or less aligned with the street, about 5 metres wide, that runs through the cemetery from north-east to south-west and with paths along the bank of the River Fiora.[54] As at Caere, these tombs are approached by corridors. One of the tombs in this area is covered by a tumulus, but the rest are without tumuli; and a characteristic tomb-form is the long, narrow type in which the entrance-corridor is continued right through to the room at the back and has symmetrical series of rooms opening off it to right and left. One of them has as many as thirteen compartments on either side of its corridor and ten compartments opening off the room at the end. The François Tomb in the Ponte Rotto necropolis at Vulci is a signal instance of the balanced and complex planning of a late-Etruscan chamber-tomb.[55] The long, narrow entrance-corridor widens into a room at its head and throws off, just before the widening, two lateral rooms to right and left. The widened portion of the corridor is connected by a passage with the central room, shaped like an inverted T, from which seven subsidiary rooms radiate symmetrically. The only asymmetry results from a second lateral room thrown off, perhaps at a later stage, by the corridor on its western side.

All the Etruscan chamber-tombs so far discussed consist of, or comprise, rooms that are rectangular, or virtually rectangular, in form. Volterra provides examples of the circular or *tholos* type, with the roof upheld by a central pillar. Some of these are of masonry, with walls built up in blocks or slabs and pseudo-vaults composed of concentric rings of overlapping slabs converging on the point at which the summit of the supporting pillar, formed now of many small, now of a few large, hewn stones, meets them. Such are the Casal Marittimo,[56] and Casaglia Tombs.[57] The Inghirami Tomb, on the other hand, is wholly rock-cut.[58] (*Pl.* 7)

Among the simplest Etruscan tombs built of masonry blocks wholly above ground are those ranged in a 'terrace' of small, contiguous houses of the dead along a street in the Tufa Crucifix necropolis at Orvieto.[59] These have 'front-doors', with plain façades above them, and have only a light spread of earth over their roofs, on each of which was placed a cone-shaped *cippus*. Examples of free-standing, masonry, above-ground tombs are the oval one, the so-called Tomb of Pythagoras, at Cortona[60] and the rectangular, temple-like structure, with a pitched roof, at Populonia.[61] The particular significance of all these above-ground Etruscan tomb-types for Roman developments will become obvious at a later stage in this study (*cf.* pp. 117–18, 130–43).

In addition to the rock-cut Etruscan tombs that were completely hollowed out below ground level, or partially sunk into the rock's horizontal surface, there are those that are bored deep into the vertical face of a steep hill or cliff. Most of these have more or less austerely worked façades.[62] But there are some striking instances of tomb-entrances equipped with elaborately carved pillars and entablatures.[63] Many Etruscan tombs of this cave-like type were reused by the Romans, who also imitated them in central Italy by cutting similar burial places of their own, with façades mainly shaped in an unpretentious, simple style. But the most spectacular Roman-age counterparts of the complex Etruscan forms, with their columned porticos and figured friezes, arose independently on the Empire's eastern outskirts (*cf.* pp. 188–99).

One of the most important examples of the latest Etruscan, Romanized, sepulchral architecture is the Tomb of the Volumnii family, dating from the early-first century BC, some three miles from Perugia.[64] It is cut into the tufa of a hillside, and was approached by steps leading down from ground level and entered through a doorway that consists of heavily fashioned lintel, jambs, and threshold. An inscription on the right-hand jamb records the foundation of the tomb by Arnth and Larth Volumnius; and in the gable-shaped space above the doorway is carved in low relief a Medusa on a shield between two dolphins. The tomb itself reflects the layout of a Roman house, with an *atrium*, measuring 7·33 metres in length by 3·6 metres in width, in the centre. The pitched ceiling of the *atrium* simulates wooden beams and its long walls are lined with tufa benches. At the far end of the *atrium* a doorway leads into the principal room or *tablinum*; and in the gable-shaped space above that doorway is carved in relief a Medusa on a shield flanked by two human busts and two swords, on each of which a bird perches. Another Medusa is cut in relief in the central coffer of the *tablinum*'s flat ceiling. The general layout of the whole hypogeum is symmetrical. Two *alae*, with a portrait-bust in relief in the central coffer of the ceiling of each, open out on either side from the end of the *atrium* and each is connected with another room, one on either side of the *tablinum* and extending to the line of the latter's back wall. Four more rooms, approached by short passages, open off the *atrium*, two on either side, two half-way along the *atrium* and two near the entrance-doorway. (*Pl.* 6)

The Tomb of the Volumnii was obviously intended to serve for an extended period, perhaps for a century or more. But its interior decoration was never completed and the burials were confined to the *tablinum*, every other room being found empty by the excavators. It would seem that some unforeseen disaster overtook the family: possibly it came, partially at least, to grief at the time of the destruction of Perugia in 40 BC, after which date only one burial was introduced, that of the wholly Romanized Publius Volumnius Violens, whose marble ash-chest, shaped like a little temple with gabled roof, has relief-ornamentation in the Augustan manner. The other six ash-chests are of stone and are all of the same character and worked in the same, more or less contemporary, style—within about twenty-five years, although four generations of the family are covered by them. Five of them, to judge from the way in which their relief-work is distributed, were designed explicitly for the positions in which they stood in the room when brought to light. In all, the ash-chest proper is raised upon a high pedestal, which, in five cases, is decorated at the corners on the front with four huge nail heads and, with one exception, with a central Medusa head in relief. The pedestal of the most imposing ash-chest, that of Arnth Volumnius, bears on its front two striking figures of Vanths, sculptured almost in the round, who flank a tomb door. Five of the ash-chests, those of men, take the form of a heavily draped funerary bed, on which the dead personage reclines at the heavenly banquet. The chest of the only woman buried in the tomb, Velia Volumnia, is in the shape of a draped, high-backed chair, on which the departed is seated. The grave-goods that were found include a bronze kottabos, arms, bronze jugs, terracotta vessels, and terracotta lamps. The Tomb of the Volumnii and its funerary iconography (apart from the Vanths), with its emphasis on Medusas, elaborate couches, and portrait-like effigies, may be said to rank as one of the most significant of the latest links in the chain that binds Roman to Etruscan burial customs.

1, 2 *Above*, Etruscan dead, men and women, feasting: a wall-painting in the Tomb of the Leopards, Tarquinia. The leopards appear above (p. 12). *Below*, Etruscan husband and wife on a funerary couch, the former reclining, the latter seated at his feet: a wall-painting in the Tomb of the Shields, Tarquinia (p. 12).

3, 4 *Above*, Etruscan stone sarcophagus. On the lid the deceased sleeps on his back. On the trough are carved the sacrifice of Polyxena (centre) and winged underworld deities, etc. (pp. 13, 14). *Below*, the Tomb of the Atian family, Volterra. Terracotta ash-chests, decorated with reliefs and surmounted by effigies, are arranged round the wall and at the base of the central pier (p. 15).

5, 6 *Right*, the stone-vaulted corridor in the seventh-century BC chamber-tomb, the so-called 'La Montagnola', found at Quinto Fiorentino in 1959 (*cf.* p. 18). *Below*, the Tomb of the Volumnii near Perugia. The ash-chests of members of the family can be seen in the *tablinum* at the back. A shield with a Medusa mask and arms are carved above the entrance (pp. 22-4).

7 The *tholos* tomb at Casal Marittimo, Etruria. The wall consists of small masonry blocks. The vault is composed of overlapping rings of masonry converging at the summit of the central supporting pier, which is formed out of four huge stone blocks (pp. 21, 22).

8, 9 *Above*, the stone sarcophagus of Lucius Cornelius Scipio Barbatus. The inscription is surmounted by a Doric frieze (pp. 39, 40, 113). *Below*, marble relief from the Tomb of the Haterii, depicting a lying-in-state in a house (pp. 44, 45).

10, 11 *Above*, marble relief found in Paris, showing a dead girl lying on a couch and mourned by her family (p. 44 and n. 119). *Below*, marble relief from Amiternum depicting a funeral procession. The deceased, lying on his funerary couch, is carried on a bier, preceded by hired mourners and musicians and followed by relations (pp. 46, 47).

12, 13 *Above*, marble statue of an Augustan man carrying ancestral busts (p. 48). *Below*, marble tomb relief showing two profile ancestral busts in little cupboards (pp. 47, 48).

14–16 *Above*, cremation burial from Caerleon. The ashes are in a lead canister, walled and roofed by stone slabs, into which a lead libation pipe leads down from the surface (p. 52). *Below*, the reverses of two *sestertii*, each showing a funerary pyre built up in tiers, struck for the consecration of Antoninus Pius (*left*) and Septimius Severus (*right*) (p. 61).

CHAPTER II

# ROMAN BELIEFS ABOUT THE AFTERLIFE. CREMATION AND INHUMATION

## (A) ROMAN BELIEFS ABOUT THE AFTERLIFE

A FULL-DRESS HISTORY of Roman-age beliefs about the life beyond the grave is obviously not to be expected in this book. Such a history would, in fact, involve a sifting of all the literature and inscriptions, Greek and Latin, belonging to the ancient Roman world, and the study, from the standpoint of the views that they express, of all the surviving works of its funerary art in every medium—sculptures, paintings, mosaics, stucco reliefs, and so forth. Parts of this vast body of material, literary, epigraphical, and artistic, have already formed the subjects of specialized and general treatises on the notions about life after death that were current under the late-Republic and Empire in both pagan and early Christian circles.[65] Here our primary concern is with the evidence, written and archaeological, for funerary practice. But inasmuch as practice depends on faith, in this as in every other aspect of religion, a summary account of the leading trends of thought during this epoch about the nature of the afterlife must precede the detailed analysis of burial customs, of feasts and cult of the dead, and of sepulchral buildings and monuments that will be attempted in the following chapters. In particular, it is in the development of this 'other-worldly' thought that we have to seek the reason for the striking and enduring change in the method of disposing of the dead, from cremation to inhumation, which appeared in Rome and Italy round about the turn of the first and second centuries AD and then spread gradually throughout those areas of the Empire where cremation had hitherto been the normal habit.

With the Romans, as with the Etruscans, the survival of the soul after death was an ancient, deep-seated belief.[66] It is true that during the first centuries BC and AD the sceptical attitude to immortality of the Epicurean and Stoic systems had its repercussions in Rome and Italy and elsewhere in the Roman world. As is very well known, these philosophies taught, on the one hand, that the soul, being itself material, is wholly dispersed at death, on the other, that it loses all individuality and consciousness by absorption into the impersonal life-force of the universe. That such denials of survival were also sometimes to be found outside the ranks of the committed adherents of the schools would seem to be proved by a number of the epitaphs. For example: 'sumus mortales, immortales non sumus';[67] 'omnia cum vita pereunt et inania fiunt';[68] 'nil sumus et fuimus. mortales, respice, lector,/in nihil a nihilo quam cito recidimus';[69] the recurrent formula 'non fui, fui, non sum, non curo';[70] and the Greek sepulchral poem that repudiates the other world and rejects all offerings at the grave as useless, since the dead exist no longer.[71] Such explicitly negative sentiments are, however, by and large, exceptional. Many other epitaphs, if they do not definitely affirm a future life, do not definitely deny it; and Tacitus, for instance, at the end of the *Agricola* leaves the question of another world open.[72] But among the great majority of people of the Roman age, as literature, epigraphy, and the structure and furnishing of tombs make clear, there persisted and prevailed the conviction that some kind of conscious existence is in store for the soul after death and that the dead and living can affect one another mutually. Human life is not just an interlude of being between nothingness and nothingness.

The bulk of our evidence, written and archaeological, for Roman afterlife ideas is not earlier than the first century BC. For the preceding period Plautus (*c.* 250–184 BC) is our chief literary authority. His *Mostellaria* implies, of course, belief that the spirits of the dead can haunt the dwellings of the living; and two of its lines convey the notion that the lower world is barred to the souls of those who have died before their time.[73] He also refers to paintings that depict the tortures of Hades, but does not tell us whether they were Greek, Etruscan, or Roman.[74] For the rest, our knowledge of the views held in early- and mid-Republican times is mainly inferential, derived from Ovid's descriptions in the *Fasti* of the traditional festivals of the dead and from the ancient term *di Manes*. From these sources, and in particular from a passage in Cicero,[75] it can be deduced that the dead at this epoch were regarded as a collectivity, divine and to be venerated as ancestors, but colourless and undifferentiated. If duly propitiated they were capable of aiding their descendents, but were harmful and spiteful to the living if kinless and neglected, under the aspect of *Lemures* and *Larvae*, as Plautus again bears witness.[76]

In Homer and in classical Greek literature and art the dead in the underworld, if condemned to a shadowy and tenuous condition, as contrasted with the fullness of human life on earth, retained their names and were still to some degree themselves. Of this belief in the survival beyond the grave of a person's identity the earliest known evidence in Rome dates from the first century BC, when Cicero, Livy, and Virgil use *Manes* of the souls of individuals;[77] while from the Augustan age onwards tomb inscriptions combine the traditional formula of collectivity, *D*(*is*) *M*(*anibus*) or *D*(*is*) *M*(*anibus*) *S*(*acrum*), with the personal name or names of the deceased in the nominative, genitive, or dative case. The same trend appears at this period even in the most intellectualized theories of astral apotheosis, whereby the soul was believed to rejoin at death the pure fiery element from which it came. This is strikingly illustrated by Cicero's *Somnium Scipionis*, where the starry being Africanus is described as dwelling among the blessed dead in the Milky Way.[78] But he still keeps his recognizable shape;[79] and he takes an eager interest in the fortunes of his descendant Aemilianus. The same insistence on continuing identity of bodily form and on lively concern for mundane pursuits and family affairs is found in Virgil's picture of the heroes in Elysium.

Closely linked with the belief that the individual dead remember with affection their ties with living friends was the notion that a person's conduct and deeds in this world had some bearing on his or her destiny hereafter. Catalogues of virtues and achievements both in literature and in inscriptions were, of course, partly intended to ensure that the dead lived on with honour in their survivors' memories; and the same was doubtless partly true of the countless scenes from professional, intellectual, or daily life that are met with in funerary art. Nevertheless, it is clear that there was developing among the Romans the sense that the survival of the individual implies some kind of moral responsibility on his or her part as regards afterlife destiny; and that all men must expect a reckoning and judgment after death, when an earthly life well spent, with duties successfully performed and talents made the most of, would reap its reward. A vivid instance of this is the address to Lucius Aemilius Paullus, censor of 22 BC, composed by Propertius for Paullus' dead wife Cornelia, daughter of Scribonia: Cornelia's soul on trial lists her virtues and good works;[80] and there can be little doubt that the art motifs above-mentioned were also meant to state that useful toil and cultural accomplishments can merit a happy immortality. This interpretation of such subjects on sepulchral monuments is not incompatible with the fact that many epitaphs treat work and care as burdens from which death brings release.[81] So does 'blessed are the dead who die in the Lord: they rest from their labours' in a context in which the activities and ordeals of this world, if faithfully carried out and patiently endured, are regarded as very relevant to the soul's condition in the next.

Roman-age speculations as to where the world of the dead was located were many and various. So far as we know, Virgil, in *Aeneid* vi, was the first Roman writer to employ the Greek mythological picture of the underworld with its elaborate topographical décor and tripartite division into 'Limbo', the region just inside Hades' portals, to which infants and others who had died before their time are relegated; Hell, where legendary criminals of superhuman stature undergo torture; and Heaven, the Elysian Fields, where heroes, exempted from every pain and care, enjoy for ever all the pleasures that had been their delight on earth. But among the Romans this picture remained, for the most part, a poetic one, used as a literary convention by Virgil's successors in the line of Roman poets from the Augustan epoch down to the end of pagan civilization and by the writers of some verse epitaphs.[82] Prose epitaphs, on the other hand, and funerary art ignore it almost totally. These, and the rites that were practised at the tomb, suggest that the mass of people who composed most ranks of society were largely unaffected by this literary tradition and had other views on afterlife abodes.

Early Roman ideas as to where the *Manes* dwelt, after the body had received due burial, are not explicitly recorded. It is, however, likely that they were thought of as being underground, at or near their burial place, where they could be given nourishment. From later periods there is, indeed, abundant evidence of an urge to keep the dead 'alive' by offerings made to them of food and drink, oil, and even blood and by their share in the funerary meals partaken of at the tomb by the survivors (see Chapter III (A)(*iv*)).[83] For this purpose holes were pierced and pipes provided so that the offerings and portions allotted to the dead could penetrate to the burials (*cf.* pp. 41, 51, 52). There the departed were believed to rest in the kindly bosom of maternal Earth, to whom they had descended. Hence the representations of Terra Mater in sepulchral art.[84] Hence the reiterated prayer of the epitaphs 's(it) t(ibi) t(erra) l(evis)'. Hence, too, the notion of immortality as union with the Earth-Goddess—'cinis sum cinis terra est terra dea est ergo ego mortua non sum';[85] and the imagery of bones or ashes giving birth to flowers: 'hic iacet Optatus pietatis nobilis infans/cui precor ut cineres sint ia sintque rosae, /terraque quae mater nunc est sibi sit levis oro/namque gravis nulli vita fuit pueri' ('Here lies Optatus, a child noble and dutiful. I pray that his ashes may become violets and roses and that the Earth, who is his mother now, rest lightly on him, who in life weighed heavily on no man').[86] There would seem to be no reason to hold that such thoughts deny individual survival or involve 'renunciation of personality', absorbed into the pure life-essence of earth.[87] Rather, they imply the continuance of the dead's identity.

According to another, closely related view, the tomb itself was the place in which the dead in some sense or at some times resided. Hence the fact that the architecture of some mausolea and the form of some sepulchral monuments recall the houses of the living (see Chapter V(G) and p. 253). Hence also, as with the Etruscans (see Chapter I), the attempt to make the dead feel at home in the tomb by renderings in paint, marble, stone, or stucco of the useful and familiar objects—toilet articles, vessels for food and drink, furniture, tools, writing materials, and so forth—which had once served them.[88]

Others placed the other-world dwellings of the dead in the sky, in the hemispheres, of which the Dioscuri, who figure not infrequently in tomb art, were looked upon as representatives,[89] in the atmosphere, or in the moon.[90] Others yet again threw open to all human souls the Blessed Isles across the Ocean (reserved in the literary tradition only for heroes), to judge from the constant representations in sepulchral art of Oceanus and of the homeward journey of the happy dead on ships or in the guise of Nereids or Cupids carried safely over the waves on the backs of friendly, frolicsome sea-lions, sea-bulls, sea-horses, sea-griffins, sea-Centaurs, Tritons, dolphins, and other Ocean-born creatures.[91]

However conflicting and confused may have been the current idea as to where the other world was situated, two things seem to emerge quite clearly—during the late Republic and throughout the Empire (outside certain philosophic schools and the circles that they influenced) belief in the survival after death of personal individuality prevailed and views on the nature of the life that awaited the soul beyond the grave were, in the main, optimistic. Both literature (to some extent) and funerary art (to a high degree) do, in fact, reveal that there was in this age a deepening conviction that the terror and power of death could be overcome and that a richer, happier, and more godlike life than that experienced here was attainable hereafter, under certain conditions, by the souls of the departed. Such conditions were a virtuous, useful, and well-ordered life on earth, or membership of one of the mystery-cults inherited by Rome from classical and Hellenistic Greece or from the East, or some looser form of adherence to one of the saviour-gods, of whom Dionysus was regarded as the most powerful and received the most widespread veneration. Mystic union or 'marriage' with themselves, ecstatic bliss in a paradise that teemed with flora and fauna, and the total victory of life over death were the 'other-worldly' gifts promised by these saviours to their worshippers. Hence the recurrence in the picture language of Roman-age tomb art of such themes as marriages, real or mythological, Dionysus' triumphal progress and the revels of his followers,[92] lively scenes of hunting and of animal pursuits and combats, the slaying of savage foes or ravening beasts, trophies of arms, Victories,[93] victorious charioteers, palm trees, palm branches, Cupids, Psyches, and other children in gardens glowing with flowers, fruits, and gorgeous birds,[94] and flocks and herds feeding peacefully in idyllic landscapes—gardens and landscapes that far outdistance in luxuriance the 'amoena virecta' of Virgil's heroes.[95] It is true that these motifs have relatively few explicit counterparts in surviving literature. But most of the tombs where they occur belonged to types of persons who expressed their ideas less easily in writing than visually.

It is in the light of these beliefs about the character and state of the human soul after death that we have to face the problem, already alluded to (*cf.* pp. 33, 34), of the revolution in burial rite in Rome and in her world.

## (B) CREMATION AND INHUMATION

According to Cicero[96] and Pliny,[97] inhumation, not cremation, was the primitive burial rite in Rome. But the Sepulcretum in the Roman Forum, dating from the eighth to the sixth century BC, contains both cremations and inhumations; [98] and from the Law of the Twelve Tables it is evident that both rites were practised side by side in the fifth century BC.[99] According to Lucretius,[100] three types of burial were known in the late Republic—cremation ('ignibus impostum calidis torrescere flammis'), embalmment ('aut in melle situm suffocari'), and inhumation ('urgerive superne obtritum pondere terrae'). Pliny says[101] that many Roman families kept to inhumation, notably the Gens Cornelia (also singled out by Cicero),[102] of which Sulla was the first member to be cremated; and in the subterranean Tomb of the Cornelii Scipiones on the *Via Appia* outside Rome were found the inscribed sarcophagi of members of the family who died between the early-third and the mid-second century BC (see Chapter V(B)).[103] But in republican Rome as a whole, from about 400 BC onwards, cremation was the normal practice and it remained so throughout the first century of our era, to such an extent that Tacitus, writing of the burial of Nero's empress Poppaea in AD 65, describes cremation categorically as the 'Romanus mos'.[104] *Columbaria* with niches for ash-urns (see Chapter V (C)), ash-chests and funerary altars containing cremated remains (see Chapter VII(C)) are the regular features of first-century BC and first-century AD custom. But during the reign of Hadrian the sudden flowering in the Roman world of the art of sarcophagus carving (see Chapter VII(E))[105] spelt the beginning of a gradual, but steadily increasing, supersession of cremation by inhumation during the second century AD, a process which by the middle of the third century had won its way throughout the provinces.

The view that mere fashion or a purely ostentatious taste for elaborate and expensively decorated coffins could have brought about a change in burial rite so widespread and lasting is not convincing,[106] despite the fact that ashes have occasionally been discovered in sarcophagi.[107] Carved Roman ash-chests, funerary altars, and independent effigies of the dead (see Chapter VII(C) and (D)) were also striking works of art and costly monuments; in Etruria, where the two rites ran side by side (see Chapter I), the ornamentation on ash-chests could be as detailed and rich in symbolic meaning as that on the sarcophagi contemporary with them: there we have no evidence for a vogue for display through inhumation that ousted cremation. On the other hand, the pagan thought of this period gives no hint of any dogma of bodily resurrection for mankind as a whole; and the fact that, for a time, in imperial Rome the two rites could coexist in the same mausoleum suggests that the change in custom did not imply any significant change in actual doctrine. The abandonment of cremation was, moreover, too general to owe anything to Semitic, in particular to Jewish, habit and too early to be due to Christian influences. The explanation has, therefore, to be sought elsewhere.

In the end, of course, interred bones and burnt bones come to much the same thing. Grave-goods, whether real or imitated in art (*cf.* pp. 52–4, 142, 143), involving some belief in conscious survival, accompany cremations as well as inhumations, just as holes and pipes enabling dead and living to share a common meal (*cf.* pp. 37, 51, 52) are found with both. But inhumation could be felt to be a gentler and a more respectful way of laying to rest the mortal frame which has been the temple and mirror of the immortal soul and enduring personality. For this matter of sentiment neither funerary inscriptions nor the literature of the time provide explicit evidence. Nonetheless, the change of rite would seem to reflect a significant strengthening of emphasis on the individual's enjoyment of a blissful hereafter.

Although embalmment, a special way of honouring the body, was a method of burial known, as Lucretius states, to the late-republican Romans (*cf.* p. 39), in Rome and Italy it was looked upon by some as a foreign custom and was, on the whole, not extensively practised. However, the empress Poppaea's corpse was, according to Tacitus, not only inhumed, instead of being burnt, but also embalmed—'corpus . . . regum externorum consuetudine differtum odoribus conditur';[108] and one remarkable instance of such a burial, which cannot, it seems, be attributed to an emperor's vagaries, came to light in February 1964 near the *Via Cassia* on the outskirts of Rome. This burial, which appears to have taken place in about the middle of the second century AD, consisted of the mummified and perfectly preserved body of a girl of about seven or eight years old, who, when the corpse was unwrapped, was discovered to have suffered from rickets: she may have died of tuberculosis. She was wearing a necklace, a finger-ring, and earrings; and with her were her toys—an ivory jointed doll and some miniature pots (*cf.* pp. 52, 53). The body is said to have been lying in a large marble sarcophagus, carved with hunting scenes in second-century style; but according to another account it was only associated with the sarcophagus.[109] The suggestion has been made that this child was the daughter of a Roman official stationed in Egypt and that she had died and was embalmed there and was then brought back to Rome for burial. On the other hand, since it is clear that there were persons in Italy skilled in embalming after the Egyptian fashion,[110] she could have died and been mummified in Rome.

Furthermore, there is archaeological evidence, additional to the *Via Cassia* find, to suggest that embalmment, if expensive and generally regarded as somewhat exotic, was practised, occasionally at any rate, outside Egypt both in Italy and the provinces. Two mummies were discovered on the *Via Appia* near Rome in the Renaissance, both of women, one under Sixtus IV, the other under Alexander VI: the latter mummy was very well preserved, with Egyptian-style wrappings and a painted face-mask.[111] In Pannonia three mummies came to light at Aquincum in 1912, 1929, and 1962 respectively; one was discovered at Carnuntum in 1939, another at Intercisa in 1963.[112] Finally, a Gaulish instance, now in the Musée de l'Homme in Paris, was found at Martres d'Artie near Riom (Puy-de-Dôme) in 1756.[113] That all these mummies were made in Egypt is difficult to believe. It is possible that in some at least of these cases the embalmers were Egyptian priests attached to local shrines of Isis and Serapis, their clients being either immigrant Egyptians or Italians and provincials who had been converted to the cults of Egypt or other persons, not so converted, who fancied this method of disposing of their dead.

## CHAPTER III

# FUNERARY RITES AND THE CULT OF THE DEAD

### (A) FUNERARY RITES

THE TERM *funus* can be used to cover all that took place between the hour of death and the performance of the last post-burial ceremonies. In its social range it denotes the final offices accorded to the very poor and to ordinary citizens of moderate or considerable means (*funus translaticum*), to soldiers (*funus militare*), to persons who had given the State distinguished service (*funus publicum*), to emperors and members of their families (*funus imperatorium*). *Funus* includes, furthermore, the questions of who paid the expenses of the funerals of these various types and of the extent to which the State regulated funerals by legislation.[114] All Roman funerary practice was influenced by two basic notions —first, that death brought pollution and demanded from the survivors acts of purification and expiation; secondly, that to leave a corpse unburied had unpleasant repercussions on the fate of the departed soul. The throwing of a little earth upon the body was the minimum requirement for burial, could nothing more be done. But custom ordained that in normal circumstances the obsequies should be carried out with as much solemnity as circumstances in every case allowed.

### (I) FUNUS TRANSLATICUM

(*i*) *Rites preceding the Obsequies.* When death was imminent relations and close friends gathered round the dying person's bed, to comfort and support him or her and to give vent to their own grief.[115] The nearest relative present gave the last kiss,[116] to catch the soul, which, so it was believed, left the body with the final breath.[117] The same relative then closed the departed's eyes (*oculos premere*, etc.),[118] after which all the near relatives called upon the dead by name (*conclamare*) and lamented him or her, a process that continued at intervals until the body was disposed of by cremation or inhumation.[119] The next act was to take the body from the bed, to set it on the ground (*deponere*),[120] and to wash it and anoint it.[121] Then followed the dressing of the corpse—in a toga, in the case of a male Roman citizen,[122] the laying of a wreath on its head, particularly in the case of a person who had earned one in life,[123] and the placing of a coin in the mouth to pay the deceased's fare in Charon's barque.[124] All was now ready for the body's exposition or lying-in-state (*collocare*=προτιθέναι)[125] on a grand bed (*lectus funebris*), if the family was well-to-do, with the feet towards the house-door.[126] (*Pl.* 10)

The best representation in Roman art of the lying-in-state of a well-off personage is a marble relief of late-Flavian or early-Trajanic date from the so-called Tomb of the Haterii family, a few miles south of Rome, on the *Via Labicana*, and now in the Lateran collection.[127] The deceased, to judge from the style of the clothing, which is certainly not a toga, would seem to be a woman. She is laid out in the *atrium* of her house, which is crowned by a tiled and gabled roof, but is here shown opened out to the spectator's view along its long axis. She lies flat on her back, on two mattresses, which are superimposed one upon the other on a couch with carved ends and elaborately turned legs. The dead woman wears rings on her left hand and is draped from neck to foot: at her feet are a pile of tablets, those of her will, no doubt. The couch itself is reared on a high platform, most of the front of which is covered by a curtain. Four large flaming torches are planted two at the head and two at the foot of the bier; and to right and left of each pair of torches is a *candelabrum*, each topped by a lamp and a minute female figure, in the one case clasping a bag, in the other holding a flask. Above the couch and the recumbent corpse are two tall vases tapering towards the top, but ending in wide, spreading mouths. Tied to the vases are two rich, sagging garlands of fruit and flowers, symbols, it may be, of afterlife fertility; while the two shells that fill the spaces above the garlands could allude to the soul's voyage across the Ocean to the Blessed Isles. Behind the couch and in front of the vases are three standing figures: on the right, a man holding a heavy flower-garland, perhaps to tie round the neck of the corpse, since the hair is already encircled by a light wreath of blossoms; on the left, two hired female mourners (*praeficae*),[128] with dishevelled hair and hands raised to beat their breasts. Below, at the foot of the couch, is a seated woman wearing the typical coiffure of the period and playing on a double pipe: a veiled woman stands beside her with hands raised and folded together. In front of the curtain hung on the platform that supports the bier are four figures, probably relatives of the deceased, walking slowly towards the right: two are men and two are women, one of whom has let down her hair behind so as to hang loose about her back and shoulders. All four beat their breasts. At the head of the couch are seated, at three different levels, three female figures with dishevelled hair: they each clasp one knee in an attitude of grief; and the tall, pointed cap (*pileus*) that each wears suggests that they are slaves freed by the dead woman's will. Between the torches and the *candelabra* on the right of the scene is a male figure walking towards the left and carrying some object on a tray. Two flaming incense-burners stand in the foreground, one at either end of the platform. The great acanthus leaf on the extreme left may represent the foliage fixed up in front of the house-door to indicate that there is a corpse laid out within. (*Pl.* 9)

In the case of members of the upper classes, the preparation of the body for its lying-in-state, which sometimes lasted for as long as seven days,[129] and the arrangements for the funeral that followed, were generally entrusted to professional undertakers (*libitinarii*)[130] and their underlings (*pollinctores*).[131] The poor were carried to cremation or inhumation on a cheap bier (*sandapila*) by *vespilliones*.[132] The actual burning of the body was normally performed by *ustores*;[133] grave-digging was done by *fossores*.[134] The *dissignatores*[135] were probably the masters of ceremonies at a rich man's or rich woman's obsequies. Very important people could have a *funus indictivum*, to which all citizens were summoned by a herald (*praeco*).[136]

(*ii*) *The Funeral Procession* (*pompa*). From the following of the corpse to the place of its disposal by relatives, friends, and other invited persons (all wearing black *lugubria*) come the funerary terms *exsequiae* and *prosequi*.[137] Traditionally, it was the ancient Roman custom for funerals to be conducted at night by the light of torches, which were still carried before the body when, in historical times, the funerals of all but children and the poor took place by day.[138] In well-to-do families the deceased, still lying on the funerary couch, was carried from his or her home on an elaborate bier (*feretrum*).[139] The bearers, on whose shoulders it rested, might be the departed's nearest male relatives or closest male friends or his or her newly liberated slaves.[140] They could be four in number, as in the case of the poor,[141] but might be as many as eight, as can be seen from the marble relief, found at Amiternum and now in the museum at Aquila,[142] which depicts the funeral cortège of a personage of consequence.

The character of the inscriptions found on the same site as this relief suggests that it may date from the late-republican or Augustan period.[143] On the bier is a funerary couch, equipped with two superimposed mattresses and pillows, on which the dead man is lying tilted up on his left side and with his head supported on his left hand. He is wreathed and dressed in a short-sleeved tunic and a toga and holds in his right hand a short staff, perhaps the emblem of the office that he held at the time of his demise. Beneath the couch, which has richly carved legs, is a low table or long seat with ornamental feet; and behind the couch appears a large rectangular, screen-like object, which may have been, in reality, a canopy fixed horizontally over the corpse, but here shown vertically in order to display its embroidered decoration—the moon in a star-spangled sky, symbolic of celestial apotheosis. Above one corner of the canopy projects what would seem to be a helmet. The living participants in the procession are arranged in superimposed tiers, the figures in the upper tiers being poised on ledges that represent ground-lines. In the bottom register are the eight bearers, advancing towards the right, the four who are furthest from the spectator being on a smaller scale than the rest; while the man who is directing them, the *dissignator*, stands facing them and grasps the end of one pole of the bier. The catafalque is preceded on the right by four pipers (*tibicines*)[144] below and by a trumpeter (*tubicen*)[145] and two horn-blowers (*cornicines*)[146] above. Again in the upper tier, between the three musicians and the bier, are two dishevelled *praeficae*, one with both hands raised, the other tearing her hair. At the same level, following the bier on the left, are the chief mourners, the widow and her two daughters, all with dishevelled hair. On the extreme left of the relief are three levels of figures—below, behind the bearers, a boy holding a palm-branch and a pail or basket, in the centre, two female relatives or servants, one armed with a spade-like implement, and above, three women, probably relatives (the third from the left may be another daughter) or friends of the family. The hired mourners and musicians in this, as in all other Roman funeral processions, were, of course, an Etruscan legacy (see Chapter I(C)). (*Pl.* 11)

The obsequies of Roman patricians in the middle of the second century BC are vividly described by Polybius.[147] If the dead was a distinguished man his corpse was placed on the rostra in the Forum, in either a standing or reclining posture, and a panegyric on him was pronounced in the presence of the citizens.[148] After the burial his portrait (εἰκών), which was a mask (πρόσωπον) resembling him as realistically as possible, was enclosed in a wooden shrine and placed in a conspicuous position in the house. In this way there were built up domestic 'galleries' of ancestral portraits, which formed part of the cortège of each member of the family when his turn came to die, the masks being worn in the procession by those relatives and friends who resembled most closely the dead individuals that they represented. The same phenomenon is mentioned by the Elder Pliny who, writing in the mid-first-century AD, states[149] that in earlier times ('apud maiores') wax masks ('expressi cera vultus') were kept in cupboards in the house to serve as portraits attending family funerals ('ut essent imagines quae comitarentur gentilicia funera'). Neither Polybius nor Pliny gives any support to the view that these masks were death-masks proper, cast directly from the faces of the dead. We would give much to possess a work of Roman art which rendered this highly original and striking feature of the upper-class Roman funerary cortège—a feature that survived into imperial times until at least as late as the second half of the first century AD.

That the traditional mask-form of the funerary *imago* was in use under the Empire we learn from Suetonius' account of Vespasian's funeral.[150] In the procession walked the *archimimus* Favor wearing his mask ('personam eius ferens') and 'according to the usual custom imitating the actions and words of the deceased during his lifetime'. Meanwhile, towards the end of the Republic, an alternative to the funerary mask had appeared in the funerary bust, of which examples, sometimes enclosed in little cupboards, are to be seen carved on tombstones dating from the second half of the first century BC (*cf.* p. 246).[151] Again, an Augustan marble statue, now in the New Capitoline Museum, shows a togate personage presumably walking in a funeral procession and holding in either hand an ancestral bust.[152] These busts, if proximately modelled on marble portraits, were obviously meant to be thought of as consisting of such portable material as wax or terracotta. In several passages of the early books of the *Annals* Tacitus cites the appearance of *imagines* at funerals—in connection with the death of Libo Drusus,[153] of the Elder Drusus,[154] of Junia, wife of Gaius Cassius,[155] and of the Younger Drusus.[156] There is no specific statement as to whether these *imagines* were masks or busts. But the fact that those at the Elder Drusus' funeral are described as 'circumfusae lecto' inclines us to believe that they at any rate were busts set on the bier around the funerary couch. (*Pls.* 12, 13)

(*iii*) *The Disposal of the Corpse*. All burials, whether of bodies or of ashes, had to take place outside the city. This regulation, laid down in the Twelve Tables,[157] was normally observed until the late Empire, although exceptions could be made for special persons[158] and for emperors.[159] Sanitary precautions and fear of defilement readily explain the law. In the case of Rome, the Campus Martius did not count as being within the city, since it was outside the *pomerium*; and some notable citizens,[160] as well as the emperors buried in the Mausoleum of Augustus (see Chapter

V(H)), had their tombs there. Similarly, the *puticuli*, the grave-pits into which the unburnt bodies of some slaves and paupers were thrown promiscuously, were in Rome situated, at least at one time, just outside the *Porta Esquilina*.[161] Rich landowners, both in Rome and throughout the Empire, had tombs for themselves and their dependants on their own estates.[162] But the great majority of people in the Roman world were laid to rest in tombs of very varied types strung along the roads beyond the city gates. For obvious reasons no cremations were allowed to take place within the city's precincts.

As soon as the funeral procession arrived at the place of inhumation or cremation, there was performed the essential rite of throwing a little earth on the corpse and, in the case of a cremation, of the cutting off of a fraction of it (*os resectum*)[163] to be subsequently buried. As regards inhumations, the poor were laid directly in the earth, generally fully extended, less often in a crouched position in simple trench-graves (*fossae*)[164] (see Chapter V(A)); or, in the case of the Jews, other Semitics and early Christians, on shelves (*loculi*) cut in the rock walls of hypogea and catacombs (see Chapter VI(F) and (G)). The wealthy were placed in richly carved sarcophagi (see Chapter VII(E)), the moderately well-to-do in less elaborate sarcophagi of marble, stone, terracotta, lead, or wood. Lead sarcophagi were usually placed in outer ones of stone or wood.[165] Not infrequently gypsum was poured over the body, forming a cast of it and sometimes preserving fragments of the textile in which it had been wrapped.[166] Sarcophagi could be placed in chamber-tombs or under tumuli or be merely buried in the earth. A common custom in the case of inhumations was to place a coin—the traditional Charon's fee—in the mouth of the deceased (*cf.* pp. 119, 124). This practice, familiar in burials in Mediterranean countries, is also sometimes found in those on the Empire's peripheries, for example, in Britain[167] and in the cemetery of the Nabataean city of Kurnub.[168]

The burning of the corpse, and of the couch on which it lay, took place either at the place in which the ashes were to be buried (*bustum*) or at a place specially reserved for cremations (*ustrina* or *ustrinum*)[169]. The pyre (*rogus*) was a rectangular pile of wood, sometimes mixed with papyrus to facilitate the burning.[170] The eyes of the corpse were opened when it was placed on the pyre,[171] along with various gifts and some of the deceased's personal possessions. Sometimes even pet animals were killed round the pyre to accompany the soul into the afterlife.[172] The relatives and friends then called upon the dead by name for the last time: the pyre was kindled with torches; and after the corpse had been consumed the ashes were drenched with wine.[173] The burnt bones and ashes of the body were collected by the relatives[174] and placed in receptacles of various kinds—in marble altar-shaped ash-chests, small ash-chests of marble, stone, or terracotta in the shape of houses or of baskets or of round or rectangular boxes or caskets (all of them richly adorned with reliefs) and in marble, alabaster, gold, silver, or bronze vases or urns (the well-to-do); or in lead canisters, glass vessels, and earthenware pots[175] (the relatively poor). According to their nature and the status of the dead whose remains they held, these receptacles could be either set up free-standing inside house- or other chamber-tombs, in the case of the altar-shaped chests (which sometimes have a recess for holding a vase or urn—*cf.* p. 254), or, in the case of the small, casket-like ash-chests, placed in niches and recesses in the walls of *columbaria* and of house- and other chamber-tombs (see Chapter V(C) to (G)); or, in the case of the humbler, undecorated containers, they could be buried in the earth, under masonry tombs of different kinds or under tumuli (see Chapter VI(D)) or under gravestones of varying sizes and degrees of elaboration (*cf.* pp. 246–53) or with just a large pot to mark the spot (*cf.* p. 101).

(*iv*) *Post-Funeral Practices and Services Rendered to the Dead.* Various statutory regulations had to be complied with on all occasions of death and burial. Only when a pig had been sacrificed was a grave legally a grave.[176] There were also a number of other acts to be performed by the family. On returning from the funeral the relatives had to undergo the *suffitio*, a rite of purification by fire and water.[177] On the same day there began a period of cleansing ceremonies (*feriae denicales*) held at the deceased's house;[178] and again on the same day a funerary feast, the *silicernium*, was eaten at the grave in honour of the dead.[179] There was also the *cena novendialis* eaten at the grave on the ninth day after the funeral, at the end of the period of full mourning, when a libation to the *Manes* was poured upon the actual burial.[180] Offerings of food were left at the tomb for the dead and were sometimes eaten by the hungry.[181] The domestic Lar was purified by a sacrifice of wethers.[182] To disturb in any way the last resting-place of human relics that had been finally and solemnly buried was a criminal offence. Official dispensations from the penalties could be granted. But there are a number of known instances of unofficial breaches of the law (*cf.* p. 76 and pp. 296–7, Notes 273–6).

Throughout the year there were occasions on which the dead were commemorated by funerary meals eaten at the tomb by their relatives and friends—on their birthdays and when the annual festivals of the dead were celebrated (see pp. 61–4). The mausolea of the well-to-do often contained chambers for this purpose, sometimes equipped with kitchens (see Chapter V(G), p. 136). At all of these banquets, as at those held at the time of a death, the departed had their share set apart for them. Their disembodied spirits, it was thought, could somehow partake of the fare with which they were thus provided and, indeed, be nourished through the medium of their bones or ashes (*cf.* p. 37). Hence the fact that graves, whether for inhumation or for cremation, with holes or pipes through which food and drink could be poured down directly on to the burial (*profusio*), so as to reach the remains, are a not uncommon feature of cemeteries in very diverse areas of the Roman world. For example, in the necropolis excavated under St Peter's in Rome several instances have come to light. In Tomb F, inset into the border of a mosaic pavement, is a series of small, square marble slabs each pierced with a hole for pouring sustenance down on to the dead beneath; and there are similar holes in the mosaic pavement of Tomb C.[183] In the floor of Tomb O there is a marble roundel pierced by four holes;[184] and Grave $\gamma$, a child's inhumation burial of Hadrianic date, near the reputed tomb of St Peter, contained a terracotta coffin, partly encased in a rectangular block of masonry, which was penetrated by a vertical tube for pouring.[185] Another child's inhumation burial, this time at Syracuse and with the bones laid directly in the earth under tiles set gable-wise, was connected with the surface by a vertical terracotta pipe, closed at the top by a movable stone stopper.[186] A small stone, oblong chest from Faleroni, in Italy, containing a cremation burial and grave-goods in the form of glass vessels, ornaments, and so forth, bears in the centre of its lid a vertical leaden pipe.[187] Among provincial examples are a lead sarcophagus for inhumation found at Colchester, near one end of the lid of which is a lead pipe passing down into the interior, where vessels of glass and pottery accompanied the bones;[188] and a cremation burial from Caerleon in Monmouthshire.[189] In the latter case the tomb consists of a horizontal slab of stone carrying a packing of rammed earth, on which stands a circular lead canister that contained the remains. The canister is walled round by slabs of stone; and between one wall and the slab that covers the canister is a lead pipe that leads down from the surface into the inside of the vessel (*cf.* pp. 37, 41, 101, 123). (*Pl.* 14)

The grave-goods discovered in some of the burials just described illustrate a widespread Roman practice, for which abundant archaeological evidence has come to light. Goods of this kind include jewellery and other personal adornments, arms and pieces of armour and other items of military equipment, toilet boxes and toilet articles, some in precious metals, eating and drinking vessels occasionally of gold and silver, more often of bronze, glass, and pottery, lamps, cooking vessels and implements, dice and gaming-counters, children's toys (*cf.* pp. 41, 53), small funerary portraits, and small images of other-world deities. Many of the objects in this list occur so often and are so familiar that individual examples need not be cited here. Some, on the other hand, are less ubiquitous; and of those a few may be illustrated at this point by specific instances.

Dice and gaming-counters were yielded by the Roman cemetery at Ospringe in Kent.[190] Just to the west of the Roman villa at Lullingstone, also in Kent, there was a species of temple-mausoleum with a subterranean chamber containing two adult burials in lead coffins. These were accompanied by goods, laid out in a row, in the shape of two flagons, one of bronze, the other of pottery, two identical groups consisting of two glass bottles with dolphin handles and a knife and spoon, and the bases of two glass bowls. On the head of one coffin lid (the other lid had been removed in late antiquity) were the carbonized and pulverized remains of a wooden gaming-board with bronze angle-pieces and a set of thirty glass gaming-counters, fifteen white and fifteen brown, all adorned with spots. There were also some carved bone objects and a bone roundel incised with a head of Medusa.[191] Toys, often in the form of animals, found in cremation graves where the age of the deceased cannot be determined, would appear to indicate children's burials. Such are the terracotta figurines discovered in a wooden chest in a grave, dated to *c.* AD 45, at Camulodunum (Colchester) in Essex. These comprise nine human figures, eight male and one female, intended to compose a dinner-party scene with diners and reciters; and various animals—for example, a dog with collar and bell, a pig, two lions, a bull, three apes, and a hare and an ibex, the last two lead-glazed. With these playthings was a small statuette of Hercules, doubtless in his other-world capacity, and the bust of a young boy on a much larger scale than the rest and possibly intended as a funerary 'portrait' of the dead child.[192] Almost certainly a toy was the miniature jet bear found with an infant's skeleton at Malton in Yorkshire.[193] Another instance of the image of an other-world deity that functioned as a protective grave-good comes from the Ospringe cemetery. This is a two-dimensional bronze bust of Minerva terminating in a short pilaster which is attached to an iron strip: its exact counterpart came to light in a funerary context at Remagen in Germany.[194]

The purpose of these grave-goods was partly to honour the dead, but mainly to serve them and help them to feel at home in the afterlife; while the 'portraits' and images symbolized death and the realms beyond it. As with the Etruscans (*cf.* pp. 12, 16), so occasionally with the Romans personal possessions could be counterfeited in works of art in various media. For example, in the Tomb of the Valerii under St Peter's the stucco figure of Gaius Valerius Herma is accompanied by writing materials rendered in the same material, while the stucco figures of women of his family are provided with stucco mirrors, a jewel casket or cosmetic box, a perfume bottle, a distaff, and a spindle[195] (*cf.* pp. 142, 143).

(*v*) *Cenotaphs.* If a person's body was not available for burial, in such eventualities as drowning at sea or death in battle, a *cenotaphium* was made to provide the soul with a dwelling-place, which it was invited to enter by being called upon by name three times.[196] A familiar example of a tombstone possibly erected above a cenotaph is that, now in the Rheinisches Landesmuseum, Bonn, of the centurion Marcus Caelius, who fell either in the Varian disaster of AD 9 in the Teutoburger Forest or in some other battle in Varus' campaign.[197] Here the half-length figure of Caelius is portrayed in military dress, with his decorations and staff of office and a bust of two of his freedmen, one on either side of him. A cenotaph, known as a *honorarium sepulcrum* or *honorarius tumulus*, could be put up for some person whose remains were buried elsewhere. The Elder Drusus, buried in Rome, had such a cenotaph in Gaul.[198]

(*vi*) *Funerary Laws and Regulations.* Legislation and magisterial regulations attempted to restrict the amounts spent on private funerals and, in particular, ostentation in the arrangements made for the cortège to the place of cremation or inhumation.[199] There was also laid down a list of persons who had the duty of celebrating the funeral rites:[200] (*i*) the friend whom the deceased had designated in his will for this purpose; (*ii*) in default of (*i*), a person designated by the friends of the deceased; (*iii*) in default of (*i*) and (*ii*), the heir, if the deceased had been the head of the family, otherwise the head of the family. The persons on whom the cost of the obsequies devolved were also fixed by law—the heir, or the head of the family, if the deceased was not in a position to appoint an heir; a married woman's father, if she had no dowry out of which it could be paid; or her heir or her husband, if she had been emancipated from her father.[201]

(*vii*) *Burial Clubs.* Among the numerous clubs or associations in the Roman world (*collegia, sodalicia, sodalitates*)[202] those that were generally tolerated by the government were the burial clubs (*collegia funeraticia*) of the lower orders of society (*tenuiores*), mainly slaves and freedmen, whose members, theoretically, met only once a month for the payment of the contributions that they made to provide for their funerals.[203] Most of these clubs had some religious connections—for example, that of the *cultores Dianae et Antinoi* at Lanuvium;[204] and, in practice, they also engaged in some social activities such as dining together on certain occasions. The members of a club were sometimes men who all practised the same craft or trade; or they were all the dependants of some great family[205] or of the Imperial House.[206] The remains of persons belonging to these groups were often laid to rest in communal *columbaria* (see Chapter V(c)).

## (2) FUNUS MILITARE

Soldiers killed on the battlefield were collectively cremated[207] or buried.[208] The funeral expenses of those who died while on service were paid by their comrades, contributions from the soldiers' pay being set aside for this purpose.[209] A general could be honoured by a *decursio* in the form of a ride or march round his funeral pyre or cenotaph.[210]

## (3) FUNUS PUBLICUM

A special kind of *funus indictivum*, to which all citizens were invited, was the *funus publicum* decreed to a benefactor of the State and paid for by the State treasury.[211] A panegyric and a sung dirge were part of the honours accorded.[212] Notable foreign prisoners also qualified for such obsequies.[213] Sulla's public funeral was conducted with particular magnificence.[214] His corpse was carried on a golden litter and was accompanied by more than two thousand golden crowns and by axes and other symbols of the offices held by him in life. In the procession were trumpeters and pipers, Vestal Virgins, the senators and magistrates, and vast crowds of soldiers, horse and foot, as well as of citizens.

In Italy, outside Rome, and in the provinces public funerals were decreed to citizens who had rendered signal service to their cities.[215] Here a woman might qualify for the honour.[216] Sometimes a rich family would accept the honour but remit the charge on the city.[217]

Under the Republic a feature (possibly borrowed from Etruria viâ Campania, although no explicit evidence of this exists) of the funerals of public men, but not of public funerals in the strict sense, were gladiatorial combats, sometimes combined with other games and free feasts, which were offered as a commemorative spectacle to the Roman people generally by the sons of the deceased. The earliest instance of this was at the funeral of Decimus Iunius Brutus Pera in 264 BC.[218] In 216 at the funeral of Marcus Aemilius Lepidus twenty-two pairs were set to fight,[219] twenty-five pairs in 200 at that of Marcus Valerius Laevinus;[220] a hundred and twenty men fought in 183 at the funeral of Publius Licinius[221] and seventy-four fought in 174 at that of Titus Quintius Flamininus.[222]

## (4) FUNUS IMPERATORIUM

Under the Empire public funerals in Rome were reserved almost exclusively for emperors and members of their families. There were, however, some exceptions. Augustus gave one to his freedman and one-time tutor Sphaerus;[223] and in AD 32 the senate decreed one to Lucius Piso.[224] Such a funeral is sometimes described as a *funus censorium*, as in the case of that of Tiberius' friend Lucilius Longus in AD 23,[225] of Aelius Lamia in AD 33,[226] and of Flavius Sabinus in AD 70.[227] The term *funus censorium* could be used for the funeral of an emperor, of Claudius, for example, who had actually been censor;[228] while Septimius Severus gave a *funus censorium* to the *imago* of Pertinax, whose corpse was not available for burial.[229]

We have brief descriptions of the funerals of some imperial persons who never reigned as emperors. The body of the Elder Drusus, who died in the Rhineland in 9 BC, was brought back to Rome by Tiberius, who walked on foot all the way, while Augustus himself met it at Ticinum and accompanied it to the capital. The deceased's ancestral *imagines* surrounded his funerary couch (*cf.* p. 48) in the procession. The corpse was taken to the

Forum, where there was mourning and a eulogy was delivered by Tiberius; and another eulogy was delivered by Augustus in the Circus Maximus. Knights carried the body to the Campus Martius, where it was burnt and its ashes deposited in the Mausoleum of Augustus.[230] On the day in AD 20 on which Germanicus' ashes were buried in the same place, the Campus Martius blazed with torches and the streets were packed with mourning soldiers, magistrates, and citizens; but the procession of *imagines* and the eulogy seem to have been omitted.[231] The funeral of the Younger Drusus in AD 23 was especially noteworthy for the great number of ancestral *imagines* that were displayed in his cortège (*cf.* p. 48).[232] Of Hadrian's intended successor, Aelius Caesar (Verus), it is stated: 'sepultus est imperatorio funere'.[233] As regards imperial women, the public funerals of Atia, mother of Augustus,[234] of Livia in AD 29,[235] and of Poppaea in AD 65[236] are recorded.

In the case of those reigning emperors whose funerals are described in the literary sources, some accounts are very summary. Of Tiberius we only know that the body was carried from Capri to Rome by soldiers and that it was given a public funeral with a eulogy pronounced by Gaius.[237] Of Claudius we learn, in addition to the fact that his *funus* was *censorium* (*cf.* p. 56), that he had a public funeral befitting an emperor, on the same lines as that of Augustus, and that his eulogy, composed by Seneca, was delivered by Nero.[238] Of Vespasian's funeral Suetonius, in addition to describing the antics of the actor Favor (*cf.* p. 48), tells us that it cost ten million sesterces.[239] Antoninus Pius, before being buried in Hadrian's Mausoleum, was accorded a magnificent funeral procession, accompanied by a *iustitium*, the closing of the law courts as a sign of mourning: Marcus Aurelius and Lucius Verus each delivered an oration on their adoptive father.[240] For complete and colourful details of imperial funerals we must turn to the accounts of the obsequies of Julius Caesar,[241] Augustus,[242] and Septimius Severus.[243]

After his murder Julius Caesar's corpse was carried to the Forum by magistrates and ex-magistrates and a lengthy speech was delivered in its presence by Mark Antony. Dio says that the body was exposed to public view, covered in blood and full of gaping wounds. But according to Appian the actual body, lying on its back on a bier, was not visible; and above the bier was placed a wax image of Caesar, on which his many wounds were counterfeited and which could be turned in all directions by a mechanism. A pyre had been prepared in the Campus Martius, but it was decided to burn the corpse in the Forum. Pipers and actors took off the clothes that they had taken from the Dictator's triumphal equipment and assumed for the occasion, and threw them on the flames. Women threw on to the pyre their jewels and the amulets and robes of their children. After the cremation Caesar's freedmen gathered up his bones and deposited them in his family tomb.

The body of Augustus, who died at Nola, was carried to Bovillae in night stages by the senators of the *municipia* and *coloniae* through which it passed and rested by day in the basilica or chief temple of each city on the route of the cortège. At Bovillae it was met by knights and carried by them to Rome, where it was placed in the vestibule of the emperor's house. The funeral procession proper from the Palatine to the Campus Martius then took place, the body being borne by senators, according to Suetonius, by the magistrates designate, according to Dio. The funerary couch was made of ivory and gold and adorned with coverings of gold and purple. In it the body itself was hidden from view: what the spectators saw was a wax image dressed in triumphal garb. Another image of the emperor, in gold, was brought from the Senate House and yet another was drawn along in a triumphal chariot. Behind these images came those of Augustus' ancestors and dead relations (except for that of Julius Caesar, who had become a demigod) and those of prominent Romans beginning with Romulus and including Pompey the Great, whose image was accompanied by figures personifying all the peoples that he had added to the Empire, each figure being distinguished by some local characteristic of the people that it represented. Arrived at the Forum, the couch was laid on the *rostra vetera*, from which the Younger Drusus read a eulogy, while Tiberius read another from the *rostra* at the temple of Divus Julius. Then the couch was carried by the consuls designate and other magistrates as the procession continued on its way to the

Campus Martius. The procession included the senators and knights with their wives, the praetorian guard, and all citizens who were in Rome. The body was placed on the pyre and first the priests and then horsemen and infantry passed round it (*decursio circa rogum*). All those who possessed triumphal decorations cast them on the pyre, which centurions lighted from beneath with torches; and an eagle released from it flew heavenward to symbolize the emperor's apotheosis. Livia remained for five days by the pyre. The leading knights, barefoot and ungirt, gathered up the bones and placed them in Augustus' Mausoleum. A *iustitium* was decreed. Women observed mourning for a whole year.

Septimius Severus died at York and in the *Life* of him in the *Historia Augusta* are given two versions of the fate of his remains. Some said that his body was brought to Rome to be cremated; others that only his ashes travelled to Rome in a golden urn to be buried in Hadrian's (the Antonine) Mausoleum, his corpse having been cremated in Britain.

The latter is the version accepted by Herodian, who records that the body was burnt in Britain, his ashes being placed in an alabaster urn and conveyed by his sons to Rome. On reaching the capital Caracalla and Geta donned the imperial purple for the funeral procession and were followed by the consuls carrying the urn, to which reverence was done by all who met the cortège. The urn was then deposited in the Antonine Mausoleum; and the ensuing ceremonies in the city were a mixture of mourning, feasting, and religious rites. The manner in which the ashes were laid to rest was that of an ordinary burial. But a life-size, realistic wax image of the emperor was made, laid on a great ivory couch, covered with golden coverlets, and placed for all to see in the vestibule of the palace. The face of the image was that of one sick and suffering. The lying-in-state of this εἰκών lasted for seven days; and for most of each day the senators, in mourning, sat on the left of it, the most illustrious matrons, without their necklaces and other gold ornaments, on the right of it. Every day the doctors came, approached the couch, inspected the image, and announced that the patient was growing progressively worse.

When they finally declared that death had taken place, the most distinguished members of the equestrian order and selected youths of senatorial rank took up the couch, carried it along the *Via Sacra* to the Forum, and exposed it there. Steps were erected on either side of the couch and on one set of steps stood a company of high-born youths, on the other, one of eminent women. Each company sang solemn, dirge-like hymns and paeans in the deceased emperor's honour.

Then the couch was taken to the Campus Martius, where a huge square pyre, as big as a house, had been constructed of logs. This pyre was filled inside with faggots and adorned on its exterior with golden hangings, statues of ivory, and elaborate paintings. It was built up like a lighthouse in five storeys diminishing in size, the topmost one being the smallest of all. The couch on which the image of the emperor lay was placed in the second storey and all kinds of spices and unguents were put in with it, together with fruits, herbs, and sweet-smelling juices piled up beside it. There was no race or city, no person of prominence or position who did not give generously of these gifts to honour the dead ruler. When a great heap of spices had been raised and all the space was filled, a cavalry parade took place round the pyre, each company of horsemen riding round it with orderly and rhythmic movements. With the same orderliness chariots were drawn round it, bearing passengers dressed in purple garments and wearing masks that were portraits of famous Roman generals and emperors. Then the new emperor took a torch and kindled the pyre, while others also set a light to it on all sides. The faggots and all the spices that were inside made it burn easily; and from the topmost and smallest storey an eagle was released and flew upwards with the fire towards the sky, the bird being believed to carry the emperor's soul heavenward.

Imperial funeral pyres of the lighthouse type described by Herodian in connection with Septimius Severus' ceremonial obsequies are represented on the reverses of consecration coins of the middle Empire, nearly always accompanied by the legend CONSECRATIO. The earliest known instance of such a design, but without the usual legend, on a *denarius* and *sestertius* of Aelius

Caesar, known respectively only from a sale-catalogue and from a cast in the British Museum, but believed to be genuine, shows a pyre of six storeys, with horsemen in relief on the outside of the bottom storey, arcades on that of the second storey, and figures and garlands on the exteriors of the third, fourth, and fifth storeys.[244] But most of these pyres are composed of four tiers, reckoning the high base as the bottommost. Such is the pyre on the *sestertius* struck for Faustina the Elder by Antoninus Pius (in AD 141): its base is garlanded, the second and tallest storey is arcaded, and on the summit is a chariot-group, presumably denoting the deceased's apotheosis.[245] All the types struck by Marcus Aurelius for Antoninus Pius (in 161),[246] for Lucius Verus (in 169),[247] and for the Younger Faustina (in 176)[248] show much the same details: the base is garlanded, the second and third storey have arcades, doors, and figures, and the fourth storey is draped, flanked by torches, and surmounted by a chariot-group. Almost precisely the same type of pyre is featured on the coins struck for Marcus Aurelius by Commodus (in *c.* 180).[249] Of the four-tiered pyre on the *sestertius* struck for Pertinax's consecration (in 193) the details are obscure on the British Museum specimen.[250] Especially magnificent are the five-storeyed pyres on the consecration coins of Septimius Severus (struck in 211).[251] On these the base, or lowest tier, is either draped or garlanded, the second, third, and fourth tiers have niches and figures, and the fifth tier, with its surmounting chariot-group, is either niched or draped or garlanded. With the type struck by Severus Alexander for the consecration of Julia Maesa (in 225)[252] we return to the four-storeyed pyre: the base is draped; in the second storey is seen the image of the dead on a funerary couch, flanked by figures in niches; figures in niches occupy the third storey; and the fourth storey, topped by the usual chariot-group, is draped and flanked by torches. (*Pls.* 15, 16)

## (B) THE CULT OF THE DEAD

The Roman cult of the departed, whether public or private, had a double purpose: it provided that the dead survived in the memories of relatives, descendants, and friends; and it also sought to ensure, through the medium of devout attention to their mortal relics in the tomb, comfort, refreshment, and perennial renewal of life to their immortal spirits.

An insistent urge to secure for oneself or for one's closest relatives such commemoration and attention after death is abundantly attested by funerary inscriptions. Those who could afford it left in their wills capital sums of money, the interest (*reditus*, *usura*) from which was to be expended on the offering at the tomb of food (*cibus*, *esca*, *edulia*), bread (*panis*), wine and grapes (*vinum*, *escae vindemiales*), cakes (*liba*), sausages (*tuceta*), ceremonial meals (*epulae*) thought of as shared by the living with the dead, incense (*tus*), fruits (*poma*), flowers of all kinds, particularly violets (*violae*) and roses (*rosae*, *escae rosales*).[253] Numerous representations of the funerary banquet carved on gravestones or painted on the walls of mausolea and hypogea bear witness to the special importance of the ceremonial meal eaten at the tomb; and this element in the cult of the departed also features prominently in the lengthy will of a citizen of Andematunnum (civitas Lingonum: Langres), in which the testator left elaborate and minute directions for the maintenance of, and rites to be carried out at, the *cella memoriae* (memorial shrine) which he seems to have had erected for himself in his lifetime.[254] Near this shrine there was to be an *exedra* and on the same spot the man's seated statue worked in the best imported marble or in the best bronze and not less than 5 feet high. The *exedra* was to contain a litter (perhaps for the use of his spirit) and two seats of imported marble; and in the *exedra*, on the days on which the *cella* was opened, were to be spread two coverlets, two cushions for diners, two cloaks, and a tunic, all for use at funerary meals. The testator's bones were to be placed in a beautifully carved altar of Luna marble, set up in front of the shrine, which was to be closed with a slab of Luna marble that could be easily opened and put back into position. On the shrine were to be inscribed the names of the magistrates during whose term of office the shrine had been begun and the number of years of the testator's life. No unauthorized person was to have access to the shrine, and the remains of no one else, whether cremated or inhumed, were to be buried within a specified distance of the shrine. The testator's freedmen and freedwomen were to contribute to the upkeep of the tomb; and his grandson and the latter's heirs were to pay an annual sum to cover the cost of food and drink for a meal to be celebrated there. Offerings at the funerary altar were to be made every year on the Kalends of April, May, June, July, August, and October. Finally it was laid down that all the testator's hunting equipment, his sailing boat, and his best clothes were to be cremated with him—presumably to serve him in the afterlife (*cf.* pp. 52–4).

Roses, the last item in the list set out above (p. 62) of offerings to the dead, are one of the gifts most frequently mentioned, along with food and drink, in funerary inscriptions—gifts for which the departed person's fellow members of a burial club (*cf.* pp. 54, 55) were often made responsible.[255] That roses were regarded as pledges of eternal spring in the life beyond the grave is suggested by one of Ausonius' epitaphs:

*Sprinkle my ashes with pure wine and fragrant oil of spikenard:*
*Bring balsam, too, stranger, with crimson roses.*
*Tearless my urn enjoys unending spring.*
*I have not died, but changed my state.*[256]

The same idea must have lain behind the painted showers of roses and rose-gardens on the walls and vaults of tombs.[257] These counterfeited flowers perpetuated, as it were, all the year round the offerings of actual roses that were often associated with the Feast of Roses (*Rosalia, Rosaria*) held in May and June when roses are chiefly in season (*suo tempore*) in the Mediterranean world.[258] Although by no means exclusively connected with the dead, the *Rosalia* (*dies Rosalium, Rosariorum, Rosationis*) undoubtedly afforded specific occasions for scattering roses on the grave and decking the funerary portrait-statue with them.

There were doubtless many other private family occasions for cult at the tomb—for instance, the departed's birthday (*dies natalis*); and provision could be made for the lighting of lamps at the grave on the Kalends, Ides, and Nones of every month.[259] But the annual official commemoration of the dead was the *Parentalia* or *dies Parentales*, lasting from 13–21 February, of which the last day, the *Feralia*, was reserved for public ceremonies, while the other days were for private celebration by the family. All these days were *dies religiosi*, during which magistrates did not wear the *toga praetexta*, temples were closed, and no weddings took place. Unlike All Souls' Day, on which all the faithful departed are commemorated, the *Parentalia* was the feast, not of the dead in general, but of parents and other kinsfolk of individual families, and it is often mentioned in inscriptions along with the *Rosalia*, birthdays, and so forth, as one of the times prescribed for offerings at the graves of relatives and friends.[260] Ovid describes in some detail the rites of the *Parentalia*, the regulations that accompanied it, and the traditions connected with it.[261] The gifts brought to the grave should, he says, be small and uncostly—such things as a tile wreathed with votive garlands, a sprinkling of corn, a few grains of salt, and loose violets, all of which gifts could be set on a potsherd in the middle of the road that was lined with tombs. On the other hand, larger gifts were not forbidden. The last day of the feast was called the *Feralia* because it was then that the living publicly carry their dues to the dead; and Varro confirms this.[262]

The second festival of the dead, held on 9, 11 and 13 May, was the *Lemuria*, when the apparently kinless and hungry ghosts, the *Lemures*, and the mischievous and dangerous *Larvae*, were supposed to prowl round the house.[263] It may have been a public festival, in view of the fact that it is entered on some calendars, although there are no records of any public celebration on those days and the rites described by Ovid are of a private and domestic character. At midnight the worshipper made a sign with his thumb in the middle of his forehead, washed his hands in clean spring water, turned, took black beans and threw them away with averted face, saying nine times: 'these I cast, with these I redeem me and mine.' The ghosts were thought to gather the beans and follow unseen behind the worshipper, who then touched water, clashed bronze, and asked the ghosts to leave the house. During the *Lemuria* temples were closed and marriages were not allowed.

17 Marble relief from the Tomb of the Haterii. The picture is dominated by a great temple-tomb with a stepped *podium*, a columned portico, and elaborate carving. Below is an enclosure surrounding a small domed tomb. Above is a scene in a tomb with a woman lying on a funerary couch. On the left workmen erect an obelisk (pp. 81, 132, 268–9).

18, 19 Two views of the Isola Sacra necropolis, showing burials of the poor. *Above*, the upper portions of *amphorae* planted erect in the ground to mark the graves. *Right*, two graves each marked by an *amphora*. Between them is an inhumation grave covered by *tegulae* (tiles) set gable-wise and with a tile at each end. In the background of both views are the mausolea of the well-to-do (pp. 101–2).

20, 21 The tomb enclosures, with pilasters set diagonally, of the Concordii at Reggio Emilia (*above*) and of the Statii at Aquileia (*below*) (pp. 80, 81).

22, 23 Two cremation graves from Colchester, each in the form of a 'box' made of tiles. *Above*, the ashes are in glass and terracotta vessels, *below*, in a large terracotta 'face-urn' (p. 101).

24, 25 *Above*, an inhumation grave from York covered by large roofing-tiles set gable-wise, four a side, with a similar tile closing each end and a row of *imbrices* (pantiles) along the top: *cf*. Pl. 19 (pp. 101–2). *Left*, another inhumation grave from York, which consists of a rough stone cist, sunk in a cavity in the ground, with walls of unevenly cut coursed stones. The skeleton rests on a floor of three slabs and was originally covered by a slab lid (p. 102).

26 *Left*, the tomb of Sabinus Taurius at Isola Sacra, built up against one wall of mausoleum No. 55. There is a rectangular brick base, carrying the inscription, on which rests an *aedicula* flanked by colonnettes and topped by a pediment. Within the *aedicula* are rendered the open doors of a tomb, revealing between them the figure of Taurius worked in intarsia (p. 103).

27 *Right*, an above-ground *columbarium* at Ostia, a rectangular chamber that once had a barrel-vaulted roof. It has *opus reticulatum* walls, one of which contains the entrance and an inscription frame worked in intarsia Part was reserved as a crematorium (pp. 115-16).

28 *Columbarium III* ('Colombari di Vigna Codini'), west wing. This underground *columbarium* takes the form of a corridor with three branches running off at right-angles from it. The projecting blocks of stone probably supported wooden galleries for reaching the upper niches (p. 114).

29, 30 *Above*, a travertine slab, carrying portrait-busts (two male, one female) set in the tufa façade of the late-republican double tomb of freedmen and freedwomen of the Clodia, Marcia, and Annia families beside the ancient *Via Caelimontana*. Beneath the busts, each of which is in an arched niche, is the inscription naming the deceased. *Left*, a view of the façades of the adjacent *Via Caelimontana* tombs. A second inset slab bears two busts (pp. 117–18).

# CHAPTER IV

# THE LAYOUT OF CEMETERIES AND OWNERSHIP OF TOMBS. WALLED CEMETERIES. FUNERARY GARDENS

## (A) THE LAYOUT OF CEMETERIES AND OWNERSHIP OF TOMBS

IN THE COUNTRY DISTRICTS of the Roman world rich and poor alike could be laid to rest in more or less isolated graves ranging in character from the simplest types of cremation or inhumation burials (*cf.* pp. 100–3) to those that were marked by, or contained in, elaborately carved or architecturally impressive monuments (see Chapters V, VI, VII). A city, on the other hand, has always needed its communal necropolis or necropoleis, at least one dependent city of the dead, more often several such cities, situated on its ourskirts. Roman law strictly prescribed that a city's cemeteries should be outside its walls or other formal boundaries (*cf.* p. 48); and for obvious reasons of accessibility they normally developed alongside of, or at least in association with, the roads that led from the gates into the open country. Familiar examples of straggling roadside cemeteries, with a single file of tombs of very varied types and sizes, and often with spaces between them, bordering the roadway on either side, are on the Via Appia Antica near Rome, where the tombs run for some miles southwards from the *Porta Appia*,[264] and on the Via dei Sepolcri outside the Herculaneum Gate of Pompeii.[265] Most cities of the Empire have produced at least some evidence of cemeteries of this sort. But in Italy, in particular, the Romans were heirs to the

Etruscan system of more expansive necropoleis, with networks of regular streets along which continuous rows of tumuli or blocks of chamber-tombs were aligned (*cf.* pp. 19–21). And it is Italian cities that provide some of the most interesting instances (three are described below) of the more compactly laid out Roman cemeteries, in which blocks or groups of contiguous tombs of similar shapes, each group following a common alignment, are seen (so far as they have yet been excavated) to be set in a line, sometimes with one or two parallel, or very roughly parallel, lines of blocks behind them, on one side, or on both sides, of a road.

The alignments of the various groups of tombs in a single cemetery are, however, sometimes so different from one another that we can only deduce the absence of any public control of a cemetery's growth and of any overall rational planning of it as an entity. Furthermore, it is by no means always the case that in a cemetery, whether of the strung-out or of the more densely built-up kind, the earliest tombs are nearest to the city. There was, it seems, no custom or rule that imposed a progressive extension of the burials outwards from the gates, although there are places in which precisely this phenomenon occurs. For example, at the Liburnian city of Argyruntum in Dalmatia there runs for more than half a kilometre on both sides of the road leading from the city's south gate an uninterrupted series of rectangular grave-plots enclosed by walls and separated from one another by narrow passages. Of the numerous burials discovered there all are cremations and many are accompanied by grave-goods that mainly represent Italian importations. To judge by the coins placed in these graves, those nearest to the city are of Julio-Claudian date, the next group is of Flavian and early-second-century date, while those furthest from the city are of the third century.[266]

The appearance of all city cemeteries was, naturally, largely determined by the tombs of the wealthy and reasonably well-to-do who could afford to buy a piece of land on which a personal or family grave-monument or house-tomb could be erected—or, it may be, to secure one of a series of ready-made house-tombs put up by a speculator on a building plot that he had purchased for that purpose. There is some literary, and a great deal of epigraphical, evidence for the frequent practice of placing on a burial plot or tomb a notice to define the width of its frontage on the road or cemetery-street (*in fronte*) and its depth reckoning back from that line (*in agro*, *retro*). This definition was often followed by some such formula as *H(oc) M(onumentum) H(eredem, -eredes) N(on) S(equitur, -equetur)* or *H(oc) M(onumentum) H(eredem) E(xterum) N(on) H(abebit)*, designed to prevent the property from passing to the owner's heir or heirs or to the heir or heirs of someone else. Horace mentions a grave-pillar (*cippus*) thus inscribed:

> *mille pedes in fronte, trecentos cippus in agrum*
> *hic dabat: heredes monumentum non sequeretur;*[267]

and Trimalchio requested, apropos of the *monumentum* that Habinnas was to build for him, 'ut sint in fronte pedes centum, in agro pedes ducenti', adding that the words 'hoc monumentum heredem non sequitur' should on no account be omitted.[268] Actual tomb-inscriptions enshrining these simple formulae are so abundant that no particular example need be cited.

There are, however, numerous inscriptions which contain more specific statements of the precautions that were taken to obviate the alienation of tombs, as in the cemeteries of Ostia and of Portus Augusti at Isola Sacra, north of Ostia, where monetary penalties are prescribed for such offences. For instance:

> Marcus Antonius Vitalis and his son Marcus Antonius Verus built this tomb for themselves, their freedmen and freedwomen, and their descendants. But if after the death of Marcus Antonius Vitalis anyone should sell or give or in any way alienate this tomb or introduce into it or within one of its enclosure-walls the body or bones of a person with a name other than is contained in the above list, he shall pay a fine of 3000 sesterces for each body to those who have charge of the cult of the Lares of Portus Augusti;[269]

and

> Lucius Cocceius Adiutor built (this tomb) for himself and declares that no one should burn or bury a body on the left side as one enters. If he does so, he shall pay 50,000 sesterces to the city of Ostia. The informer shall receive the fourth part.[270]

The tomb-inscription of a pearl merchant (*margaritarius*), found in Rome, combines a prohibition of misappropriation ('ex testamento in hoc monumento neminem inferri neque condi licet nisei eos lib(ertos) quibus hoc testamento dedi tribuique') with the request that the tomb itself should not be harmed ('rogo te, viator, monumento huic nil male feceris').[271] As regards the latter, the most common formula is *H(uic) L(oco)* or *M(onumento) D(olus) M(alus) A(besto)*; while another inscription from Rome reads: 'Pontia Prima heic est sita nolei violare.'[272]

Of the tomb-owners' two anxieties, misappropriation and injury, the second probably weighed on them more heavily, since interference with the structure and, in particular, any act that involved disturbance of the actual burial, spelt, it was believed, distress for the soul when it visited or dwelt in its body's resting-place (*cf.* p. 37). *Violatio sepulcri* was, indeed, a criminal offence and the subject of repeated imperial enactments, as the legal compilations testify. But there is a mass of evidence to show that fear of it was all too well grounded and that the sacrosanctity of tombs was frequently disregarded. Examples of this are the constant reuse of sarcophagi for secondary burials;[273] the ruthless employment of carved and inscribed gravestones as building material in the walls of cities, fortresses, and forts;[274] and even, on at least one occasion, in late-Roman Ostia, the cutting up of tomb-inscriptions to serve as seats in a public latrine.[275] In view of all this it is not, perhaps, surprising to find a sepulchral text from Rome in which a curse is prepared for possible violators of the author's burial place:

> Gaius Tullius Hesper made for himself this altar in which his bones are to be placed. If anyone disturbs them or removes them from here I pray that he may, while alive, endure prolonged

pains of body and that, when he dies, the gods of the lower world will reject him.[276]

It may have been partly in the hope of diminishing the risk of alienation or spoliation that members of two or more different families sometimes arranged to own a tomb conjointly. Tomb 94 in the Isola Sacra cemetery was owned by Valeria Trophime, who, at a later stage, added to its façade an enclosure, which she sold off in four portions to other people for the building of four separate little tombs.[277] The inscriptions put up by three of these purchasers survive, two in Tomb 94, while one was found nearby:

> Gaius Galgestius Helius, having bought a vacant burial-space from Valeria Trophime, made for himself and for members of his family a tomb-chamber joined to the wall on the right as one enters, in which are fourteen urns [= urn-niches?], apart from one urn [= urn-niche?], which Trophime gave to Galgestius Vitalis. He gave one of these urns [= urn-niches?] to Pomponius Chrysopolis.[278]

> Trophimus, slave of our emperor, and Claudia Tyche built this tomb for Claudia Saturnina, their loving daughter, who lived fifteen years, six months, and thirteen days, and for their freedmen and freedwomen, and their descendants. They bought as a burial-place a quarter of this monument from Valeria Trophime.[279]

> Euhodus, slave of our emperor, and Vennonia Apphis, having bought a burial-space from Valeria Trophime, built (this tomb) for themselves, their freedmen and freedwomen, and their descendants.[280]

At Ostia a tomb was shared between Manius Acilius Marianus and Cognita Optata.[281]

A more complicated division at Isola Sacra appears to involve two tombs: one was built by Marcus Ulpius Artemidorus for his father, Marcus Ulpius Hilarus, and his wife, Atria Fortunata, and it looks as if the latter had, after Artemidorus' death, married as her second husband Publius Afranius Callistus, to whom she gave burial-rights in the half of the tomb that had been allotted to her; meanwhile, Artemidorus had, it seems, acquired another burial-place for himself, in respect of which he took into partnership Lucius Domitius Callistion and Domitia Eutychia, who built in their half a tomb for themselves and their children.[282] No less complicated were the arrangements for the burial-plot at Isola Sacra, now Tombs 75 and 76,[283] a large enclosure acquired by Marcus Cocceius Daphnus for himself, Marcus Antonius Agathias, and Marcus Ulpius Domitus.[284] Two chamber-tombs were built in it, that to the south (76) being taken over for occupation by Agathias, Daphnus' heir, who, having made a division between himself and his co-heirs, built a wall right across the enclosure, continuing the line of the north wall of his tomb, and cut an independent entrance in the east wall of his share of the enclosure.[285] Tomb N in the Vatican cemetery under St Peter's gives yet a further instance of tomb dividing. It was built by Marcus Aebutius Charito for himself and his family, but either while it was under construction or just after its completion Lucius Volusius Sucessus and Volusia Megiste bought half of it for their son, Caius Clodius Romanus.[286]

Another practice (of which we have actually already seen an instance in the case of Tomb 94 on Isola Sacra: *cf.* p. 77) was for the owners of a family tomb to give to friends belonging to a different family a vacant grave-space for the burial of a relative.

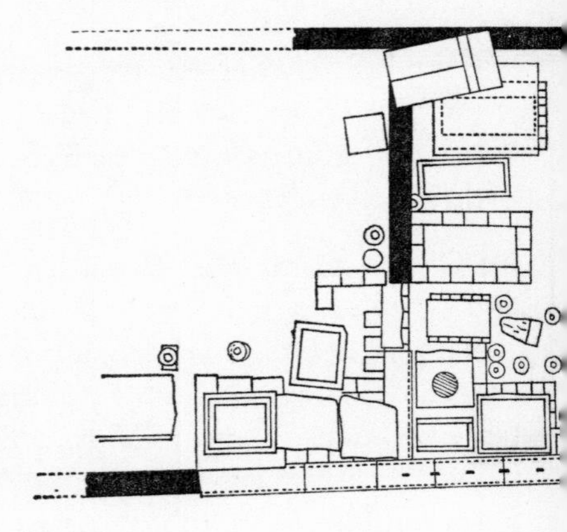

*Fig. 2 Part of the western cemetery at Aquileia*

For example, at Ostia, Flavia Marcellina made a tomb for her sister, Flavia Hilaritas, in a place granted to her by Plotius Hermes and Valeria Saturnina;[287] and Primitivianus and Volusia made one for their son, Lucius Kacius Volusianus, in a place granted to them by Gabinius Adiectus.[288] In the Vatican cemetery, in Tomb C, the mother of Tullia Secunda ceded part of her daughter's burial-place to Passullena Secundina;[289] and in Tomb H Valerius Philumenus and Valeria Galatia gave Titus Pompeius Successus a place in their mausoleum in which to bury his son, Titus Pompeius Successus junior.[290]

At **Aquileia** in north-east Italy there has been excavated a compact row of five contiguous tomb-enclosures, originally planned and built in the late-first or early-second century AD, but remaining in use for several centuries after.[291] The group was obviously part of a cemetery that had developed just outside the gate near the southern end of the west city-wall and it must have been aligned along a Roman road running westward from the gate, although no actual traces of that road have come to light. The five enclosures that have been examined, together with a fragment of a sixth, also contiguous to the east of them, are of unequal width *in fronte* but have a common frontage-line, a common depth *in agro* of 30 Roman feet (8·87 metres), and a common wall at their rear. Although it is clear that these tombs were not all put up in a single building operation, their common

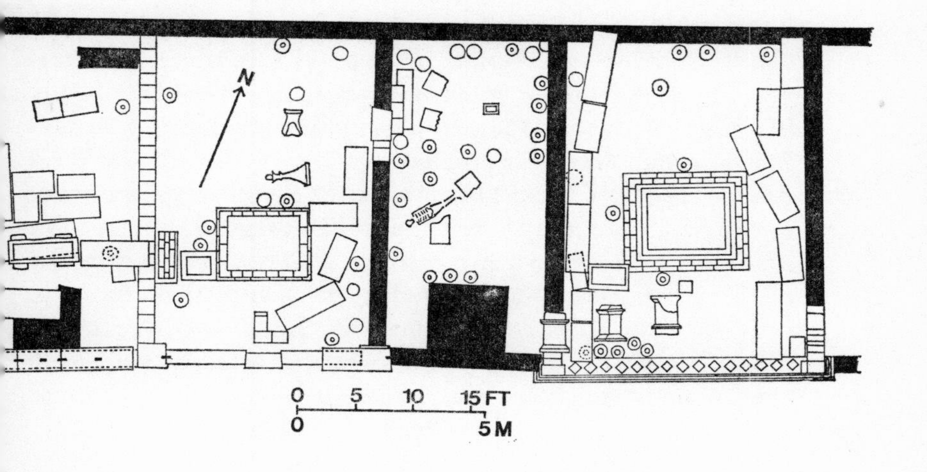

back wall is continuous and of the same type of masonry throughout. It must have been erected, to mark out the sepulchral area between it and the now-vanished road, by a speculator, who may have divided the area into plots and sold them to various individuals or families. Such purchasers would have then built at their own expense the side walls (*maceriae*) and façades that defined their burial-precincts, since all of these differ from the back wall in build.

Each plot when occupied consisted of a walled enclosure open to the sky, with a large, dominating altar-like monument reared on a base (*cf.* pp. 123–5) and surrounded by other burials. In the easternmost of the investigated tombs, measuring 25 Roman feet *in fronte*, only the three-stepped base of its great, centrally-placed altar has survived, together with a few fragments of its carved crowning feature. The risers of the top and middle steps of the base are richly carved in relief with floral ornament that can be dated stylistically to the late-first or early-second century. But if the main altar and its inscription have been lost, the tomb can be attributed without much doubt to the Statii family on the score of two inscriptions found inside it. One, cut in what is probably early-second-century lettering on one long side of a small stone sarcophagus, reads: 'L(ucio) Statio L(uci) f(ilio) Firmo'; the other, cut in what may be slightly earlier lettering on the face of a small grave-altar, reads: 'Fabricae Severinae an(norum) XVI mens(ium) X Hermes August(alium) et VI vir (orum) ark(arius=treasurer) et Sentia Severa parent(es) l(oco) d(ato) a Statiis'—yet another instance of a tomb's proprietors granting a burial-place within it to members of another family (*cf.* pp. 77, 78). Besides the sarcophagus there are fifteen cremation burials in the precinct, whose side walls are constructed of three courses of squared stones at the base and then of twelve courses of bricks, which are topped by a continuous rounded coping. Most striking is the façade, which is made up of fifteen small rectangular pilasters, 0·87 metres high, set diagonally with slight intervals between them. Of these the two sides that were visible to the spectator on the road side are elaborately carved in relief with floral designs—foliated stems, candelabra, and *thyrsoi* (Bacchic wands) and running floral scrolls. At each angle of the façade is a rectangular base or pilaster similarly carved on the front and on the outer side, the front in each case showing an ornamental chalice amid floral work; while on top of each base stood an altar again with the same type of carving on its front and two sides—running floral scrolls, chalices, and other floral patterns. All this decoration is in a style identical with that of the carving on the steps of the central altar. Along the top of the pilasters, between the angle bases and their crowning altars, runs a flat coping. The angle bases and pilasters were found still standing; and the rest can be restored with confidence from the fallen portions. (*Pl.* 21)

Of this façade the most unusual feature is the series of diagonally-placed pilasters, for which only two parallels are so far known, but in the case of both of them the pilasters are completely lacking in carved ornamentation. The earlier of the two is the façade, with sixteen pilasters, of the famous tomb-enclosure of the Concordii found at Boretto, seventeen miles north-west of Reggio Emilia, in whose public garden it has been re-erected: its funerary portraits are of the middle of the first century AD.[292] The second example is on one of the well-known reliefs from the so-called Tomb of the Haterii near Rome. Here there seems to be depicted a section of a closely built-up cemetery, dominated by a great temple-mausoleum on a high *podium* (*cf.* pp. 132, 268–9), in front of which is a small tomb-enclosure with six diagonally-set pilasters in its façade and a grave-altar, reared on a high base and topped by a domed canopy, as its central monument: this relief is of late-Flavian or early-Trajanic date.[293] (*Pls.* 17, 20)

The second excavated tomb-enclosure, passing westwards, in the Aquileia group is the narrowest and most modest of the five. It was obviously not envisaged when the Statii tomb and the third tomb towards the west were built, but was crammed into the plot, 14 Roman feet *in fronte*, that had been left vacant between them and it utilized their eastern and western side walls respectively as its own side walls, while the two ends of its rather shoddily made façade each mask the carved or neatly finished-off outer side of one angle base of its predecessors' façades. Of one build with the centre of this second tomb's façade is the base of its now lost, large funerary altar. The burials inside the enclosure are all cremations, with the exception of one inhumation trench-burial. The third tomb, measuring 23 Roman feet *in fronte*, has again preserved only the plain base of its large, centrally-placed altar, but it has, on the strength of the inscription on a small altar found inside —'Venusto ser(vo) rarissimo C(aius) Iulius Trophimus'—been assigned to the Julii family. Its façade, although not richly decorated like that of the Statii tomb, was built of well-cut, rectangular blocks and orthostats of stone, with corner blocks or bases. It contains several cremation burials and one inhumation. The fourth tomb, known as that of the Trebii from a sarcophagus within it bearing the inscription 'Trebia Pothusa', is the largest of the fully excavated series, with a frontage of 34 Roman feet. Its owner used for its eastern side wall the western side wall of the Julii tomb, building its western side wall himself, and its façade is made of large, well-cut, rectangular blocks crowned by a coping. The base of its lost main altar is not centrally sited and most of its burials are inhumations, with sarcophagi on three superimposed levels, the topmost being probably as late as the fifth century. The fifth tomb westwards, whose owners, like those of the second tomb, are wholly unknown, could not be completely investigated and the line of its western side wall has not been located, so that the extent of its frontage remains uncertain. It used the western side wall of the Trebii tomb, the line of whose façade its own façade continues, and its main grave-altar is off-centre. It has not proved possible to determine how far this 'terrace' of attached tombs ran in a westerly direction. But the section available for study has thrown valuable light on layout and ownership in one of the necropoleis of an important north-Italian Roman town.

The great cemetery of **Isola Sacra** served the town of Portus Augusti during the second and third centuries AD, after the construction of Trajan's inner hexagonal harbour. It takes its name from its situation at the northern end of the flat island that is bounded on the west by the Mediterranean, on the north by the *Fossa Traiana*, the artificially cut canal that linked the Tiber with the sea just south of the harbour, and on the east and south by the windings of the Tiber itself as it flows towards its mouth beside the northern boundary of Ostia.[294] Sporadic finds of tombs on this island, combined with the systematic excavations of the late-twenties and the thirties of the present century, have indicated that the cemetery as a whole occupied an area of about 40,000 square metres and was roughly triangular in shape, the base of the triangle being parallel with Trajan's canal, while the last tombs in the Ostia direction formed its apex. That apex is, in fact, represented by the complexes of tombs, running for some 330 metres from north to south, which Calza's investigations have revealed.

The tombs, whose chronology can be deduced from the details of their construction, from the styles of their internal decorations, and from the dated brick-stamps incorporated in them, range from about 100 to about 250 AD. They lie on either side, mainly on the west side, of the uncovered metalled section of the *Via Severiana*, the coast road linking Portus Augusti with Ostia, a road that was made, at any rate in its present form, in the early years of the third century, as its name indeed implies; and the line of this road clearly forms the cemetery's axis. However, only the third-century tombs lie close beside its margins (e.g. No. 12). All the earliest (Trajanic) tombs that have been unearthed are at quite a considerable distance to the west of it, a few as much as about 45 metres away from it: most of the Hadrianic tombs lie roughly 17 metres back from it; and the interval between it and the bulk of the Antonine tombs averages 5 metres. Thus, despite a number of exceptions to these general rules, there would seem to have been a gradual filling up of the ground between the earliest tombs and the roadside, the last comers wedging themselves in where they could. Apart from a very few, all the tombs, those of the second century no less than those of the third, face towards the highway or (in rarer cases) along it. And since it is unthinkable that no communication between Portus Augusti and Ostia existed before the Severan age, an earlier road must have run along much the same line as that of the *Via Severiana*. The Severan tombs are, in fact, on a level that is about 30 centimetres higher than that of the tombs of the second century. The land on Isola Sacra was not, so far as we can tell, required for other building purposes or for agriculture, but was completely untenanted. There was therefore nothing to prevent the owners of the earlier tombs from choosing plots well away from the busy thoroughfare, where they had space either to construct their burial-places inside roomy enclosures or to add at will enclosures in front of the façades of tombs that were already built. Another motive for such siting may have been the laying out of funerary gardens (*cf.* pp. 94–100).

In its completed state the Isola Sacra necropolis is a veritable 'city of the dead' after the Etruscan style (*cf.* pp. 19–21), with row upon row and block upon block of 'homes of the dead' all of the same general types—rectangular brick, or mixed brick and masonry, house-tombs with barrel-vaulted or (less frequently) flat roofs and impressive façades—often forming *insulae* (blocks) that are separated from one another by streets, lanes and open squares. The overall pattern of the excavated area and some of the means by which this pattern was achieved are outlined in the following paragraphs.

Among the most northerly and westerly tombs, at the greatest distance from the road, is a large Trajanic enclosure (No. 110) containing four burial-chambers (Nos. 106–9) and with its main entrance facing away from the highway. Further to the south, with a wide space between it and the last, but on much the same alignment, is a smaller Trajanic enclosure holding several burial places (Nos. 112–17), while to the west of it, and on quite a different alignment, is a pair of large, single house-tombs that share a common frontage, but are of different dates, one Trajanic (No. 128), the other Hadrianic or Antonine (No. 127). This north-western group of tombs spreads sporadically southwards (Nos. 129–42). But the great concentration of serried blocks of mausolea to the west of the *Via Severiana* begins some 25 metres to the south of these outliers, each block taking its own alignment, although all are more or less parallel to the highway. Amid the Severan tombs that fringe the kerb are two that take the form of ample precincts embracing several sepulchral chambers (Nos. 47, 34). But the great majority of them are relatively small, self-contained, single chambers huddled together in little clusters

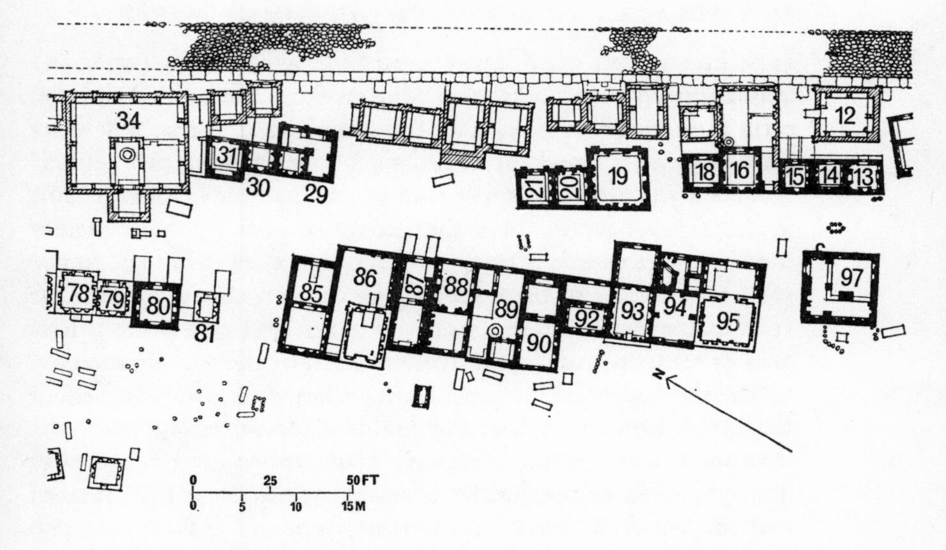


*Fig. 3 Part of the cemetery at Isola Sacra. Plain outline indicates tombs of the early-second century; solid colour, those of the mid- and later-second century; hatching, those of the third century*

of two, three, or four tombs, with narrow passages between the clusters. Somewhat similar Severan nuclei of tombs line the road's eastern edge; and a few of the second-century tombs behind them have been brought to light.

To return to the western side of the highway, the Antonine mausolea, whose façades were, in some cases, almost completely masked by the Severan tombs in front of them, fall into six nuclei, strung out at intervals and all on slightly different alignments. Between the Severan tomb-enclosures Nos. 47 and 34 are first a single mausoleum (No. 46) and then two contiguous tombs (Nos. 42, 39) of unequal size, but with a common back line. Immediately to the south of No. 34 are three adjacent house-tombs (Nos. 31, 30, 29), which shared a common frontage until an enclosure holding further burials was added to the east and south of No. 29. Eighteen metres further south is a block of three contiguous mausolea, two small (Nos. 21, 20) and one large (No. 19), all with a common back wall; then a space; and then a 'terrace' of five adjacent tombs (Nos. 18, 16, 15, 14, 13), all with a common back line and all small, apart from No. 16, which is larger and was equipped with a narrow annexe on the south and, on the east, with a great enclosure, into whose south-eastern corner a Severan burial-chamber was later intruded. A lane separates this 'terrace' from a nucleus of two small contiguous mausolea (Nos. 11, 10); and directly beyond these the excavated area of the cemetery terminates, towards Ostia, in a complex of Severan tombs (Nos. 3–9), some of them set back at the same distance from the road as the Antonine series just described and two preceded by enclosures that reach to the western kerb of the *Via Severiana*.

The third and earliest range of mausolea, that which is furthest from the western side of the highway, is separated from the Antonine range by a wide empty space running the whole way along in front of the façades, a space that is open at the southern end, but now closed at the northern end by a Severan tomb (No. 72) interlarded between the Severan tombs on the kerb and one small Hadrianic tomb (No. 55) and three large Hadrianic tombs with enclosures (Nos. 76, 75, 54). These four adjacent tombs make up the northern end of the most northerly of the two great, more or less similarly aligned blocks of which this series of mausolea is composed and they are built up against, and on the same alignment with, three small contiguous Trajanic house-tombs (Nos. 77, 78, 79), which share a common back line both with one another and with a still smaller Trajanic tomb (No. 81) that had been put up at some distance to the south of them. Between this tomb and the trio 77–9 a Hadrianic tomb (No. 80) was inserted, adjacent to the trio and sharing a common frontage with the one that is its immediate neighbour to the north (No. 79); and thus the whole block now contains nine contiguous tombs. On the ground occupied by the more southerly of the two great blocks in this range, a block now consisting of ten tombs, there seem to have been originally two widely separated, but similarly aligned, Trajanic tombs (Nos. 86, 95). In the Hadrianic period precincts were added to these and the interval between them was filled with seven new mausolea, five with a common frontage (Nos. 92, 90, 89, 88, 87), two with enclosures projecting from their façades (Nos. 93, 94), while an eighth (No.

85) was built up against the northern side of No. 86. Two isolated Hadrianic tombs were erected to the south of the southern block, Nos. 97, 100; and there is a scatter of small, isolated Trajanic and Hadrianic mausolea to the west of the northern block. But the Hadrianic age would appear to have witnessed, at least in this cemetery, a deliberate tendency to fill up gaps and so to produce large, compact, and self-contained *insulae*.

Sprinkled haphazardly in the spaces between the blocks of house-tombs, of which only the earliest were equipped internally solely for cremations, are the burial places of the humbler folk—small square monuments with pyramidal roofs, small chest-shaped tombs with rounded lids, trench-burials covered by tiles set gable-wise, and other simple burials each marked on the surface by the upper half of an *amphora* (*cf.* pp. 101–3). After the Severan period the reoccupation and reconditioning of the second-century tombs for new burials began to take place on an extensive scale, the original owners' families having by then presumably died out. But throughout its history the social pattern of the cemetery remained unchanged, as inscriptions and 'professional' tomb-reliefs reveal. It was, in the main, essentially a city of the bourgeois dead—of shopkeepers, merchants, surgeons, craftsmen, and so forth, persons of comfortable means and artistic taste, nearly all Latin-speaking and thoroughly Roman in background, even if many had Greek names and were ultimately of east-Mediterranean stock.

Roughly contemporary with the Isola Sacra necropolis and reflecting much the same social *milieu* is that which was excavated in 1939 and during the decade following on **The Vatican**, under the nave of St Peter's Basilica.[295] The section that has been unearthed and remains accessible to visitors runs for about 70 metres in an east–west direction and is about 18 metres wide from north to south. Its eastern termination is roughly half-way between the Papal Altar and the church's eastern façade, and on the west it extends for about 8 metres beyond the niche, immediately below the Papal Altar in a north–south red-stuccoed wall, that is generally believed to mark what the Roman Christians of the mid-second century venerated as St Peter's grave. All the tombs are rectangular in shape, range in size from about 10 by 6 metres (H) to about 2 by 1·7 metres (M), and are mostly cross-vaulted, single, enclosed chambers built of brick (*cf.* pp. 138–43). One mausoleum (H) had an open forecourt, surrounded by a low wall, in front of its façade, while in the case of two (B and D) the front half of the tomb was open to the sky and formed a forecourt behind the façade and separated from the tomb proper by a wall reaching to the roof (*cf.* pp. 135, 139). With one exception ($R^1$—the court annexed to the back of R), which has an entrance opening to the east on to a partly inclined, partly stepped, north-south alley (the so-called *Clivus*), all the tombs face south. They stood on the lowest portion of what was once the steep southern slope of the *Mons Vaticanus*; and not much further south of them, in the *Vallis Vaticana*, must have run, after the mid-second century, when Nero's circus ceased to exist,[296] an east–west road, probably the *Via Cornelia*, of which the Vatican excavators found no trace opposite the tombs, although a substantial stretch of it had come to light further east in the sixteenth century.

The eastern half of the excavated area consists of two parallel rows of tombs with a narrow street between them. The earlier row, that to the north, the only row that existed while Nero's circus was in action, is furthest away from the presumed east–west road and was once only separated by the narrow street from the imperial gardens and circus. Its tombs, which are all contiguous and probably of Hadrianic date, contain mixed cremation and inhumation burials, whereas the four (*Ψ* to *Z*) in the southern row, each of which is separated from its neighbour by a narrow passage, are for inhumations only and must have been put up later in the second century. In the northern row the first six mausolea, reckoning from the east, that have been revealed have an absolutely even common frontage, which suggests that a speculator had, as at Aquileia (*cf.* p. 80), bought up a strip of land large enough to hold at least six mausolea (there may have been more belonging to the same 'terrace' further east) of slightly varying widths and depths; and that he either built the tombs himself and sold them prefabricated to different families or sold just the plots, the actual building of the tombs being undertaken by the individual

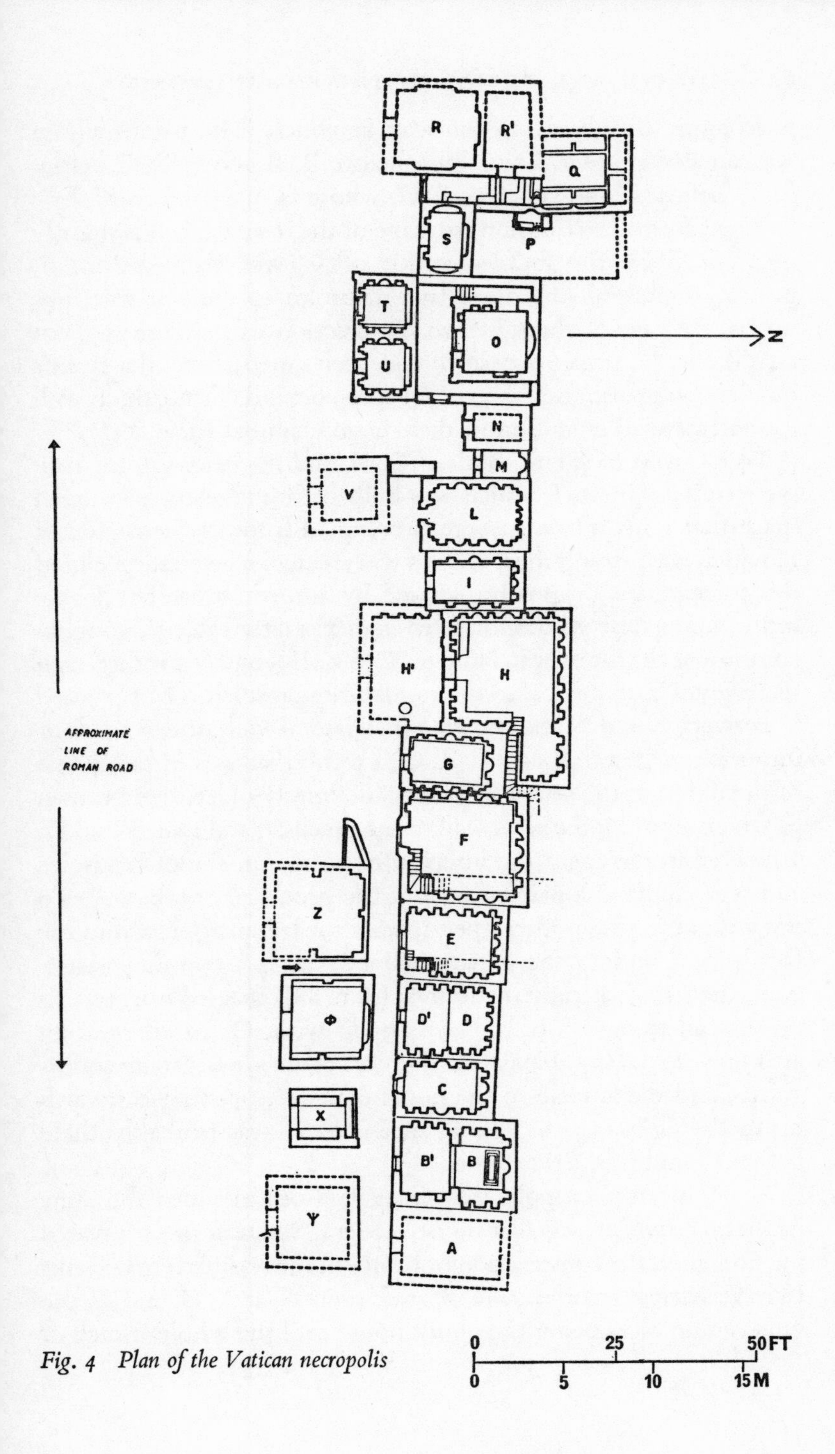


*Fig. 4 Plan of the Vatican necropolis*

purchasers. By observing the way in which these tombs adjoin we can deduce that A was built before B, B before C, C before D, D before E, and E before F. G, whose façade projects slightly forward from the common frontage of the 'terrace' and is slightly overlapped by the façade-cornice of F, was there before F, possibly before all the other five mausolea to the east were put up: it was, again, there before the erection of its large western neighbour, H, since its cornice had been cut back by the latter's builders, who also used the vacant space behind G's northern wall for an eastward extension of their main chamber (*cf.* p. 142).

To the west of *Z* and south of G, H, and the latter's immediate western neighbour, I, which was built before it, there is an open space that leads into a passage running in front of the façade of L, which was already there when I was erected. The western end of this passage was originally blocked by a north–south bench-like tomb, up against whose southern end was later built V, roughly continuing the interrupted line of *Ψ* to *Z*. Beyond V another open space gives access to N, to the miniature mausoleum M squeezed in between L and N and utilizing their lateral walls, and to the door into the precinct that surrounds O, a tomb that was certainly one of the oldest in the whole cemetery, definitely older than N, than S, which abuts on the west wall of the precinct, and than T and U, which continue again the interrupted southern line of mausolea and were built as a pair up against the precinct's south wall. To the west of T yet another open space afforded an approach to the façade of S and to the partly inclined, partly stepped, passage-way, the *Clivus* already mentioned (*cf.* p. 88), that led northwards up the hill to, and is of the same build with, Q, an inhumation area open to the sky. Finally, to the west again are R, facing south-wards, and the annexe to the north of it, $R^1$, opening eastwards on to the *Clivus* (*cf.* p. 88). R, at any rate, was probably there before Q and its *Clivus* existed.

The Vatican necropolis was, then, laid out in much the same haphazard style as was that on Isola Sacra. So far as the excavated portion goes, the construction of tombs in the northern row seems to have started at three quite separate points—at A, G, and O, the intervening plots being then built upon until the whole stretch of ground from A to O presented one long, continuous, solid block of mausolea. Only the 'terrace' A to F suggests deliberate planning. The later tombs had to take such spaces as were left nearer to the presumed highway (*Ψ* to *Z*) or up an incline (Q), the former leaving between them narrow passages and small 'piazze' giving access to their predecessors to the north. If on the Vatican the alignments of the various groups of tombs in both rows run parallel to one another, instead of at acute angles, as on Isola Sacra, that is likely to be due to this cemetery's restricted terrain, penned in between a road and a steeply sloping hillside.

A very large number of necropoleis attached to towns is known throughout the Roman world; and obviously only a minute fraction of the total mass of available material is represented by the three Italian samples that have been selected for description here. It can, however, be claimed that few other Roman funerary sites have yielded so vivid and informative a picture of the growth and arrangement of some of these elaborate Roman cities of the dead as have those at Aquileia, on Isola Sacra, and on the Vatican.

## (B) WALLED CEMETERIES

The walled funerary enclosure open to the sky and housing several or many burials is, as we have seen, a feature of Roman city-cemeteries in Italy, where it either forms, as at Aquileia, the entire tomb (*cf.* pp. 79–82) or is an adjunct, as on Isola Sacra, to the main, barrel-vaulted sepulchral chamber (*cf.* pp. 88, 90). In both of these cases such enclosures are integral parts of rows or blocks of contiguous tombs; which are again but constituent elements of whole necropoleis; whereas the unroofed precinct surrounding the tomb of the Concordii in the countryside north-west of Reggio Emilia, with its lofty carved and inscribed stele in the centre of its front wall, is a free-standing, independent little cemetery in itself, measuring 10·60 by 9 metres (*cf.* p. 81). (*Pl.* 20)

Akin in form and internal arrangements to these Italian sepulchral precincts, but more closely resembling, for the most part, the Concordii type of structure in the self-contained independence of their siting, are the unroofed walled cemeteries of the northern

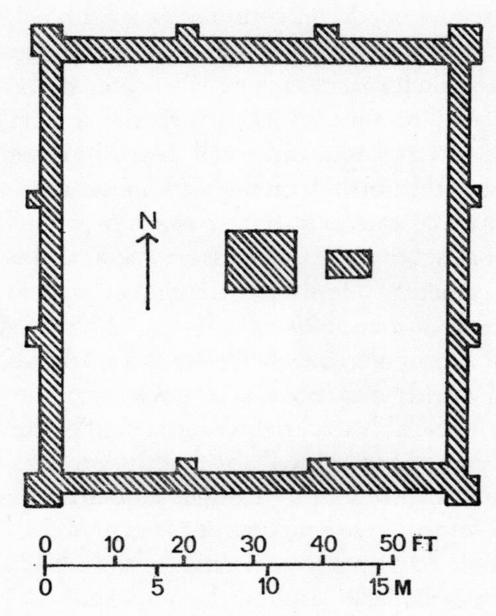


*Fig. 5 Plan of the Southfleet walled cemetery*

and western provinces, particularly of Britain and Gaul. These vary greatly in size; and they range in character from what could be described as mausolea, that is, enclosures containing a large central grave monument, sometimes with a few other burials around it inside the precinct walls, to those that hold as many as a hundred different interments. In Britain[297] such cemeteries are mainly, but not always, to be found in the south-eastern areas of the province; they are frequently aligned on Roman roads; and are often in the neighbourhood of country villas and farmsteads, whose owners were presumably the persons buried within the enclosures. Much rarer is the appearance of these cemeteries in association with cities or other urban centres.

Among the British examples of the mausoleum type of walled cemetery with a conspicuous central structure are those at Harpenden in Hertfordshire, at Southfleet in Kent, and on Shorden Brae, to the west of Corbridge, in Northumberland. At Harpenden[298] the enclosure is about 100 feet square, with rubble walls of flint and clay, an entrance in the middle of one side, and a

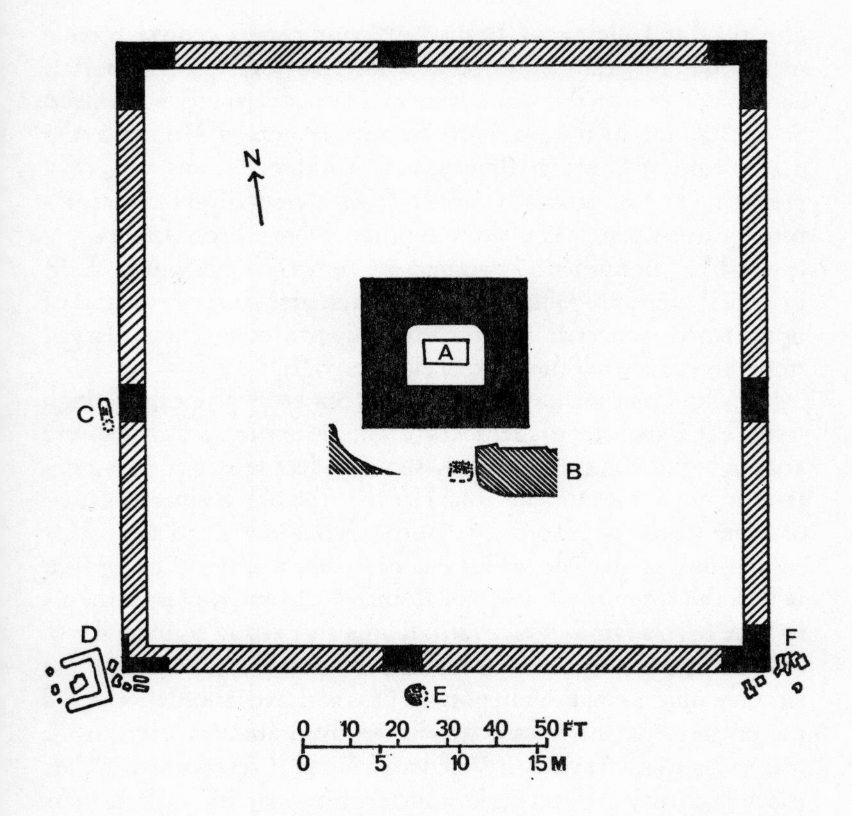


*Fig. 6 Plan of the Shorden Brae mausoleum. A, primary burial. B, building debris. C, grave. D, tomb fountain. E, pit. F, lion*

V-shaped ditch outside it on three sides. The central monument is circular and 11 feet in diameter. The precinct at Southfleet[299] is about 50 feet square, with massive external buttresses at the four corners of its walls and two small, intermediate buttresses on each of its four sides. The central burial was in a stone sarcophagus under a pavement of ragstone, on which some superstructure must once have stood. Aligned with this and between it and the eastern precinct wall was another stone sarcophagus containing two lead coffins with a skeleton in each. A Gaulish walled cemetery at Ladeuze in Brabant[300] comprises a central monument, hypothetically restored as a lofty tower, and five burials and is not unlike the cemeteries at Harpenden and Southfleet. So far unique in the northern frontier region of Britain is the mausoleum at Shorden Brae near Corbridge,[301] consisting of a precinct 135 feet square which encloses a centrally-placed structure 35 feet square. The latter appears to have been originally a tower-like monument covering an underground burial-shaft, in which were probably interred the remains of some person of importance connected with the township of Corstopitum. Carved stone lions once adorned the enclosure walls.

Less like a mausoleum and more of a cemetery proper, although restricted, it may be, to members of a single family, is the enclosure at Langley in Kent,[302] which is about 80 feet square and contains two principal monuments, one circular, the other square, neither of them centrally placed, two square stone cists, and five other cremation burials. The walled enclosure, measuring 38 by 27 feet, within the western cemetery of Roman Colchester,[303] is also likely to have been a family graveyard. It appears to have contained, not only a monument set up in its central internal bay, but also not less than nine cremations in pottery urns and five inhumations; and the pottery suggests that it was in use from about AD 100 to the fourth century. At Sutton Valence in Kent[304] there was a walled precinct forming a rectangle some 60 feet long by 15 feet wide, with one long side bowed out in a shallow curve. Near the straight long side was a cist or vault of stone, 4 feet square and containing cremated remains; but the other half of the enclosure was occupied by about a hundred cinerary urns arranged in three straight, parallel rows, two of the rows running across the whole length of the precinct, the third half-way across it. This must have been the cemetery of a whole community, including perhaps its leading family or most important member.

## (C) FUNERARY GARDENS

Among the directions given by Trimalchio for his future tomb (*cf.* p. 75) was that for the laying out around it of an orchard and vineyard—'I should like to have every kind of fruit growing round my ashes and plenty of vines';[305] and numerous sepulchral inscriptions bear witness to a widespread interest in the Roman world in the endowing of funerary gardens consecrated to the dead as holy and inviolable domains. The texts make it clear that these gardens were enclosed by walls, planted with a great variety of trees and flowers, equipped with wells, pools, and so forth for watering the plants and refreshing visitors, and furnished with buildings such as dining rooms and species of summer-houses in which meals in commemoration of the departed could be eaten by the survivors. Arrangements of this kind were wholly in keeping with the social and religious patterns of Roman life and thought in late-republican and imperial times. They reflected both the general passion of the Romans for gardens,[306] a passion that the dead when dwelling in the tomb did not, so it was believed, cease to experience,[307] and also the notion that Elysium, with its idyllic landscape, natural amenities, and heavenly banquets, could have its symbolic counterpart on earth.

The technical term *cepotaphium* or *cepotafium* (= κηποτάφιον or κηπόταφον), or, very occasionally, *cepotafius*, which in itself implies that sepulchral gardens were common in the Greek-speaking provinces, is relatively rare in inscriptions in the West, in Rome and in other parts of Italy; and, to judge by such names of imperial freedmen as occur in the texts that contain the term, it was not much employed there before the second century AD. In the East, on the other hand, and in Alexandria in particular, these Greek forms are attested in literary, papyrological, and epigraphic Greek sources from Augustan times and from later periods in the first century of our era. For example, Strabo describes the district west of Alexandria as containing κηποί τε πολλοὶ καὶ ταφαί.[308] An Augustan papyrus mentions persons who combined in a group for the leasing of three κηποτάφια near Canopus, one of the conditions being an annual payment of the best produce of these gardens (τῶν ὄντων ἐν τοῖς κηποταφίοις [τ]ὰ κράτιστα καὶ βέλτιστα) namely a large and very profitable quantity of vegetables and fruits.[309] An inscription found in Alexandria and cut in lettering of the second or third century refers to legal proceedings conducted between AD 89 and 91, when Mettius Rufus was Prefect of Egypt, in respect of a funerary garden which had been dedicated, obviously at some earlier date, by one Pomponia Mousa for her son Maximus and her husband Marcus Antonius Theophilus:[310] this garden was to be 'held in common, undivided, inalienable, not to be burdened legally, and not to be transmitted by will, for all time' (*κηπόταφον . . . ἐγγόνοις κοινὸν καὶ ἀδι[αίρετον καὶ] ἀνεξαλλοτρίωτον καὶ ἀκαταχρηματιστον ἐκ παντὸς τρό[που καὶ ἀκληρο]νόμητον εἰς τὸν ἀε[ὶ] χρόνον*). An inscription, probably of the first half of the second century, discovered at Ilias in Asia Minor, records the erection by a man, whose name is lost, for himself, his wife, and his children of a tomb complete with its own funerary garden (*ἰδίῳ κηποτάφῳ*).[311] An instance of the Greek form in a Greek inscription in the West came to light in the *Via Tusculana* region near Ponte Lungo to the south of Rome.[312] The slab, whose lettering suggests the second century, was put up by a husband and wife, Ortorios Eleis and Ortoria Eutychis, clearly persons of the east-Mediterranean freedmen class, in memory of their ten-year-old son, Markos Ortorios Eleutheros: they were also adherents of an Egyptian mystery-cult, since the text includes a prayer to Osiris to give the dead boy refreshment (*[δ]οίη σοι ὁ ῎Οσειρος τὸ ψυχρὸν ὕδωρ*). They made for their son an 'eternal bridal chamber' (*αἰώνιον νυμφῶνα*: for mystic marriage with the god?) and for themselves in expectation of their death a tomb and garden (*[ἑα]υτοῖς θανάτου προσδοκίαν τοῦτο τὸ [μνη]μεῖον κηπόταφον*).

Examples of the use in the West of the Latinized version of the Greek terminology are 'hoc cepotaphium muro cinctum',[313] 'hoc munimentum [*sic*] sive cepotafium',[314] 'aedificium cum cepotafio et memoriam a solo fecerunt',[315] 'cepotafius intus q(ui) cont(inet) p(e)d(es) pl(us) m(inus) CC' (one of the few instances in which the area of the garden is recorded),[316] 'cepotafium sibi donatum muro cinctum fecit',[317] and 'in hoc cepotaphio maceria cinctum' [*sic*].[318] There is also the diminutive *cepotafiolum*.[319] Far commoner is the appearance of the Latin *hortus*,[320] *horti*,[321] and *hortulus*;[322] and these, like the whole sepulchral plot (*locus*) or tomb or grave-monument (*monumentum*), are frequently described, as are the *cepotaphia*, as surrounded by an enclosure-wall (*murus*, *maceria*).[323] In addition to the general words for buildings cited in the inscriptions in association with the gardens, such as *aedificia* and *monumenta*, which perhaps sometimes in the first case, and certainly always in the second, refer to the actual tombs or grave-monuments, there are some words that suggest more specifically places for the eating of funerary meals, for keeping provisions, or for other forms of social activity. There are references to *cenacula* (dining-rooms),[324] *tabernae* (eating-houses),[325] *tricliae* (summer-houses),[326] *diaetae* (bars or lounges), one with as many as five different apartments,[327] *solaria* (sun-terraces),[328] *horrea* (stores),[329] and even, in one case, to *stabula* and *meritoria* (rooms to let?, brothels?).[330] Paths (*itinera*) in the garden are sometimes mentioned.[331] Water-supply was catered for by *cisternae* (cisterns),[332] *piscinae* (basins),[333] *canales* (channels),[334] *putei* (wells),[335] and *lacus* (pools).[336] In some cases the sepulchral garden is described as a *praediolum* (small estate)[337] or *ager* (field).[338] Other gardens are designated *pomaria* or *pomariola* (orchards).[339] Indeed, as further inscriptions also show, Trimalchio was not alone in his desire for *poma* and *vineae* planted around his final resting-place (*cf.* pp. 94, 95). The owners of one tomb are said to have 'adorned it with the seeds of vines, fruit-trees, flowers, and plants of all kinds'.[340] Another man 'made his mausoleum fruitful by planting trees, vines, and roses'.[341] Marcus Rufius Catullus, styled *curator nautarum Rhodianeorum*, 'built for himself and for his son and daughter a tomb with a vineyard and enclosure-walls'.[342]

Plantations of this type had sometimes a practical, as well as an aesthetic and mystical, value (*cf.* p. 95). Their produce could be turned to good account to provide the wherewithal for celebrating the festivals of the dead and other commemorations of the departed. For example, we hear of 'a half-acre of vineyard for celebrating the *Parentalia*'.[343] A north-Italian, Lucius Ogius, declares that 'he will give, during his lifetime, gardens, with a building, adjoining his tomb, so that from their yield a greater abundance of roses and eatables may be offered to his patron and eventually to himself.'[344] Another north-Italian provided 'gardens

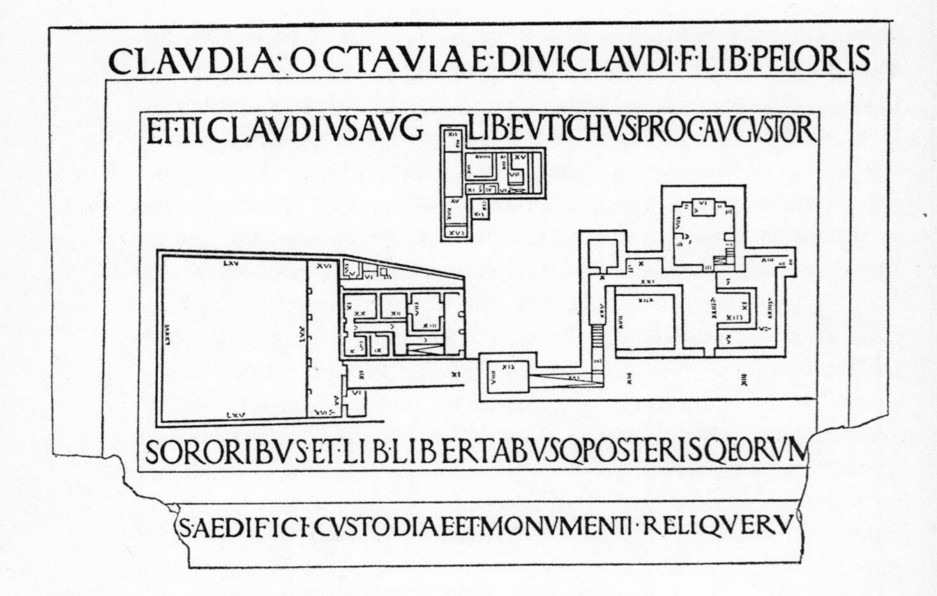


*Fig. 7 Marble plan at Perugia of a funerary garden*

from whose yield my survivors may offer roses to me on my birthday for ever—gardens which, I direct, shall not be divided up or misappropriated'.[345] A Gaul, Publicius Calistus, equipped his tomb with 'a vineyard two-thirds of half an acre in area, from whose yield I wish libations of no less than fifteen pints of wine to be poured for me each year'.[346]

Some idea of how these funerary gardens were laid out may be gleaned from two Roman marble slabs each incised with the plan of one.[347] A slab of uncertain, but probably metropolitan, provenance, now in the Archaeological Museum at Perugia, shows the family sepulchral plot of Claudia Peloris and Tiberius Claudius Eutychus.[348] On the right-hand side are various groups of tomb-chambers; in the centre are two large rooms divided into small apartments, perhaps *cenacula*, *tabernae*, *diaetae*, etc.; and on the left is an empty walled space, almost certainly a garden, roughly rectangular in shape, two of its parallel sides measuring

65 Roman feet, the other two sides 76 and 70 feet respectively. The second slab was found in the cemetery of Helena on the *Via Labicana* near Rome.[349] In the centre of one long side of this plan is a circular, tower-like tomb-monument on a square base, flanked on either side by an open space which has a row of dots, presumably denoting trees, on two of its sides. The central part of the area of the slab is occupied by five rectangular (one very narrow) and two small square spaces, possibly representing lawns

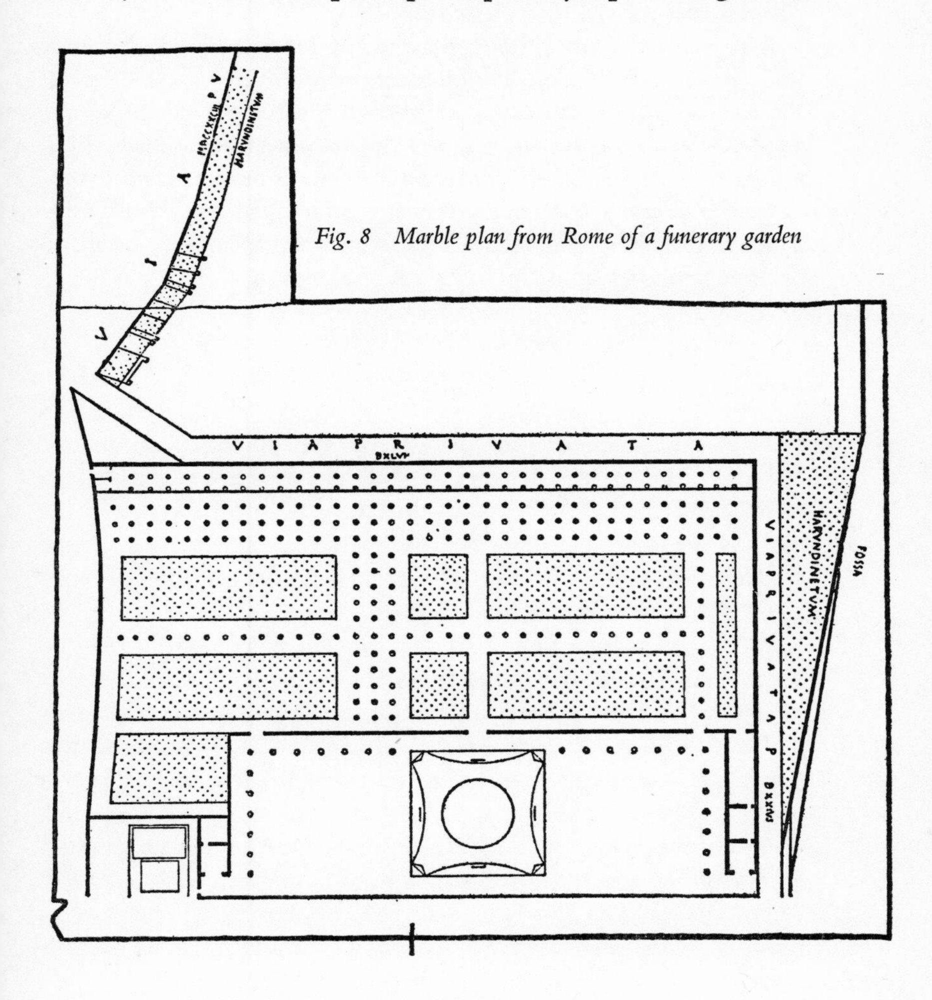


*Fig. 8 Marble plan from Rome of a funerary garden*

or flower-beds: between these spaces are absolutely straight rows of dots; and five more such rows lie between the spaces and the long side of the slab that is furthest from the tomb-monument. What strikes one most about these trees, if indeed it is for trees that the dots are meant, is the mathematical regularity with which they are planted: all are exactly equidistant from their neighbours, each tree in each row being exactly in line with the tree in the row in front and behind. Whether all *cepotaphia* were so primly planned we cannot, of course, tell.

It is possible that some suggestion of a funerary garden may have been intended on a military tombstone found at Chester. Below the inscription is a scene showing three gabled buildings, a tall one in the centre and a lower one on either side, which could represent either a block of contiguous mausolea or, more probably, the actual tomb flanked by subsidiary sepulchral buildings. In front of each of the lateral buildings is a stylized tree or shrub planted in the ground.[350]

# CHAPTER V

# SELECTED TYPES OF TOMBS I

## (A) SIMPLE CREMATION AND INHUMATION TOMBS

THE SIMPLEST TOMBS of the Roman world were holes in the ground, unadorned by any form of structure, in which were placed either the receptacle containing the deceased's burnt bones and ashes or his or her unburnt skeleton. It is likely that above such burials there was always once, at ground level, some kind of marker, which, in the case of the humblest graves, took the form of a plain standing stone or even of a large clay pot. For example, numerous upper portions of *amphorae*, down the necks of which libations could be poured (*cf.* pp. 37, 41, 51, 52), mark the sites of the burials of the poor that occupy the spaces between the rows of the house-tombs of the well-to-do in the Isola Sacra cemetery north of Ostia (*cf.* pp. 134–8).[351] Some of the inscribed and often richly carved stone or marble stelai (see Chapter VII(B)) in other cemeteries could have marked the positions of structureless cremation graves or of coffins, or possibly bare skeletons, sunk directly in the earth. On the other hand, it is extremely probable that the more elaborate of these stelai stood above human remains that were protected under ground by some type of built-up covering, since even unsophisticated burials were often provided with unpretentious structures. Cremation burials, where the burnt bones and ashes have been placed in a terracotta pot or glass jar, accompanied by a few inexpensive grave-goods, are frequently enclosed in a 'box' composed of large clay *tegulae* (tiles), or of large flat bricks, or of stone slabs (*cf.* p. 52). As provincial instances of the tile- or brick-made type of 'box' may be cited burials from Trier and Bingen in Germany[352] and from Colchester in Britain.[353] For inhumations the simplest method was to lay the body in the earth, but to cover it with pairs of flat *tegulae* set gable-wise and generally with *imbrices* (curved and hollow roofing tiles) along the ridge. Such was Tomb $\theta$ in the Vatican necropolis, near St Peter's shrine;[354] and a burial at York was protected by four large *tegulae* along each side, by a similar *tegula* at either end, and by a ridge of *imbrices*.[355] A group of tombs precisely similar to the tomb at York just quoted came to light at Rheinzabern in Germany.[356] In the case of another York inhumation the body was placed in a wooden coffin that lay inside a rectangular construction consisting of tiled walls and a flat tiled roof.[357] At Isola Sacra, interspersed among the *amphora*-marked cremation graves, are inhumations in the bodies of huge *amphorae* cut in half and laid on their sides. One half served as a receptacle, sunk in the ground, for the corpse, the other as a barrel-vault-like covering projecting above the surface.[358] Yet another inhumation burial found at York comprises a rough stone cist constructed in a cavity in the ground with walls of unevenly cut, coursed stones, a base of three slabs, on which the body was deposited, and a slab lid.[359] (*Pls.* 18, 19, 22–5)

The tile- and stone-built tombs that we have reviewed are representative variants of a class of funerary structures that all but the very poorest could afford. Their materials were cheap and in making them little skill was needed. Still simple, but more costly, because requiring more exacting workmanship, are the small chambers constructed of masonry or brickwork to house the relics normally of a single person, but sometimes of two or even three dead people. A further feature of those areas of the Isola Sacra cemetery in which the less well-to-do were laid to rest are the so-called 'tombe a cassone', built of bricks, completely sealed up, and shaped like chests with semi-cylindrical roofs. One of the smallest of these when turned over on its side was found to contain a terracotta vessel holding burnt bones;[360] and although the largest examples, whose interiors could not be probed, may well have held inhumations,[361] the rest probably housed cremations. The inscribed marble tablet on one records, in fact, its erection 'cineribus Claudiae'.[362] These chests all projected above the surface of the ground, as did also tombs of another relatively modest type exemplified by the monuments of Gaius Annaeus Atticus, a painter from Gallia Aquitania,[363] and of one

Bassus,[364] both set up among the humbler graves. Each consists of a square, sealed brick 'box' topped by a pyramidal roof: in view of their shape they are likely to have held cremations. More ambitious in its structural and decorative elements, but basically unpretentious, is the tomb of Sabinus Taurius at Isola Sacra, which is built up against one wall of house-tomb 55.[365] It comprises a brick rectangular base, carrying the inscription slab and presumably containing the cremated remains (unless there is an inhumation in the ground below), and above that an *aedicula* (literally, 'little house') flanked by a colonnette on either side and topped by a pediment. Within the niche of the *aedicula* are rendered the open doors of a tomb, disclosing between them the figure of Taurius worked in brick intarsia. (*Pl.* 26)

Carefully built, but lacking decoration and inscriptions, are some provincial variants of funerary structures of this simple kind. Roman York again provides examples and all are for inhumations. Some at least were in all probability subterranean originally. One neat brick tomb is large enough to hold three or four corpses.[366] Of other brick-built tombs one had a barrel-vaulted roof; and there are also tombs made of upright stone slabs, some divided internally so as to take two bodies.[367] Another funerary chamber, containing a single coffin, has walls of coursed limestone blocks and a vaulted roof turned in tiles: the entrance, blocked up after the burial had taken place, has a lintel and threshold each of a single limestone slab.[368] Similar to the last-cited York example, but designed to hold a pair of coffins, is a probably once subterranean chamber, built of well-cut stone blocks and originally covered by a barrel-vaulted roof, at Efferen in Germany.[369] Tombs of this type must have been extremely common throughout the northern and western Roman provinces.

## (B) THE TOMB OF THE CORNELII SCIPIONES IN ROME

From the humble or at least relatively simple tombs of a single individual or of two to four individuals, cremated or inhumed, we turn to more developed types. First, we consider a large and elaborate early family tomb on the southern outskirts of Rome, some 300 metres inside the *Porta Appia* of the Aurelian Wall.

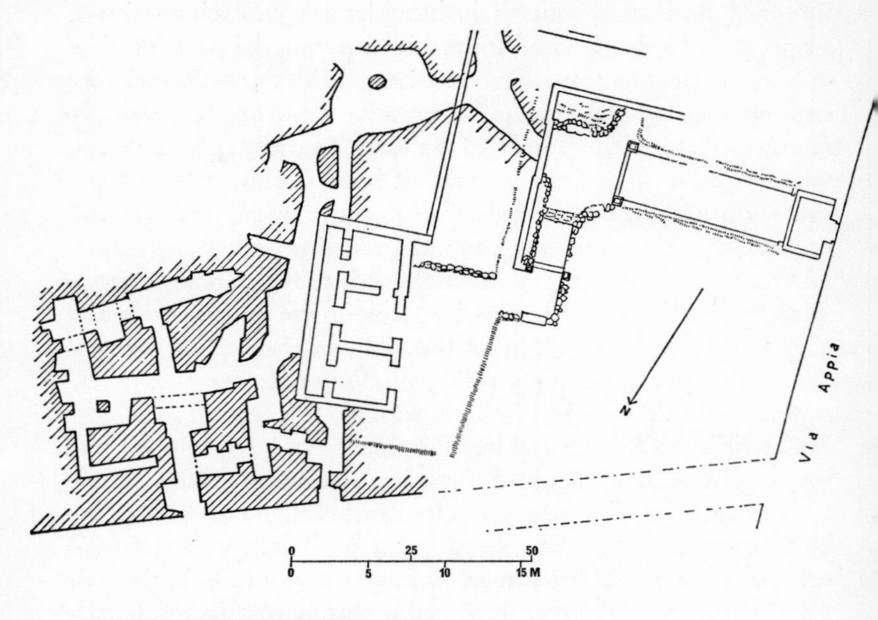


*Fig. 9 Plan of the Tomb of the Scipios*

This is the burial place of the Cornelii Scipiones beside the *Via Appia*, hollowed out of the tufa after the manner of the Tomb of the Volumnii near Perugia (*cf.* pp. 22–4), but dating back to the first half of the third century BC.[370] The façade, which faced towards the *Via Appia* and was approached by a private side road leading off it, was cut in the face of the living rock and embellished with simple architectural elements and paintings. The two entrances to the tomb itself, within the rock, opened off the side road. The western one gives access to a main single gallery, with burial niches on either side of it, whose original appearance was greatly changed when a house was built on top of it in the third century AD. The eastern entrance leads into a large, roughly square chamber consisting of a central gallery and of a gallery on each of its four sides, while two more or less regularly shaped masses of rock are left on either side of the central gallery. The burial niches are cut in the walls of the galleries.[371]

31, 32 *Right*, the Mausoleum of the Julii at St Rémy (Glanum) in Provence. It consists of a square base carved with four pictorial reliefs, an intermediate square storey with an arch piercing each side, and a 'canopy' of twelve columns sheltering statues of the dead beneath a conical roof. *Below*, the Street of the Tombs at Pompeii, running into the country from the Herculaneum Gate (pp. 118-27).

33 The Augustan tomb of Gaius Cestius, near the *Porta Ostiensis*, takes the form of a pyramid made of brick-faced *opus caementicum* sheathed in marble. Inscriptions on the outside give Cestius' names and titles and the circumstances of the tomb's erection (pp. 127–8).

34, 35 The late-republican tomb of the baker, Marceius Vergileus Eurysaces, near the Porta Maggiore (*below*). Trapezoidal in shape, it has a series of vertical cylinders (representing corn-measures?) in its lower storey and of horizontal cylinders in its upper one. *Above*, a detail of the tomb's frieze showing bread-making operations—sorting grain, kneading, rolling, placing loaves in an oven (p. 128).

38 'La Conocchia' (the distaff), a mausoleum at Santa Maria Capua Vetera (*opposite*). The masonry is of small irregular pieces of stone set in cement. There are a square base; a rectangular storey with concave sides, closed *aediculae*, and a rounded engaged column at each corner; and a circular structure with engaged columns (pp. 129-30).

36, 37 *Above*, detail from a fourth-century Christian sarcophagus depicting the Raising of Lazarus, whose tomb takes the form of a little temple with stepped *podium* (p. 132). *Right*, the restored temple-tomb of Asfionius Rufus in the Sarsina Museum. It stands on a high *podium* and consists of a *cella* and a *pronaos* of four free-standing columns. There is a false door in the front wall of the *cella*, which has engaged Corinthian columns along the exterior of its sides and back. There was a pyramidal roof (p. 131).

39, 40 *Above*, the so-called 'Tomba degli Orazi e Curiazi' near Ariccia. Its base is surmounted by a central circular pyramid and a truncated cone at each of its four corners (p. 129). *Below*, the rectangular brick house-tomb, probably of Annia Regilla. near the *Via Appia* (p. 133).

41 The façades of two of the three brick-built house-tombs under the Church of San Sebastiano. On the right, the Tomb of Marcus Clodius Hermes, on the left, the Tomb of the Axe, the former with painted interior decoration (pp. 133–4).

42 Interior of the Tomb of the Axe, with handsome stucco decoration (rosettes and vine-scrolls) on its ceiling and back wall. In the case of all three tombs (mid-second-century AD) the interior is at a lower level than the façade (pp. 133–4).

Unlike most republican Romans, members of the Gens Cornelia inhumed, instead of burning, their dead throughout the third and second centuries BC (*cf.* pp. 39, 40); and in this family tomb the bodies were laid in inscribed sarcophagi placed in *loculi* (shelf-like niches) carved, as has been said, out of the rock walls of the galleries. The inscriptions record the names of eight members of the Gens belonging to this period,[372] of whom Lucius Cornelius Scipio Barbatus, believed to have been consul in 298 BC, was the earliest and Paulla Cornelia, wife of Hispallus, who died *c.* 130–120 BC, was the latest .There are also the burial of an unidentified Scipio and the *loculi* of two first-century AD persons, Cornelia Getulica and Marcus Iunius Silanus, son of Getulicus.[373] Many of the sarcophagi have been badly damaged. But that of Barbatus is well preserved and is now in the Vatican. It was also the only one to be decorated, carrying a Doric frieze along the upper part of the trough, and a large Ionic volute at either end of the lid.[374] (*Pl.* 8)

### (c) COLUMBARIA

The *columbarium* proper is a large tomb, either partly or wholly underground, whose walls contain hundreds of niches, semicircular or rectangular, set closely together—hence its name 'dovecot'—and intended to contain the ashes of the dead in urns or chests. Since the fifteenth century great numbers of these *columbaria* have come to light in the area between the *Via Appia* and *Via Latina* within the Aurelian Wall of Rome. But of those only four are preserved today, the three so-called 'Colombari di Vigna Codini' being structurally the most impressive.[375] All three served as burial-places for connections of the imperial family and for freedmen of members of the Julio-Claudian dynasty. *Columbarium I* is a rectangular room, measuring 7·50 by 5·65 metres, with a massive rectangular pilaster at its centre,[376] in whose sides, as in those of the walls of the chamber, regular rows of serried niches have been cut, larger rectangular ones occasionally interrupting the series of semicircular niches. The walls are of *opus reticulatum* (small facing-blocks set diagonally in a net-like pattern), stuccoed and painted. There is also a 'step' running round the base of the walls in which *ollae* (urns) have been sunk. Inscriptions record the selling and buying of these *ollae*. The chamber could have held some 450 cremation burials and it has produced 298 epitaphs referring in particular to freedmen, slaves, and workmen who died in the principates of Tiberius and Claudius.

*Columbarium II* is a regular cube, with nine rows of nine semicircular niches in each of the four walls and the same 'step' containing *ollae* at their base as in *Columbarium I*.[377] Here nearly all the dead had been slaves or freedmen of Livia, the Elder Drusus, Marcella I, and Marcella II. An inscription states that two freedmen had the chamber's mosaic pavement laid in AD 10. Notable among the deceased persons mentioned in the epitaphs are members of a *collegium symphoniacorum*, *socii coronarii*, a female obstetrician called Hygieia, and an imperial bodyguardsman (*corporis custos*). Some of the niches hold portrait-busts of the departed. Much of the stuccoed and painted decoration of the niches still survives. The vaults both of *Columbarium I* and *Columbarium II* are modern restorations.

*Columbarium III* is the most remarkable of the trio in view of its size and of the mainly rectangular shape of the niches in its subterranean galleries: only those in the walls of its stairs are semicircular.[378] The manner in which these large rectangular niches are lined and embellished with marble, and the richness of the carving of the marble ash-chests that many of them contain, suggest that this *columbarium* belonged to people wealthier than were the owners of *Columbaria I* and *II*. This tomb takes the form of a corridor with three branches running off at right angles from it. From the upper part of the walls project horizontal blocks of stone. These probably supported wooden galleries on which, on feasts of the dead, the survivors could mount, from the head of the stairs, to visit and decorate the upper niches. All the corridors are roofed with cross-vaults that are painted with garlands, other floral motifs, animals, and so forth, worked in roundels and squares in the early-first-century AD style. Most of the dead were freedmen of the Julio-Claudian dynasty; but a few burials date from the period of Trajan and Hadrian, presumably placed in niches that had not been used in earlier times. (*Pl.* 28)

The fourth well-preserved *columbarium* in the *Via Appia–Via Latina* area within the Aurelian Wall is known as that of Pomponius Hylas from the coloured mosaic panel inscribed with his name that is erected above the stairs which lead down to the subterranean burial chamber.[379] Hylas may have founded the *columbarium*; but it does not seem to have remained in his family's possession, since none of the names in its other funerary inscriptions show any connection with him or, indeed, with one another. The tomb is chiefly notable for the paintings and architectural features of its main chamber. But the usual rows of semicircular niches appear in that chamber's walls on either side of the *aedicula* at the apex of its apse and in the walls that flank the stairs that give access to it. The inscriptions reveal that the *columbarium* was built under Tiberius and remained in use until the principate of Antoninus Pius. But no inhumations have been discovered in it.

Much closer to the centre of Rome, but still outside the line of the Servian Wall, is the *columbarium* found in 1886 in the Villa Wolkonsky, in the angle between the Via Statilia and the Via di Santa Croce in Gerusalemme. This is a partially subterranean three-storeyed structure, built for Tiberius Claudius Vitalis by members of his family, two of whom are styled *architectus*.[380] The inscription recording this is on a heavily framed marble slab let into the brick façade, above the door of the tomb. The upper storey comprised a rectangular room, once cross-vaulted, which may have served for funerary banquets and other rites. From this stairs lead down to the middle storey, whose walls are filled with semicircular niches for cremation burials, as are also the walls of the lowest storey, which is approached by stairs from the door in the façade on the level of the floor of the second storey. This third storey is completely underground and lighted from above.

Unlike these early-imperial burial places on the outskirts of, and in, Rome that could be excavated in the tufa, contemporary tombs at Ostia are built wholly above ground. One type is a rectangular roofless enclosure, with plain reticulate walls some metres high and no entrance, ladders being the only possible means of access. Inside such an enclosure the dead were cremated (*cf.* p. 49) and their ashes were placed in urns sunk in the ground along the

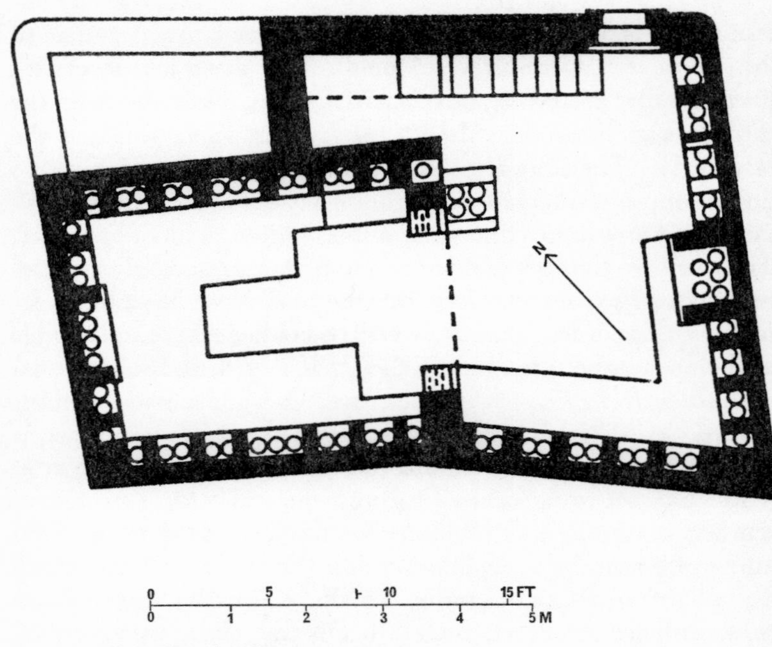


*Fig. 10 Plan of a* columbarium *at Ostia*

walls.[381] Variants of this type have some kind of stone architectual feature—occasionally quite elaborately carved—in the centre of its most important side.[382] A second type of Ostian tomb, exemplified by Tomb 18 in the Laurentine cemetery, ranks as a *columbarium*, although no part of it is underground and it contains a far smaller number of cremation burials than do the *columbaria* of Rome.[383] This type takes the form of a rectangular chamber with a barrel-vaulted roof. It has high *opus reticulatum* walls, one of which contains the entrance and carries on the outside a decorative frieze and inscription-frame worked in terracotta and pumice inlay. One corner of the rectangle is cut off from the rest and reserved as a place for cremating the dead, whose ashes were placed in rows of rectangular niches built into the inner faces of the chamber's walls. (*Pl.* 27)

### (D) LATE-REPUBLICAN CHAMBER-TOMBS IN ROME

From the Porta Celimontana (Arch of Dolabella and Silanus) on the line of the Servian Wall there once ran an ancient road (*Via Caelimontana*) to the site of the Porta Maggiore in the Aurelian Wall. Along this road, near the intersection of the modern Via Statilia and Via di Santa Croce in Gerusalemme, remains of Roman tombs came to light in 1881, 1899, and 1914, mostly on the road's southern edge. These discoveries have disappeared. But a row of four adjacent tombs that were excavated in 1916–18, also on the southern edge of the old road, in the north-east corner of the Villa Wolkonsky, have been preserved and offer features of special interest.[384] The façades of the easternmost two of the quartet, made of tufa blocks, present a continuous frontage (*cf.* pp. 85, 88): the façade of the next tomb westwards has been wholly destroyed; while the westernmost is constructed of well-worked blocks of peperino. Behind each façade, and lower than it in height, is a rather irregularly rectangular *cella*, cut out of the tufa of the rising ground. Built against the inside of the southern wall of the easternmost tomb, which has an empty space behind it, is a bench; and its *cella* was roofed by a simple, asymmetrical vault. On the blocks of the façade are inscribed the names of the owners of the tomb: Publius Quinctius, a *librarius* and freedman of a certain Titus, his wife Quinctia, freedwoman of Titus, and his concubine and freedwoman Quinctia Agatea. The lettering of these inscriptions is that of the late Republic. Also on the façade are two plain shields carved in low relief. The *cella* as found contained eight burials, four cremations and four inhumations; and, curiously enough at that date, the original three owners of the tomb would appear to have been inhumed.

The next tomb, although built as one structure on a single foundation, contains two *cellae*, each with its own doorway and with a partition wall between them. Both the walls and the roofs of both *cellae* were found in a ruinous state. In the northern portions of the east *cella*'s lateral walls were discovered six niches, three on each side and each niche holding two urns. In the east *cella* are fourteen cremation urns, set along the walls: there is also a *fossa* for inhumation. On the tufa blocks of the façade there are inscriptions in the same type of lettering as on the Quinctii tomb, recording the deceased freedmen and freedwomen of the Clodia, Marcia, and Annia families. But the chief interest of this double tomb lies in the two inset travertine slabs, one at the top of each *cella*'s façade which carry in the one case (east *cella*) a row of three busts, two male and one female, in the other case (west *cella*) a row of two busts, male and female, each bust being in relief and framed in an arched niche. All these busts are in the late-republican portrait style. In view of this evidence it would seem to be extremely probable that most of the numerous stone or marble late-republican portrait-busts worked in relief on square or horizontal slabs were originally set in the façades of tombs, similar to those of the group here described (*cf.* p. 245); their structures have disappeared, while the portraits, preserved as works of art, are now housed in the museums of Rome and in other European and American public and private collections. The great majority of these reliefs came to light in or near Rome. Some bear a single bust, some a row of two or three busts, others four, five, or even six busts.[385]

Of the two remaining tombs of the *Via Caelimontana* group, that immediately to the west of the double tomb was already largely destroyed at the time of its discovery. Its inscriptions recording the names of its owners have vanished; but it was found to contain a number of cremation burials in niches and the tile-built inhumation burial of an infant. Only the façade of the fourth tomb has been excavated. In the centre is a rectangular frame, which probably once contained a slab with portrait-busts in relief; and a travertine block bears the names of Aulus Caesonius Paetus, of his freedman Aulus Caesonius Philemo, and of a freedwoman Telgennia Philumina. (*Pls.* 29, 30)

### (E) LATE-REPUBLICAN AND EARLY-IMPERIAL MASONRY TOMBS OF VARIOUS TYPES IN ROME AND ITALY

The tombs of the wealthy and of the relatively well-to-do that have been considered so far—the rock-cut hypogeum of the Scipios, the *columbaria*, and the chamber tombs of the *Via Caelimontana*—all fall into clearly definable types that are easy to classify. Other tombs designed for comparable social strata in Rome and Italy are much more individual; and even those that share the same general characteristics tend to differ from one another in their details to a far more marked extent. For example, the Street of the Tombs at Pompeii outside that city's Herculaneum Gate, presents to the eye, for the most part, a varied spectacle of funerary structures of very divergent shapes and sizes juxtaposed.[386] These Pompeian tombs, and some parallels to them drawn from elsewhere, will be discussed first. We shall then turn to the much less numerous, but in some cases more self-consciously ambitious, specialized monuments within the area of ancient Rome; and finally to a few unusual tomb-forms elsewhere in Italy. (*Pl.* 32)

One of the simplest types, architecturally, among Pompeian tombs is the unroofed enclosure generally entered by a door on one side. It is exemplified by the burial place of the aedile Titus Terentius Felix, provided, according to its inscription, by the city (*publice*) and situated on the north side of the Street of the Tombs, a short distance from the city gate.[387] Felix's remains were found in a glass urn placed inside a leaden case, which was in turn protected by a terracotta jar. It had been buried in the earth under a small masonry table set against the enclosure's south wall, on the left of the entrance. Coins of Augustus and Claudius are recorded as being in or near the urn—presumably Charon's fee (*cf.* pp. 49, 124 and p. 291, Note 168). Along the interior face of the north wall is a bench containing the burials of members of Felix's household. The discovery of shells suggests that funerary meals took place in the enclosure's central area. More elaborate is another unroofed enclosure in the fork between the Street of the Tombs and the 'Vesuvius Road' that branches off the former to the north-west.[388] This is a regular sepulchral *triclinium* with painted walls (perhaps once sheltered by some form of penthouse at the top), a broad, sloping bench along each side wall, on which the banqueters reclined, a table between the benches, and in front of the table a small round altar for offerings to the dead. Small pyramidal towers crown the walls. The tomb was built by a freedman, Callistus, for his patron, Gnaeus Vibius Saturninus,

*Fig. 11 Plan of the Street of Tombs, Pompeii*

A HERCULANEUM GATE

B CITY WALL

C BAY ROAD

D ROAD ALONG CITY WALL

E VESUVIUS ROAD

KEY TO THE LEFT SIDE

24 VILLA OF DIOMEDES

16–23 TOMBS—GROUP III
- 16 Unfinished tomb
- 17 Tomb of Umbricius Scaurus
- 18 Round tomb
- 19 Sepulchral enclosure
- 20 Tomb of Calventius Quietus
- 21 Sepulchral enclosure of Istacidius Helenus
- 22 Tomb of Naevoleia Tyche
- 23 Triclinium Funebre

5–15 SO-CALLED VILLA OF CICERO

1–4a TOMBS—GROUP I
- 1 Sepulchral niche of Cerrinius Restitutus
- 2 Sepulchral bench of A. Veius
- 3 Tomb of M. Porcius
- 4 Sepulchral bench of Mamia
- 4a Tomb of the Istacidii

KEY TO THE RIGHT SIDE

33–43 TOMBS—GROUP IV
- 33 Unfinished tomb
- 34 Tomb with the marble door
- 35 Unfinished tomb
- 36 Sepulchral enclosure with small pyramids
- 37 Tomb of Luccius Libella
- 38 Tomb of Ceius Labeo
- 39 Tomb without a name
- 40 Sepulchral niche of Salvius
- 41 Sepulchral niche of Velasius Gratus
- 42 Tomb of M. Arrius Diomedes
- 43 Tomb of Arria

31–32 SAMNITE GRAVES

10–30 VILLA
- 10, 11, 13, 14 Shops
- 12 Garden belonging to Tombs 8 and 9
- 15 Street entrance of Inn
- 16–28 Rooms belonging to the Inn
- 29–30 Potter's establishment

1–9 TOMBS—GROUP II
- 1 Tomb without a name
- 2 Sepulchral enclosure of Terentius Felix
- 3, 4 Tombs without names
- 5 Sepulchral enclosure
- 6 Garland tomb
- 7 Sepulchral enclosure
- 8 Tomb of the Blue Glass Vase
- 9 Sepulchral niche

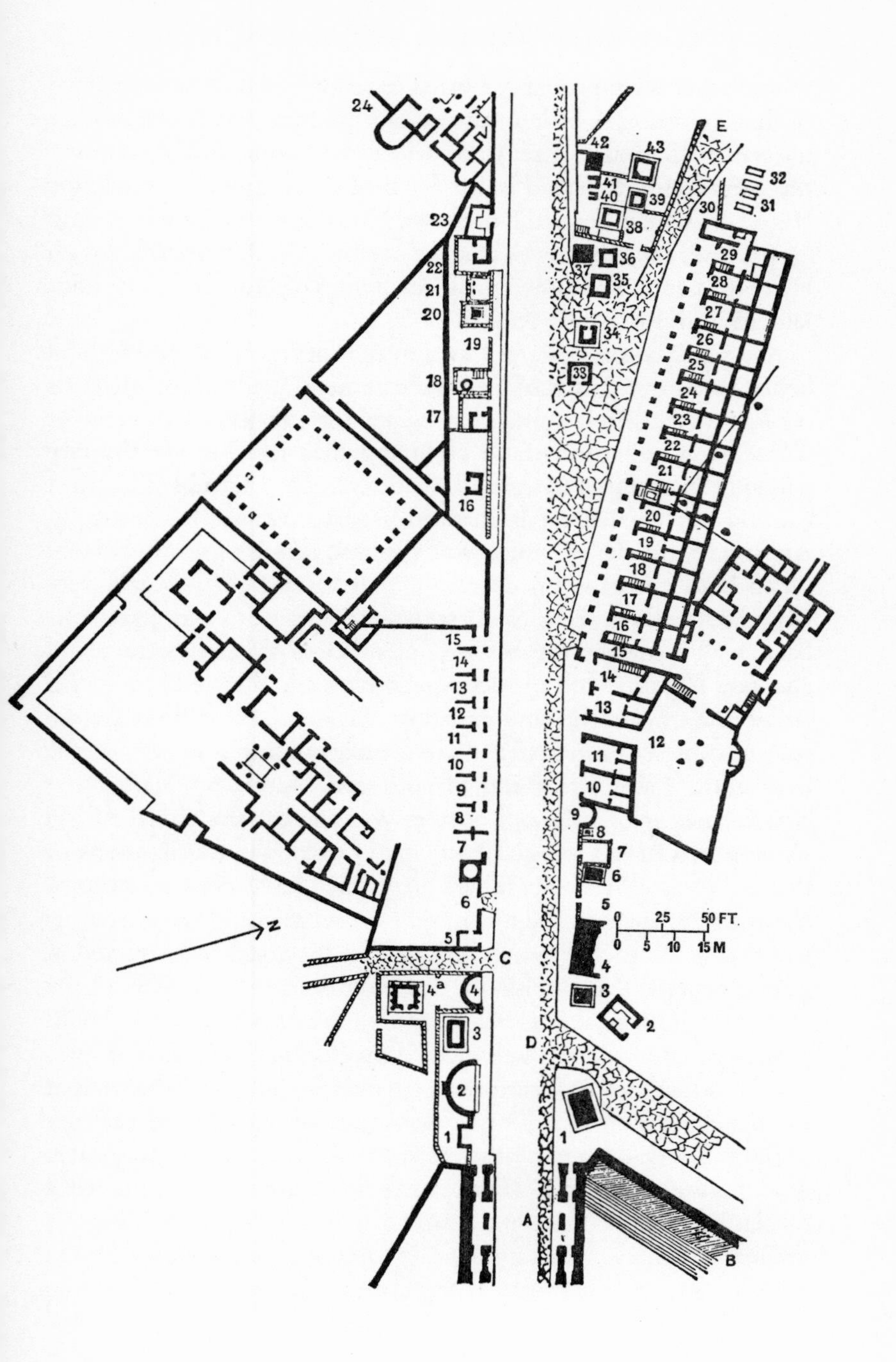

A
B
C
D
E
N
0 25 50 FT.
0 5 10 15 M

whose ashes were probably buried in an urn sunk below the floor of the enclosure. A little to the east of the *triclinium* is yet another unroofed enclosure, this time without a door and containing three gravestones shaped in the form of stylized human busts, the largest of which bears the name of Numerius Istacidius Helenus. (*cf.* pp. 124, 125).[389] A tablet on the enclosure wall is inscribed with Helenus' name, combined with the names of Numerius Istacidius Januarius and Mesonia Satulla.

A type of tomb designed to win the survivors' gratitude, and hence to ensure that the dead were remembered, is the niche or *exedra*, which often contains a bench for the use of passers-by. Three such structures stand close together just outside the city gate on the southern margin of the Street of the Tombs. The most easterly of the quartet is the tomb of Cerrinius Restitutus, an Augustalis, the site of which was voted to him by the city council ('loco dato decurionum decreto').[390] It consists of a small, rectangular, vaulted niche with seats along its sides and against its back wall a marble tombstone, intended to take a portrait, and an altar. The urn with the deceased's ashes could have been buried either underneath the altar or below the stone. Next door are the two unroofed, semicircular niches, each holding a bench, of the magistrate Aulus Veius and the priestess Mamia respectively.[391] The former is of tufa and 20 feet wide across the chord of the semicircle. Carved winged lion's paws mark the terminations of the niche on either side. There may once have been a statue of Veius at the apex of the niche; and on what could have been its pedestal is an inscription recording that the tomb was erected at public expense ('ab populo ex decurionum decreto'). Behind the apex of the niche is a small, unwalled space where Veius could have been interred. Mamia's niche is smaller, but has the same lion's paw terminations. Its inscription, cut in large letters on the back of the bench, tells us that Mamia was a *sacerdos publica* and that her burial place was given by the city council ('locus sepulturae datus decurionum decreto'). Two large semicircular niches, very similar to those of Veius and Mamia, are on the edge of Pompeii's Stabian Road, near the city gate.[392] One of these, to judge by the inscriptions on two stones at the corners of the burial plot, was provided for Marcus Tullius by the city council ('ex decurionum decreto'), which also granted the site of the second niche, that of Marcus Alleius Minius ('locus sepulturae publice datus ex decurionum decreto'). On the north side of the Street of the Tombs, about half-way between the city gate and the branching off of the 'Vesuvius Road', is a large semicircular niche, of unknown ownership, with a rounded entrance arch, flanked by two pilasters and topped by a pediment, and a vaulted roof.[393] In the angle between the Street of the Tombs and the 'Vesuvius Road', and facing towards the former, are two small, vaulted rectangular niche-tombs, designed for children and once adorned with stucco reliefs. The urn in each case was sunk in the earth beneath the apex of the niche, with a small libation pipe leading down to it (*cf.* pp. 37, 41, 51, 52, 101, p. 292, Note 187).[394]

A third type, the cylindrical drum (*cf.* p. 127), is represented in the Street of the Tombs by a single example, situated in the row of monuments that stand on the southern edge of the road, just to the east of the Villa of Diomedes.[395] Its owner is not recorded. It is reared on a square base and is built of brick with a white stucco facing drafted to counterfeit marble blocks. Within the cylinder is the sepulchral chamber which contains three niches. In the low walls of the tomb's enclosure, which carry little pyramidal towers, is an entrance doorway on the street side. Another, more substantial cylindrical tomb on a low, square base stands outside the Nocera Gate.[396] These are small versions of the huge 'gasometer' mausolea of imperial times, erected for private persons or for emperors and other rulers (*cf.* pp. 143–63).

The most homogeneous group of Pompeian funerary structures is that of the tombs that take the form of a monumental altar, generally raised on a base, which varies in height from tomb to tomb, and surrounded by low enclosure walls. This type of monument we have already met with in the regularly laid out portion of a cemetery at Aquileia (*cf.* pp. 79–82). At Pompeii the earliest example is the tomb, between the *exedrae* of Veius and Mamia, of Marcus Porcius, whose funerary plot is known from its inscription to have been 25 feet square and granted to him by the city council ('ex decreto decurionum in frontem ped(es) XXV in agrum ped(es) XXV').[397] The altar, which is hollow inside and made of tufa blocks, with travertine volutes on top, has been severely damaged. The ashes would appear to have been buried in the earth below it. Very similar, no doubt, was the unnamed altar-tomb next to the city gate on the street's north side.[398] Here, however, the burial chamber is in the base and entered by a narrow passage that had been blocked up in ancient times. In the chamber were discovered remnants of a pyre, various grave-goods, and two cinerary urns covered with earth, each in a case of lead and each containing a coin of Augustus (*cf.* pp. 49, 119 and p. 291, Note 168). But the most impressive altar-tombs are the four, two to the east of the cylinder tomb and two to the west of it, on the southern margin of the street.[399] In all these cases the altar is reared upon a high base, with marble steps at the top, and is itself faced with marble. Low walls, with a door on the street side, enclose the plot; and in the base is the sepulchral chamber entered by a door either at the back or in one of the sides.

The most easterly altar-tomb of this group was not yet completed when the eruption took place. Not all of its marble veneering was in position and the five niches inside, intended for urns, were found empty. In the plot outside the altar a bust-stone (*cf.* pp. 122, 125) inscribed 'Iunoni Tyches Iuliae Augustae Vener[iae]' came to light. The next altar, that immediately to the east of the cylinder tomb, is of notable size and bears the name of its owner, Aulus Umbricius Scaurus, a magistrate, whose burial plot and funeral expenses were provided by the city council ('huic decuriones locum monum[enti] et sest[ertios] MM in funere... censerunt'). The upper part of this altar's base was decorated with stucco reliefs, which have now virtually gone, depicting gladiatorial fights and an arena hunt. But the painted inscription associated with one of the scenes reveals that the shows were given, at least in part, by another man, Numerius Fistius Ampliatus. Here the burial chamber is low, with plain white walls and a stout pillar supporting its vaulted roof. On this pillar are four burial niches and fourteen more are on the walls. The first altar west of the cylindrical tomb is that of Gaius Calventius Quietus, an Augustalis, to whom, as the inscription states, the city council had voted a *bisellum* (double seat) in recognition of his *munificentia* (generosity). On the front of the altar this *bisellum* is carved in relief and an oak wreath, also in relief, appears on either side. In this case there is no sepulchral chamber either in the base or in the superstructure of the solid altar, from which it may be inferred either that the urn had been buried in the earth beneath the monument or that the latter was a cenotaph. The small towers on the plot's walls are adorned with reliefs. The last and most westerly tomb in this altar series is that built in her lifetime by a freedwoman, Naevoleia Tyche, for herself, for one Gaius Munatius Faustus, probably her husband, and for her and his freedmen and freedwomen. Like Quietus, Faustus had been granted a *bisellum*, which is shown in relief on one of the altar's sides. On the other side a relief depicts a sailing ship—symbolic of the dead reaching the haven of death after the storms of this life. Both of these pictorial panels and also the inscription panel on the front are framed by broad borders of running acanthus scroll. In the sepulchral chamber are a large niche, holding an urn, opposite the entrance and smaller niches, also filled with urns, in the walls, while more urns, each accompanied by a lamp, were discovered in the benches that run along the sides: these were of glass, in leaden cases.

The basic features of the last type of Pompeian tomb to be considered here are a heavy rectangular base and a light surmounting 'canopy', which consists of a ring of columns probably topped by a conical roof and perhaps intended to shelter the funerary portrait statues of the dead.[400] The largest example is the tomb of the Istacidii, behind the *exedra* of Mamia on the south side of the Street of the Tombs.[401] It is raised on a small terrace and surrounded by a balustrade. The rectangular base is adorned externally with engaged half-columns that give it the look of a pseudo-peripteral temple. In it is the burial chamber, entered by a door at the back and roofed with a vault, which a central pillar supports. On one side is a large niche to hold two urns, and smaller niches are cut in the other sides. Of the upper feature enough remains to indicate that it was a colonnaded 'canopy'. Bust-stones (*cf.* pp. 122, 124) in the plot outside the monument give the names of members of the Istacidii, Melissaei, and Buccii families.

On the opposite side of the street, further west, stands the 'Garland Tomb', so-called from the swags of flowers and leaves that dangle between the flat pilasters on the exterior walls of its substantial base.[402] Its upper feature has vanished, but we may safely guess that it was a columned 'canopy' on the analogy of the Istacidii monument.[403] In the case of yet another Pompeian tomb of this variety, that known from its inscription as the tomb of Ceius Labeo, standing in the fork between the Street of the Tombs and the 'Vesuvius Road', there is certain evidence that the now largely disintegrated upper storey was a columned 'canopy' perhaps with funerary statues.[404] Here again flat pilasters adorn on the outside the walls of the base that contains the burial chamber.[405]

Of the same general type as these base-and-'canopy' Pompeian tombs is the large unnamed monument of Augustan date from Fiumicello which now stands restored beside a modern street (Via Giulia Augusta) in Aquileia.[406] The massive rectangular base is raised on steps and carries a ring of columns mounted on a low round *podium* and topped by a conical roof, below which stands a funerary statue. Figures of lions are poised on two of the corners of the low enclosure walls.

The most imposing instance of the base-and-'canopy' Italian type of funerary structure dating from the period with which we are concerned here is not actually in Italy, but in Narbonnese Gaul, the most highly Romanized of all the provinces—'Italia verius quam provincia' (Pliny, *Nat. Hist.* iv, 105). This is the so-called mausoleum of the Julii at St Rémy, outside the ancient city of Glanum.[407] Over 19 metres high it consists of a square base, reared on steps and carved with four large pictorial reliefs, one on each side, depicting battles and hunts; of an intermediate storey (absent on the tombs in Italy that have been described), which takes the form of a square with an arch piercing each side, a pilaster at each corner, and a figured entablature; and of a 'canopy' of twelve Corinthian columns enclosing the statues of the dead beneath its conical roof. In its size and in the elaboration of its architectural and sculptural features this Gaulish monument far outdistances all its counterparts in Italy. (*Pl.* 31)

Of the upper- and middle-class tombs in Rome that do not belong to any of the categories described in earlier sections of this chapter (pp. 103–4, 113–15, 117, 118) four may be considered here in virtue of their strongly individual characteristics. The funerary monument of Gaius Poplicius Bibulus stands to the north-east of the Capitol, just outside the line of the Servian Wall, and dates from the first half of the first century BC.[408] Only part, perhaps the major part, of its south-east façade is standing, but the remains of the tomb's foundations show it to have been rectangular. Both base and superstructure are of travertine-faced tufa. The surviving façade has a tall central window, in which a portrait statue may once have stood. A flat pilaster relieves the plainness of the wall on either side of the window and at each corner; and two small panels with projecting frames occupy the spaces between the window and the end pilasters. The frieze, of which a fragment is left above one pilaster, carried a repeating design of swags and rosettes between *bucrania*. Where the burial was does not seem to have been recorded; and the nature of the architectural features above the window and the frieze remains unknown. Still less is known of the totality of the tomb of Cornelia, daughter of Lucius Scipio and wife of Vatienus, which dates from Augustan times and stands today, not on its proper site, but just outside the Aurelian Wall between the *Porta Salaria* and the *Porta Pinciana*.[409] Its interest lies in its shape, that of a cylindrical drum (*cf.* p. 123) on a circular base, which in turn rests on a square one. All is marble-faced, apart from the square base, which is of plain travertine. Part survives of a boldly projecting, circular, moulded cornice, and there can be little doubt that it once crowned a drum of which only the lower portion is preserved.

More original in character than the Bibulus and Cornelia monuments and perfectly preserved is the tomb of Gaius Cestius, a contemporary of Augustus, which takes the form of a pyramid 36·40 metres high and is now a very familiar landmark on the line of the Aurelian Wall near the *Porta Ostiensis*.[410] The pyramid rests on a large travertine foundation and is itself of brick-faced *opus caementicum* sheathed in marble blocks. A brick-lined corridor leads from the north-west side into the burial chamber in the interior. This has painted walls. It provides no evidence as to the manner and precise spot of Cestius' burial. Inscriptions on two sides of the pyramid give Cestius' names and titles: another inscription, on one side only, states the circumstances of the tomb's erection. Two bases found near it record the names of Cestius' heirs, one of whom was Marcus Agrippa. The annexation of Egypt to the Empire after Actium, and the consequent fashion in Rome and Italy for things Egyptian, may well have suggested this monument's unusual shape. (*Pl.* 33)

No Roman tomb is more exotic in appearance than that of Marceius Virgileus Eurysaces, 'pistor et redemptor' (master-baker and contractor), as the inscription styles him.[411] It dates from the late Republic, to judge from this inscription's lettering and spelling, and stands close beside the Porta Maggiore. It is trapezoidal in shape and comprises a base, on which stands a series of vertical cylinders. Above those runs the inscription cornice; and above that again come three rows of horizontal cylinders with large round openings on the monument's exterior. The uppermost row is topped by a frieze carved with reliefs depicting in a 'popular' and lively manner the various operations involved in bread-making—sifting and grinding corn, sorting grain, kneading, rolling, and placing loaves to bake in a domed oven with a long-handled shovel. It would seem that the great cylinders, which form such conspicuous features of the structure, were intended to represent stylized corn-measures. The inscription, found nearby, of Atistia, Eurysaces' wife, describes the tomb as a 'panarium' (bread-basket—perhaps in this case, bakery). The walls are of travertine on the outside, with plain flat pilasters at the corners. No marble is used, not even for the sculptured frieze. Of the burial chamber in the upper portion of the tomb, that with the rows of horizontal cylinders, nothing remains. There also came to light near the monument the funerary standing figures, worked in high relief and in the late-republican portrait style, of Eurysaces and Atistia. (*Pls.* 34, 35)

Larger and grander versions of the relatively humble brick

box'-tomb with a pyramidal roof at Isola Sacra (*cf.* pp. 102, 103) are the impressive marble-faced 'boxes' raised on (occasionally stepped) bases and almost certainly once provided with pyramidal roofs, of which there are examples at the fifth milestone on the *Via Appia* and at Sarsina. The *Via Appia* structures, as restored and drawn by L. Canina and his *La prima parta della Via Appia*, 1853,[412] had on the exterior flat pilasters at their corners and along their walls. This is also the case with the 'box'-tomb of Publius Verginius Paetus found in the Pian di Bezzo cemetery of Sarsina and reconstructed in the local archaeological museum.[413] Here a frieze of metopes and triglyphs runs above the pilaster-caps and on one side, between the pilasters, are carved in low relief Verginius' military and civil insignia—a round shield and a spear, two magisterial seats and *fasces*.

Most individual is what might be described as the 'tall-pointed-cap'-tomb, built in *opus reticulatum*, at Quarto di Marano near Naples.[414]. The high base is circular and has an arched doorway at ground level leading into a square sepulchral chamber with niches in its walls. Above this rises a very narrow, straight-sided pyramid tapering to what must once have been a sharp point. The tomb seems to have had tiers of rounded upper windows.

Another peculiar and more complex structure is the so-called 'Tomba degli Orazi e Curiazi' by the *Via Appia* near Ariccia.[415] It is built throughout of squared blocks of stone; and its high, square base is surmounted by a central circular pyramid and a tall truncated cone at each of its four corners. This curious effect appears to have been modelled on the tomb of Porsenna near Chiusi, which was, according to Pliny (*Nat. Hist.* xxxvi, 86) a 'monimentum . . . lapide quadrato quadratum' with 'piramides . . . quinque, quattuor in angulis et in medio una'. (*Pl.* 39)

Similar in many respects to the tomb of the Julii at St Rémy is the mausoleum at Santa Maria Capua Vetere known as 'La Conocchia' (the distaff: *cf.* p. 156).[416] The masonry of this building consists of small irregular pieces of stone set in cement, which must have been heavily stuccoed all over and probably painted, while some of the minor decorative architectural features, such as pilasters, cornices, and the pediments of *aediculae*, are worked in brick. The tomb is composed of three main elements—a high, square base containing the burial-*cella*; above that, a rectangular storey, which, instead of being straight-sided and pierced by four open arches, as at St Rémy, has concave sides, with a rounded engaged column at each corner and a pedimented, closed *aedicula* at the centre of each side; and at the top a circular structure comprising a plain round base surmounted by a ring of columns, which, instead of being free-standing and forming an open 'canopy', as at St Rémy, are engaged in a solid, circular wall. Its whole appearance is powerfully massive and 'baroque'. (*Pl.* 38)

### (F) RECTANGULAR TEMPLE-TOMBS

Since the Greek dead were heroized and the Roman departed accorded the title of *di Manes* it was natural that some Hellenistic and Roman tombs should assume the form of shrines. A Hellenistic mausoleum at Mylasa in Caria, for instance, has a high *podium* with steps at its base on all four sides, a cornice along its top, and a door giving entrance to the sepulchral chamber; while above the *podium* is what might be termed a peristyle without a *cella*, topped by a pyramidal roof.[417] The 'peristyle' consists of square pilasters at the corners and two elliptical columns on each side between those pilasters. By contrast, the early-imperial Tomb of the Volumnii at Padua presents a *cella* without a peristyle or columned porch.[418] Reared on a high base it comprises solid walls at back and sides and a Corinthian pilaster at each of the four corners. Above the open front is a pediment carved with a chariot race in relief and surmounted by a Sphinx. The family busts, originally ten in all, are ranged in tiers on the insides of the walls of this temple-like *aedicula*, whose total height is 3·90 metres.

A type of early-imperial tomb that might be described as a pseudo-temple is exemplified by the monument of Aulus Murcius Obulaccus from the Pian di Bezzo necropolis of Sarsina.[419] Its full height is 8·92 metres from the bottom of its stepped *podium*, on which its inscription is cut, to the finial on its pyramidal roof. Above the *podium*, in front, are two free-standing Corinthian columns supporting an entablature, while at the back is a solid wall, flanked by two square Corinthian pilasters and carved with a false door, intended as the entrance to a non-existent *cella*.

Another Sarsina monument, that of Asfionius Rufus, is a true temple-tomb, raised on a high *podium* that contained an ossuary, and consisting of a *cella* as well as of a *pronaos* of four free-standing Corinthian columns.[420] Here again there is a false door in the front wall of the *cella*, which is pseudo-peripteral, with engaged Corinthian columns along its sides and back. There was a pyramidal roof; and the overall height of the tomb has been reckoned as 14·15 metres. Very similar in structure, but with a pedimented roof, is a mausoleum at Haidra in Tunisia, with its high *podium*, *cella*, and tetrastyle *pronaos* supporting the entablature.[421] Of the same type again is the tomb of Mamastis, dated by its inscription to the middle of the second century AD, at Termessos in Pisidia.[422] In this case, however, the pediment surmounting the entablature is broken by an arch. None of the *podia* of these tombs has a flight of steps in front. At Fabara in Hispania Tarraconensis the temple-tomb of Lucius Aemilius Lupus, whose name is inscribed on the pediment, stands on a low *podium*, again without steps giving access to its portico.[423] The tomb is built in fine ashlar masonry and consists of a very shallow *pronaos*, preceded by four unfluted, free-standing Tuscan columns, and of a large room behind. Externally, at each corner of the back and at the centre of the back and of each of the sides is a flat, fluted Tuscan pilaster. The frieze is Ionic. Immediately inside the entrance-door, on the left, a stairway leads down to the vaulted sepulchral chamber, which is partly in the *podium* and partly underground. (*Pl.* 37)

The monument of Gaius Lusius Storax from Chieti, restored as a tetrastyle temple-tomb during its sojourn in the Museo Nazionale Romano,[424] was most probably not a temple-tomb at all, since not a vestige of a column, whether of shaft, capital, or base, came to light among the debris of the structure.[425] The earliest known temple-tomb that shows a *podium* with steps leading up to its floor in front in the Italic manner is the so-called 'Oratorio di Falaride' at Agrigento in Sicily, which dates from the first half of the first century BC and is stated by its inscription to have been the tomb of a Roman matron.[426] Its rectangular *cella* is preceded by a tetrastyle porch, to which steps, now largely vanished, once ascended. Apart from this Sicilian monument, and the little church of Sant' Urbano near the *Via Appia* to the south of Rome, which may have been a temple-tomb with a rectangular *cella*, a tetrastyle *pronaos*, and steps leading up to it,[427] temple-tombs with steps at the front of their *podia* are so far documented only by representations in art. The familiar relief from the so-called Tomb of the Haterii in the Lateran collection[428] depicts a most elaborate temple-tomb of this type (*cf.* pp. 81, 268–9). The *podium*, with its steps leading up to the porch, is very high and is very richly carved on its visible side, in which is the door of the sepulchral chamber. The tetrastyle *pronaos* shows column-shafts with delicately ornamental spiral bands worked in very low relief, heavy Corinthian capitals, topped in each case by an eagle of apotheosis, and a pediment, in which is carved the veiled bust of the deceased woman who presumably occupied the tomb. The visible side of the *cella* has decorated flat pilasters and, between them, three tiers of figured reliefs, the top tier containing the funerary busts of three children, each in a shell. The entablature is very intricate and the gabled roof is tiled. The existence in the fourth century AD of temple-tombs of a simpler kind than that on the Flavian relief, with a high, stepped *podium*, but only two columns upholding the entablature and pediment, is proved by the scene of the Raising of Lazarus on early Christian sarcophagi[429] and on the walls and vaults of catacombs.[430] (*Pls.* 17, 36)

## (G) RECTANGULAR HOUSE-TOMBS OF THE MIDDLE EMPIRE

At about its third Roman milestone from Rome, near the point of its convergence with the Via Appia Nuova and the railway, the *Via Latina* is preserved for a short, but impressive, section on its original line, with some of its paving intact and with its flanking brick-built Roman tombs.[431] These tombs date from the second century AD and take the form of large rectangular houses, normally with a subterranean burial-chamber and, originally, two storeys above ground containing rooms for funerary cult and family or club reunions: several of these upper storeys have been restored in modern times. The most famous of the group are the so-called Tombs of the Valerii and Pancratii, whose underground chambers have richly painted and stuccoed decoration on their walls and vaults—figures of deities, mythological scenes and personages, animals, and so forth,[432] all in lively contrast with the sober, not to say austere, exteriors of their neighbours: their own original above-ground portions have disappeared. A similar tall house-tomb on the *Via Nomentana*, popularly known as the 'Sedia del Diavolo', has an underground sepulchral chamber and two upper storeys.[433] More ornamental externally than the tombs on the *Via Latina* is the so-called 'Temple of Deus Rediculus', in fact, probably the gable-roofed tomb of Annia Regilla, wife of Herodes Atticus, on whose estate it stood by the Via della Caffarella, which branches off to the left from the Via Appia Antica, just to the south of the Domine Quo Vadis? church.[434] Here a gaily colouristic effect is produced by the yellow brick of the walls, by the red brick of the flat pilasters at the corners and along the sides, and by the red and yellow terracotta in which are carried out the meander border that runs round the walls at half the building's height and the decorative features of cornice, door, niches, and windows. (*Pl.* 40)

The basilica of San Sebastiano, near the third milestone on the right-hand side of the Via Appia Antica as one travels southward, is erected above the site of an ancient quarry-cemetery whose roof collapsed at some date during the first half of the second century AD. The rest of the quarry was then demolished and the debris levelled to form an oval courtyard round which were built, on the segment of a circle, three contiguous house-tombs.[435] These stand today well below the floor of the present church. While their façades are on the level of the courtyard, their interiors are tunnelled at a lower level which is reached by steps leading down from their doors. The tombs date from about the middle of the second century and were obviously planned as a single unit. The walls are of brick; the doors have stone (travertine) sills, jambs, and lintels; above each door is a panel for an inscription (two of the panels are, in fact, blank); above each panel is a pediment; and above each pediment is a massive rectangular attic. The easternmost tomb is that of Marcus Clodius Hermes, whose name appears in the façade inscription. Inside, its walls, ceiling, and *arcosolia* (arched recesses) for inhumation burials are brightly painted with figure scenes, including an 'ascension', a Medusa head, birds, flowers, baskets of fruit;[436] and the floor mosaic shows an *emblema*-like scene of birds in a chequered surround.

The next tomb is known as that of the Innocentii, members of a burial club, whose name is painted in Greek characters on the plaster sealing of their graves;[437] while the tomb furthest to the west bears the title of the Tomb of the Axe, from the axe symbol (*ascia*) worked into the brickwork of its façade. Both of these tombs have handsome stucco ornament on the vaults of their internal stairs and burial-chambers—rosettes in octagons and roundels, a peacock in a shell, vine-scrolls, and so forth.[438] Here again, in the case of all three mausolea, severe exteriors are counterbalanced by richly adorned interiors. At a later date the attic of the Tomb of Hermes was plastered and painted with scenes that may very well be Christian in content.[439] (*Pls.* 41, 42)

By far the most prolific and informative series of mid-imperial house-tombs are those in the Isola Sacra and Vatican necropoleis, whose layout and chronology have been discussed in Chapter IV (*cf.* pp. 82–91). Here we are concerned with the architecture, decoration and burial arrangements of the individual tombs and with the light that they throw upon the cult of the departed.[440]

The mausolea of the Isola Sacra cemetery are built either entirely of brick or of brick and *opus reticulatum* masonry combined. Most of them have one storey only, the façade containing a door with stone (travertine) sill, jambs, and lintel, above which is a central marble panel intended to hold, and often actually holding, an inscription giving the names and titles of the tomb's occupant or occupants. Above the panel comes a cornice and finally, in the great majority of instances, a triangular pediment. Occasionally it appears that, where there is a very large and heavy cornice, the front of the barrel-vaulted roof forms a rounded pediment, with decorative edging, above the cornice and slightly behind it. On some tombs the main central panel is flanked by two smaller lateral panels for reliefs and by two slit-like windows which are cut in marble or terracotta slabs inserted on either side of the inscription panel or pierced at either end of the inscription panel itself. Sometimes the slit takes the form of a double T. Other tombs have a single window cut in a marble slab above the central panel. There are cases of inscription panels framed by quite elaborate decorative patterns carried out in terracotta and pumice intarsia. The lateral reliefs, worked in brick or terracotta, present scenes from the dead men's professional lives. We are shown the deceased plying his trade as obstetrician, surgeon, manufacturer of iron implements, hardware dealer, knife-grinder, boatman, miller, water-carrier, water-seller, wine-merchant, carpenter, and so forth. Such scenes, while chiefly designed to commemorate the past, could also suggest a happy afterlife earned by honest toil (*cf.* p. 36).

Very rarely there is evidence that part at least of a tomb had an upper storey, as in the case of a portion of the precinct of No. 29. The façade of this tomb and that of No. 86 are adorned with flat brick pilasters topped by ornamental terracotta capitals. Nos. 20 and 21 have pilasters with marble capitals. Also very rarely these relatively sober exteriors could be further relieved by niches flanked by brick pilasters that rested on decorated terracotta brackets. The colour of the bricks employed, now red, now yellow, also provides an element of cheerfulness to the dwellings of the dead. The roofs of these mausolea are normally barrel-vaulted; and even where they are flat externally they are always vaulted inside.

Often the façades described above lead directly into a roofed *cella* or sepulchral chamber, whose walls are lined with burials. In other cases, e.g. Nos. 75, 76, 87, 88, 89, there is a generally unroofed precinct, of one build with the *cella*, between the latter and the façade (*cf.* pp. 88, 139), also containing burials. Some precincts, e.g. those of Nos. 11 and 94, were built up against the *cella's* façade at a later date. In the *cellae* cremation burials were in *aediculae* or semicircular niches in the upper portion of the walls, inhumations in *arcosolia* below. Since the burials in the great majority of precincts are cremations, still the cheaper and more traditional method of disposing of the dead, even when the *cellae* hold

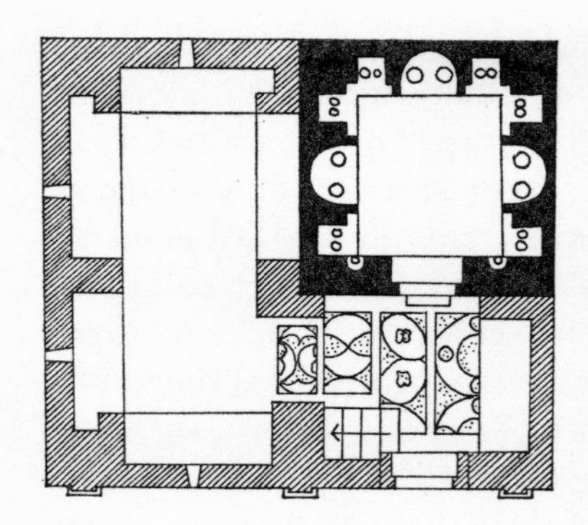
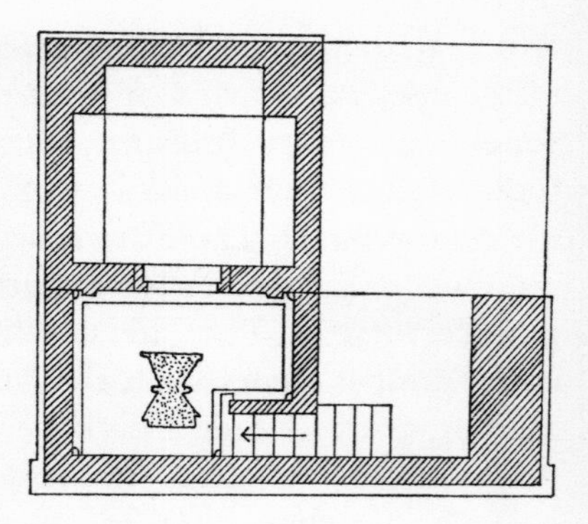

*Fig. 12 Tomb 29 at Isola Sacra, second century* AD: *left, ground floor; right, upper floor*

inhumations, it may be deduced that these outer areas, open to the sky, were destined as resting-places for the humbler dependants of the families who built and owned the tombs and whose remains were in the *cellae*. Other features of these precincts are wells for supplying water for cult and purification purposes, as in Nos. 16, 34, 47, 75, and ovens and small kitchens, as in No. 11, for the preparation of food for the sepulchral banquets that were probably held in the precincts (*cf.* p. 51). The precincts of some tombs do not only precede the *cella* but also flank one of its sides, as in Nos. 16, 78, 86, 89. In the case of No. 29 there is a vestibule preceding the *cella*, while the precinct to the left of it has a vaulted ceiling which supports the upper floor already mentioned (*cf.* p. 135). No. 34 has a large square precinct with only a small funerary *cella* at the centre of its back wall.

The structural arrangements of these mausolea behind their façades and walls do, then, vary quite considerably. But all alike, whether they stand alone, isolated from their neighbours, or are set contiguously in rows or terraces, present externally the appearance of the substantial, but unpretentious, dwellings of a well-to-do urban bourgeoisie. (*Pl.* 43)

As with some of the house-tombs on the *Via Latina* (*cf.* pp. 132, 133) and those below San Sebastiano (*cf.* pp. 133, 134), so here on Isola Sacra these plain exteriors can mask a riot of ornament and

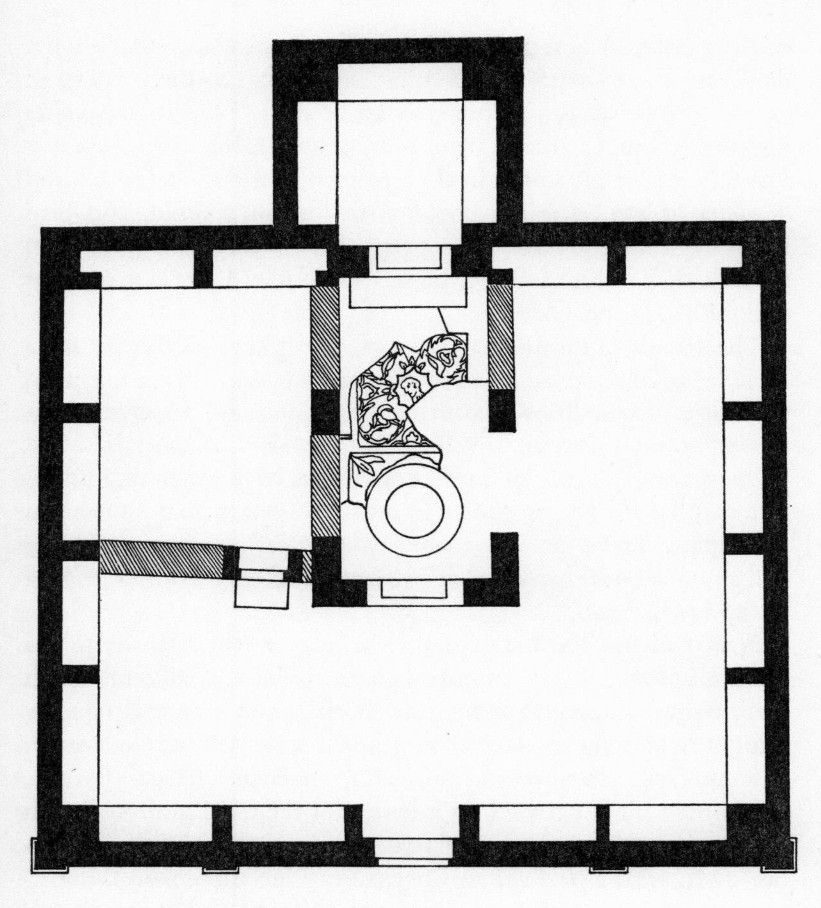

*Fig. 13 Tomb 34 at Isola Sacra, third century* AD

colour within.[441] In addition to the small semicircular and rectangular niches of the usual *columbarium* type, there are large *aediculae*, some with flat roofs, others with semi-domes, flanked by two colonnettes and often supported on heavy brackets, e.g. Nos. 17, 19, 57, 87, 95. No. 90 has a pair of exceptionally elaborate *aediculae*, one on either side of the door, where the arches are surmounted by richly corniced triangular pediments. The fluting of the pilasters or colonnettes of niches of this type is worked in stucco relief, as is also the coffering of some of the vaulted ceilings of the tombs. In No. 95 is a frieze of panels in white stucco relief depicting the Labours of Hercules: No. 94 has a stucco frieze of architectural features, colonnettes and panels; No. 93 has niches containing single stucco figures in relief. Often the stucco is brightly coloured; and indeed every inch of the walls, vaults, and *arcosolia* of the *cellae* is painted with human, animal, and bird figures against a yellow, blue, or red background and with plain areas washed in the same gay hues, while dados are of red, grey, or yellow bands and panels.

The marble sculptures that have come to light inside the mausolea include sarcophagi adorned with garlands and such subjects as marriage scenes, lions devouring other animals, funerary banquets, business scenes, revelling Cupids, and shepherds. Most striking are the figure of a priest of Magna Mater reclining on his funerary couch (*cf.* pp. 268–70) and two reliefs that show him officiating. There are also some quite good funerary portraits and mythological groups that convey an other-worldly meaning (*cf.* pp. 215, 277–9).

Nearly all the house-tombs of Isola Sacra were originally paved with black-and-white or polychrome mosaics, many of which were largely destroyed when new burials were dug through the floors towards the middle of the third century. Some, however, have survived; these show figure-scenes such as Charon's barque, confronted birds perched on a basket of fruit, a lighthouse with two ships coming into port (*cf.* p. 125) accompanied by the inscription *ΩΔΕ ΠΑΥΣ[Ι]ΛΥΠΟΣ* ('here there is no more pain'). Endymion and Selene, the Muses, a marine *thiasos*, and the Genius Saeculi with the Seasons—all well-known motifs of the funerary repertoire. These houses of the dead are, indeed, lavishly adorned from floor to ceiling; and the language that these adornments speak is less that of death than of life abundant beyond it. (*Pl.* 44)

Contemporary with, and almost identical in character, both outside and inside, with, the Isola Sacra house-tombs are those in the cemetery under St Peter's on the Vatican. To judge by what Constantine left of the roofs of these burial places when he reared his basilica over them, they were cross-, not barrel-, vaulted—apart from the miniature mausoleum of the Julii, whose shallow saucer dome was not molested by the emperor's architects. Furthermore, none of the Vatican tombs has the spacious type of precinct that is attached to some of the tombs on Isola Sacra, although three of them, namely the Tomb of Fannia (B), the *opus reticulatum* tomb (D), and the Tomb of the Valerii (H), have forecourts, open to the sky, equal to or smaller than the *cellae* in size, while the Tomb of the Matuccii (O) has a quite narrow open court in front of it. These are the only significant differences between the two series.

The Vatican façades are of the same style of neat pink brickwork as are those of Isola Sacra. The doors have the same heavy sills, jambs, and lintels of travertine surmounted by inscription slabs of marble that are set in frames of elegant terracotta mouldings or of inlay, carried out in red terracotta and black pumice-stone, and are flanked by loophole windows (except in the cases of Tombs B and D, where an open court lies behind the façade) and, on the First Tomb of the Caetennii (F), also by terracotta figured panels. Two of the non-contiguous tombs in the southern row have flat brick pilasters at their corners: so has the Tomb of the Matuccii in the northern row; but only one tomb, that of the Valerii, has similar pilasters spaced along its façade. One façade, that of the Marcii in the southern row, carries an unusual adornment, a mosaic panel depicting the death of Pentheus. Above their inscription panels and windows the Vatican mausolea have either crowning mouldings or more elaborate entablatures; and it would seem to be highly probable that in most cases these were topped by triangular pediments, after the manner of the tombs under San Sebastiano and on Isola Sacra. But only on the Tomb of the Steward (G) does any trace of such a pediment survive: the builders of Constantine's church would have destroyed the rest. (*Pl.* 48)

Externally the Vatican tombs are, for obvious reasons, less imposing today than are their counterparts on Isola Sacra. But when the cemetery under the basilica was packed with earth it is remarkable how much of the internal decoration of its mausolea was preserved; and this far surpasses that of the Isola Sacra interiors in the finish, refinement, and exuberance of style and in the novelty of content displayed by the paintings, mosaics, sculptures, and stucco-work which the clearing of the tombs brought to light. Indeed, it may be claimed that in no Roman house-tombs of a middle-class *milieu* were more thought and artistry lavished on the dead than in those beneath St Peter's.

Of the paintings some are unique, so far as our present knowledge goes, and of special interest. For example, in the Tomb of the Egyptians (*Z*) there are three large-scale figures of an Egyptian god in national costume and holding national attributes. Of Tomb G the focal point on the north wall opposite the entrance is the picture of a steward, presumably the owner, making a financial reckoning with an underling. The highlights of Tomb U are the attractive, youthful figures of Lucifer and Hesperus, each on a snow-white mount; while from the walls of the Tomb of the Marcii (*Φ*) brood the awe-inspiring forms of two Sileni, nimbed and emerging from calyces of luxuriant acanthus.

It is true that in the field of mosaic pavements the Vatican mausolea have less to offer us than have those on Isola Sacra. This may be partly due to the very extensive digging of secondary inhumation graves through the floors of the tombs, and only one figured pavement has, in fact, survived, that in the Tomb of the Quadriga (I), where the Rape of Persephone is drawn in black against a white ground and within a border of wild beasts—excerpts from the animal paradise. Nonetheless, this dearth of floor mosaics in the cemetery is compensated for, not only by a very unusual wall-panel, the mosaic of the death of Pentheus already mentioned (p. 139), but also by the presence in the miniature mausoleum of the Julii of the earliest Christian vault- and wall-mosaics so far known. On the ceiling of this tomb, over a bright yellow background, is a spreading vine, rendered in three shades of brilliant green, and framing a central octagonal space which contains the majestic figure of Christus-Helios in his chariot. On the walls (where the *tesserae* have fallen out, leaving their impressions and revealing the painted sketches that guided their setting) are an angling scene (symbol of Baptism), Jonah and the Whale (symbol of Death and Resurrection), and the Pastor Bonus (symbol of Salvation). These mosaics belong to the period of the tomb's reconditioning about the middle of the third century, either when the Julii embraced Christianity or when a new, Christian family took over the burial-place. (*Pls.* 45, 47)

In interest and quality the marble sarcophagi found in the Vatican cemetery outstrip by a long way those on Isola Sacra. Only a few of them can be cited here. On an infant's sarcophagus of Hadrianic date, found stacked in the street between the two rows of tombs, the realistic seated figures of the grief-stricken parents strike a homely and peculiarly touching note. In the Tomb of the Egyptians a late-second-century piece carved with the scene of Ariadne's discovery by Dionysus is a sculpture of exeptionally skilful virtuosity. Outstanding is the very large, early-third-century Dionysiac sarcophagus in the Tomb of the Marcii, remarkable for its vividly rendered sculptural groups and for the life-like portrait-busts on its lid of its occupants, Quintus Marcius Hermes and his wife Marcia Thrasonis. Another fine portrait is that of Marcia Felicitas in a roundel at the centre of her coffin, which again came to light in the cemetery street. No sculpture in the round from Isola Sacra can rival the veiled head, once belonging to a full-length statue, of a beautiful and distinguished lady, which was found near the Tomb of the Valerii and is perhaps a work of the early-fourth century, when the Faustina Major hair-style that she affects was once more in vogue.

Some of the white and painted stucco work in the Vatican mausolea—in the coffering of vaulted ceilings and in wall-panels showing small-scale figures of Cupids, birds, masks, floral scrolls, and *candelabra* (generally in white against a brightly coloured ground)—is of much the same kind as that already described in the Isola Sacra tombs (*cf.* p. 138). But the Tomb of the Valerii provides examples of this elegant and all-too-perishable field of Roman craftsmanship that nothing in the other cemetery, not even the frieze of Herculean Labours (*cf.* p. 138), can equal. Even the exquisitely accomplished figured stuccoes of the Tombs of the Valerii and Pancratii by the *Via Latina* (*cf.* p. 133) appear conventional by comparison with the large-scale relief works of quite unprecedented content and complexity which form the main decoration of this large mausoleum beneath St Peter's, whose principal chamber has an annexe projecting eastwards behind the rear wall of Tomb G (*cf.* p. 90).[442]

Each of the tall curved niches in the north, east, and west walls—eight in all—and each of the two tall rectangular niches which flank the curved niche that marks the centre of the north wall of the principal chamber is occupied by a single, full-length, statuesque figure worked in high relief. The three figures on the north wall opposite the entrance are probably those of Apollo and of Isis and Minerva on either side of him. In the curved niche on the north wall of the annexe is Hypnos equipped with bat's wings and holding a torch and drinking-horn. In the lunette above him two Cupids are upholding a golden *cornucopiae*, beneath which is a golden pomegranate spray. The six other full-length figures, in the niches on the north, east, and west walls of the principal chamber, are all mortals and must portray members of the Valerii family, since the dedicatory inscription on the tomb's façade records that it was built by Gaius Valerius Herma for himself, for his wife Flavia Olympias, for his daughter Valeria Maxima, and for his son Gaius Valerius Olympianus. (This boy, so we learn from an inscription inside the tomb, died at the age of four.) Two male Valerii appear on the north wall beside Minerva and Isis respectively. In the lunette above the former man is a splendid relief of Mother Earth reclining to the right, wreathed with corn-ears and grasping a loaded *cornucopiae*. Corresponding to her, on the lunette above the other man, is Oceanus reclining to the left, with rudder and anchor and crab's claws in his hair. The figure in the tall curved niche on the east wall may be identified as that of Herma himself, for he holds a tablet on which [HER]MAE is inscribed. In the lunette above him are the writing materials of a literary man. In the central niche on the wall opposite is another male member of the family, perhaps once a priest, since he wears a high headdress, is veiled for sacrifice, and pours a libation. He, too, has in the lunette above him a scholar's emblems. In view of the fact that his niche is equal in size to Apollo's and larger than that of any other human, he must have been a very important personage, possibly the founder of the family who died before the tomb was erected and was buried elsewhere. He is flanked by two women, each with toilet articles and other feminine objects in the lunette above her. It is tempting to equate them with Flavia Olympias and Valeria Maxima.

But these stately figures of gods and men and the delicate lunette reliefs by which seven of them are surmounted do not exhaust the stucco-worker's repertory in this tomb. On the back wall of every one of the twenty smaller square-headed recesses that alternate with the full-length niches is modelled in low relief a swiftly moving member of the Bacchic *thiasos*. There are also the Bacchic heads and the strangely Romanesque-looking heads, virtually in the round, that crown the herms between the niches and recesses. Finally there are also the heads of completely free-standing portraits of other Valerii, including the gilded head of a young boy wearing an Isiac curl, who could be the four-year-old Gaius Valerius Olympianus. (*Pl.* 46)

The mausoleum of the Valerii under St Peter's is perhaps the most informative existing document of how a family house-tomb could express, to the fullest possible extent, by its decoration and furnishings the honours due to the departed, the cult of the deities on whom they and their survivors relied, their need beyond the grave of the familiar objects that had served them in this life, and their hope for prosperity, ecstasy, and bliss, whether in the bosom of the earth or across the ocean, after the sleep of death.

### (H) LARGE CIRCULAR AND POLYGONAL TOMBS

The great series of circular masonry and brick tombs (including a few polygonal examples), which constitutes one of the most imposing features of Roman sepulchral architecture, spans intermittently a period of more than three and a half centuries, from Augustus to the sons of Constantine I. Despite an ingenious, but unconvincing, attempt by R. R. Holloway to derive these mausolea from the tumuli of the Romans' and, in particular, Augustus' Trojan ancestry, as described in the *Iliad* and *Aeneid*,[443] there can be little doubt that the generally accepted theory that finds their models in Etruscan cemeteries (see Chapter I) is most likely to be the right one. Caere, for instance, is little over thirty miles from

Rome; and in that city's monumental round tumuli, with ring-walls of masonry retaining their cone-shaped earthen mounds, high-born and wealthy Romans had close at hand a type of princely tomb that could be readily adapted to their needs.

As Holloway correctly demonstrates, none of the surviving Roman mausolea of this class can be proved to be pre-Augustan. And it may very well be that it was Augustus' tomb in the Campus Martius that inaugurated the whole series.[444] This had been built by the emperor in 28 BC between the *Via Flaminia* and the Tiber[445] and was about 87 metres in diameter. Inside, in the centre of the sepulchral chamber, was a pillar rising to the total height of the monument, calculated as about 44·65 metres, and supporting the statue of Augustus that crowned the apex of the tomb. Around this medial point were five concentric ring-walls, which probably supported superstructures and decreased in height from the centre to the perimeter. The outermost circle was the retaining wall of the mound which would have been piled on top of the tomb so as to cover all the internal structures, including the central pillar. This wall was faced externally with travertine. The sepulchral chamber contained three niches for the burial of the tomb's most important occupants and was approached by a narrow passage leading from the outside. Several different restorations of the mausoleum's external appearance have been proposed, with varying heights for the retaining wall and varying positions for its cornice or cornices. According to the view of some the drum or double drum (the two portions parted by a cornice) was surmounted by a simple mound with straight or slightly convex sides. Others postulate two cypress-planted earthen slopes, the upper one divided from the lower by a masonry drum considerably smaller than that at the base. Others, again, superimpose an upper and only very slightly smaller drum on a lower one, separate them by a cornice, envisage cypresses planted on a flat terrace above the upper drum, and reduce the mound to a relatively small one at the top of the monument. In the absence of any conclusive evidence it is difficult to choose between these divergent ideas. (*Pls.* 49, 50)

Of special interest are the funerary inscriptions brought to

43, 44 Tombs in the Isola Sacra cemetery (often flooded). *Above*, exteriors, showing doors, windows, and pediments. *Below*, part of an interior (pp. 134-9).

45–7 The St Peter's necropolis. *Above*, the painted and stuccoed interior of Tomb I. *Below, left*, a stucco relief of a Maenad in Tomb H (Valerii); *below, right*, part of the vault mosaic in Tomb M (Julii), showing Christus-Helios in a vine-scroll (pp. 138–43).

48 The brick façades and doors with travertine lintels, jambs, and sills of the tombs in the northern row in the St Peter's necropolis, looking west. Tomb C (Tullii), in the foreground, has a framed inscription panel, flanked by two windows, above the door (pp. 138–43).

49, 50 *Above*, an aerial view of the Mausoleum of Augustus in the Campus Martius. The ancient remains have been cleared and cypresses planted round them. *Below*, a close-up view of the same (pp. 144, 153).

51, 52 *Above*, the Tomb of Caecilia Metella by the *Via Appia*, probably of Augustan date, with medieval work at the top. *Below*, a restoration of the Augustan Tomb of Lucius Munatius Plancus at Gaeta (pp. 154–5).

53 Interior of the round Church of St George at Salonika, with fourth-century mosaics, originally the Mausoleum of Galerius (p. 160).

4 Interior of the fourth-century imperial mausoleum, perhaps originally
agan, converted into the round Church of Santa Costanza (pp. 160–1).

55 The early-fifth-century Mausoleum of Theodoric at Ravenna, built in the tradition of the great Roman circular tombs (p. 163).

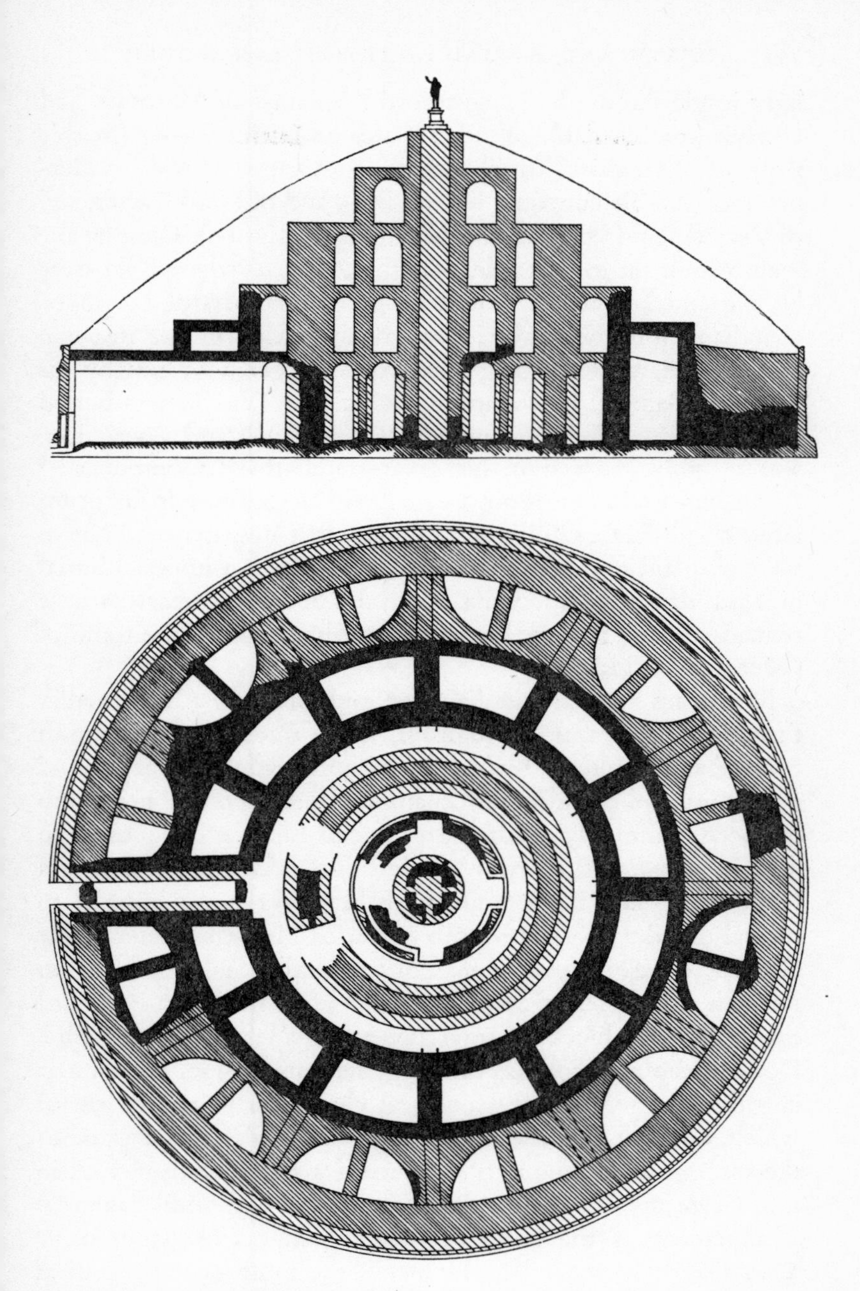

*Fig. 14 Section and plan of Mausoleum of Augustus*

light inside the tomb. These record the names of Marcellus and Octavia (marble slab), of either Gaius or Lucius Caesar (marble slab), of Germanicus (marble slab), of Agrippina, wife of Germanicus (marble container for her urn), and of Nero Caesar, son of Germanicus (recorded, but now lost, inscription). Close to the mausoleum, on its east side, was the *ustrinum*, where *cippi* have been found bearing the names of other members of the Julio-Claudian House who were presumably buried in the imperial tomb. In view of the magnificent funeral given to him by his successor Gaius, it is practically certain that Tiberius was buried there;[446] the same must apply to Claudius;[447] and Gaius, too, was possibly interred in his great-grandfather's monument.[448] According to Tacitus, Poppaea, wife of Nero, 'tumulo Iuliorum infertur'.[449] Further inscriptions suggest that Vespasian and Nerva were also laid to rest in the mausoleum. The last imperial burial in it was that of Julia Domna, Septimius Severus' empress, whose remains are said to have been temporarily placed 'in the tomb of Gaius and Lucius'.[450]

Measuring 83 metres in diameter, and thus only a little smaller than the mausoleum of Augustus, is the so-called 'Torrione di Micara' at Tusculum,[451] which has an outer casing of peperino and a wide internal corridor with chambers opening off it. This tomb has been commonly attributed to Lucius Licinius Lucullus, who died in 56 BC. But there is no clinching evidence for this; and Holloway[452] and Lugli[453] are probably right in assigning it to several decades later. The tomb of Lucius Munatius Plancus near Gaeta is a gasometer-like masonry structure built in about 20 BC with a diameter of 29·50 metres.[454] Here the drum is dressed externally with blocks of travertine and is adorned above with a Doric frieze and cornice carrying merlons. Inside, an annular corridor surrounds four sepulchral chambers, in the centre of which, as in the mausoleum of Augustus, a pilaster once rose to the summit of the tumulus and carried a statue or trophy. Also near Gaeta and of the same size and type and with similar internal arrangements is the tomb of Lucius Sempronius Atratinus.[455] Very similar in general appearance is the tomb of the Plautii at Ponte Lucano near Tivoli.[456] It stands on a low square base and is faced with travertine. Only the lower part of the drum up to the cornice is original. Inside is a small apsidal burial chamber opposite the entrance. The so-called 'Casal Rotondo' at the sixth milestone on the *Via Appia* is held to be the tomb of Valerius Messala Cotta.[457] Its cylinder measures 27 metres in diameter: it has a simple cornice near the top; and it was originally faced with travertine. Closely akin in its external look to the tomb of the Plautii is the so-called tomb of the Acilii Glabriones at Alife on the *Via Latina*.[458] From ground level to conical roof the structure is original, although it has been largely despoiled of the blocks of stone that faced it. About a third of the way up the drum is girdled by a projecting limestone cornice. Inside, in the thickness of the drum's wall, are eight rectangular sepulchral niches. Also near Alife is the so-called 'Torrione', a circular tomb badly ruined: of the wall of the drum only the rubble core remains.[459] It stands on a low base and had a conical vault within. (*Pl.* 52)

A variant of the class of mausoleum with which we are dealing is that in which the round drum is reared on a high square *podium*. The most famous instance of this is the tomb of Caecilia Metella, a conspicuous landmark beside the *Via Appia* a few miles south of Rome.[460] Commonly dated to the middle of the first century BC, it need not, as Holloway cogently argues, be pre-Augustan.[461] The relief-sculpture of its frieze, on the side facing the highroad, shows barbarian shield devices which could as well refer to Germanic and Dacian as to Gallic victories; and he suggests that the tomb's inscription[462] should be interpreted as meaning that Caecilia Metella was the mother of the Marcus Licinius Crassus who in 27 BC was accorded a triumph for his conquest of Germanic, Dacian, and Moesian tribesmen in 29 or 28. The *podium* is 22·30 metres square and the drum 29·50 metres in diameter: both were once faced with travertine blocks. The frieze just below the cornice of the drum is of marble and contains, in addition to the military panels, a series of festoons suspended from *bucrania*. The medieval work above the cornice incorporates traces of the Roman *cippi* which functioned as the tomb's original merlons. (*Pl.* 51)

Campania provides some notable instances of this variant of tomb, three of which may be noted here. One, at Pozzuoli, near

San Vito, has two internal storeys, both of whose walls are lined with *aediculae* and niches.[463] Here the drum is relatively low in proportion to the *podium*, whose external walls are simply, but attractively, adorned with brickwork (no doubt originally stuccoed)—pilasters flanking panels topped by pediments and half-pediments and a cornice above. The tomb may date from the late-first or early-second century AD. Very similar, and likely to be of about the same date, is the mausoleum at Marano, near Naples.[464] In this case, again, there is the same type of decorative facing on the *podium*—brick pilasters separating panels of *opus reticulatum* masonry that are surmounted by pediments and half-pediments in brick. Along the top of the *podium* runs a quite elaborate terracotta cornice. The drum is wholly in *opus reticulatum* with encircling terracotta bands at the base and half-way up. A vivid colouristic effect, of pink, yellow, and two tones of grey, almost an effect of inlay-work, is thus obtained. Internally the tomb has two superimposed sepulchral chambers connected by a stairway. The third Campanian tomb of this type, that known as 'La Conocchia' ('the distaff': *cf.* p. 129) at Capodimonte (Scudillo) near Naples,[465] is probably roughly contemporary with the two just described. Its drum is relatively low in proportion to its high *podium*, which is crowned by a particularly elegant and rich terracotta cornice. The funerary chamber in the *podium*, approached from the outside by a broad passageway, is circular, with five rectangular niches opening off it. Each niche has in its floor a round hole in which a cinerary urn was deposited. The most striking provincial example is that at Adalia (Attalia) in Pamphylia, which has been dated to the end of the first century AD.[466] In the massive *podium* is a cross-shaped sepulchral chamber connected by stairs with the upper storey. Both *podium* and drum, which are of more or less equal height, are built in ashlar masonry and carry along their upper edges simple cornices, that of the drum being topped by merlons.

Thus Augustus, in all probability, set the precedent for the building by private citizens, known and unknown, of great, round, soaring monuments of the dead, conspicuous in any kind of landscape setting. No tombs of any class express more forcibly the Roman taste for size and magnificence in honouring their departed with enormous structures that housed, in the case of the early-imperial examples, the handfuls of ashes of the relatively small number of persons buried in each tomb. Many of these mausolea are difficult to date with any certainty, where epigraphical and other external evidence is lacking. But the series undoubtedly continued, if rather more sporadically, into the middle Empire; while in the late-antique period it flourished anew under the patronage of emperors and of members of their families.

Just as Augustus' mausoleum had dominated the circular tombs of the early Empire, so in the middle Empire was the same role played by Hadrian's (Castel Sant' Angelo), built by the emperor for himself, his relatives, and his successors on the right bank of the Tiber in an area that had once formed part of the imperial gardens, while a bridge that was also his work gave access to it from the city.[467] Obviously inspired by its imperial predecessor, it consists of a great cylinder 64 metres in diameter in its lowest portion, above which there may have risen three more drums of progressively diminishing diameters, the uppermost carrying a cypress-planted mound crowned at its apex by a statuary group on a lofty *podium*. The interior arrangements were, however, very different from those in Augustus' tomb. From the vestibule a circular ramp between walls of brickwork winds up to the level of the square, central burial chamber, which has three arched niches and whose tufa walls were lined with marble veneering. From the top of the ramp a stairway may have given access to a second central chamber, also square, above which is a third chamber, circular and encircled by a staircase. The wall of the drum is of concrete faced with tufa *opus quadratum* (squared blocks), incorporating some courses of travertine blocks. There was also originally an outer skin of Parian marble. The great precinct-wall, 89 metres square and about 15 metres high, which surrounded the drum, may have been added by Antoninus Pius. Caracalla is the last emperor whose burial in Hadrian's mausoleum is recorded.[468]

Despite the prestige of this great imperial monument, the number of circular tombs, whether in Italy or in the provinces, that have been attributed to the second and third centuries is relatively small. The comparatively modest cylindrical mausoleum of the Lollii near Constantine (Cirta, Constantina) in Numidia, 10·20 metres in diameter, 5·50 metres high, and built of squared blocks of stone, has been dated by some in the time of Antoninus Pius:[469] others, however, place it in the late-first century.[470] Two tombs have, indeed, been tentatively assigned to the Severan epoch—the co-called 'Monte del Grano' near Rome and the so-called 'Tempio di Portuno' at Porto.[471] The former, which was robbed of the travertine casing of its drum during the Middle Ages, has at its centre a circular chamber, 10 metres in diameter and divided into two storeys, both of which were vaulted and approached by a corridor. The latter has a circular *podium*, the top of which is reached by a flight of steps and on which stands an external colonnade of twenty-four columns carrying a penthouse roof. The thick wall of the drum supports the shallow dome; and inside are eight niches, four rectangular (including the entrance) and four semicircular, alternating with eight columns.

Possibly of second- or third-century date and similar in their external embellishment with a 'false' arcade, but not necessarily all contemporary, are one Italian and two North African mausolea. The Italian example is the largest and most imposing of all the Roman tombs in Campania, the so-called 'Le Carceri Vecchie' at Santa Maria Capua Vetera.[472] It consists of two superimposed drums, the upper and smaller one separated from the lower and larger one by a terrace. In the outer wall of the lower drum (now partly below the modern ground level) are twenty-two arched niches flanked by engaged Doric columns, whose shafts, built up in alternating rings of brick and stone, were once cased in stucco fluting. Spaced along the outside of the upper drum are very plain flat pilasters without caps or bases. All these ornamental features were presumably designed to relieve the austerity of the spreading girth of the cylinders. Inside, in the centre, is a cross-shaped sepulchral chamber approached from the entrance by a narrow corridor. How the building was roofed, whether by a mound of earth or by a cone of masonry, remains unknown. To turn to Africa, the so-called 'Medracen' south of Constantine is

58·86 metres in diameter and 18·35 metres in height and has a drum adorned externally with engaged Doric columns.[473]

Larger (64 metres in diameter and 33 metres high) and much better known is the so-called 'Tomb of the Christian' near Cherchel (Iol Caesarea) in Mauretania.[474] Commonly held to have been built by Juba II or by one of his predecessors, it has recently been attributed to late-antique times. But a date in the middle Empire, between those two extremes, would seem to be equally possible. Sixty engaged Ionic columns decorate the outside of the drum; and four of the spaces between the columns are filled with 'false' doors, elegantly carved. Above the cornice that surmounts the capitals the 'mound' of the tumulus rises to its apex in a series of masonry steps of progressively diminishing diameters. The door of the hypogeum below the drum opens, beneath the 'false' door on the east, into a vaulted passage that leads to a rectangular vestibule. From one side of the vestibule seven steps give access to a vaulted gallery that circles round the interior of the *podium* to end at its centre in the funerary chamber, which could have held only two or three inhumation burials.

Of the certainly late-antique mausolea of the large, centrally planned class that were erected in Italy and the central Mediterranean provinces most are of Tetrarchic or Constantinian date. The so-called 'Tor dei Schiavi' on the *Via Praenestina*, once believed to be the burial-place of the Gordians on account of the proximity of their villa, is proved by its brick-stamps to be Constantinian or at any rate not earlier than Diocletian.[475] Who were buried here, whether members of the imperial House or private persons, we do not know. It would seem to have been closely modelled on the Pantheon, for its drum, raised on a low circular *podium*, adorned near the top with two cornices, and roofed with a shallow saucer-dome, was preceded by a rectangular pedimented portico. Very similar in structure is the mausoleum beside the *Via Appia*, of Romulus, son of Maxentius, who died in 309.[476] Romulus' funerary shrine in the Roman Forum is also circular, but is preceded by a curved vestibule and flanked by two apsidal chambers.[477] The mausoleum of Diocletian, which forms the centrepiece of the south-eastern quarter of his palace at Split (Spalato) and is now the city's cathedral, is octagonal externally and stands upon a *podium* that contains the domed sepulchral chamber.[478] Outside the drum there was once an octagonal colonnade of twenty-four columns, carrying a penthouse roof (*cf.* the 'Tempio di Portuno', p. 158), and a rectangular columned and pedimented porch (*cf.* the 'Tor dei Schiavi' and the tomb of Romulus by the *Via Appia*). The interior is round, with eight niches, four rectangular (including the entrance) and four semicircular, opening off it. They are cut into the 10-foot-thick wall of the drum. Between the niches there stand against the wall eight columns carrying an entablature; and above them there are eight smaller columns, also bearing an entablature. At about 4 feet above the latter starts the spring of the dome, which is transformed externally into an octagonal pyramid.

As originally built by Galerius in *c.* 300 as a mausoleum for himself, the round church of St George at Salonika was a simple circular structure, whose hemispherical brick dome is carried on eight piers, each 6·30 metres thick, with rectangular vaulted niches in between them: above each niche is an arched window.[479] The mausoleum of Helena on the *Via Labicana* outside Rome, popularly known as the 'Tor Pignattara' from the *amphorae* incorporated in the structure of its dome, was erected in 329 or 330 and is divided internally into two superimposed zones by a cornice, with alternating rectangular and semicircular niches on the ground floor and windows above.[480] On the exterior the drum is correspondingly divided by a cornice, the upper part being smaller in diameter than the lower and containing a series of eight shallow curvilinear niches that frame the windows. A colonnaded *aedicula* once formed the entrance. (*Pl.* 53)

The originality of the large brick-and-concrete building by the *Via Nomentana*, now known as the church of Santa Costanza, lies in the fact that its hemispherical dome rests on a drum borne on an internal arcade of twelve pairs of columns placed radially to the circumference.[481] The wall of the drum rises with clerestory windows above the penthouse roof of the barrel-vaulted ambulatory which runs round the lower part of the building and gives access to the main central space below the dome through arches

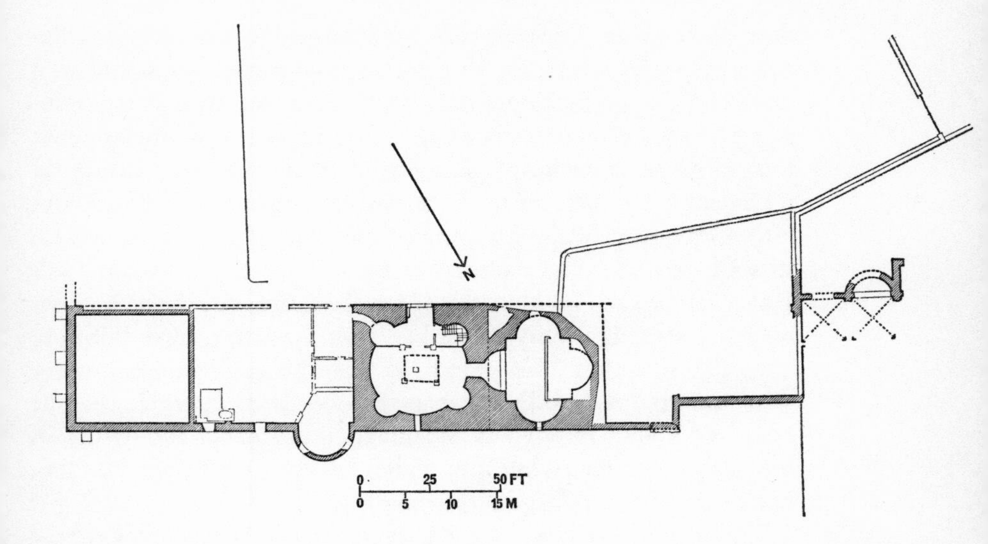


*Fig. 15 Plan of the Centcelles mausolea*

that link the pairs of columns. In the thickness of the ambulatory's solid outer wall are contrived three large and twelve small niches, some curved, others rectangular, the large ones, at least, no doubt intended for burials in handsome sarcophagi. For the building was certainly a mausoleum, in which Constantine I's two nominally Christian daughters, Constantina and Helena, were laid to rest. But the surviving early-fourth-century vault-mosaics of the ambulatory are completely 'neutral' in content, without any trace of direct Christian influence: seventeenth-century drawings of lost dome-mosaics with biblical scenes are counterbalanced by eighteenth-century drawings and descriptions of mosaics of a Bacchic character; and the place may have been originally a pagan tomb, to which the Christian scenes were slightly later additions. (*Pl.* 54)

Identifiable as mausolea are the two remarkable interconnected buildings, dating from the middle of the fourth century and enclosed in a common rectangular precinct, at Centcelles, five kilometres inland from Tarragona in north-eastern Spain, where they formed an integral part of a large fourth-century villa-complex.[482] The building to the east, now encased in a square of walls and topped by a pyramidal roof, all of later date, was originally a domed circular structure, *c.* 10·7 metres in diameter, with four large symmetrically placed semicircular niches opening off it. Below the centre of its floor is a rectangular vaulted 'crypt', into which some steps descended. The door of the building is on its southern side; and from its western side a short passage leads into a four-conch building on much the same scale as the circular one and, since it is only accessible from the latter, once fulfilling a similar purpose. The 'crypt', which is clearly contemporary with the eastern building, can only have been intended for the burial of a very important personage, presumably the owner of the villa-complex; while the niches of the four-conch building could have housed large sarcophagi.

The sepulchral character of these two adjacent buildings is fully borne out by the figure-decoration on the upper part of the interior wall and on the inside of the dome of the circular member of the pair. Round the wall, below a painted meander band, is a painted frieze, partly interrupted by windows, of which but scanty fragments now survive. An animal, a group of houses, probably a villa-complex, and the head and bust of a richly dressed girl can be discerned—not enough to determine the general significance of what was represented. But of the three mosaic figured zones encircling the dome much of the subject-matter is clear. The lowest zone presents a lively hunt, starting from, and returning to, a villa-building. In the central zone are a series of Christian figures and episodes—Adam and Eve, Daniel, Jonah (three episodes), the Good Shepherd, Noah's Ark, the three youths refusing to worship the golden image, the three youths in the fiery furnace, and the Raising of Lazarus. The upper zone held personifications of the Four Seasons, of which those of Spring and Autumn largely survive, with human figures, some seated, who cannot be identified, in the panels between them. Another mosaic figure-scene, of which only two human heads remain, filled the circle at the apex of the dome. The biblical figures and scenes are all among those that are familiar from works of Christian funerary art of the third and fourth centuries—in catacomb-painting and sarcophagus-carving; figures of the Seasons occur as symbols of the endless cycle of eternity or of celestial blessings in Christian, as in pagan, sepulchral and cultic contexts; and in similar Christian, as in similar pagan, contexts hunting scenes have their place as allegories of the joys of paradise or of victory over the powers of death and evil.

It would seem, then, that the builder and owner of the Centcelles fourth-century villa and its mausolea was a Christian and a very special Christian at that. For the mausolea are as yet unparalleled in Spain and, indeed, throughout the western Roman world; and they and their decoration are unlikely to have been the creations of merely local architects and artists. It has been suggested that this Christian was none other than the emperor Constans I, who, after the death of Constantine II, was master of all the western provinces until his own death in 350. In the impressive and very individualized frontal head of 'the master of the hunt' in the mosaic hunting-frieze, with its upward glance and furrowed brow, we may have Constans' portrait.[483]

One more round mausoleum, related to the present series, but chronologically outside it, is the stone, gasometer-like tomb of the Gothic King Theodoric at Ravenna, where he died in 526.[484] The drum is two-storeyed and decagonal in the lower storey and in the lower part of the upper storey, while the topmost part is circular and ringed by two projecting cornices. An external gallery is formed by the upper storey being smaller in diameter than that below. On the outside of the lower storey are ten deep, arched niches, one of which is the entrance; and immediately above that is the entrance from the gallery into the upper storey. The shallow dome is a monolith and carries twelve corbel-stones inscribed with the names of the Apostles. The lower storey would have housed the king's sarcophagus and other burials: the upper storey could have served for commemorative services or banquets. Although built for a Germanic king and carved with barbaric ornament on the cornice immediately below the dome, this mausoleum is architecturally wholly Roman; and it marks the end of the long tradition that began with Augustus' tomb. (*Pl.* 55)

## CHAPTER VI

# SELECTED TYPES OF TOMBS II

### (A) TOWER-TOMBS

TOWER TOMBS may be characterized as tall masonry structures, square or rectangular in shape, and rising from bases, that are often stepped, in two or several storeys. With them may be classed what might perhaps be described as 'pseudo-towers', namely tombs of the same general shape and style as towers proper, but consisting of never more than one storey. The majority of true tower-tombs are incomplete. Many have lost one or more of their upper storeys, for whose one-time existence evidence survives; and the nature of their roofs can only be conjectured. Where roofs do exist they are either pyramidal or flat. Towers are predominantly provincial or peripheral funerary monuments. Some occur in the western provinces of Gaul, Spain, and Africa. But the most important groups lie on the Empire's eastern fringe—at Palmyra, Dura-Europos, and other Syrian sites.

A late-Hellenistic precursor of the Roman tower-tomb is the so-called 'Tomba di Terone', standing more than 9 metres high outside the south gate of Agrigentum.[485] Two square storeys survive. The lower storey, whose base is formed by a single step, is composed of seven courses of neatly cut blocks and is devoid of decoration apart from a crowning cornice. The upper storey has an engaged Ionic fluted column at each of its four corners and, above, a Doric frieze of metopes and triglyphs: a false door occupies the centre of each side. The entrance to the funerary chamber in the lower storey was blocked up after the burial. The whole tower tapers slightly towards the top.

Of western tower-tombs the most familiar is the monument of the Secundinii family which stands to its original height in the village of Igel a few miles to the south-west of Trier.[486] From the much ruined inscriptions it appears that Secundinius Aventinus and Secundinius Securus erected it 'parentibus defunctis et sibi vivi'; and from some of the reliefs adorning its walls it can be gathered that cloth-making was the Secundinii's business and the source of the wealth that made the building of the tower possible. The monument, which is square, made of sandstone, and about 23 metres high, has four main parts: a four-stepped base; a relatively low *podium* carrying figure-scenes and topped by a projecting cornice; a tall storey, at the angles of which are flat Corinthian pilasters with decorated shafts and supporting an architrave, a sculptured frieze, and a very heavy cornice; a species of attic, on each face of which is a sculptured scene in a shallow niche crowned by a pediment that is also carved; and finally a pyramidal roof at the apex of which is a pine-apple carrying a group of the Rape of Ganymede. In all this extremely rich and elaborate carving are combined scenes from that successful daily and professional life, which won for the family its reputation here and now and a well-earned, blissful afterlife (the making, examination, and sale of cloth, the cording and transport of bales, travelling in a two-wheeled carriage, rent-paying, a kitchen scene, and a meal), and episodes from mythology as allegories of victory over death and immortality (the Rape of Ganymede, the Rape of Hylas, Perseus and Andromeda, Mars and Rhea Silvia, Achilles' Bath in the Styx, the Apotheosis of Hercules, and the deities of Sun and Moon). There is no external evidence for the tower's date, but the first half of the third century is suggested by the sculptural style. The dead whom the monument commemorates were probably laid to rest in graves dug near it. (*Pl.* 57)

Another well-known western tomb is the so-called 'Torre de los Escipiones' which stands about four miles from Tarragona beside the Roman road to Barcelona.[487] Square and built entirely of ashlar masonry, it rises, 26 feet high, in three slightly receding storeys, the first and second being separated by a simple moulding, the second and third by a plain projecting cornice. The upper portion of the third storey is gone; but it has been plausibly restored as surmounted by a heavier and more elaborate cornice and crowned by a pyramidal roof. While there is here, as at

Igel, no external evidence for the tomb's date, its ascription to the early Empire would seem to be reasonable, in view of its austerity of form and its sparseness of ornament. Only on the side facing the highway is any decoration attempted—a very shallow arched niche on the third storey and on the second storey two hooded, Atys-like mourning figures, each standing cross-legged on a ledge. (*Pl.* 56)

To pass from Europe to the western provinces of Roman North Africa, many of the tower-tombs of what is now Algeria have long ago been catalogued and described.[488] The tower at Khamissa (Thubursicum Numidarum) has a high, square basement containing the funerary chamber and above that another chamber, whose rubble walls are faced with squared blocks of stone.[489] At Ksar el Ahmar the tower, set on a low base, consists of two storeys with a cornice between them. The burials were in a hypogeum below. There is no entrance to the above-ground chamber in the lower storey; but on the east side there is a false door, flanked by two niches, in each of which a mourning Cupid with reversed torch is carved in relief. An inscription, flanked by similar Cupids in relief, states that this was the family tomb of Marcus Anniolenus Faustus. The upper storey, which is incomplete, was probably vaulted internally.[490] The tower at Ksar Tenaceft, near Timgad, has a low base and two storeys. The lower storey, inside which are two interconnected chambers, is crowned by a cornice; and the upper storey has fluted Corinthian pilasters at the angles and a curved pediment.[491]

In the case of some of these Algerian tower-tombs the front wall of the upper storey is not flush with that of the lower and closed, but set back and open and probably nearly always preceded by a portico of columns. At Setif (Setifis) the tower-tomb is rectangular and set on a two-stepped base. The chamber in the lower storey containing the burials—in urns set in eight semicircular niches—is approached by five steps leading up to a sill and then by five steps down, and is lighted by windows. Here the upper storey's set-back front is a great open arch; and the other faces of its walls are adorned with flat pilasters.[492] A similar architectural arrangement appears in towers at Lambaesis,[493]

Morsott (near Tebessa),[494] and Mdaourouch (Madauri).[495] The square 'pseudo-tower' at Abkou de l'oued Sahel has one storey only, resting on a four-stepped base. The entrance to the funerary chamber inside it is on the north side: on each of the other three sides is a false door with ornamental panels. A pyramidal roof crowns the whole. Within the chamber, on each wall, are two niches flanked by engaged Ionic columns.[496] Other 'pseudo-towers' are at Ksar Tebinet, near Tebessa,[497] and Morsott.[498] At Henchir el Hamman is the four-stepped base of what may well once have been a tower-tomb. Below it is a hypogeum consisting of a central chamber, on one side of which is the entrance, and of three lateral chambers opening symmetrically off the other three sides of the central one. All the chambers are vaulted and each of the lateral ones has eight semicircular niches in its walls. An inscription records the building of the tomb by Flavius Sedatus and Flavius Urbicus.[499]

Examples of other African tower-tombs are those at Mactaris and at Kasserin in Tunisia. The former, very well preserved, stands on a three-stepped base and has two storeys, each surmounted by two projecting cornices and each adorned externally with flat Corinthian pilasters. The roof is a pyramid.[500] The latter has a four-stepped base and three storeys. On one side of the unadorned lower storey is the door of the sepulchral chamber. Flat Corinthian pilasters, resting on a projecting cornice, relieve the outer walls of the second storey; while the third storey, which is smaller than the other two, has on its front side a large arched opening.[501]

In the Roman East, it is on ancient sites in modern Syria and neighbouring countries that tower-tombs survive most abundantly as a standard type of funerary structure; and in these Semitic lands all housed inhumations. At Dura-Europos on the Euphrates excavations in the necropolis just outside the city's western wall have produced the remains of eight tower-monuments, all much ruined and lacking dating evidence, but of which three, Tombs A, B, and C, still form a conspicuous group beside the ancient road to Antioch-on-the-Orontes.[502] Of Tomb A all that remains is the square, five-stepped base and a small portion of the tower's central pillar. Into the exterior of the base on the north-west and south-east sides were cut, at a right angle to the face of the base, five *loculi* (shelves for inhumation burials), two below and three above; and on the south-west and north-east sides, five *loculi*, four below and one in the centre above. After the insertion of the coffins the *loculi* were sealed. There are traces of a stairway winding round the central pillar, of engaged angle pilasters, and of a door, with engaged flanking columns, on the south-east side. The tomb was built of irregular stones set in mortar and plastered.[503] Tomb B is of the same general plan as is Tomb A, but is in a much more dilapidated state. Of Tomb C only two of the originally five steps of the base remain intact. But the north-east wall of the tower was discovered lying on its face almost undamaged; and from this it has been possible to reconstruct much of the monument's outer look. On the lower storey there were angle pilasters and three engaged columns on each wall between the angles. This storey was topped by a simple cornice; above that were seven vertical slits or grooves and above these again three false windows with grooves between them. Here, also, the walls were of irregular stones plastered over; and there was a continuous internal staircase round the central pillar.[504] Another tower-tomb, D, which is nearer to the city's main gate, has a ruined four-stepped base which contains a small vaulted chamber. By combining the evidence of the fallen wall of Tomb C with that of other tower-tombs in the Euphrates valley, most of whose lower storeys show traces of exterior engaged columns, for example, the 'Abu-Zimbel', 'Abu-Gelal' and 'Erzi' tombs at Baghuz,[505] a conjectural restoration of the external appearance of the first two and a half receding storeys of the Dura tower-tombs, including the decorative elements noted above, can be arrived at.[506]

At Palmyra the tower-tomb was a traditional and favourite form of funerary monument, whose surviving examples, some of which are precisely dated by inscriptions, are mainly to be seen in the 'Valley of the Tombs'.[507] They are of four main, chronologically successive types. Type I goes back to the first half or middle of the first century BC and is characterized by one row or several rows of external *loculi*, cut, as at Dura, at a right angle to

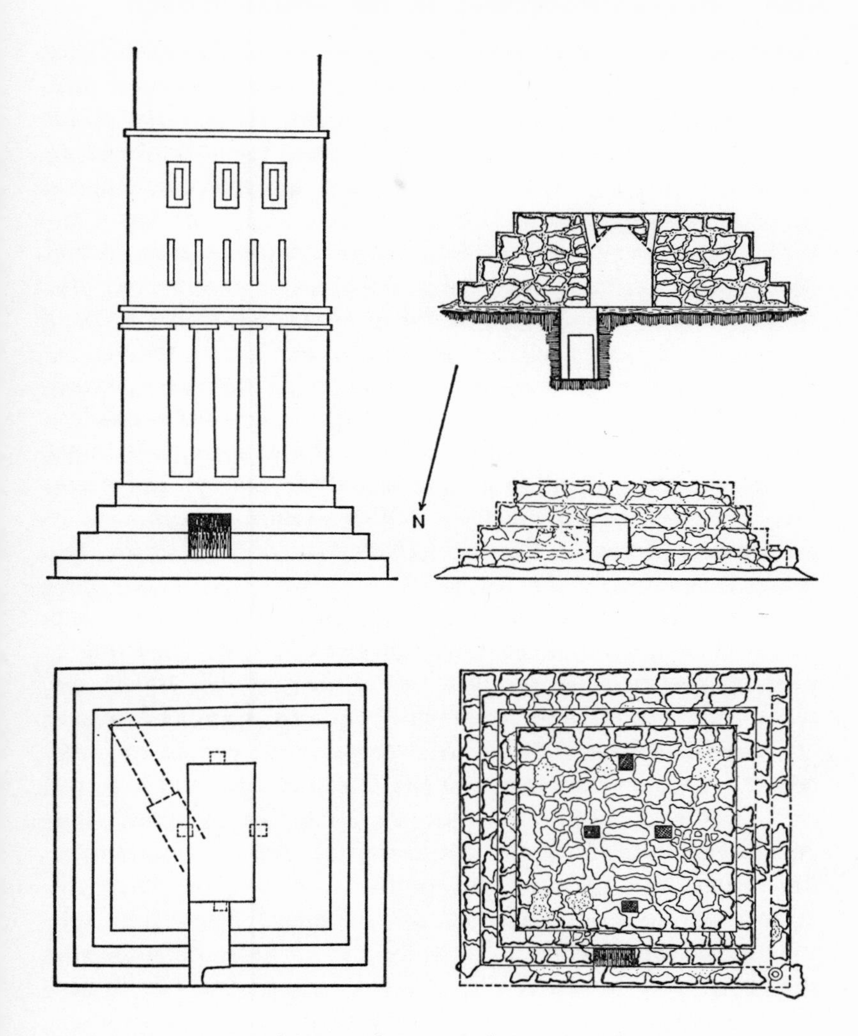


*Fig. 16 Restoration and sections of Tower-tomb D at Dura-Europos*

the face of the base. There are generally no burials in the tower itself, although a few tombs, marking a transition to Type II, have some internal *loculi* as well. The square body of the tower is solid-built of stones and tiles, with a facing of irregularly shaped blocks of stone; and it is slightly smaller in area than is its base. Tombs of this type were uneconomical, in that they could only take a few burials. With the need for family tombs that could serve εἰς τὸν αἰῶνα ('for ever') there emerged, towards the end of the first century BC, tombs of Type II, that is, towers containing a series of superimposed chambers, connected by a turning staircase, up to the building's total height, thus enabling many bodies to be accommodated inside. An example of this class is the tomb of Kithôt (No. 44), founded in AD 44, which has a door, approached by steps up the base on the side facing the valley, that leads into the ground-floor chamber, whose walls are pierced by two rows of *loculi*. Similar chambers, but progressively smaller, since the tower's walls slant markedly upwards towards the top, occupy the first, second, third, fourth, and fifth storeys. The facing blocks are still irregular in shape. Other dated tombs of Type II are those of 'Atenatan, founded in 9 BC (No. 7)[508] and of Hairan, founded in AD 33.[509] (*Pl.* 60)

Tombs of Type III, which appeared about the middle of the first century AD, are in every way more regular—in the build of their internal stairs, in the plans of all their storeys, and in the shape of their external facing-blocks.[510] Tombs of Type IV, which are known to have first occurred towards the end of the first century AD and continued into the third century, are perfectly regular towers, faced with quite regularly shaped blocks and embellished both inside and outside with restrained architectural decoration. Examples are the tombs of Sabeis (No. 68),[511] of Iambelicus (No. 51), founded in AD 83,[512] and of Elahbêl (No. 13), founded in AD 103.[513] In some of these tombs the funerary chambers have moulded and coffered ceilings and Corinthian pilasters, carrying an epistyle, along their walls;[514] and some could take as many as two hundred burials.

Externally the towers of Palmyra are soberer than those at Dura in that they lack the latter's angle pilasters, engaged columns in the intervening spaces, and decorative rows of grooves and windows.[515] The external masonry is mostly bare, apart from narrow slit-like windows lighting the stairs and upper storeys, some richly moulded door-lintels (e.g. the tombs of Iambelicus and Elahbêl), and, on the upper part of some towers, a kind of balcony, with projecting lower ledge and arched top, within which, below a small window, is carved in high relief a funerary banquet-scene. Some tombs have a larger window in the upper part and beneath it a projecting cornice about half-way up. The roofing of the Palmyrene tower-tombs presents a problem, since nearly all the surviving examples lack at least one storey. Roofs could well have been either pyramidal or flat. (*Pl.* 58)

The internal *loculi* were normally cut into two of the sides of the sepulchral chambers, corresponding in number and position on each side and rising in three or more superimposed tiers. Sometimes the ends of the tiers of *loculi* were closed by continuous vertical panels, up the wall's full height, flanked by Corinthian pilasters;[516] or the end of each *loculus* was sealed by an individual slab carrying a 'portrait' of the deceased. The *loculi* are generally 0·5 metres square in section and penetrate the wall to a depth of 2 metres. The back door of Elahbêl's tomb led down to a kind of cellar containing *loculi*, while the four extant above-ground storeys were full of sarcophagi.

Eastern tower-tombs are found, either singly or in less concentrated groups, on many other sites—in Syria, Cilicia Trachaea, Lebanon, the Euphrates valley, and Mesopotamia.[517] At Qanaouat (= Kanatha) in the Hauran, tower-tombs have been noted in the necropolis beside the road to Soueida. One of these is square with two storeys left, separated by a simple projecting band. It has a heavy lintel, surmounted by a small relieving-arch, above its door. Inside, in its vaulted chamber, is a sarcophagus at the far end and in its side walls there are tiers of *loculi*.[518] In Cilicia Trachaea the oldest tower-tomb, of the first century BC, is at Diocaesarea. It is square, stands on a two-stepped base, is built of very regular masonry blocks, has Doric angle pilasters with a Doric entablature, and is crowned by a stepped pyramidal roof: inside there is a single chamber with no floors above it.[519] One of the most spectacular towers of this series is that at Hermel in the Lebanon, which has been restored with certainty with its original materials.[520] This is a massive structure, built of well-cut stone and 10 metres square. It rests on a pedestal of three black lava steps and has two high storeys, slightly tapering towards the top. The lower storey carries flat angle pilasters, between which, in the upper half, are hunting scenes, symbols of the pleasant pastimes of paradise or of the soul's victory over the powers of evil. The upper storey has four flat pilasters, including those at the angles, on each side. The whole is surmounted by a tall, pointed pyramid. The tomb was probably put up about the turn of the second and first centuries BC. A tomb of similar type was built at Homs (Emesa) for Gaius Julius Sampsigeramus in AD 78–9, but is now known only from a drawing. Its lower storey had engaged columns; then came an attic carved with *bucrania* and garlands; and then an upper storey. The tower seems to have been built in *opus reticulatum*, unique for the region. Its vaulted inner chamber had niches in its walls. At El Bara in Syria is a large square tower standing on a low base. In its lower storey, which has angle pilasters and a cornice between it and the upper storey, is a large and elaborate door. The upper storey has angle pilasters, windows, and a cornice at the top. Above this is an entablature with low angle pilasters and a pyramidal roof crowns the whole building.[521] (*Pl.* 59)

At Hatra in Mesopotamia there are tower-tombs of the 'pseudo' kind, square or rectangular, with no upper storey outside, but sometimes with two storeys inside. They are built of dressed stone, with corner pilasters and engaged columns in between. In no case has the roof been preserved.[522]

### (B) CELEIA

Peculiar to themselves are the tombs of the Roman cemetery excavated between 1952 and 1955 in the village of Šempetru near the ancient town of Celeia in the province of Noricum (now Jugoslavia).[523] The remains of the tombs consisted of inscriptions, sculptured reliefs, and architectural features, found in fragments, but capable of reconstruction as more or less complete funerary monuments. The five most spectacular of these monuments, all family tombs, will be considered here. None bears a date. But the character of the lettering and of the sculpting and the hair- and beard-styles of the men and women whose portraits are preserved on the tombs reveal that the series falls within the second and third centuries AD.

The Ennii monument was built by Quintus Ennius Liberalis and Ennia Oppidana for themselves, their daughter Kalendina, who died aged 17, and for their son Vitulus, who died aged 30.[524] Reared on two steps is a high, rectangular base or *podium*, topped by a cornice. Above this is a low *podium*, the front of which carries the inscription and on which stands a tall *aedicula* with a solid back and short, solid side walls and in front an open porch of two Corinthian columns, with plain shafts, whose capitals support directly the arch at the outer face of the *aedicula*'s vaulted and coffered ceiling. The roof above this arch and ceiling takes the form of a triangular pointed structure; and that in turn is topped by a gabled roof with projecting eaves and elaborate cornice mouldings along the front. The tomb is very richly carved with reliefs. On the front of the ridge of the gabled roof is a Medusa mask. Six-petalled rosettes and other floral motifs occupy the coffers of the vault. On the back wall of the *aedicula*, inside, are carved the family portraits—deep busts of Quintus Ennius Liberalis and Ennia Oppidana above and, below them, in a gabled niche and flanked by mourning Cupids, the deep bust of Kalendina (her brother Vitulus is not portrayed). Both mother and daughter have the coiffure of Faustina I. The flat pilasters at the corners of the lateral walls of the *aedicula* carry floral scrolls and other plant motifs. On the horizontal friezes above the column- and pilaster-capitals at the sides are processions of marine beasts. On the front of the base is the Rape of Europa, flanked by two panels of vine scrolls. The right-hand side shows the Rape of Ganymede flanked by panels of floral scrolls, while on the left-hand side are a Satyr and Maenad making love and similarly flanked. (*Pl.* 61)

The family tomb of the Prisciani was put up by one Gaius Spectatius Finitimus, duumvir of Claudia Celeia, to his son Gaius Spectatius Priscianus and was also dedicated in a secondary inscription to Gaia Septimia Iusta, wife of Spectatius Priscianus, who died at the age of 55.[525] The monument is composed of the same main elements as is that of the Ennii—steps, in this case three, a rectangular base, topped by a heavy cornice, a low *podium*, on which is cut the secondary inscription, and then an *aedicula*, whose two Corinthian columns have shafts with spiral fluting and are linked with the short side walls by arches, instead of by horizontal friezes. Each of these side walls has, again, two decorated, flat pilasters; and, again, the arch at the outer face of the *aedicula*'s vaulted ceiling is borne directly by the column-capitals. But the structure above this arch is rectangular, not pointed, and carries the heavy horizontal cornice of a pediment, with heavy raking cornices, overhanging eaves, and, again, a Medusa mask at the apex. The sculpture is even more elaborate than that of the Ennii tomb. Within the *aedicula* are the seated figures of three members of the family, carved in very high relief—a woman in the centre and a man on either side of her. The base is divided into two superimposed zones, separated by a narrow band that is carved with animals, masks, and so forth. On the front, in the lower zone, is a scene from the *Iphigeneia in Tauris*, flanked by two panels each containing the figure of a Dioscurus. In the centre of the upper zone is the primary inscription, between two panels that each depict a Satyr and a Maenad. On the sides of the base the four main panels, two, one above the other, on either side, show further scenes from the story of Iphigeneia, flanked on one side by narrow panels each of which contains the figure of a hero, on the other side by narrow panels each adorned with the personification of a Season. (*Pl.* 62)

The Vindoni tomb is structurally simpler than are the two tombs just described and consists of only two main superimposed parts. Above is an altar-like feature, raised on three steps, which rest on a low *podium*, and topped by a very heavy projecting cornice below the focus. On the front of this altar is the inscription recording the erection of the monument by Gaius Vindonus Successus, aedile of Claudia Celeia, for himself and his wife Iulia Ingenua, who died at the age of 50.[526] In a panel on the right-hand side is the figure of Vindonus wearing a short tunic and holding an open ledger(?) in both hands, while a large cylindrical box stands on the ground at his feet. On the left-hand side, also in a panel, is Iulia, dressed in a long, voluminous, wide-sleeved tunic, and holding a rectangular box: her hair is dressed in Iulia Domna's style. On the *podium* below the altar's steps D M is inscribed in monumental characters. The lower and larger element of the tomb is a rectangular base resting on two steps and topped by a heavy projecting cornice just below the altar's low *podium*. The relief on the front depicts Hercules leading Alcestis back from Hades, flanked by two narrow panels of vine and ivy scrolls. On each side there is a single figure, one of a man carrying a hare on his shoulders, the other of a man holding a brace of birds in one hand, while with the other hand he balances on his shoulder a *pedum*, on which a basket is slung. These figures may be Seasons—Spring and Winter(?)

Of the Secundiani family two monuments have come to light. The most impressive of them is a tall, rectangular, single structure, resting on three steps, with solid walls on all four sides, a flat Corinthian pilaster at each of its four corners, an attic, carrying D M in bold lettering, above the pilaster-capitals, and, finally, a pedimented roof, which has strongly projecting cornices and a Medusa mask in relief at its apex. It was built by Gaius Spectatius Secundianus for himself, for his wife Tutoria Avita, who died aged 55, for Gaius Spectatius, son of Cerva, who died aged 28, and for his grandson Gaius Rusticus Tutor, who died aged 12.[527] This is the content of the primary inscription cut on the front wall of the monument between the legs of a funerary table, behind and above which, under a four-arched canopy, appear the busts of three of the deceased—a woman with mid-third-century coiffure, presumably Tutoria Avita, a man, the outline of whose bust is only roughly blocked out, presumably Gaius Spectatius Secundianus, and a young boy, presumably Gaius Rusticus Tutor. At a later date more names were added—those of Spectatia Severina, who died aged 25, and of Rusticius Albinus(?), who died aged 30, on the main panel, and those of Spectatius Avitus, who died aged 80, and of Aurelia Severina, on the edge of the funerary table.[528]

The second Secundiani monument is actually not so much a tomb as a large, tall, oblong stele (see Chapter vii (B)), carved on one face. It was erected by Statutius Secundianus and his wife Cerva for their son Statutius Secundus, who died aged 4.[529] The face of the stele has four superimposed elements—a plain *podium* at the bottom, then a panel carved with a three-legged funerary table, set out with food and drink and flanked by a male and female attendant, then the inscription panel, and finally a gable-topped niche, in which are the busts of father, mother, and child, the adults having mid-third-century hair-styles, while the spandrels of the gable bear the letters D M.

The subjects of the reliefs on all five monuments are patient of a funerary interpretation. The very high degree of sophistication displayed by the sculptures of the Ennii, Prisciani, and Vindoni tombs, with their classical style and content, suggests that artists from Italy may have been responsible for carving them. Moreover, the architectural elements of the first two tombs, with their solid back and side wall and open porticos in front and their high, rectangular bases or *podia*, recall in some ways the 'pseudo' temple-tomb at Sarsina (*cf.* pp. 130, 131). Similarly, the upper part of the Vindoni monument is reminiscent of the large, rectangular, funerary altars, carved with figures of the deceased, at Aquileia (*cf.* pp. 79–82). The first tomb of the Secundiani is also somewhat temple-like architecturally. But its sculpture, like that of the second Secundiani monument, is distinctively provincial in style.

## (C) GHIRZA

Another local group of tombs which merits separate discussion is that at Ghirza in the interior of Tripolitania, 150 miles south-east of Tripoli. Here two cemeteries, about a mile apart, served a large settlement of fortified farms dating from the third and fourth centuries AD and situated at the junction of the Wadis Ghirza and Zemzem.[530] The mausolea, built of local limestone and obviously those of well-to-do people living at an important centre for caravans and commerce between the Mediterranean coast and the heart of Africa, are of two main types—temple-tombs and obelisk-tombs, the former being both architecturally and sculpturally the richest and most spectacular.

Of the temple-tombs in the more northerly of the cemeteries the largest and most impressive takes the form of a peripteral temple raised on a *podium*, the north and south sides of which are prolonged at the east end to enclose the flight of steps that gives access to the front porch.[531] The square *cella* had a false door with panels and a decorated lintel and cornice. It is surrounded on all four sides by a free-standing colonnade with four columns at the front and back and five on each side, if those at the angles be counted twice, all the columns having moulded bases, plain shafts, and very debased composite capitals. Above the columns is a Doric frieze of triglyphs and metopes, each of the latter being filled with either a rosette or a round shield carved in relief. Pediments are lacking. The real entrance to the *cella* is on the south side; and a sliding stone closed it when the burial had taken place. In the *podium*, below the *cella*, is a crypt. (*Pl.* 63)

Another form of temple-tomb at Ghirza consists of a high, square *podium* and, on it, a solid *cella* surrounded by free-standing columns that carry an arcade, each arch springing directly from the column-capitals, as at Celeia (*cf.* pp. 173, 174). The best-preserved example is also in the northern cemetery.[532] At the corners of the *podium* are flat Corinthian pilasters carrying a frieze which is carved with a running scroll containing grapes, pomegranates, and other fruits. A flight of steps leads up the eastern side of the *podium* to the *cella*'s false door. On each side the arcade is composed of four columns and three arches, whose spandrels are carved with rosettes and stylized floral motifs. Above the arcades a tall frieze is crowned by a projecting cornice and richly carved with hunting-scenes and episodes from agricultural life. The burial chamber is below the tomb.

Other arcaded temple-tombs at Ghirza, some of them in the southern cemetery, have five, three, or two columns on each side and are, like the tomb just described, lavishly carved in a crude, but vivid, style.[533] These reliefs reflect the daily life, funerary practice, and afterlife ideas of the settlement's inhabitants.[534] They show us people reaping, winnowing, and threshing; ploughing with camels, oxen, and horses; hunting lions, leopards, antelopes, and ostriches; and swarming up date-palms. There is a dead chieftain surrounded by members of his family and servants; and there is another dead chieftain's ceremonial funerary banquet.

There is also the familiar Roman funerary theme of Hercules' Labours and other achievements (*cf.* pp. 138, 141, 175, 244, 274, 279); and there is a striking slab on which eight large fishes, symbols of the dead, encircle, and nibble at, a central rosette, symbol of life beyond the grave. The funerary iconography of this settlement on the Empire's southernmost periphery is, in fact, as completely Roman in its motifs and imagery as the architecture of its temple-tombs is classical. (*Pl.* 65)

Of the obelisk-tombs of Ghirza a characteristic instance in the southern cemetery was, when intact (its upper portions were destroyed by an earthquake), about 14 metres high and it rests on a base about 1·50 metres square.[535] It was divided into three storeys by two projecting cornices. The lowest storey has a false door on one side and flat Corinthian corner pilasters carrying a frieze carved with figures and decorative motifs. The second storey was an *aedicula* standing on a low *podium* and consisting of a shallow, open-fronted *cella*, with an arcaded porch of two free-standing Corinthian columns in front and an engaged Corinthian column at each corner at the back. The third storey was a slender pyramid crowned by a finial. With this tomb may be compared obelisk-mausolea from other Tripolitanian sites. That at Gsar Umm el-Ahmed in the Wadi Nfed[536] stands on a moulded base; its lowest storey has Corinthian corner pilasters and a Doric frieze of metopes topped by a projecting cornice. The second storey is a solid *cella* with a false door and engaged three-quarter Corinthian columns carrying a frieze adorned with a running floral scroll. Then comes another cornice and finally the pyramid. The obelisk-tomb at Mselleten in the Wadi Merdum stands on a similarly moulded base and consists of the same three elements separated by cornices, but is completely plain.[537] Of the obelisk-tomb in the Wadi Mesueggi[538] the base and lowest storey resemble those of the Wadi Nfed obelisk, but the former's frieze is carved continuously with human busts, animals, and birds. Its second storey is made up of nine free-standing Corinthian columns, arranged in three rows of three and standing on a *podium*. Above the capitals is a square intermediate element, then another cornice, and finally the pyramid. In the elegance of their proportions these Tripolitanian obelisk-mausolea are unrivalled among all existing works of Roman funerary architecture. (*Cf. Pl.* 64)

### (D) PROVINCIAL TUMULI

In Chapter V it was suggested (pp. 143, 144) that it was most probably the monumental round tumuli of the Etruscans that served originally as the models of the great circular tombs with masonry and brick drums erected in Roman Italy during imperial times. These often enormous structures had also in Italy their lesser counterparts, doubtless of the same derivation, namely the round tombs with cone-shaped mounds of earth and low retaining-walls of stone of which there are familiar instances beside the ancient *Via Appia* just to the south of Rome.[539] For tombs of this humbler sort, as for their large and small Etruscan ancestors, the accepted term is 'tumulus'; and this term is further properly applied to the so-called 'Roman barrows', the circular burial-mounds of varying sizes put up, mainly in the course of the first two centuries AD, by the populations of the northern and north-western Roman provinces. But if the same word describes both an Italian and a provincial type of tomb, that must not be taken to imply that the provincial series invariably stemmed from Italian prototypes and that local, pre-Roman traditions played no part in their development. One of the major problems of these 'barrows' is, indeed, the problem of their origins.[540] (*Pl.* 66)

Burials in round tumuli were, of course, prevalent among the Early and Middle Bronze Age peoples of the countries in which the relatively widespread use of mounds of the circular type began to emerge with some suddenness under the early Empire. In the Late Bronze Age the practice of tumulus building was largely abandoned in the central European areas, while persisting in certain parts of Britain and of western and northern continental lands.[541] In north-western France, for example, tumuli survived through the Late Bronze Age and the Hallstatt period into La Tène times;[542] as also, in the form of richly furnished aristocratic graves, by the Middle Rhine and in the Marne region of France.[543] Again, in La Tène pre-Roman Britain small round tumuli covered the remains of chieftains;[544] and in the cemetery at Lexden near Camulodunum are two great round Belgic 'barrows' dating from the last years before the Roman conquest, one of which, found to contain extremely rich grave-goods, may well have been the tomb of Cunobelinus himself.[545]

There was, then, in certain regions some slight thread of temporal continuity linking the prehistoric with the Roman-age tumuli. At the opening of our era the 'barrows' of the Early Bronze Age (and such later prehistoric 'barrows' as were built) would obviously have been far more conspicuous and imposing features of the British and continental landscapes than they are today—features that could still invite imitation on an extensive scale, even after the passage of many centuries, given some special stimulus. That stimulus can hardly have come from elsewhere than from Augustan Italy, where, as we have seen, the long series of circular Roman tombs and mausolea took its rise and with which Britain as well as northern Gaul and the central European provinces and borderlands were in close cultural contact. It is undoubtedly a far cry from the Mausoleum of Augustus to even the largest and most impressive provincial tumuli. But all the latter shared with their distant Italian relatives their circular shape and earthen mounds; while some, in which the mound is combined with quite substantial masonry elements, approximate much more closely to Etruscan and Roman prototypes. Provincial 'barrows' are, in fact, notable for their structural variety, for their inability to be reduced to any fixed formula. A large number of them were, like many of their pre-Roman precursors, aristocratic in character, built for local magnates and for the wealthy owners, whether Romans and Italians from the south or local people, of big country estates; and were lavishly equipped, in many cases, with costly tomb-furniture. Some appear to have been the tombs of veterans and of officials in the provincial administration. The main concentrations of Roman-age tumuli are in Britain,[546] Belgium,[547] the Treviran region,[548] parts of the Danubian provinces,[549] and Thrace.[550] None of these countries are among the most highly Romanized provincial areas; and it is precisely in such less Romanized lands that we should expect to find imitations and adaptations of just that type of Italian tomb which could be readily acclimatized in a native, pre-Roman tradition. For immigrants from the south the type had its counterparts in their own homelands; while provincials found in it a means of blending a new taste for Roman fashion with something older and more familiar to them.

In Britain by far the most common form of tumulus was the plain circular mound of earth, conical in shape, steep-sided, and often truncated at the top. It was surrounded by a ditch, inside which there was sometimes a small earthen bank. No stone walling or reveting has a place in tombs of this simple kind. Their distribution is mainly in the region bounded on the west and north by the Fosse Way, with special concentrations in what are now Hertfordshire, Essex, and Kent. Outlying instances occur in Yorkshire (Hovingham), in Lincolnshire (Riseholme and Lincoln itself), Dorset (Woodlands), and just possibly in Northumberland (Carvoran). They are found either singly or in groups, such as the single row of six along a roadside at Stevenage in Hertfordshire[551] and the two rows of four and three respectively at Bartlow in Essex.[552] This latter group yielded exceptionally rich grave-goods. The surviving eastern row of four contains the largest extant tumulus in Britain, 45 feet high and about 144 feet in diameter—as contrasted with the smallest in the province, that at Godmanchester in Huntingdonshire, whose diameter is only 32 feet. Five of the 'Bartlow Hills' produced evidence that wooden chests held the cremated bones: one contained a tile-built burial chamber.[553] The vast majority of British tumuli covered cremations. There are, however, a few examples of inhumations, for instance, at Richborough in Kent, where the remains were in a wooden coffin sunk in a pit below a stone chamber,[554] and at Rougham in Suffolk, where the body was laid in a wood-encased lead sarcophagus, placed in its turn in a chamber of rubble and tiles.[555] In the central area of the tumulus at Holborough in Kent there was a long, narrow wooden coffin containing the dead man's cremated bones. Here the cremation had taken place elsewhere, whereas in other cases the tumulus had been heaped up over the actual pyre. The Holborough tumulus also provides one of the rare British examples of a secondary burial—that of a child in a decorated lead sarcophagus of early-third-century date, which had been inserted into the southern part of the mound (*cf.* pp. 276, 277).[556] The number of 'barrow' tumuli so far known in Britain is about one hundred. (*Pl.* 67)

Much rarer in Britain are the round tombs in which a ring of stone marks out the circumference of the roundel. There can be little doubt that here we have a type of tumulus in which a revetment or species of low masonry drum contained the cone of earth after the Italian style. Plain circular foundations exist in tombs at Pulborough in Sussex (external diameter 60 feet; wall 11½ feet thick)[557] and at High Rochester in Northumberland (circumference 50 feet), the latter presenting two courses of off-set masonry, the relics of a drum, resting on the foundation.[558] It could be that the tombs with circular foundation-walls, the so-called 'towers', at Lockham (Langley) in Kent and at Harpenden in Hertfordshire, both surrounded by precinct-walls, were small tumuli with surmounting earthen cones;[559] and the same could be true of the circular portion of the sepulchral complex at Witchampton in Dorset.[560] The round tomb at Keston in Kent is very likely to have been a small drum-and-cone tumulus, despite a recent assertion to the contrary.[561] It has an overall diameter of 29 feet, with a flint ring-wall 3 feet thick and uninterrupted by any entrance, and six large radiating external buttresses. The purpose of these buttresses, which were stuccoed and painted red and may have carried low columns or pilasters adorning the drum's exterior, must have been to counteract the thrust of a mass of earth inside; and they are paralleled by the twelve exterior ones on the much larger tumulus, 65 feet in overall diameter and with a ring-wall 3 feet thick, at West Mersea in Essex.[562]

This tomb, which is close to the remains of a large and rich Roman house, is of the so-called 'cartwheel' type, with a small central hexagonal 'hub' from which six 'spokes' radiate to join the ring-wall and correspond to alternate buttresses. The superstructure reared on these foundation lines was of tile and mortar. The 'spokes' have their counterparts in tumuli by the *Via Appia* near the fifth milestone from Rome, one with eight 'spokes' and one with only four.[563] A tumulus by the *Via Tiburtina* has eight radiating 'spokes', but no 'hub'; and another tomb by the *Via Appia* has neither 'spokes' nor 'hub', but eight contiguous recumbent arches just inside the ring-wall; while a tomb on the *Via Salaria* has six 'spokes' joining a series of curving walls.[564]

All these tombs are probably Augustan in date. 'Spokes', recumbent arches, and curving walls were clearly intended, as were the external buttresses, to help the ring-walls to withstand the pressure of the earthen cone; and the 'hub' could have supported a pilaster reaching to the top of the mound and crowned by a projecting monument on the summit. These features obviously recall, however remotely in the cases of Keston and West Mersea, the concentric circles of walls, and radiating 'spokes' below Augustus' Mausoleum in Rome—possibly also its crowning monument. Three British tumuli at Overton Down in Wiltshire may represent a combination of native and Italian structural elements, inasmuch as their retaining-walls were not of stone but of close-set, stout wooden posts (*cf.* p. 184).[565]

In Belgium, where about 340 'barrow' tumuli are known, the main concentrations are north of the Meuse, in the provinces of Brabant, Limbourg, Namur, and Liège, the most important group being in the area of Tongres.[566] The Belgian tumuli are structurally the same as those in Britain, but are on the whole larger, ranging in diameters from 40 feet (4 feet high) to 145 feet (40 feet high). Most of them date from the second century. Two remarkable examples are at Koninksem, just south-west of Tongres, beside the Roman road that runs between Maastricht and Bavay.[567] The burials are invariably cremations, often accompanied by remains of pyres and by very rich grave-furniture; some tumuli had burial-chambers walled with stone, tiles, or wooden planks, and none appear to be later than *c.* 180. Tumuli with circular walls of masonry are known at Avernas-le-Bauduin, Hottomont, Glimes, Koninksem, Penteville, Waremme-Longchamps. Quite outstanding is the tumulus excavated by M. Amand in 1954 at Antoing, a short distance to the south-east of Tournai.[568] This tumulus, whose mound has been levelled since the seventeenth century, has an overall diameter of 30 metres, with a huge circular retaining wall of great heavy blocks of stone that rested on a deep and broad foundation. An underground corridor, resembling the *dromos* of a Greek tomb, 12 metres long, 1·75 metres high, and 0·75 metres wide and once roofed with large stone slabs, led to two burial chambers at the centre. This implies that the tomb was intended to be entered, and that new burials could be placed in it or funerary rites conducted there, after the primary burial had taken place.[569] Similar entrance passages of masonry exist in the Treviran tumuli at Oberkail, Strotzbüsch, and Flaxweiler, but all of these lack stone retaining walls.[570] The builders of these tombs clearly followed a Mediterranean practice in providing entrances of this type. (*Pl.* 68)

There can, indeed, be little doubt that for the Antoing tumulus, for the three Treviran tumuli just cited, as well as for the Keston and West Mersea tumuli in Britain, the provincial builders had at their disposal architectural sketch-books or manuals compiled in southern lands. This must also apply to those who erected four other Treviran tumuli, two near Trier (the smaller of them has now disappeared), one at Nennig, and one at Fremersdorf (now also vanished), which form a homogeneous group.[571] They vary in size from 51·15 to 9·1 metres in diameter and all are characterized by strong retaining walls of carefully squared masonry and, just inside them, recumbent arches, 22, 32, and 17 respectively in number (the precise number in the lost tomb near Trier is unknown), while the extant tumulus near Trier has at its centre a substantial square pilaster to support a crowning monument of some kind and the tumulus at Fremersdorf had a 'hub' from which four 'spokes' radiated to join the circle of recumbent arches. It is true, as H. Koethe points out—and the same applies to the Keston and West Mersea tumuli—that in all four cases the ring-wall is basically of the nature of a 'fence' designed to support and restrain the earthen cone, unlike the high, monumental masonry drum, topped by a mound, of the great Italian circular mausolea (of Augustus, Caecilia Metella, Hadrian, etc.), and that these stone 'fences' recall the palisades round the 'beaker-culture' tumuli, and the dry stone walls surrounding the Bronze Age and Hallstatt period tumuli, of the district. But Koethe admits that the recumbent arches and 'spokes' are purely Roman features and that the small tumulus (probably a cenotaph) at Nickenich had a moulded cornice of Italian type crowning its quite substantial drum.[572] And since the whole resurgence of tumulus building here, as elsewhere, coincided with the Romanizing of the local population, it is hard to agree with him that southern influence on this funerary practice was but a superficial one ('äusserlich romanziert').

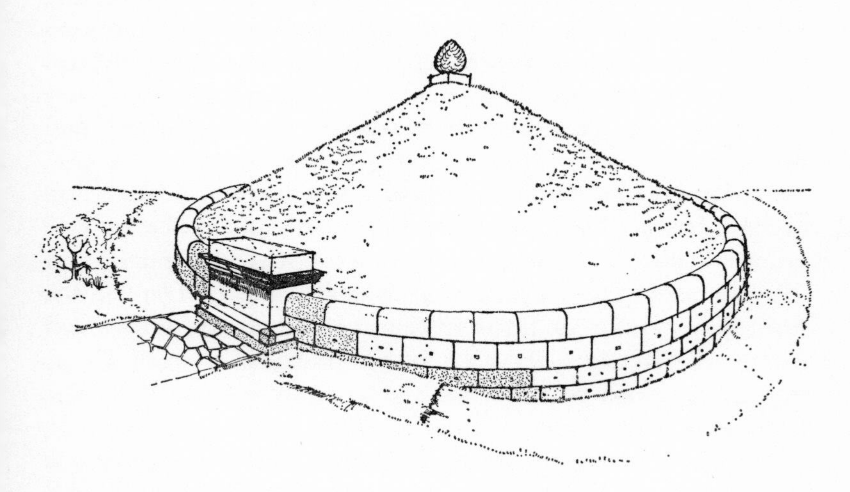

*Fig. 17 Restoration of the tumulus at Bill* (see Note 569)

In 1939 Koethe catalogued about 145 Roman-age tumulus sites in the territory of Trier and its neighbouring areas, a small proportion of them doubtful, a few of them consisting of a group of several mounds—in one case, fifteen. He prefaced this catalogue by an introductory essay on Roman-age tumuli in general and on those in the Treviran region in particular, pointing out that in this area the revival of tumuli seems to have been largely connected with elements of what he terms the 'Hunsrück-Eifel culture' and to have been least significant in those localities in which La Tène culture was most firmly rooted. In this important paper we have abundant evidence both of the popularity of tumulus burials with the Treviri taken as a whole and of the unevenness of their distribution among them.

The Roman-age tumuli of the Danubian provinces have so far formed the subject of fewer studies than have those of Britain, Belgium, and Germany. In the meantime two tumuli, both for cremations, that have been investigated in the Salzburg district, may be cited as among the best-known examples.[573] In one of these, at Maxglan, no stone internal structure was found: the burial had been on the ground or in a sinking. But in the other tumulus, that at Köstendorf, a masonry burial chamber came to light. Here in what is now Austria the presence of pre-Roman tumuli of the Hallstatt and Le Tène periods may have contributed to the revival of this type of tomb in the first and early-second centuries AD.

Further evidence of the native background of tumulus building in the Danubian regions under the early and middle Empire appeared in 1961–2 with the discovery of a *villa rustica* and adjacent necropolis at Cineis in Rumania (Transylvania), the one-time province of Dacia.[574] The villa buildings, which had been badly damaged by the plough, contained pottery of the second and third centuries and were probably owned by the Roman or Romanized manager of some of the iron works in which that district abounded. In the centre of the cemetery, which presumably served both the family of the owner of the villa and its Dacian dependants, is a rectangular walled precinct divided by a cross-wall into a main burial chamber and a smaller ante-chamber, with a stone-paved platform at the latter's entrance that probably supported funerary statues after the Roman style. But of the four burials within the main chamber (one was an inhumation in a trench grave) three were cremations in tumuli whose earthen mounds were contained by roughly constructed ring-walls of irregularly shaped stones; while outside the precinct, no doubt reserved for members of the villa-owning family, are seventeen more tumuli of varying sizes and of the same construction as the three inside. One of the tumuli inside and five of those outside have lost their ring-walls. All the external tumuli housed cremations, the dead in each case being burnt on a pyre

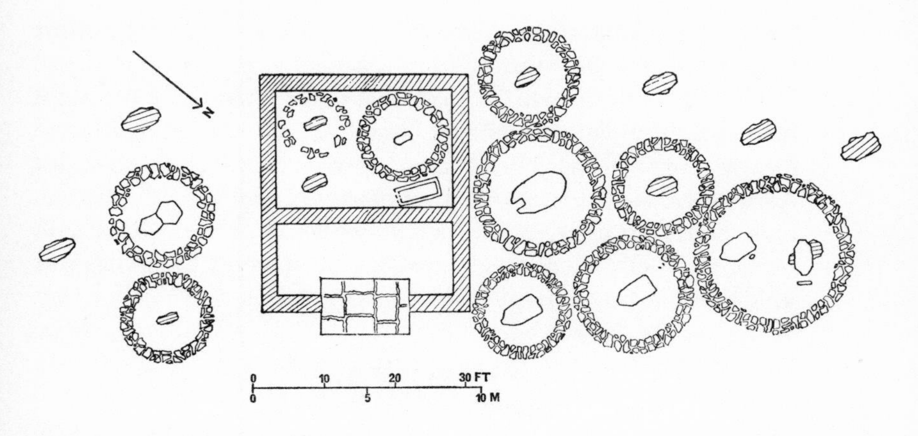


*Fig. 18 Plan of the Cineis cemetery*

on the spot. The grave-goods included local Dacian as well as Roman pottery.

Of the Thracian Roman-age tumuli two groups, remarkable for the outstanding richness of their imported grave-goods, have been excavated in the eastern (now Turkish) area of the country.[575] All these tombs were simple mounds of earth without stone ring-walls and all housed cremations. Of the three at Lüleburgaz one, 11 metres high and 65 metres in diameter, contained two burials, whose furniture included gold and bronze jewellery; bronze discs bearing human masks and small bronze human busts—all mounts in high relief for wooden chests; a bronze jug and a bronze skillet; two bronze mirrors whose backs are adorned with mythological figure-scenes in relief; and a bronze two-handled basin. At Vize (the ancient Bizye) is a group of four tumuli, of which the largest and most important from the viewpoint of its contents is 9·50 metres high and 55 metres in diameter. In the centre of the mound is a rectangular barrel-vaulted burial chamber built of carefully squared blocks of local limestone. In it was a stone sarcophagus, painted on one of its long sides, which held the ashes of the dead accompanied by a dazzling wealth of works of Roman art. These comprised a silver one-handled mug embossed with Bacchic motifs; four silver chalices embossed with naturalistic birds; and a magnificent, elaborately decorated face-mask-visor 'sports' helmet of bronze, with decidedly portrait-like facial features. There can be little doubt that this was the tomb of a local king or prince, dating from the years that immediately preceded the organization of Thrace as a Roman province in AD 45–6. Another of the Vize tumuli, 30 metres in diameter and 4 metres high, contained grave-goods of a less costly type. A third mound, 50 metres in diameter and 2·5 metres high, covered the remains of someone's favourite horse.[575a]

## (E) EASTERN TOMBS WITH ROCK-CUT FAÇADES: JERUSALEM AND PETRA

Of the tombs that are typical of the Empire's eastern borderlands none have a greater fascination than those whose façades are carved in the vertical surface of a cliff or wall of rock, with burial chambers that are tunnelled deep into the heart of the living rock behind or at the side. The most impressive examples, which combine to a remarkable degree Semitic burial custom with Graeco-Roman architectural and sculptural ornament and sometimes with Graeco-Roman funerary symbols, are those on the outskirts of Jerusalem, in the Kedron Valley and to the north of the ancient city, and at Petra, the Nabataean capital and later one of the leading cities of the Roman province of Arabia.

In Jerusalem the Kedron Valley tombs include two particularly notable rock-cut complexes, to both of which have been assigned dates as widely separated as the third century BC and the Herodian era.[576] One of these complexes comprises a large square block cut free from the rock face of which it once formed part, so that an open corridor surrounds it on all four sides. This is the so-called 'Tomb of Absalom', which serves as the 'façade' or monumental 'marker' of the eight-chambered rock-cut 'Tomb of Jehoshaphat' behind it. In the pediment over the entrance leading from the 'Tomb of Absalom' to the main chamber of the 'Tomb of Jehoshaphat' is carved in low relief an elegant floral scroll containing olive-branches, grapes, flowers, and leaves and springing to right and left from a central acanthus calyx—all motifs that are symbols of life and refreshment after death.[577] Of the group of chambers on the west side one has three *loculi* cut into the rock at right angles to its west wall; while three of the other chambers have windows opening on to the corridor surrounding the 'Tomb of Absalom', proving that the latter and the 'Tomb of Jehoshaphat' are contemporary and planned as a single unit. The 'Tomb of Absalom' contains a central burial chamber (to which no ancient entrance is visible today), including *arcosolia*, and is thus a tomb in its own right, as well as a 'marker'. Externally it is composed of three sections. The bottom one, which is the tallest, is carved from the surrounding rock and its walls are sculptured with engaged Ionic columns and corner pilasters, surmounted by a Doric frieze of triglyphs and shields in the metopes, which is in its turn topped by a projecting cornice. The rest of the monument is worked in finely dressed ashlar blocks, rising above the summit of the rock face. The second section is a square *podium* with a projecting cornice at bottom and top; the third is a circular drum with two cornices girdling its upper portion and a cone-shaped roof crowned by a finial. (*Pl.* 70)

The second Kedron Valley complex, a short distance to the right of the first as one faces the line of tombs from the modern road, comprises the so-called 'Tomb of Zechariah' and the so-called 'Tomb of Jacob', the latter being in reality the tomb of the sons of Hezir. Both are on the same alignment along the cliff face, the former being a free-standing monumental 'marker' connected with the 'Tomb of Jacob' by a stairway at the side leading to the latter's vestibule, whose exterior façade consists of a portico of two free-standing columns and two corner pilasters of the Doric order supporting an epistyle, a Doric frieze of triglyphs and empty metopes, and a heavy cornice. Behind the vestibule is a central hall from which radiate, cross-wise, three burial chambers with *loculi* at right angles to their walls. The 'Tomb of Zechariah' is possibly a solid block, without any chamber inside it, hollowed completely from the rock, whose vertical walls box it in on three sides, surrounded by a corridor, and adorned with two engaged Ionic columns and two Ionic corner pilasters on each face of its exterior. These carry an epistyle with two very heavy projecting cornices; and the whole is crowned by a simple pyramidal roof.

The most impressive rock-cut tomb in the cemetery to the north of the ancient city is the so-called 'Tomb of the Kings', actually, as an Aramaic inscription proves, that of Helena, queen of Adiabene, and her son Izates.[578] According to Talmudic sources Helena settled with her family in Jerusalem during the second quarter of the first century AD and became a proselyte; and Josephus states (*Ant.Iud.* xx, 4, 3) that she and Izates were buried 'by the pyramids that she had set up'. These pyramids or pavilions with pyramidal roofs[579] may have stood above the extant façade of the tomb, which is on the west side of a great forecourt cut 9 metres deep into the heart of the rock. The wide opening of the façade may once have formed a two-columned portico, to judge from the surviving fragments of shafts, bases, and capitals, as well as of angle pilasters. Still in place are portions of the opening's border, carved in low relief with floral motifs and framing the opening above and at the sides. Over the opening runs a Doric frieze of triglyphs and metopes, broken at the centre by a bunch of grapes flanked by garlands and terminating at either end in an acanthus calyx, while *paterae* (shallow bowls) occupy the metopes. A heavy projecting cornice tops the frieze.

In both the Kedron Valley tombs and that of Helena and Izates the use of decorative motifs largely, but not entirely, culled from classical copy-books, yet often somewhat unclassically combined, goes hand in hand with the Semitic practice of inhumation at a time when the Roman world as a whole, apart from its Semitic areas, was cremating its dead. Here the bodies were laid in *loculi* cut, as we have seen, at right angles to the walls of the burial chamber or placed in *arcosolia* or on benches in niches cut parallel to the walls. Sometimes, as in the Adiabene tomb, sarcophagi were employed. These have semi-cylindrical lids and are carved with running floral scrolls or with large rosettes.[580] According to the normal Jewish rule only non-figured ornament of this kind was allowed; but as in the pagan world, so here and on the Jewish tomb façades (see above), these motifs could be interpreted as symbols of new life beyond the grave. Similar in content is the decoration worked in 'intaglio' or 'Kerbschnitt' technique on the stone *ossuaria* (bone-chests) that have been discovered in many Jewish tombs of this period.[581] In these chests could be collected the bones of the bodies that had decomposed in the tomb and space thus saved for further burials. Or they could contain the bones of Jews who had died and been buried abroad, sent to Palestine for a second burial in the fatherland.

The famous tombs, or temple-tombs, of Petra, carved in the soft sandstone of the locality, have, since their rediscovery for the modern world by Burckhardt in 1812, formed the subject of a large and still increasing body of writings, both learned and popular.[582] Only a summary account and discussion of their character and chronology can be given here. None of them have independent, monumental 'markers' of the 'Absalom' and 'Zechariah' type. All have true façades sculptured in relief on the rock face, although some have free-standing rock-cut columns; and in one case the topmost storey of the façade, reared above the summit of the cliff, is completed in masonry. These façades fall into three main classes, two of which may be described as 'oriental', the third as 'classical'.

Of the 'oriental' tombs, which are very numerous and are most impressive as seen rising tier above tier up the cliff-face to the south of the theatre, one class, described as 'Assyrian', shows a fairly plain façade. It is pierced by a single doorway, often flanked by an engaged column or pilaster on either side, and is surmounted by either a single or a double row of small, triangular, crow-stepped 'merlons' of the kind found very much earlier, for instance, on the rock-cut tomb at Dau Duktar in Persia, dating from between 650 and 550 BC. Both in Persia and at Petra these 'merlons' are backed against a smooth, perpendicular attic of rock. Tombs of the second 'oriental' class, the 'corniced' class, have, above a somewhat more elaborate façade that can be decorated with a row of four engaged columns, either one very heavy projecting cornice or two such cornices, obviously Egyptian in origin, surmounted by a pair of large, half-triangular 'merlons', backed in the same way as are the small 'Assyrian' ones and with crow-steps on their inner diagonal sides. There can be little doubt that both classes of 'oriental' tombs originated at

Petra during the time of the city's independence, perhaps early in the first century BC if not before. A number of them are unfinished and these provide a clear demonstration of how the carvers went to work, beginning at the top, since in these cases the 'merlons' and cornices have been completed, while the rest of the façade has only been roughly blocked out. Sometimes the face below the cornices has been smoothed, but not cut back to the required depth, there is no door, and the positions of the angle pilasters, which should eventually have projected slightly beyond the surface between them, are merely pecked in. In other cases the doorway with its pediment has been carved, but not opened out, and the flanking engaged columns have been cut to their final shape, but still lack their details.

Much rarer and much more controversial as regards both their prototypes and their chronology are the temple-tombs with 'classical' façades. Some of these, while definitely classical in character, are relatively unpretentious, for instance, the 'Lions Tomb' cut in the western wall of the mountain-girt valley in which the city lies. Its door is flanked by two flat pilasters which carry an epistyle surmounted by a shallow pediment—elements that recall the plain pedimented doorways of the Hellenistic rock-cut tombs at Termessos in Pisidia. On the Petran tomb two lions carved in low relief, standing and facing inwards, keep the door as guardians of the dead or as symbols of death's ravening jaws, both common concepts in funerary art throughout the Roman world. More ornate and combining local with classical features (if indeed a single tomb and not a pair of separate tombs is in question) is the 'Obelisk Tomb' cut in two parts on two terraces of the rock face near the entrance to the narrow Syk or gorge that leads from the south through the mountain barrier to the city area. On the upper terrace, mounted on a *podium* which is pierced by a central doorway, is a row of four obelisks, emblems of the Nabataean god Dusares. On the lower terrace, which projects in front of the upper one, is a closed portico of six engaged columns, three on each side of a door, which carry an epistyle and a shallow pediment, rounded at the centre and straight at the sides. Above this are six flat engaged pilasters, of which the four central ones support a broken pediment. The upper part with the obelisks would certainly appear to have been carved first, since the lower part suggests that its design was squeezed rather uncomfortably into space that was left for it. A comparatively austere, but imposingly monumental, classical façade is that of the 'Tomb of the Roman Soldier', so-called from the statue in the central niche above the doorway (there are two other niches, each holding a statue, one on either side of the soldier) and situated to the south of the main city area. This façade projects as a solid block beyond the vertical rock face and consists of two engaged columns flanking the door, a heavy square pilaster at each corner, an epistyle, a pediment, and an attic. Associated with this tomb is a large rock-cut *triclinium* for the funerary feasts which seem to have played an important part in the Petran cult of the departed. Its interior walls are adorned with engaged columns that alternate with niches. (*Pls.* 71, 72)

But by far the most conspicuous fruits of the Hellenization and Romanization of the Nabataeans, which began early in the first century BC and continued through the second century AD, after the annexation of Arabia by Rome in 106, are Petra's six great intricately carved classical tomb façades—the Khazne opposite the northern end of the Syk, the 'Deir Tomb' on the top of the Jebel el Deir, one of the mountains that closes the valley on the west, and the 'Urn Tomb', the 'Corinthian Tomb', the 'Palace Tomb', and the 'Florentinus Tomb' (to pass from south to north), all cut along the wall of cliffs that terminates the valley on the east.

The Khazne is almost certainly the earliest and undoubtedly the finest of the six. Its two-storeyed façade stands some 90 feet high in a deep niche cut for it in the slightly sloping, smoothed-down surface of a rose-red cliff; and it begins 7 metres back from the edge of a level terrace or plinth raised about 3 metres above the floor of the gorge. The lower storey is an open portico of six unfluted Corinthian columns, two of them completely free-standing, three on either side of steps that lead into a vestibule, wider than it is deep. At the back of the vestibule another flight of steps gives access through a richly carved doorway to the main chamber, which is square and whose rear and side walls are each pierced at the centre by a door opening into a small, narrow, *loculus*-like room. In each short side of the vestibule is an ornate door flanked by two flat pilasters that carry an epistyle, over which is a circular window. These doors each give entrance to a lateral chamber rather more than half the size of the main one. Although all traces of burials (and these as elsewhere in Semitic Petra would have been inhumations) have long since vanished, there can be little doubt that some at least of these rooms once held bodies. The central square room could, perhaps, have served for funerary meals.

To return to the details of the Khazne's façade—between the two outer columns of the portico on each side on the projecting piece of wall that unites them, is carved in relief the figure of a Dioscurus, guardian of the dead; and the entablature above the columns contains a frieze of rinceaux and pairs of griffins that confront one another from either side of a vase. All these are well-known Roman funerary motifs. In the centre of the pediment above, which runs across the four central columns only, is a bust flanked by floral scrolls. This pediment is backed against an attic, which forms the *podium* of the upper storey. Here the centre-piece is a circular *tholos* or pavilion with a conical roof and engaged Corinthian columns on its wall. It is free-standing for two-thirds of its circumference; and it is flanked on either side by a square feature with a Corinthian engaged column at each of its three visible corners and a broken pediment crowning each of its two visible sides, namely the front and the side that runs back opposite the *tholos*. On the epistyle of the *tholos* and of both lateral features is an exquisite frieze of flowers, leaves, and fruit, interrupted by masks at intervals. On the wall of the *tholos*, in its central inter-columniation, is the figure of a goddess holding a *cornucopiae*, perhaps Abundantia, symbolizing afterlife prosperity. The side intercolumniations of the *tholos* and the front and side inter-columniations of the square lateral features each carry the figure of an Amazon triumphantly brandishing a battle-axe; and at the back of each of the two deep recesses, flanked by engaged columns, that separate the *tholos* from the lateral features, is carved a Victory. Both Amazons and Victories suggest the vanquishing of death by the souls of those who were buried in the tomb.

The wholly Graeco-Roman character of both the architectural and the sculptural ornament of the Khazne's façade is immediately obvious. Whether the designers and executants were Nabataeans accustomed to sculpting in rock or immigrant artists and craftsmen from east-Mediterranean lands or even from lands further west, who learnt their expertise in this technique at Petra, the models that they used all formed part of the late-Hellenistic and early-imperial repertory. Comparisons drawn between a façade of this type and Campanian mural paintings, Roman *scaenarum frontes*, and such a façade as that on the great peristyle in the 'Colonnaded Palace' at Ptolemais in Cyrenaica are a familiar feature of Petran literature. No actual building of either Hellenistic or Roman times with a *tholos* in its upper storey is so far known. But there would seem to be no reason why the individual elements of the Khazne and related façades should not have been ultimately derived from various real, three-dimensional buildings, here combined in the unreal or pictorial manner possible in two-dimensional art. Such combinations we find, of course, in the wall-paintings of Pompeii and Herculaneum. But we need not suppose that the Petran sculptors worked from direct copies of Campanian paintings. The Campanian wall-painters and the Petran façade designers and, indeed, workers in other media, could all have used common, circulating copy-books containing sketches of a wide variety of architectural features and of figural and floral motifs; artists of many kinds could have worked these models at will into compositions of their own devising. (*Pl.* 73)

Very imposing in view of its enormous height, over 140 feet, and commanding position about 4000 feet above Mediterranean level, is the 'Deir Tomb', whose façade has many points of similarity with that of the Khazne, but lacks the latter's slim elegance and refinement of sculptural detail. This tomb, too, is recessed deep into the face of a massive cliff with a level terrace in front of it, and is, like the Khazne, composed of two distinct storeys. The lower storey here is also a six-columned portico, with three columns on either side of a central, pedimented door. But all the columns (which have the bossed, 'Nabataean' capitals) are engaged in a wall that is tightly closed, apart from a shallow niche in each of the two outer intercolumniations. The upper storey, which is somewhat top heavy in effect, has a central, circular, columned *tholos*, whose conical roof is surmounted by a large, round, rock-cut urn; and here again are the two square lateral features, each crowned by two broken pediments, but at each extremity is added in this case a very heavy rectangular pilaster. Above the 'Nabataean' capitals of the columns on the *tholos* and lateral features and of the pilasters are quasi-Doric friezes of triglyphs and circular shields in the metopes. Very deep recesses separate the *tholos* from the lateral features and the latter from the terminating pilasters. In the back wall of the burial chamber behind the façade is a large, arched niche holding a low platform on which a coffin must once have rested. (*Pl.* 69)

To pass to the four classical tombs carved on the valley's eastern wall—the 'Urn Tomb' is cut back so deeply into the rock that it has in front of its façade a great unroofed forecourt, reared on a platform, with a portico of free-standing, quasi-Doric columns on either side of it. The door through the façade is flanked by flat pilasters which carry a Doric frieze of triglyphs and round shields in the metopes and a pediment above. Four immensely tall engaged columns tower above the doorway, two on either side of it. These support an architrave and a high attic crowned by another pediment, at the apex of which stands the urn that gives the tomb its name and which is backed by yet a further attic reaching to the top of the smoothed-down surface of the rock. In the back wall of the chamber behind the façade are arched niches containing *podia* for coffins long since lost.

The 'Corinthian Tomb', so-called from the fact that all the columns of its façade have Corinthian capitals, has in its lowest storey a closed portico of three engaged columns on either side of the central doorway that gives access to the burial chamber. Above their capitals is a species of intermediate attic; and above that again a central *tholos* flanked by two square lateral features of the same type as those on the Khazne and Deir façades.

As on the 'Urn Tomb', so on the façade of the 'Palace Tomb', believed, with some probability, to imitate that of a late-Hellenistic or Roman palace, the *tholos* and its lateral features find no place. Here, again, the lowest storey is closed apart from its four doors, which are pierced through four tall and elaborate *aediculae*, flanked by pilasters and crowned two by triangular and two by rounded pediments. The second and third storeys are composed of a series of closed, flat-topped arches carried on pilasters. Those parts of the third storey that project above the summit of the cliff are worked in masonry. Behind the façade of this tomb are three chambers of which the central one had a burial niche in its back wall with four rock-cut blocks, emblems of Dusares, above the place where the dead once lay.

Finally, a short distance to the north-east of the 'Urn', 'Corinthian', and 'Palace' tombs and on a different alignment is the 'Florentinus Tomb', called after Sextus Florentinus, whose name and career are inscribed on the façade and whose last appointment was that of governor of the newly founded province of Arabia.[583] The bottom portion of this façade is plain and pierced by a single doorway with a triangular pediment. Above is an attic adorned with five engaged columns whose capitals support the epistyle on which the Latin text is cut. Above that again is a rounded pediment carved with a central bust and floral scrolls on either side of it. There are three burial niches in the back wall of the internal chamber, the central one being larger than its neighbours.

It goes without saying that all of these large, classically adorned and presumably very expensive temple-tombs were cut for highly cultivated and important persons. With the question of who those persons were—Nabataean kings or high-ranking Roman officials or wealthy Nabataeans under Roman rule—is obviously bound up the thorny problem of their chronology. With regard to this problem there are several schools of thought, one that ascribes all the classical tombs to the time of Petra's independence, another that assigns them all to her Roman period, and a third that would place some before, some after, the Roman annexation. None of the tombs has produced external dating evidence, apart from the 'Florentinus' and 'Roman Soldier' tombs. But even there the possibility cannot be ruled out that the first was an earlier tomb reused for the Roman *legatus*, the inscription being later than the carving of the façade; while it was the view of the late Ian Richmond, a specialist in Roman military equipment, that the cuirass of the statue of the Roman soldier is of Julio-Claudian type, not, as might have been expected, of a second-century form.[584] According to Strabo (xvi, 4, 21) many Romans were already domiciled in Petra in Augustus' time.

The Khazne façade, the most beautiful and best proportioned of the Graeco-Roman group, is far more likely to have served as the model for the rest than *vice versa*. The Nabataean kings were well known for their philhellenic tastes. Aretas III, who was reigning round about the middle of the first century BC, styled himself 'the Philhellene'; and from the first half of the first century BC onwards Hellenic types were issued on the royal coinage. Nothing would appear to be more probable than that some of these rulers were buried on the outskirts of their metropolis in sumptuous tombs worked in native technique but of classical design. On the face of it, there is nothing in the decoration of the Khazne's façade to exclude the tomb from having been just such a royal burial place, not later in date than the first century of our era. Against such a dating two main objections have been raised. The first is that at the Nabataean city of Hegra (Medain Saleh), where the making of rock-cut tombs ceased before the close of the first century AD, no classical façades are found and that therefore those at Petra must be later.[585] But since Petra was the royal capital where one would expect to find costly work entailing special skill that could not be afforded elsewhere, it may validly be held that the presence of such façades at Petra could well be contemporary with the absence of them at provincial Hegra. The second objection raised against a pre-Roman-annexation date for the Khazne is based on a similarity between the floral decoration on the capitals of the pilasters framing the doors leading to the Khazne's lateral chambers and that on the angle pilasters of the central passageway of the Triple Arched Gate that spanned Petra's colonnaded street—a gate that has been assigned on typological grounds to the middle of the second century AD.[586] To this it may be replied that decorative motifs of this kind are often found in use over a period of several generations: something very like the scrolls on the Khazne, carved, let us say for the sake of argument, *c.* AD 50, could have appeared on a gate erected *c.* AD 150—if indeed the gate is really so late. For typology is not always an infallible guide to dating. For instance, Petra's single extant free-standing temple, the Qasr Bint Far'un, at the eastern end of whose precinct the Arched Gate stood, once dated with some assurance on typological grounds to the Antonine period,[587] has now been shown by the discovery of a Nabataean inscription built into its precinct wall to date from the latter part of the first century BC.[588]

Whatever their precise date, and whoever their owners may have been, the classical rock-cut tombs of Petra, both those of the plainer kinds and those with the highly ornate, 'baroque' façades, are of unique importance for the study of death and burial in the Roman world. They provide an outstanding instance of the intermingling of local technique and sepulchral tradition with Graeco-Roman funerary art and afterlife ideas in the cult and honours that were paid to the high-ranking dead on the Empire's eastern outskirts.

### (F) SOME HYPOGEA OF IMPERIAL TIMES IN ROME AND THE PROVINCES

The most complex and spectacular funerary hypogeum that has yet come to light within the circuit of **Rome's** Aurelian Wall is that of the Aurelii discovered in 1920–1 beside the modern Viale Manzoni, a short distance to the west of the Porta Maggiore.[589] This situation obviously dates the monument to before the building of the Wall between AD 270 and 275; and since the latest brick-stamps found in its structure belong to Caracalla's reign, it is unlikely to be later than the first quarter of the third century. The place is chiefly famous for the very ebaborate and sometimes enigmatic paintings on the walls and vaults of its burial chambers —paintings which appear to be of a mixed Christian and pagan, possibly Gnostic, character. But since our main concern here is with the hypogeum as a type of tomb and as evidence for sepulchral customs, these pictures will merely be mentioned as part of the description of the rooms that they adorn, without any detailed discussion of their style and meaning.

The name of this hypogeum is derived from a mosaic inscription on the floor of one of its principal chambers. This reads: 'Aurelio Onesimo/Aurelio Papirio/Aureliae Prim(a)e virg(ini)/ Aurelius Felicissimus/fratris [*sic*] et colibert(is) b(ene) m(erentibus) f(ecit).' The wording suggests on the face of it that the tomb was the burial place of a single family. But this interpretation is rendered unlikely both by the size, complexity, and grave-capacity of the structure and by the nature of the paintings. More probably is was made (and later enlarged) to serve the needs of a whole religious community, the *fratres* being 'brothers' in the sense of all belonging to a sect whose members were of the freedman class and in which persons named Aurelii played a leading role.

Above ground the tomb appears to have been marked by some distinguishing feature (now completely lost) standing on a brick-built *podium*, whose lower portion has survived. This stands within a small precinct, in the eastern wall of which is the door from which a flight of steps gives entrance to the upper of the two main underground levels that the hypogeum comprises. This upper level consists of a single chamber whose door is on a landing at the bottom of the stairs. It measures 2·65 by 3·51 metres and only the lower parts of its walls remain. Here, as throughout the hypogeum, all the burials are inhumations. There is a large *arcosolium* in each of the side walls; on the back wall, opposite the door, a *loculus* was cut at a later date; and apart from two light-wells, one near the door and one near the back wall, the area of the floor is occupied by six 'troughs' or *formae* for burials with brick walls between them. Originally there seems to have been an upper tier of three *arcosolia*, one on each side wall and one on the back wall. The paintings on the lower part of the back wall, through which the *loculus* was cut, include the Creation of Man and the Fall—immediately proclaiming the tomb's quasi-Christian character, since nothing distinctively Jewish is displayed in any of its decoration.

56, 57 *Right*, the tower-tomb near Tarragona, known as the 'Torre de los Escipiones'. It is built of well-cut blocks of ashlar masonry and has on one side two mourning figures in relief (pp. 165-6). *Below*, two reliefs, probably of the third century AD, from the tower-tomb of the Secundinii at Igel, near Trier. The upper picture shows cooking operations; in the lower one the landlord's tenants are presenting payments in kind—game, fish, etc. (pp. 164-5).

58-60 *Above, left*, the tower-tomb of Elahbêl at Palmyra (p. 170); *right*, the tower-tomb at Hermel in the Lebanon (pp. 171-2). *Below*, tower-tombs in the 'Valley of the Tombs', Palmyra (p. 168).

61–3 *Above*, the richly carved family tombs at Celeia in Jugoslavia of the Ennii (*left*) and of the Prisciani (*right*) (pp. 172–4). *Below*, a temple-tomb with Doric frieze at Ghirza in Tripolitania (pp. 176–7).

64, 65 *Left*, an obelisk-tomb in the Wadi Merdum in Tripolitania. It has a moulded base; a plain lower storey topped by a projecting cornice; a second storey with engaged Corinthian columns, one at each corner and carrying a frieze with a running scroll in relief; then another projecting cornice and finally a pyramidal roof (*cf.* p. 178). *Below*, a carved slab from one of the Ghirza tombs. Eight large fish, symbols of the dead, encircle and nibble at a central rosette, symbol of life (p. 178).

66, 67 *Above*, one of the cone-shaped tumuli beside the *Via Appia* (p. 179). *Below*, an aerial view of the four surviving tumuli (there were seven originally) at Bartlow, Essex. One of them is the largest in Britain (144 feet in diameter) (p. 181).

68, 69 *Left*, the stone-built corridor leading to the burial-chamber of the tumulus at Antoing, near Tournai. The tumulus is 30 metres in diameter, with a stone retaining-wall (pp. 183-4). *Below*, the rock-cut 'Deir Tomb' at Petra. The façade of this tomb consists of two storeys the lower one a closed portico of six columns, while the upper one has a central circular pavilion, crowned by an urn and flanked by two square structures, all three elements having quasi-Doric friezes (pp. 195-6).

70 The so-called 'Tomb of Absalom' in the Kedron valley, Jerusalem. The lowest storey, with its Ionic columns and pilasters, is carved from the rock. The upper portions are of masonry (p. 189).

71–3 Three Petran rock-cut tombs. *Above*, the two-storeyed 'Obelisk Tomb'. *Below*, *left*, the 'Lions Tomb', with a simple classical façade: *below*, *right*, the 'Khazne', the earliest and finest of the tombs with classical façades: above a four-columned portico is a central pavilion flanked by two square structures, all elegantly carved (pp. 193–5).

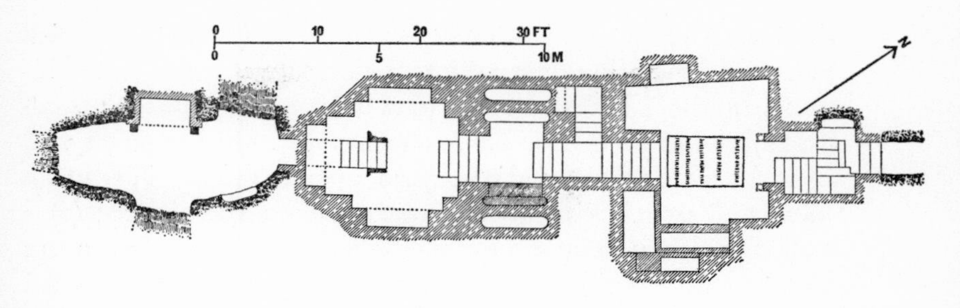


*Fig. 19 Plan of the hypogeum of the Aurelii*

From the threshold of the upper chamber a staircase, divided into three flights of four steps each, winds round a central pilaster and arrives at a landing, to north and south of which open the entrances to the two main chambers of the lower level. On the north side of the landing a flight of seven steps leads to the door of the almost square chamber labelled 'A' by Bendinelli. It is 5·20 metres below the upper chamber, measures 4·93 by 4·43 metres, and is roofed by a system of barrel-vaults with a light-well at the centre. The entrance wall has been largely destroyed. On each of the side walls are two large *arcosolia* of different sizes and asymmetrically placed. There was also once another *arcosolium* on the back wall, but this had been demolished and a rectangular doorway of decorative brickwork, with architrave, pediment, and flanking columns, cut through it and through the wall painting above and on either side of it. In the centre of the floor is the mosaic inscription of Aurelius Felicissimus (see above), surrounded by *formae* sunk into, and destroying, the rest of the pavement at a later stage. The *loculi* cut through the *arcosolia* are also a later modification. The painted subjects on the ceiling include the Good Shepherd in a roundel, four times repeated, masks and other decorative motifs. Round the lower part of the three surviving walls is a painted frieze of eleven standing male personages, reasonably interpreted as Apostles. Above them, in friezes and lunettes, immediately below the vaulted ceiling, are painted the most interesting of all the hypogeum's pictures.[590] On the west wall are: (1) a Reader seated with an open scroll on a shrub-clad hillside on which sheep are grazing; (2) the 'Triumphal Entry' of a victorious general into a city (suggestive of Rome bisected by the Tiber) through a gate (whose siting, in the case of Rome, would be that of the *Porta Flaminia*). On the north wall are: (1) a large colonnaded courtyard, open to the sky, in which is seated a Teacher with his audience standing round him; (2) a walled garden with figures walking in it. The east end of the north wall and the north end of the east wall form together a small rectangular salient that juts into the area of the room; and on the west of this salient is a banquet scene, on its south side, a group of male figures. On the east wall of the chamber, beyond the salient, are: (1) a pastoral scene (above); (2) a scene from the story of the home-coming of Ulysses to Ithaca (below).

Immediately opposite the head of the stairs that lead from the landing to chamber 'A' is a flight of four steps giving access to the two rooms that form the southern half of the lower level of the hypogeum. These rooms are on precisely the same axis as is 'A'; and there can be little doubt that the whole of the original lower level of the tomb was planned and built as a unity. The first room at the bottom of the short flight is a vestibule, rectangular in shape, with a barrel-vaulted, painted ceiling and painted walls. On each side wall is a large *arcosolium* also painted. As first cut, these *arcosolia* could have held perhaps three burials apiece. But they were later enlarged by adding niches at the sides; and parallel to the front of each were contrived, below the level of the floor, chest-like containers for yet more bodies. Of the vestibule's paintings one on the west wall is of special interest: it shows a woman pointing to a Latin cross.[591]

From the south door of the vestibule, which is exactly opposite its north door, three (as was first planned) steps lead to the second, and main, southern chamber, Bendinelli's 'B'. This is 3·31 by 4·62 metres in dimensions and is barrel-vaulted. Its back and side walls have each two superimposed *arcosolia*, with emplacements for sarcophagi; and along the walls are *formae* for further burials. The most noteworthy of the paintings in the *arcosolia* are those in the upper trio—identical rows of twelve dignified personages, six men and six women, standing on a ground-line. In the

*Fig. 20 Plan of the northern extension of the hypogeum of the Aurelii*

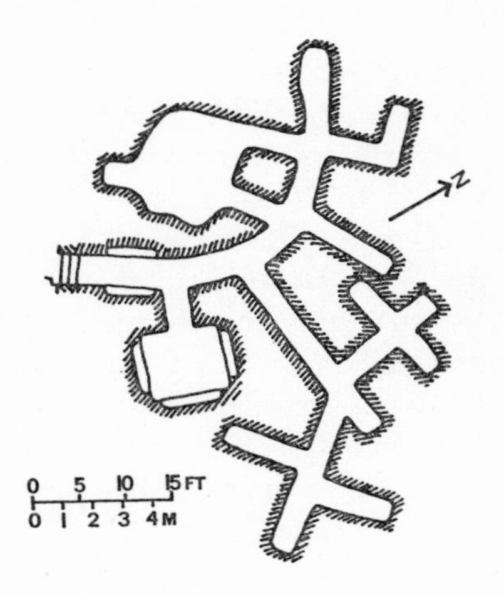


'spandrels' formed on the walls by the curves of the upper *arcosolia* are single human figures: peacocks shown in profile occupy the corresponding spaces on either side of the lower *arcosolia*. Of no less interest are the ceiling paintings of this room. Here the main design consists of three concentric circles, of which the inner one is a medallion depicting a woman flanked by two bearded men, one of whom holds a rod above her head—perhaps an initiation scene. Narrow panels forming an equal-armed cross link this roundel with the circle next to it; and that in turn is connected with the outer circle by four lunettes. Single human figures, standing or reclining, fantastic sea-beasts, and frontal peacocks occupy the fields thus formed by the circles and their linking features.

Such was the hypogeum as Aurelius Felicissimus (if it were he) originally planned it. But despite the ample provision that it made for secondary burials inserted into walls and floors, not many decades, so its seems, had passed before this proved inadequate and further underground galleries and chambers had to be opened up to north and south of, and at a slightly deeper level than, the tomb's lower storey. At the north end the brick doorway somewhat ruthlessly inserted through the north wall of 'A' (*cf.* p. 209) was designed to give access to a staircase of two flights of steps at the foot of which is a narrow landing with a *loculus* cut in its west wall. After that three more steps lead to a corridor, still on the axis of 'A', with two superimposed *loculi* in each of its walls. From this there branches off to the east a short passageway leading to a small square chamber, whose north, east and south walls each contain a *loculus* running the wall's full length. Beyond that point there came to light an irregular network of galleries and chambers, still connected with 'A', but no longer on its axis.

To turn to the opposite, southern, end of the hypogeum—the stairway between the vestibule and 'B' was increased from three to five steps in order to lower 'B's floor, through the centre of which, to the south of a landing, a staircase of seven steps was sunk. This leads to a roughly oval-shaped chamber, whose principal feature is an *aedicula*-like *arcosolium* cut into the west wall, painted and flanked by engaged columns. There are traces beyond this room of even more galleries.

What had been planned in the first instance as a compact and symmetrical burial place had, in fact, begun to develop into something that resembled, if still remotely, an extra-mural catacomb (*cf.* pp. 234–42).

While lacking both the structural and pictorial elaboration and the complex religious implications of the Aurelii tomb in Rome, the hypogeum at **Weiden bei Köln**, found in 1843 nine kilometres west of Cologne, on the north side of the Roman road that linked Cologne with Aachen, is unique of its kind north of the Alps and was clearly built by people who had close links with Italy.[592] This burial place consists today of a single underground chamber, measuring 4·44 by 3·55 metres internally and constructed throughout of unmortared blocks of local tufa, very neatly joined, apart from its entrance doorway on the east side, which is worked in red sandstone. It is 5·91 metres below the modern ground-level, with which the ancient ground-level seems to have been more or less identical, and is now approached by a modern stairway replacing the original eleven steps. The jambs and lintel of the doorway are each of a massive single block of stone; and at the side can be seen the groove for the now vanished slab of stone that formed the actual door. The chamber had a barrel-vaulted roof which was broken through apparently in

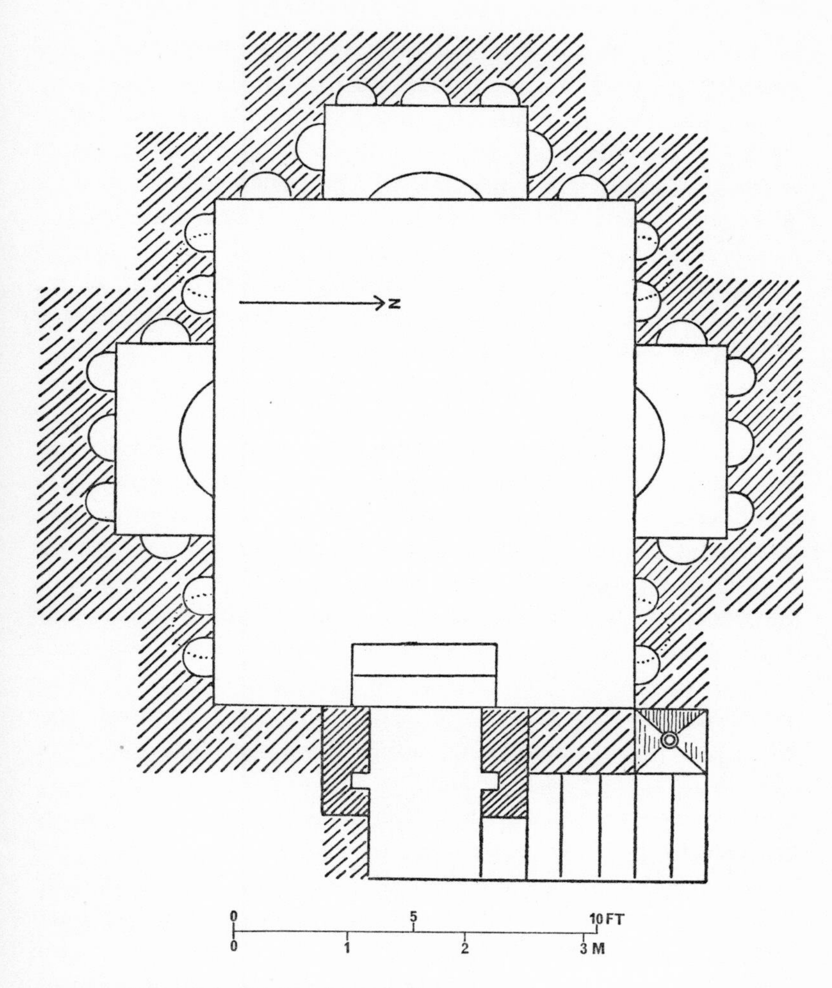


*Fig. 21 Plan of the Weiden bei Köln hypogeum*

ancient times. But enough of the original spring of the vault remains for the whole to be reconstructed (the modern parts are of a different stone) to its ancient height of 4·06 metres above the floor.

The east wall of the hypogeum, on either side of the entrance, is completely flat and unadorned. But each of the other three walls is opened up by a quite elaborate system of rectangular and rounded niches. The main feature of the system is a wide and deep rectangular niche or recess covered by a vaulted ceiling and filled, up to a short distance from the floor, by a low platform or *podium*, into the front of which is cut a crescent-shaped recess. The top of the *podium* is covered with a large slab of black carboniferous limestone, along the outer face of which runs a narrow horizontal panel of yellowish limestone, with a short, flat, carved vertical feature of the same material hanging down from it at either end. Round the three walls of each rectangular recess is a dado of slabs, again of yellowish limestone, which have something of the look of marble veneering. Above this dado in each recess are five small curved and round-headed niches, three on the back wall and one on each side wall. On the west wall of the chamber there are also two similar niches, one on either side, between the rectangular recess and the corners of the room; but on the north and south walls, being longer than the west wall, there is room for two such niches on either side of the rectangular recess, while a rather larger one of the same type is set symmetrically above them. There is thus a total of twenty-nine rounded niches for ash-urns in the hypogeum, which was obviously designed to hold cremation burials only—a fact that suggests a date for it in the first or second century AD.

The short vertical pieces of yellowish limestone mentioned above were clearly meant to represent parts of the carved legs of couches; and there can be little doubt that they, together with the black slab faced with a yellowish panel, form in each rectangular recess a *kline* or sepulchral couch on which the dead person was believed to recline unseen at the funerary cult-meals held in his honour by his relatives and friends. Such *klinai* in Roman tombs have their prototypes in Etruria (*cf.* pp. 16, 24); and there, too, we find precursors of two of the most remarkable objects that the Weiden hypogeum has produced—namely two high-backed 'wicker' armchairs, each complete with a wooden framework and a cushioned seat, carved in limestone, which were found, facing west, one on each side of the entrance in the east wall. Somewhat similar stone chairs are to be seen, for instance, in the Tomb of the

Shields and Chairs at Cerveteri,[593] where they were presumably intended to accommodate the spirits of some of the departed at funerary feasts. In Roman-age renderings of such sepulchral banquets comprising a man and a woman, the former reclines on a couch while the latter occupies a chair at one side (*cf.* p. 12). The same arrangement for the sexes holds good if two or more men and women are involved. A particularly clear example is the banquet scene depicted on the tombstone, now in the Römisch-Germanisches Museum in Cologne, of Marcus Valerius Celerinus, a veteran of *Legio X Gemina*, who had it carved during his lifetime ('vivos fecit') for himself and for his wife Marcia Procula.[594] Here the husband reclines on a *kline*, with cups on a three-legged table beside him, while his wife is seated at his feet on a high-backed chair with a basket of fruits on her lap. It is therefore natural to suppose that in the Weiden burial chamber the two armchairs were for the dead female members of the family to use, the *klinai* for the male departed. The crescent-shaped recess beneath each *kline* may have been meant to indicate that in actuality the space between the legs was hollow.

Some of the deceased who were buried in the Weiden tomb may probably be recognized in the three life-size busts of Italian marble portraying respectively a man, a woman, and a girl, that also came to light in the interior. Leading German experts in Roman portraiture have differed quite widely as to the periods in which they were carved, particularly in the case of the man. The present writer's inclination is to agree with those who assign them all to the reign of Hadrian—a time at which in Rome and Italy inhumation in sarcophagi was coming into vogue, whereas in the provinces the old practice of cremation was still prevailing. The busts could then be portraits of three of those whose ashes occupied the niches in the hypogeum.

The third major sculptural find in the tomb is a large Seasons sarcophagus, with rounded ends and probably dating from the second half of the third century, which was discovered in fragments on the floor and had clearly not got there by design. For one thing, it would have completely blocked the view of the west wall with its *kline* and pattern of cremation niches; secondly, its undecorated back indicates that the position intended for it was up against a blank wall; and thirdly, it could never have been brought in through the chamber's doorway, bits of which had to be cut away in 1947, when the restored piece was temporarily removed and taken to an exhibition. As has been already said (*cf.* pp. 212, 213), the vaulted ceiling of the hypogeum seems to have collapsed in antiquity; and the presence in the tomb of the sarcophagus can only be explained by assuming that it had fallen there from an upper, above-ground room, of which all structural traces have long since disappeared. At any rate it proves that this family burial place was still in use at least as late as the closing decades of the third century and that its owners were still men of substance and still in contact with the Mediterranean world. For neither the busts nor the sarcophagus (also of Italian marble) were carved in the Rhineland. They represent the imported products of Italian workshops.

Among the minor finds from the hypogeum are fragments of glass, some of fourth-century date; a silver bowl; four ivory plaques carved with figures in relief; and a female statuette in chalcedony.

The owners of the Weiden hypogeum were obviously wealthy and cultivated people, probably Roman or Italian by origin, who maintained their connection with the south through many generations. That their home was in Cologne is unlikely, in view of the tomb's distance from the city. They probably lived on an extensive country estate in a large, elaborate, and richly furnished *villa rustica*.

Smaller, simpler in its structure, and much later than the Weiden tomb is the hypogeum discovered by chance *c.* 1940 at **Silistria**, the ancient Durostorum, on the Danube in Moesia Inferior. It is a single rectangular chamber, measuring 3·25 by 2·60 metres, whose barrel-vaulted roof is at its centre 2·30 metres above the floor, and its outstanding interest (it appears to have been found completely empty of portable objects) lies in the (on the whole) very well preserved funerary paintings that adorn its walls and ceiling.[595] The entrance doorway, in one of the shorter walls, measures 0·90 by 0·80 metres and has a stone sill and plain

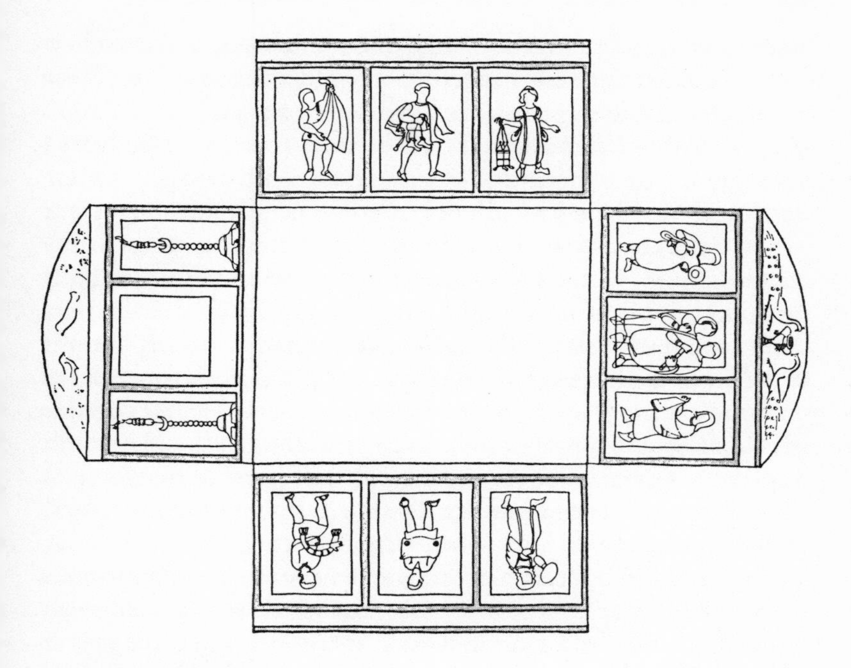

*Fig. 22 The Silistria hypogeum*

stone jambs and lintel. A stone slab once closed it. That the tomb and its paintings date from the fourth century AD is evident both from the style in which the pictures are carried out and from the costumes worn by the human personages that they portray.

The main surface of the walls is covered with a plain white ground and divided into eleven large rectangular panels, taller than they are wide, and framed by broad red bands; and inside each panel is a dark-green frame which contains a picture. The two panels flanking the entrance hold each a lighted candle on a tall candlestick which three animal-feet support. It is likely that these candles are at one and the same time counterfeit illumination for the tomb and its occupants and symbols of the light of the afterlife which the dead enjoy. Three panels fill the other short wall opposite the door. In the central one stands the married pair for whom the hypogeum was constructed and painted. The woman wears a long-sleeved tunic under a dalmatic and a bonnet-like headdress: she rests her left hand on her husband's shoulder and holds in her right hand a flower or fruit, perhaps a pomegranate, symbol of immortality. The man wears a long-sleeved tunic under an ample mantle and grasps with both hands the unopened scroll of his will—or destiny. The remaining eight panels each contain a single human figure moving towards the central group. To the left of the latter, on the same wall, is a girl carrying a jug and bowl; to the right, a girl holds a towel outspread and ready for use. On the left-hand wall (passing from right to left) are a girl, who dangles by a triple chain a three-sided perfume casket;[596] a youth carrying a large pair of *bracae* over his left shoulder and a pair of slippers in his right hand; and a youth displaying a cloak. On the right-hand wall (passing from left to right) are a girl with a mirror; a youth grasping a piece of stuff, perhaps a folded tunic, to which two small roundels are applied; and a youth who bears across his extended arms an enormous metal torc with 'buffer' terminals. All of these attendants are bringing to the dead man and wife articles of toilet, dress, and adornment for their use in the life beyond the grave.

Round all four walls, between the panels and the spring of the vaulted ceiling, runs a most unusual motif—a narrow band containing imitation beam-ends painted in perspective, so as to appear to be jutting out into the area of the room, in bright green, yellow, and red. The paintings in the two lunettes above the shorter walls symbolize the gardens of paradise by means of sprigs of flowers scattered across their fields. Against this background above the entrance two rather badly damaged birds of indeterminate species face one another; above the back wall, two peacocks confront one another from opposite sides of a wide-mouthed vase—an allegory of other-world refreshment. The vaulted ceiling, also covered with a plain white ground, shows a network of sixty square panels linked at the corners by circles and all carried out in red. Inside each square is a polygonal panel outlined in dark green: each of these contains the single figure of a hunter, or of the beast being hunted, or of a bird, while other polygons hold a single palm tree, or a bunch of grapes, or a fruit, or a group of flowers.

All these motifs are symbols of the pleasant pastimes and abounding fertility of the afterlife.

The Silistria hypogeum thus provides us with a striking instance of the persistence under the Christian Empire of pagan eschatological ideas and sepulchral practices.

The hypogea of the Roman period that have been described so far—in Rome, at Weiden bei Köln, and at Silistria—are selected representatives of a type of tomb that was not by any means the dominant form of burial place for the rich and reasonably well-to-do in those regions. It competed there with many other types of different kinds. But on the Empire's eastern fringes, and in particular on sites in Roman Syria, large and elaborate hypogea owned by wealthy families, or somewhat less sophisticated ones belonging to professional or religious groups, were the characteristic and prevailing form of sepulchre, and extremely numerous. Of this the necropoleis of Dura-Europos and Palmyra, already drawn upon for eastern versions of the tower-tomb (*cf.* pp. 167–71), offer the most prolific and impressive illustrations.

In the necropolis excavated close to the western city wall of **Dura** the hypogeum was undoubtedly the leading type of tomb for all but the very poor and inhumation, as elsewhere in Semitic lands, the usual rite.[597] Most of the Duran hypogea are marked at surface-level by a low tumulus, often surrounded by circular or square stone walls. In the majority of cases a narrow stairway of seven to twelve steps gives access to an arched or rectangular doorway cut in the rock and forming the entrance to a single chamber where a pillar or pier sometimes supports the roof. In the walls of the chamber and at right angles to them *loculi* are cut, each of which normally held a single burial, while some are large enough to have accommodated two interments. The cemetery was in use for five hundred years; and during that time the sizes and shapes of the chambers, the forms of the doorways, the number of the *loculi*, and the dimensions of the benches along the walls varied considerably. Of the fifty-eight hypogea that have been investigated only one, Tomb 47, bears a date—AD 36. But they fall into ten fairly distinct groups, for which it has proved possible to work out a tentative relative chronology running from the third century BC (some are thus actually pre-imperial) to the second century AD. One hypogeum, Tomb 4, was, to judge by the state in which it was found, made not long before the city's destruction in 255–6.

Tombs of Group I, which seems to be the earliest, are of a very simple kind—a long, narrow chamber with a roughly cut *loculus* for a single body (e.g. Tomb 10, *Report*, pl. 3). Group II tombs are small, flat-roofed chambers, approached by a short, steep *dromos* (*cf.* p. 184) and two or three steps and containing two or three burials on benches along the walls (e.g. Tombs 5, 8, 17, 19, *Report*, pl. 3: third century BC). Tombs of Group III are the most prolific in the cemetery. Here the chamber forms an irregular quadrangle, with high, wide benches, four or five *loculi* in its back and side walls, and one *loculus* on either side of the entrance, to which a *dromos* leads (e.g. Tombs 12, 14, 15, 16, 18, 20, 57, *Report*, pls. 4–7: second and first centuries BC). Group IV tombs have basically the same characteristics as those of Group III, but their chambers are more regularly shaped and there are sometimes two or three *loculi* on either side of the entrance (e.g. Tombs 3, 11, 13, 24, 37, 46, *Report*, pls. 8–11: first century BC to first century AD). Group V is characterized by a large pier of rock protruding from the middle of the back wall into the area of the chamber and containing either a small, additional burial chamber or a *loculus* (e.g. Tombs 6, 27, 36, 55, *Report*, pl. 12–14: first century BC). Tombs of Group VI are marked by their very large size, which is rendered possible by the presence at the centre of the chamber, to uphold the roof, of a square or rectangular pillar of rock, which is either flat in front or decorated with a central engaged column and corner pilasters (e.g. Tombs 7, 22, 23, 41, 51, *Report*, pls. 15–17: first century BC). Tombs belonging to Group VII have the same plan as those of Group V, but their protruding piers are smaller and contain no burial chamber (e.g. Tomb 35, *Report*, pl. 18). Group VIII comprises relatively small hypogea without either protruding piers or central pillars (e.g. Tombs 28, 40, 47, *Report*, pls. 19, 20: first century AD). Of tombs of Group

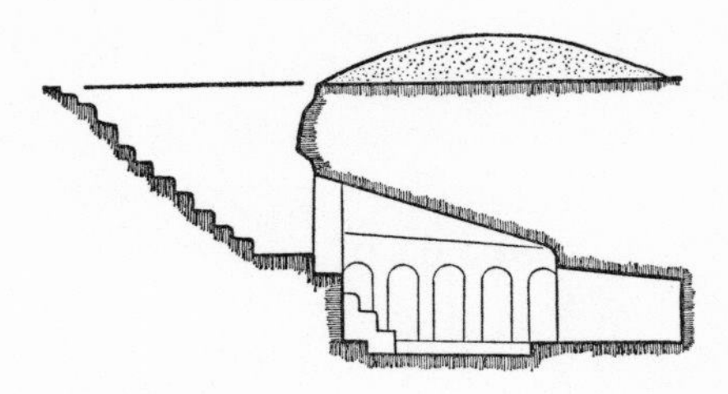

*Fig. 23 Plan of Hypogeum 24, Group IV, at Dura-Europos*

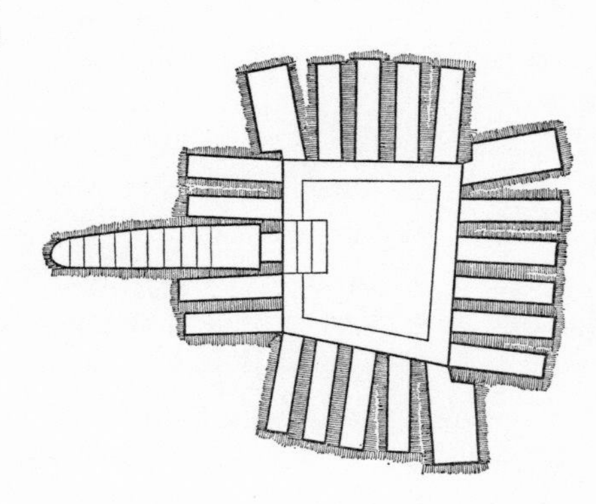

IX the only distinctive feature is the greater breadth of the *loculi* in the side and entrance walls as compared with those of the back wall (e.g. Tombs 33, 53, *Report*, pl. 21: first and second centuries AD). Tomb 4 forms a class (Group X) to itself. It is characterized by the alternation of narrow and broad *loculi* in its back and side walls and by the fact that it has a stone door that could be shut and opened, instead of the normal closing slab (*Report*, pl. 22: third century AD).

The Duran hypogea are completely lacking in inscriptions and in carved and painted decoration. It is therefore impossible to tell whether a given tomb was owned by a family or by a social or religious group or by undertakers from whom individual *loculi* could be purchased. It is, however, clear that these tombs were never used by relatives and friends for cult-feasts or reunions, since the *loculi* (which are either rounded or pointed at the top) were very seldom sealed and the coffins were often carelessly placed in them or even left lying on the benches or on the ground.

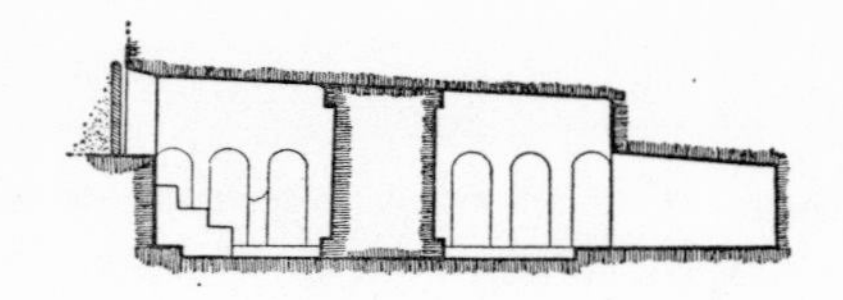

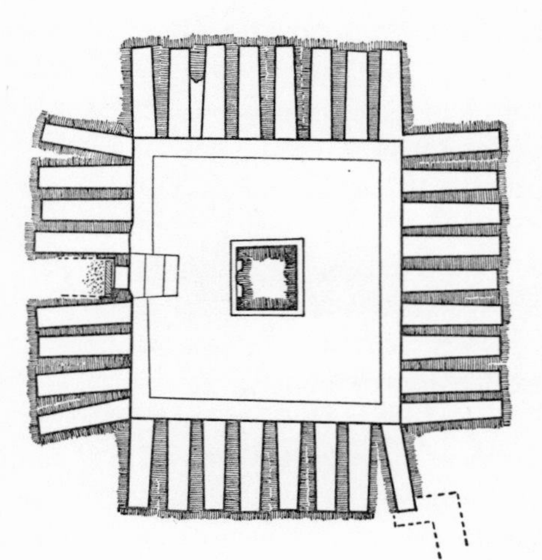

*Fig. 24 Plan of Hypogeum 23, Group VI, at Dura-Europos*

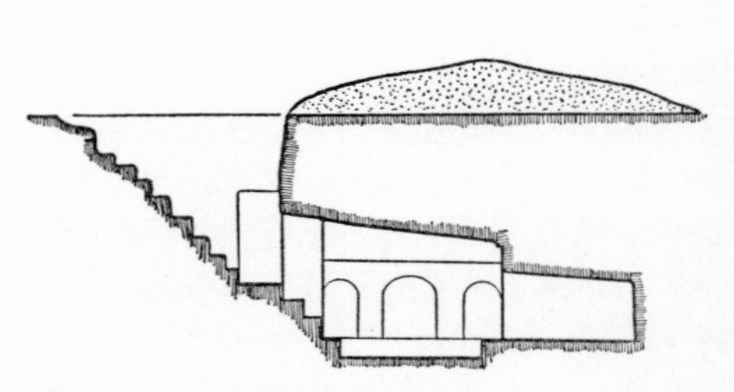

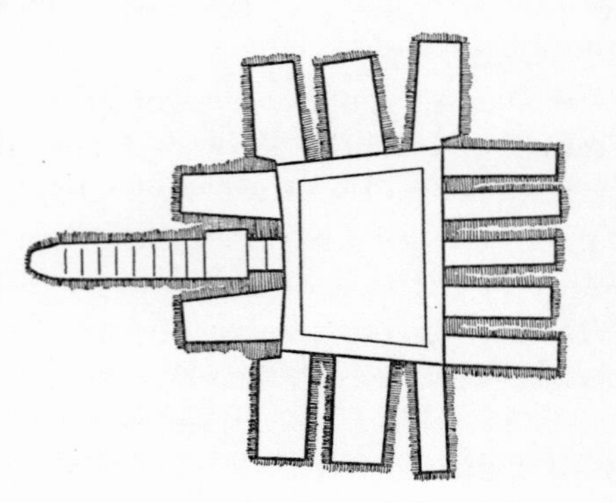

*Fig. 25 Plan of Hypogeum 33, Group IX, at Dura-Europos*

At first the coffins were all of wood, clay sarcophagi being introduced at a later stage. The head of the coffin or sarcophagus was normally towards the entrance to the *loculus*: but this rule was not always adhered to. Most of the tombs were found rifled; but such grave-goods as remained were the simpler objects of daily life for other-world use—pottery vessels (some of them deliberately 'killed'), alabaster vessels, terracotta figurines, bronze vessels, bracelets, ear-rings, finger-rings, mirrors, beads, and so forth—all suggestive of the comfortably-off, middle-class status of the departed.

A vivid contrast to these anonymous, vaguely dated, and unadorned Duran tombs is presented by the great groups of hypogea in the south-east and south-west cemeteries of **Palmyra**. Many of these Palmyrene underground sepulchres are not only larger and more complex in their plans and much more capacious in their burial accommodation than their Duran counterparts, but they often carry texts, sometimes in Greek as well as in the Palmyrene form of Aramaic, that record the names of those who built the tombs in the first instance and of those other persons to whom the ownership of certain grave spaces in them subsequently passed, with precise dates, in the first, second, and third centuries AD both for the original construction and for the later transfers. Furthermore, the *loculi* were scrupulously sealed, often with slabs that are carved with portrait-busts; the walls and vaults were sometimes brightly painted; and occasionally the dead were laid to rest in monumental, richly carved sarcophagi. Whereas at Dura burial was not infrequently casual and the dead, once interred, left unhonoured and unvisited, at Palmyra the remains of the departed were treated with the greatest care and veneration and some of the chambers were used by the survivors for cultic purposes. It would seem that the dead who were buried in the Palmyrene hypogea belonged, on the whole, to a wealthier and more cultivated stratum of society than did the occupants of the Dura tombs.

One of the most imposing hypogea in Palmyra's south-west necropolis is the tomb of the Three Bothers, built, as one of its inscriptions states, by three brothers Naʿmʿan, Malê, and Saʿedi.[598]

It is approached on the east from ground-level by a staircase and takes the form of an inverted T. Opposite the entrance, on the west, is a gallery and beyond that, at the end, an almost square chamber; and two rectangular chambers open out to north and south respectively of the entrance. The northern lateral chamber contains at its far end three sarcophagi placed *triclinium*-wise as for a meal. The southern lateral chamber appears from its inscription of AD 142–3, the earliest text found in the tomb, to have been Malê's special burial place.[599] Cut into the walls of the gallery and of the north, south, and west chambers are slots or *loculi*, contrived at right angles to the walls as at Dura and elsewhere at Palmyra normally, sixty-five in all, each of which held six simple sarcophagi tiered one above the other. There is thus a total of 390 burial spaces—far more than the three brothers needed for their and their immediate families' use; and, indeed, we learn from further inscriptions that descendants of the trio sold or transferred specified *loculi* to various Palmyrenes, for instance, in 160; again in 191 to one Sim'on; and yet again in 241 to one Julius Aurelius Malê. The building of this dwelling of the dead was, in fact, as much a speculation as is the building of a block of flats for living occupants.

An important feature of the Three Brothers hypogeum is the paintings on its walls and vaulted ceiling, to take which the surface of the native rock was plastered. In the western chamber the strips of all three walls between the slots for the coffins are each painted with the figure of a Victory standing on a globe and holding above her head with both hands a circular medallion or *clypea* which carries the portrait-bust of a man or woman. In the lunette at the end of this chamber is depicted Achilles at the court of Lycomedes (an allegory of the soul revealed at death in its true character?): on the vault is the Rape of Ganymede.[600]

Five dated Palmyrene hypogea, again in the south-west cemetery, have formed the subject of a special study by Harald Ingholt.[601] The tomb of 'Atenatan has a façade of limestone blocks and a panelled stone door, composed of two wings that turn on pivots, above which is the slab for a bilingual Greek and Palmyrene inscription. It states that 'this cave' was made in AD 98 by 'Atenatan for himself and for his brother Hairan. Another inscription, in Palmyrene only, on the lintel of the main door records that the *exedra* ('chamber' in the case of these tombs), described as 'house of eternity', inside the door on the right was added in 229 by Julius Aurelius Maqqai for himself, his sons, and their male descendants 'for ever'. The original tomb (passing from the entrance to the far end) consists of a gallery in whose walls four *loculi* are cut on either side, a rectangular chamber with five *loculi* cut in each of its side walls, and a wide, deep recess, opening off the end of the chamber, without any *loculi* and with a vaulted ceiling.

As in the northern lateral chamber of the Three Brothers tomb, so in the *exedra* added by Maqqai there are three monumental sarcophagi arranged as a *triclinium*. Of one of the three only fragments remain, but the other two are of the *kline* type. The central piece shows a man, now headless, reclining on the couch, identifiable from an inscription on the coverlet as the 'image of Maqqai who built the *exedra*'. He wears, as do all the images of the deceased in scenes of this kind, Parthian dress—in this case, long-sleeved, embroidered undercoat, long-sleeved, embroidered overcoat, open down the front, and trousers—typical oriental garments, but the floral scrolls and other patterns in the borders that enrich them are here, as elsewhere, culled from classical sources. At Maqqai's feet, facing the spectator, sits his much-bejewelled wife, also in local costume and also now headless. On the trough of the sarcophagus, between the elaborately turned couch-legs, are carved in relief three men, one of whom leads a horse, all in the same type of dress as Maqqai. It may be that the horse is to be thought of as being held in readiness for Maqqai's afterlife hunting. Of the sarcophagus on the right of Maqqai's only part of the relief-sculpture on the trough survives: it shows parts of five frontal male figures, wearing only undercoats, one of whom holds an *amphora*.

The tomb of Julius Aurelius Malê, the roof of which had fallen in, has a panelled door made from a single slab of stone; and on the cornice above a Palmyrene inscription gives the date AD 109, but does not name the hypogeum's builder. The next dated text, on the lintel, states that in 183 Malê, son of Hairan, bestowed and gave in partnership the whole of the *exedra* on the right as one enters to Taibbôl and his male descendants. Another text, also on the lintel, informs us that in 215 the same Malê, here described as Julius Aurelius Malê son of Hairan, gave in partnership to Julius Aurelius Hairan and Julius Aurelius Abbâ and their male descendants the whole of the *exedra* on the left of the entrance. Three more inscriptions on the door record the transfer of parts of the tomb to other persons in 219, 234, and 235 (two transfers). But this was not the end of these transactions. In 237 Julius Aurelius Hairan, one of those to whom in 215 Julius Aurelius Malê had transferred the left-hand *exedra*, himself transferred parts of it to two other persons, one of whom had already received three *loculi* from Julius Aurelius Malê in 235. The transfer of burial spaces was quite an industry, so it seems, at Palmyra.

The only portion of this tomb's interior into which the excavators could penetrate was a small chamber to the north-west of the door containing three *kline* sarcophagi with portraits that inscriptions identify as those of Julius Aurelius ʿAbissai, the recipient of a whole wall of the hypogeum from Julius Aurelius Malê in 219, and of members of his family, of his father Honainâ, of his wife Marti, of his brother Honainâ, and of other close relatives. The original tomb of 109 had thus become, through gifts and transfers, the communal burial place of several families.

The tomb of Malkû had also a collapsed roof, precluding the investigation of its interior arrangements and decoration. But thirteen inscriptions, one above, the rest on, the entrance doorway record a no less complicated story of partnerships in the tomb and of transfers of parts of it. The oldest inscription, on a plaque above the door, states that the 'cave' was made in AD 116 by Malkû the physician. Six other texts mention the transfer of portions of the hypogeum to other persons by the sons of Malkû in 186, again in 186, in 188, in 213–14, in 214, and again in 214. We also hear of the cession of part of an *exedra* in 213 by a certain ʿOggâ, who is probably the same as the Julius Aurelius ʿOggâ who made transfers of some *loculi* in 241 and 249. A text of 267 records the transfer of some *loculi* by a certain Dadiyôn, this time to a woman, Ammô, who, in her turn, in the same year made a transfer of part of what she had received to another woman, Julia Aurelia Agatônâ. Finally, as late as 279, seven years after Palmyra fell, yet another woman, Tammâ, transferred some *loculi* to a man, Abgar.

The tomb of Nasrallat has a complex plan, but a less involved history than have the tombs of Julius Aurelius Malê and Malkû. Just inside the entrance is a central chamber without *loculi* for burials. But the room that opens off it opposite the door has seven *loculi* in its back wall and three in each of its side walls. Symmetrically placed chambers open off the central one to right and left, each with three *loculi* in each of its side walls and three in its back wall. The tomb was thus well equipped in grave-space. The oldest inscription, on the lintel of the door, states in Greek and Palmyrene that the hypogeum was made in 142 as his 'eternal home' by Nasrallat for himself and his male descendants 'for ever'. The next inscription, also bilingual and also on the lintel, records the cession in 263 of two *exedrae* of the 'cave' by a person of another family, Julius Aurelius Yediʿbel to Julia Aurelia Amatê. A third text, just below the lintel, informs us of other transfers of other *loculi* by the same man to the same woman two years later (265).

The fifth tomb of this dated series is that of Barʿa, who, according to the Greek and Palmyrene inscription on the doorway, made 'this cave, house of eternity' in 186 for himself and his male posterity. This hypogeum has a central chamber with ten *loculi* in each side wall and at the end an *exedra*, which probably once housed three sarcophagi. The two lateral chambers, which open off the central one, just inside the entrance, are devoid of *loculi* and seem to have been never finished.

In a second paper Ingholt studied four more tombs, also in Palmyra's south-west cemetery, the names of whose owners and something of their history are known from inscriptions.[602] The tomb of Yarhai, ʿAtenûrî, and Zabdibôl was built in AD 133–4 by three brothers with these names, sons of Moqîmû, as the Palmyrene building inscription records. It consists of a gallery with six *loculi* in each of its side walls and a chamber, which was never finished or used, opening off it to the right just inside the door. Beyond the gallery, and divided from it by an arch, is a rectangular chamber with three *loculi* in its back wall, four in its left-hand wall, and three in its right-hand wall. A second Palmyrene text states that in 194 a certain Moqîmû, son of Lišamš, and a woman, Aqamate, who appears to have been the daughter of the Yarhai mentioned in the first inscription, gave in partnership some stretches of wall in the tomb to two other persons, Salman and Taimû. In the gallery came to light two sculptured slabs from sarcophagi of the *kline* type, with the dead partaking of the funerary meal—a reclining man accompanied by his wife and children. One of these slabs was for some reason never completed, but was replaced by the other slab that shows an identical scene. The presence of both the rejected piece and the replacement in the tomb strongly suggests that in this case, at any rate, the carving was done *in situ*, since a relief that had been abandoned on account, presumably, of some defects in it before it was finished would never have left the workshop had it been executed there.

The tomb of Seleukos comprises three galleries, one opposite the entrance and two to right and left of it respectively. The central gallery has five *loculi* on each side and three in its back wall: the left-hand one has six *loculi* on each side; and the right-hand one has on each side, near the entrance, only two *loculi*, beyond which the walls are empty as far as a vaulted space connecting the gallery with a square room, whose back wall has a single *loculus*. The sole inscription in this tomb, one in Palmyrene, records that in 251 Seleukos transferred two *loculi* to a certain Yarhibôlâ.

The tomb of Lišamš is somewhat similar in plan to that of Seleukos. It has a long gallery opposite the entrance with a rectangular chamber at its far end. The left-hand wall of this gallery has six *loculi*, the right-hand one four; and the chamber has four *loculi* in each of its side walls and three in its back wall. The lateral galleries to right and left of the entrance are shorter and each is linked by a vaulted space with a chamber at the end. The left-hand gallery has four *loculi* in each of its walls, but in its terminal chamber only two were cut, although there are spaces for eight. Similarly, in the right-hand gallery only six *loculi* were

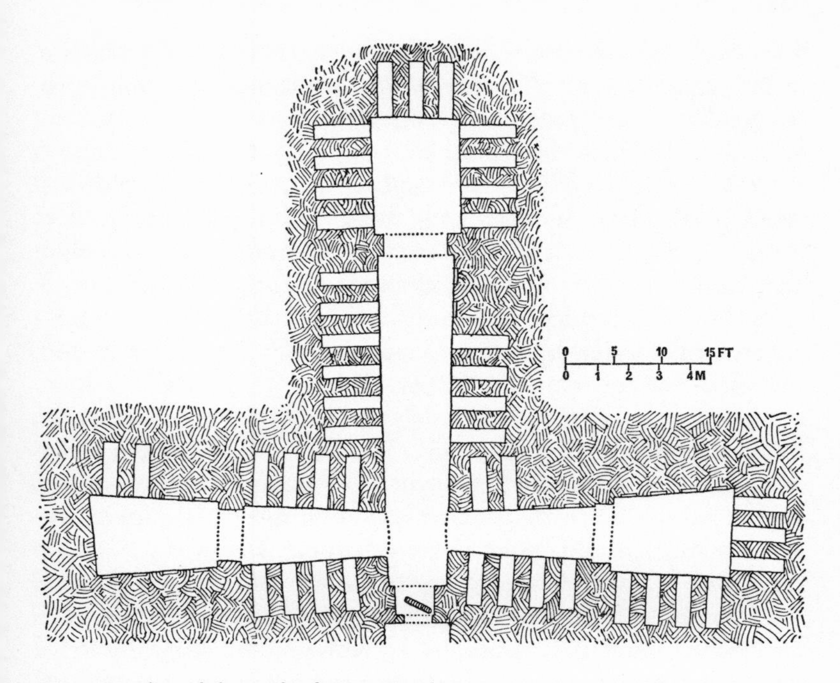


*Fig. 26 Plan of the tomb of Lišamš, Palmyra*

cut out of a possible eight; and only seven out of a possible eleven in its terminal chamber. There were thus seventeen burial spaces in the tomb that were never used. Above the door, which is a monolith, a Palmyrene inscription states that Lišamš and Amdai, two half-brothers, made Wardan a partner in the tomb in 186 and ceded to him parts of it. Two years later (188), so we learn from another Palmyrene inscription, Lišamš took into partnership one Bonnê. Finally, in 228, Wardan ceded some of the property rights that he had acquired in 186 to Aurelius Malkû. A sarcophagus found in the chamber beyond the central gallery is unique in that the funerary banquet scene is carved, not on the top, but on the long side of the trough.

The fourth tomb of this group, the tomb of ʿAbdʿastôr, has much the same plan as that of Lišamš's. The central gallery opposite the door has three *loculi* in its right-hand wall, while from its left-hand wall opens out a square *exedra* containing three sarcophagi again arranged *triclinium*-wise, one against each wall. Beyond this gallery a rectangular chamber has four *loculi* in each of its side walls and three in its back wall. The two, much shorter, lateral galleries have each five *loculi* in their side walls; and each leads to a square chamber with three *loculi* in each of its three walls. Here, then, the symmetry is complete. The building inscription in Palmyrene and Greek records that 'Abd'astôr made 'this house of eternity' for himself and his sons in AD 98. From a second, and much later, Palmyrene text we learn that in 239, the then owners of the tomb, two women, Julia Aurelia Šalmat, daughter of an 'Abd'astôr who was probably the grandson of the builder of the hypogeum, and a freedwoman, Embadû, ceded parts of it to a man and woman. The three sarcophagi in the *exedra* have all identical banquet scenes on top—two men reclining, a woman seated, and two boys standing. Below the *klinai*, on the troughs of the sarcophagi, are male and female busts in medallions. On the *exedra*'s vaulted ceiling an exquisitely naturalistic vine-design is carried out in white stucco on a light-red ground, enhancing the symbolism of the banquets below.

The hypogeum of Taai, discovered by chance in 1952, is, like the tomb of Yarhai, 'Atenûrî, and Zabdibôl, mainly extended on a single long axis deep into the rock on the west.[603] From the surface a steep flight of twenty-seven steps leads down to an external vestibule, on the further side of which a monolithic door gives access to an internal vestibule. The latter's roof had collapsed, but the piers at its four corners suggest that it was vaulted. In this vestibule came to light fragments of an inscription which ascribes the building of the tomb to Taai, but the date has not survived. To north and south of the internal vestibule open two *exedrae*, that on the north being somewhat irregular in shape and containing only two *loculi*, while that on the south is roughly square and has four *loculi* in its western wall. Beyond the vestibule runs a gallery, divided into two parts by an arch. The eastern part has four *loculi* on one side, five on the other, the western part four on each side. At the extreme west end, under an arch, is an *exedra*, which produced a large *kline* sarcophagus, on which a man with a priest's round cap reclines, with a woman seated at his feet. A special feature of this tomb is the number of slabs, for closing the burials in the *loculi*, that have been found in it. A few of these show standing figures in relief, but the majority bear portrait-busts of the deceased, sometimes inscribed with their names. Of these a few were discovered *in situ*: the rest were scattered on the ground where they had fallen from their places.

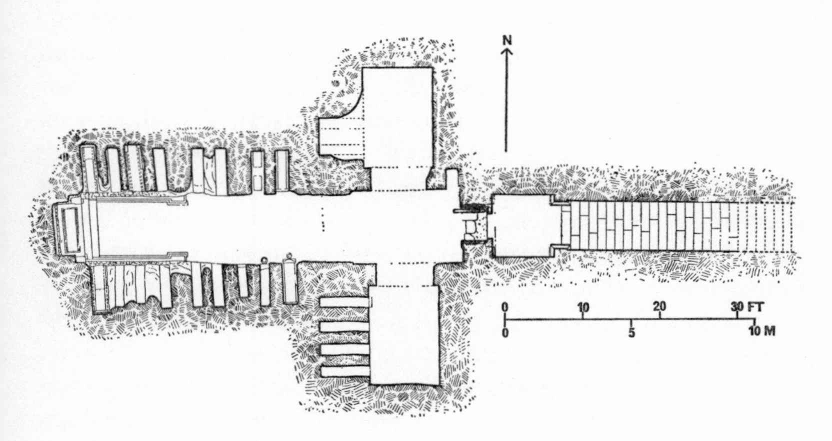


*Fig. 27 Plan of the tomb of Taai, Palmyra*

What is perhaps the richest in its sculptural decoration of all known Palmyrene hypogea is the tomb of Yarhai (or Iarhai), excavated in 1934–5 in the 'Valley of the Tombs'.[604] Its general plan is of much the same pattern as that of Taai's tomb, but it is extended on its long axis southwards from its entrance on the north. Six steps lead down to an unroofed vestibule, on whose eastern side a little door, composed of a single slab of stone and elaborately panelled, gives access to a small square chamber. The doorway of the main tomb carries a heavy entablature of classical mouldings, above which is the plaque for the dedicatory inscription; and the door itself has two leaves, each of them monoliths and panelled.

From the door ten steps descend into the tomb's main gallery;

and to left and right of the bottom of these steps are the entrances to two *exedrae*. That on the left (east) is a roughly shaped oval, which was clearly never completed or used. But the *exedra* on the right (west), which is divided by an arch into two more or less equal areas, contained, as will be seen later, some of the tomb's most impressive sculptures and was finished architecturally in every detail. The gallery, which is 14·05 metres long and barrel-vaulted, is divided into three sections by arches springing from pilasters. The northernmost section, containing the foot of the stairway of ten steps and the openings into the *exedrae*, is an internal vestibule without *loculi*. The next section has six *loculi* for tiers of burials, with flat pilasters against the strips of wall between them, on its west side, but on the east side only four *loculi* were cut between the pilasters. The third, southernmost, and most luxurious section, has four *loculi* on each side wall, that at the far end on each side being twice the length of the rest, with engaged Corinthian columns alternating with them. Each *loculus* holds six superimposed burials, the two lowest ones being masked by the *podium* on which the columns stand, while the other four were closed by slabs with portrait-busts, male and female. The *podium* and Corinthian columns on each side wall return along the back wall of this section; and between the three columns that adorn this wall open out two large triconch niches, each of which was faced by an entablature, and by a semi-dome with shell decoration, above it. The three lobes of each triconch also had semi-domes with shells. At the bottom of each niche, between the pedestals of its flanking columns, is a sculptured funerary banquet group. These groups close the ends of burials in two tiers behind, four burials to the south of the eastern group and two burials to the south of the western group; and to the south of these again traces were found of four more burials laid out on the same axis. The eastern group consists of two men reclining on a *kline* with a woman seated at their feet: in the western group a man reclines with a woman seated at his feet and a man and a woman standing in the background.

In the southernmost section of the gallery was discovered an inscription recording the building of the hypogeum by Yarhai in

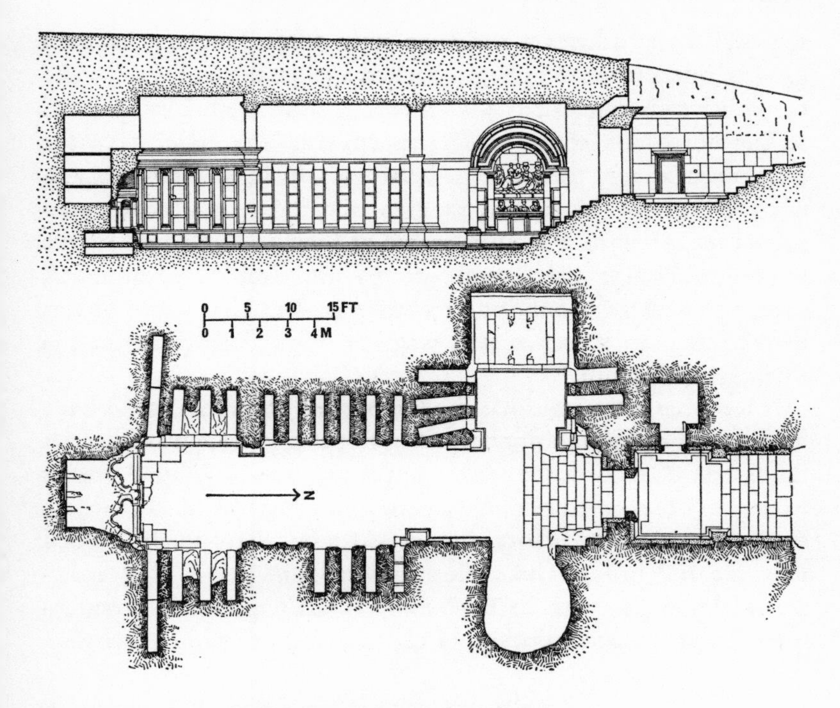


*Fig. 28 Section and plan of the tomb of Yarhai, Palmyra*

AD 108; and it would appear that the unroofed vestibule, the door, and all three sections of the gallery formed the original tomb. The west *exedra*, on the other hand, was probably an afterthought, since the steps down from the main doorway impinge slightly on the line of its entrance, where an arch marked it off from the gallery. Another arch separated its two parts, which were barrel-vaulted; and the side walls of the outer part have *podia* and flat pilasters between the *loculi*, of which there are three on the south and two on the north. Here again there are six superimposed burials in each *loculus* and again the two lowest are masked by the *podia*. There can be little doubt that here also the four upper tiers had each a closing slab with a portrait-bust. The inner portion of the *exedra* reproduces a *triclinium* with three funerary banquet groups, one a true sarcophagus backed against the end wall, while the other two concealed *loculi* running, most unusually, parallel to the north and south walls respectively. The *klinai* have the usual decoratively turned legs, between which, in each case, is a row of busts of priests and women. On the central couch two priests recline with a woman seated at their feet and two priests standing behind: the lateral groups are similarly composed, except that there is only one reclining priest. The whole of this *exedra* has been reconstructed with its original materials in the Damascus Museum.[605]

It has been estimated that the hypogeum of Yarhai could have held a total of 219 inhumations. But not every place was filled. A bilingual text records the cession in the year 240 by Julius Aurelius Malachus of specified burial places to Julius Aurelius Theophilus—some thirty years before the catastrophe that finally ruined Palmyra and brought to a close this splendid series of Roman-period hypogea, with its fascinating intermingling, in architecture, sculpture, and painting, of classical and oriental elements.

## (G) CATACOMBS

The words 'hypogeum' and 'catacomb' could, obviously, be used as convertible terms inasmuch as both denote subterranean sepulchres. There is, however, a real distinction that can be drawn between the two types of tombs that the two words represent. In the foregoing section of this chapter we were dealing with burial places that are more or less compact in plan and of a private or semi-private character, contrived for, and at the expense of, an individual family or a relatively small group of families or some select religious sect. They are mostly on one level only, although there are occasionally two, or even three, levels linked by stairs, as in the case of the Aurelii tomb in Rome. Here the term 'catacomb' is reserved for the public underground necropoleis of relatively large religious communities, namely those of Jews and Christians, in Rome and in Italian cities outside Rome, together with a few provincial instances. What marks off most catacombs from the tombs which we have classed as hypogea is their unsystematic, irregular, spreading plans forming networks of galleries that often cover quite an extensive area, the multiplicity of levels—sometimes three or four—on which some of them, the Christian ones, in particular, were dug, and the fact that, while the small chambers opening off the galleries were probably set apart for better-off individuals or families, the galleries themselves housed the remains of quantities of very poor persons who could never have afforded to make tombs or purchase tombs out of their own resources. There are indeed some public Christian catacombs that developed in the neighbourhood of family hypogea and which may or may not have had some association with them; and there are some Christian sepulchres that would seem to have been privately owned and privately planned, while resembling in many respects the public cemeteries. But it may be claimed that the line that has been drawn in this chapter between the hypogeum and the catacomb does in general hold good. It should, of course, be borne in mind that the word 'catacomb' originated with the *coemiterium ad Catacombas* (the cemetery at the 'Sunken Valley') under the present church of San Sebastiano on the *Via Appia* just to the south of Rome.

This book is clearly not the place for any detailed discussion of the iconography and style of the art of the Jewish and Christian catacombs—that is, of the paintings executed on their walls and vaults and of the sculptures, mainly carved sarcophagus-reliefs, found in their chambers and galleries. But a few quite general observations on the subject may be made. First, it is abundantly clear that in the centuries during which the catacombs were being dug and decorated neither the Jews (at any rate, not those in the Diaspora) nor the Christians took the Decalogue's ban on 'graven images' in its literal sense, but resorted to art for ornamental and didactic purposes as long as the art was 'applied' in the sense of being flat paintings on surfaces and carvings in relief, where there could arise no danger of idolatry, as in the pagan worship of cult-statues in the round. Secondly, these pictures certainly expressed, for the members of both religions, their hopes and aspirations for the welfare and happiness of the departed in the life beyond the grave.

In Jewish art part of the picture-language conveying these ideas were specifically Jewish motifs—the menorah (seven-branched candlestick), the lulab (palm-branch), the ethrog (citrus-fruit), the shofar (ram's horn), and so forth. In the Jewish catacombs no scenes that illustrate the Scriptures have so far come to light. The Christian catacombs reveal not only Christian symbols and single figures but also a somewhat restricted repertory of biblical pictures. Furthermore, such unequivocally Jewish and Christian subjects are frequently combined with figures and other motifs drawn from the other-world imagery current in contemporary pagan funerary art. These were obviously used, as the pagans themselves also used them, not for their literal meaning, implying real belief in the historical existence of Dionysus, Hermes, Cupids, Maenads, Victories, Season-personifications, and such like, but for their allegorical and symbolic value as pictorial expressions of beliefs about the nature of the afterlife. Even if they were carried out by pagan artists, these pagan subjects were undoubtedly acceptable both to Jewish and to Christian patrons. And if the artists were themselves Jews or Christians they could well have learnt their crafts in pagan workshops and have used for representations of this kind pagan copy-books.

In their homeland of Palestine the Jews had long been accustomed to lay their dead to rest in rock-cut tombs (*cf.* pp. 188–90); and in the Diaspora this practice was maintained wherever the character of the terrain permitted it. It would seem to be not unlikely that some at least of the Jewish catacombs in Rome were at any rate as early as the second century AD; and that it was from their Jewish neighbours that the Roman Christians borrowed the idea when about the year 200 (so we learn from the *Elenchos*, a work written in Greek early in the third century, perhaps by Hippolytus) Pope Zephyrinus commissioned the deacon Callixtus to found and organize the first public Christian cemetery, *τὸ κοιμητήριον* (*the* cemetery), which is represented by the oldest part of the catacomb that bears St Callixtus' name today. This is the earliest recorded date for the Christian catacombs in Rome. The subsoil of Rome and its outskirts is particularly suitable for this type of sepulchre, consisting as it does of deep and extensive layers of dark, soft tufa, easy to cut, yet strong. Both the leaders of the Jewish community and the authorities of the Christian Church would have had to acquire tracts of land outside the city for making these excavations. The method was to dig a stairway into the ground and then at its foot to excavate a gallery parallel to the surface. Other galleries were then driven off at right angles to the first one and connected with yet further galleries running parallel to the latter or roughly in the same direction. When the boundaries of a property had been reached and more burial places were needed, the digging had to go deeper, either by lowering the floors of existing galleries or by sinking more staircases or ramps and excavating another level, sometimes several other levels, below the original one.

For number, extensiveness, and complexity the Christian Roman catacombs far outdistance their Jewish counterparts. In the galleries the dead were placed in *loculi* cut parallel to the walls, normally two by two in the depth of the wall and tier above tier up its height, after the manner of bunks. Very rarely *loculi* were cut at right angles to the walls (*Via Appia* Jewish catacomb). These were sealed by stuccoed tiles (Jewish catacombs) or by slabs of stone or marble (Christian catacombs), a minority of which were inscribed with the names of the deceased and with roughly incised religious symbols. Coins, gold-glass 'medallions', lamps, and even small glass flasks could be fixed in the mortar beside the *loculi*, where they would have served identification purposes. Such were the burials of the poor. More elaborate were the arched recesses (*arcosolia*), where the bodies were walled up in species of 'troughs', sometimes cut into the walls of galleries, more often into those of the *cubicula* or chambers that opened off the galleries: there the more well-to-do were laid to rest. Not infrequently *loculi* were cut through the back walls of *arcosolia* at later dates to increase the burial space.

## JEWISH CATACOMBS[606]

Of the six Jewish catacombs on the outskirts of Rome that have so far come to light, two, those in the Vigna Cimarra and on the Via Appia Pignatelli, are very small and little of their plans is known, although the latter has been described as containing two corridors, one of which had an *arcosolium* painted with palm trees, fruit, and Cupids.[607] Of another catacomb, that on the *Via Labicana*, a plan was published by Marucchi in 1886: this shows two long galleries at right angles to each other with shorter corridors and *cubicula* opening off them.[608] The Monteverde Catacomb, just beyond the Porta Portese, first found in 1602 and rediscovered in 1904, has now collapsed and is inaccessible. The account of it does, however, record a vestibule, nearly 7 feet wide and barrel-vaulted, which led to the catacomb itself.[609]

Much better known and documented are the two remaining catacombs of the Jewish series. Of the Rondanini (or *Via Appia*) Catacomb two plans have been published, one by R. Garrucci in 1889[610] and a revised one by J. B. Frey in 1933.[611] At the entrance from the Via Appia Pignatelli on the east are two rectangular rooms, the second of which is wider than the first, has two niches in its south wall, and a bench down its centre. It has two doors at its western end, one, on the north, leading down three steps to a small room with benches round its walls, the other, on the south, to the vestibule of the actual catacomb. The eastern part of this consists of two long main corridors, the first running east–west, the second north–south, with *loculi* in their walls and *cubicula* opening off them. To the west, between the north-west main gallery and the Via Appia Antica, where there is another ancient entrance, is a further network of shorter corridors with *cubicula* It would appear to be very probable that the three rooms between the Via Appia Pignatelli and the catacomb proper were used for the burial of special persons and for the cult of the deceased. In the painted rooms in the western area of the catacomb are renderings of unequivocally pagan motifs—Victory, Fortuna, Pegasus, Cupid, and possibly an Orpheus scene. But of all the works of art from this necropolis the most important is the fragment of a Seasons sarcophagus, on which are depicted two Victories holding up between them a roundel above a grape-treading scene; and in the roundel is a large menorah.[612] There could hardly be a more impressive piece of evidence of a Jewish patron's deliberate choice of a pagan setting for his most revered religious symbol. (*Pl.* 74)

The largest Jewish catacomb in Rome was found in 1920 in the Villa Torlonia beside the *Via Nomentana*.[613] Of all the six Jewish catacombs this one comes nearest to the Christian catacombs in its extent and in the complexity of the network of its galleries. These are on two levels, which seem originally to have formed two separate cemeteries. They were clearly amalgamated at a later date, although the actual entrance from the one to the other did not come to light.[614] The upper and less extensive level on the south-east has five *cubicula*; but there is only one *cubiculum* on the lower level on the north-west, where all the other burials are in *loculi* in the walls of the galleries. Throughout the catacomb the paintings disclose an inextricable intermingling of Jewish and pagan motifs.

In Italy outside Rome the most elaborate Jewish catacomb is that at Venosa, which has two long, roughly parallel, galleries with shorter ones running off them at right angles.[615] Of Jewish cemeteries in the Roman provinces one of the most important is that at Gamart on the outskirts of Carthage. This is, however, not a catacomb in the strict sense, but according to the plan[616] comprises huddled groups of individual, unconnected rectangular tombs with *loculi* cut at right angles to all four walls, as in the hypogea of Dura and Palmyra (*cf.* pp. 219–34).

## CHRISTIAN CATACOMBS[617]

The principal features that are common to the Christian catacombs of Rome, dating from the third and fourth centuries, have been outlined in the introductory paragraphs to this section of the present chapter. They are found beside, or at a short distance from, all the main ancient highways that radiate from the city. Styger lists 35, Hertling and Kirschbaum list 36, No. 36 representing the small, probably privately owned, catacomb found in 1956 on the *Via Latina* (*cf.* pp. 242–4). The two last-named authors number all the public catacombs consecutively on their plan (frontispiece and fig. on p. 18), starting with No. 1 on the *Via Flaminia* on the north and passing eastwards, southwards, westwards, and northwards round the circuit of the Aurelian Wall to No. 35 beside the *Via Aurelia* on the west. These Christian catacombs are far too numerous and complex to be described in detail here. The best detailed account of them, accompanied by plans, is Styger's. The Touring Club Italiano volume *Roma e Dintorni* gives a useful plan of the great catacomb of St Callixtus, in which the galleries on its four superimposed levels are distinguished in different colours (e.g. 1934 ed., pp. 600–1). Chronology presents a far from easy problem. But a pre-Constantinian date may be confidently claimed for some—for instance, the oldest portions of the Catacomb of St Callixtus (e.g. the 'Sacraments Chapel'), and parts of the Lucina Catacomb (e.g. the double chamber), of the Domitilla Catacomb (e.g. the 'Gallery of the Flavians') and of the Priscilla Catacomb (e.g. the 'Cappella Greca').[618] The old romantic notion of the Roman catacombs as the scene of regular Christian worship, of the celebration of the Eucharist, has long since been discredited. The *cubicula* that open off the galleries could have held only very small gatherings of persons, probably for reunions of relatives and friends on the anniversaries of the dead, when, as the benches found in some of them suggest, meals in honour and remembrance of the departed were partaken of. And it may be that it was for the souls of the departed that the small stone chairs, which are occasionally found in the *cubicula*, were intended —the unofficial survival among some ex-pagan Christians of a pagan practice (*cf.* pp. 214, 215).[619] This interpretation finds support in the fact that the chairs are on much too small a scale to have accommodated the adult president at a funerary feast. On the other hand, a small carved *cathedra* could have been a symbol at the burial place of one who had been famed as a teacher of Christian doctrine.

Among the best-known Christian catacombs in Italy outside Rome is the catacomb of St Januarius at Naples. This comprises two storeys and is still accessible.[620] But those that come nearest to the largest Roman public catacombs for size and impressiveness are the Sicilian cemeteries, in particular, those of San Giovanni and Santa Lucia at Syracuse.[621] The latter is the largest and the earliest of these necropoleis, parts of it, those that contain the poorest burials, being definitely pre-Constantinian.[622] This catacomb consists of three main areas, one to the north, one to the

Fig. 29 *The San Giovanni catacomb, Syracuse*

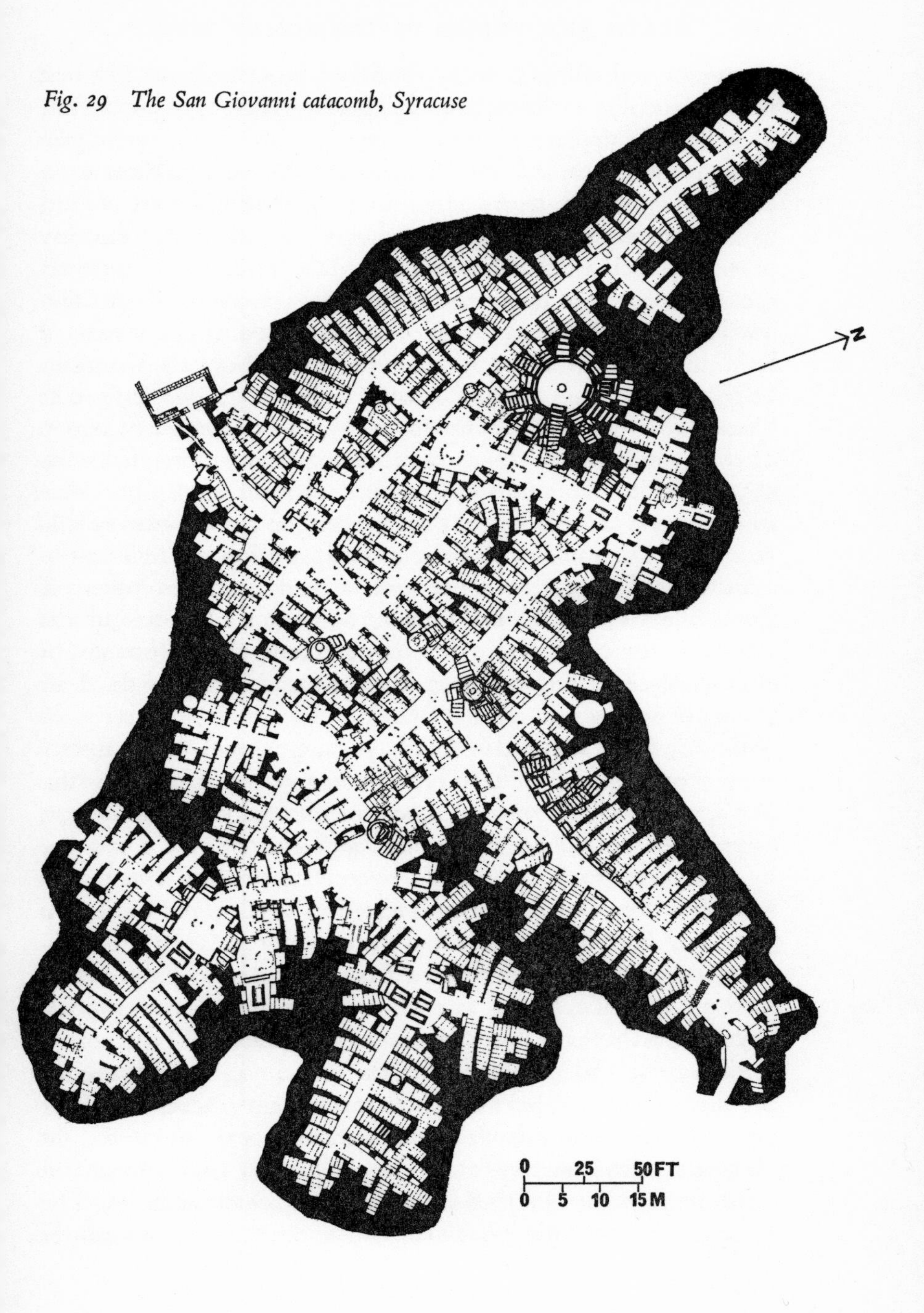

south-east, and one to the south-west of the octagonal church that contains the shrine of Santa Lucia. There are three levels of tombs, of which the upper, in the northern area, and the lower, in the south-western area, are much less extensive than is the intermediate level, which spreads over all three areas and forms a series of long galleries mainly running on a roughly north–south axis with tiers of *loculi* in their walls and *cubicula*, also holding *loculi*, opening off them. On both the upper and the intermediate levels there are a few instances of the reservation of circular spaces which may have been intended to accommodate the sarcophagi of wealthier persons. The San Giovanni catacomb has a ground plan that resembles in many respects the street-grid of a city of the living.[623] There is a long and relatively wide main gallery running from the north-west to the south-east, crossed at right angles by other galleries, one of them longer than the rest, on a south-east–north-west axis. The walls of all these galleries are full of *loculi*; and a multitude of chambers, some with arched entrances, open off them, filling up the 'blocks' (*insulae*) between the 'streets'. In this catacomb there are also a few large rectangular rooms and a number of circular spaces, more than at Santa Lucia, for the dead of wealthier families.

The Christian catacombs that have been considered up to this point would appear to have been owned, so far as concerns the tracts of land which they occupied, communally by the Church communities, although individual *loculi* and *cubicula* could be, as inscriptions show, purchased by private persons. But in the magnificently painted catacomb found in 1956 on the *Via Latina* (*cf.* p. 239) both its small size and the overall regularity and symmetry of its plan suggest that we have an example of a privately owned cemetery, planned as a whole before any excavation took place and perhaps the property of a single family or of a group of families who had combined for the enterprise.[624] The ancient entrance on the east, parts of which survive, gives access to a long gallery, with *loculi* in its walls, running roughly north–south, out of which opens on the east a large *cubiculum*, A, vaulted and containing *arcosolia*. Further to the south, and again on the gallery's eastern side, is a single *arcosolium*, a short distance to the south of

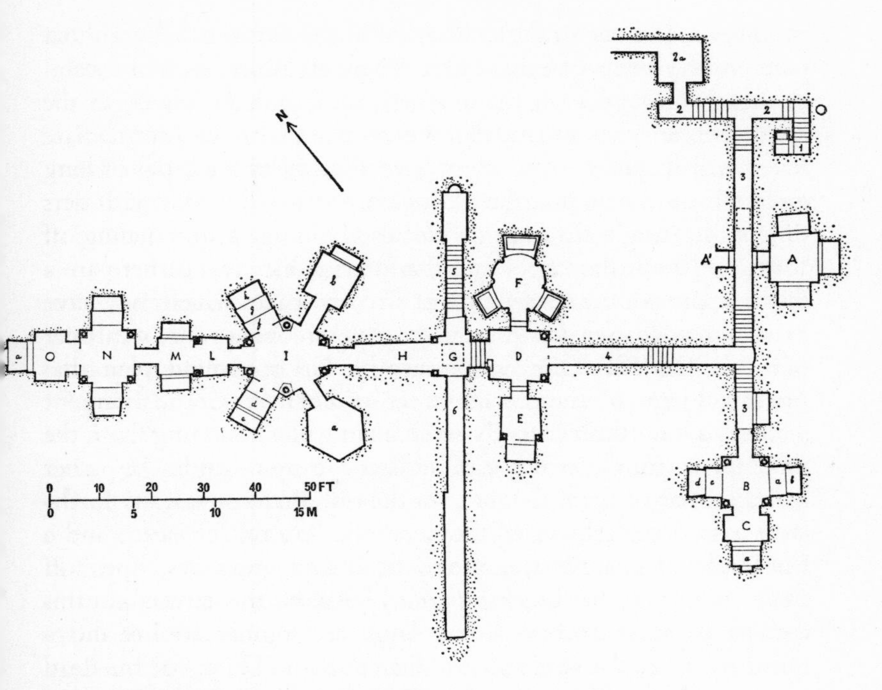


*Fig. 30 Plan of the new* Via Latina *catacomb*

which the gallery ends in an elaborate *cubiculum* consisting of an outer chamber, B, with two deep lateral *arcosolia,* and a smaller inner chamber, C, with an *arcosolium* in its back wall. About halfway between A and B another gallery branches off at right angles from the first; and from that point onwards the whole catacomb is on a single east–west axis. Proceeding along this gallery we arrive first at a large central square chamber, D, with two lateral *cubicula,* E and F, symmetrically placed, but differently shaped, F with three *arcosolia,* E with one only. From D four steps descend to a square vestibule, G, to north and south of which branches off a transverse gallery. Then comes a broad corridor, H, which brings us to the largest complex in the whole catacomb—a central hexagonal chamber, I, from which four *cubicula* radiate symmetrically, the two on the east being of different shapes, while the two on the west are identical. After that we reach the vestibule, L, to a square chamber, M, with two lateral *arcosolia* and connected by a short passage-way with a larger square chamber, N, again with lateral *arcosolia*. Finally, the catacomb terminates in a square chamber, O, intermediate between M and N in size, with shallow lateral *arcosolia* and a very deep, apsed *arcosolium* in its back wall. There can be little doubt that the entire tomb was all designed at one time with a single mind, or the minds of a single group, behind it.

From the extreme elaboration and from the style of the paintings on the walls and ceilings and in the many *arcosolia* of this catacomb we can deduce that its proprietors were wealthy people of the second half of the fourth century. The great majority of the figure-subjects of these pictures are Christian, Old Testament scenes far outnumbering those that illustrate the Gospels. Here there is a much wider range of biblical episodes than in the public Roman catacombs; and when an episode that is rendered in the latter also occurs here—for instance, the Raising of Lazarus—the *Via Latina* version has a great crowd of supplementary figures in addition to those of the protagonists. Again, in the public catacombs, while individual pagan motifs and figures are not infrequent (*cf.* p. 236), whole scenes drawn from classical mythology are never found. Here, however, in the penultimate chamber, N, are no less than six pictures that present scenes from the life of Hercules. Are these scenes to be interpreted in a Christian sense allegorically—Hercules' achievements being prototypes of those of Christ? Or were they painted for pagans? The fact that they occur in one chamber only and are not mixed up with biblical pictures would appear to indicate that the catacomb belonged to a family that was mainly Christian, but partly pagan, or to a group of families some of which were Christian, others pagan, whose members in either case had agreed to tolerate in their burial place the coexistence of different faiths. (*Pl.* 75)

## CHAPTER VII

# GRAVESTONES AND TOMB FURNITURE

### (A) BUILT-IN GRAVE RELIEFS

IN CHAPTER V, SECTION (D), it was observed that on the façade of one of the late-republican chamber-tombs in the grounds of the Villa Wolkonsky in Rome are two inset slabs carved with portrait-busts of the deceased; and it was suggested that, in view of this discovery, most of the numerous portrait-busts carved in relief on slabs, either singly or in groups, that have been found in or near Rome were once similarly built into funerary chambers which have now disappeared (*cf.* p. 118). This is very likely also to have been the case with a number of other grave reliefs worked on square slabs or rectangular slabs, broader than they are high, and relatively thin from back to front. These include later pieces with portrait-busts and pieces of various periods carved with figure scenes—all stones whose shape makes them difficult to visualize as standing independently above a burial. In this chapter they are distinguished from what are generally termed stelai, that is, free-standing stones normally, but not always, taller than they are broad and either two-dimensional, with all the interest concentrated on the front, or four-sided, or, occasionally, round. But it must be borne in mind that this distinction is by no means to be regarded as a hard and fast one. There are some two-dimensional, flat-topped stelai that could have been incorporated quite suitably in tomb-façades. And, again, there are some reliefs, broader than they are high, that may once have been mounted on pedestals or inset in square or rectangular pillar-shaped structures and could thus have stood above cremation or inhumation graves.

Among late-republican funerary reliefs with figure scenes that could have been of the built-in variety is that of Aurelius Hermia and Aurelia Philematio, found near the *Via Nomentana* in Rome and now in the British Museum.[625] In a shallow rectangular niche the full figures of man and wife stand in profile, confronted, the wife, who survived her husband, raising his right hand to her lips in a farewell gesture that recalls the groups on classical Greek stelai of the fourth century BC. A series of stones of about the same time, or slightly later, that depict the wax or terracotta *imagines* of the deceased in little wooden shrines (*armaria*) could likewise have been inset. One of these, in the National Museum, Copenhagen, is a laterally spreading slab, with a central inscription flanked by the profile portrait-busts of a man and woman worked in low relief (*cf.* p. 48).[626] The *armaria* continuing them are pedimented and their doors are flung open, as in the case of a stone in the cloisters of St Paul's-outside-the-Walls in Rome and of one on the *Via Appia*, both with frontal *imagines* in fairly high relief.[627] Another stone, in the Vatican collection, shows in the centre one Paconius directing, so it seems, agricultural operations on his estate, while on either side of the picture are a male and female funerary bust rendered in profile in a lozenge-shaped frame that may be intended for a shrine.[628] A much later piece, in Athens and carrying a Greek inscription, depicts within a deep rectangular niche, broader than it is high, the draped frontal busts of a man and wife side by side, the man being bearded and coiffured in the style of Antoninus Pius.[629] Despite its mid-second-century AD date, it bears a close resemblance structurally to a late-republican slab, now in the Museo Nazionale Romano and presumably from Rome, with the frontal busts of a married pair in an almost precisely similar niche.[630] (*Pl.* 76)

## (B) FREE-STANDING STELAI

Of the three types of free-standing stelai listed above (*cf.* p. 245), the commonest type by far is that of the two-dimensional vertical stones, normally taller than they are wide, erected on the ground above the burial.[630a] They may have flat, rounded, or gabled tops. Sometimes they carry only an inscription, filling nearly all the field, or an inscription that is accompanied by carved or incised non-figured decorative motifs. Such stones occur throughout the Roman world and particularly in the northern and western provinces.[631] More elaborate are the stones on which the text is confined to a die or panel specially reserved for it, while the field or fields above or below it, or both above and below, are occupied by figure scenes showing the deceased fighting on horseback or hunting or reclining at the funerary meal, or presenting some other group or episode or a set of objects appropriate to his career.[632] Here the picture element very often dominates the epigraphical. One such stele of unusually large dimensions, a single slab of white marble 4·04 metres high, 1·82 metres broad, and 0·30 metres thick, is the so-called 'Pranger' (whipping-post), which has stood since the sixteenth century in the market-place of Pettau, the ancient Poetovio, in Austria.[633] It is flat-topped, crowned by a bearded head, possibly Oceanus, between two recumbent lions, and its face is divided into four main panels or fields, of which the third from the top and largest is the inscription die, the other three being carved with reliefs. Above is an 'engaged' pediment containing two reclining figures difficult to identify and flanked by two flying Victories in the 'spandrels'. Below that is Orpheus and the Beasts bordered at top and bottom by two narrow friezes of birds and animals. The lowest field, now badly damaged, seems to show Orpheus in the underworld. An abnormal feature of this stele is the carving of its narrow sides—with single figures from the Bacchic thiasos in superimposed tiers. Two unusual military stelai from Cimiez (Cemenelum) in Provence, with gabled tops, are carved, each in the form of a closed four-panelled tomb door, with a ring-handle in each of the two lower panels.[634] (*Pls.* 77, 78)

Of the stelai meant to be viewed from the front alone those displaying busts of the deceased in niches cut deep into fairly thick blocks of stone or marble might be regarded as the most specifically Roman, since they recall *imagines* of wax or terracotta in *armaria* (*cf.* pp. 48, 246). A late-republican example in the Museo Campano at Capua shows a deep rectangular, flat-topped recess, crowned by an architrave and pediment and flanked by flat pilasters, which encloses the waist-length busts of Venuleia Vassa and her daughter Rufa.[635] Although only about 1 metre high in itself, this block could have been mounted on a pedestal and stood above a burial: but the possibility that it was inset in a tomb-façade cannot be wholly excluded. A stele of early-imperial date, now walled up in the Porta Nuova at Milan, has three tiers of similar deep, this time arched, niches each with a bust, one at the top and two in each of the tiers below, beneath which is the inscription die and beneath that again a small panel carved with figures.[636] A group of stelai peculiar to Danubian lands has busts in concave roundels combined with inscriptions and scenes in relief. Some carry two or three such roundels, each with a single bust, or one roundel holding a single bust or even a family group of three, four or five busts.[637] But on the great majority of two-dimensional stelai, on which busts, both short and waist-length, appear alone or are combined with either figure panels or inscription dies or with both, the busts, whether single or in groups, in one tier or in two tiers, are in relatively shallow arched or flat-topped niches or *aediculae*, the latter often flanked by colonnettes.[638] A particularly tall and well-preserved example from Walbersdorf, near Ödenburg, the ancient Scarbantia, has at the top the waist-length busts of Julius Rufus and his wife Julia Ruffla in an arched *aedicula* flanked by colonnettes and crowned by an architrave and pediment, both carved: below that is a panel with a combat scene: below that again the inscription die; and at the bottom another panel in which a gladiatorial fight is depicted.[639] All these funerary portrait-busts carry on, if more remotely than do the short busts in deeply hollowed out recesses, the old, peculiarly Roman, republican tradition of ancestral *imagines*.

More closely approximating, on the other hand, to their classical Greek and Hellenistic precursors are the Roman, Italian, and provincial stelai that show one full-length figure or a pair or a group of such figures, standing or seated, generally within some form of shallow niche or *aedicula*. These, apart from a very few examples (*cf.* p. 246), differ from Hellenic stelai chiefly in sculptors' preference for full-face, as contrasted with profile or three-quarter, poses—a preference shared, to some extent, by late-Hellenistic carvers, when in the second century BC the sculptured stele, banned in Attica about 317 BC by Demetrius of Phaleron, reappeared, mainly in east-Greek lands.[640] Two republican or early-imperial examples, which have lost such framing elements as they once possessed, present a man and wife standing to the front side by side.[641] Strongly reminiscent of late-Hellenistic stelai is a piece from Capua, now in the Naples Museum, on which is cut an arched niche, flanked by flat pilasters and surmounted by an inscribed architrave and a pediment: inside this niche a man and wife are seated frontally side by side, while another man, perhaps their son, stands in a three-quarter pose to the left of them, resting his hand on the seated man's knee.[642] A finely worked and unusual stele, now in the British Museum, has above an uninscribed inscription panel an arched niche in which stands the figure of a woman with Trajanic coiffure in the guise of Venus Victrix, half-draped, leaning on a pillar, holding a palm branch, and accompanied by a dove.[643] Provincial stelai provide innumerable examples of single figures, both military and civilian, standing in niches or *aediculae*, and of pairs or groups of figures, also both military and civilian, similarly framed.[644] Seated figures are rarer and are also normally frontal.[645] (*Pl.* 79)

Nowhere is the fusion of Greek and Roman elements in Roman-age funerary art more clearly exemplified than on the carved stelai which reappeared in Attica during imperial times.[646] These preserve the traditional forms of the Hellenic and Hellenistic stelai, being normally pedimented, with an architrave and lateral pilasters and an arched or flat-topped niche containing one, two, or occasionally three figures, standing or seated. With a few Latin exceptions, the inscriptions are in Greek and are cut on the architrave of the *aedicula* or below the pediment, if there is no architrave. The specifically Roman features are the hair- and beard-styles and the fact that, while there is a number of examples in which the figure or figures are in a profile or three-quarter pose, the frontal position on the whole predominates. Instances of the former type are the stelai of Eutychia, who is seated to the right, confronted by her little maid, who holds her toilet casket;[647] of Ianthe(?), seated to the left, while a veiled woman, standing to the right, grasps her hand;[648] of Achilleus who stands to the left in conversation with his little dog, which lifts a paw in greeting;[649]

and the piece that portrays a mother and son standing confronted and wholly absorbed in one another, she laying her left hand on his right shoulder and clasping his right hand in her right.[650] Examples of the type with strictly frontal figures are the stelai of a woman, Asklepias, who is seated with both hands uplifted;[651] of the little girl Olympias, who clasps her pet dove to her breast;[652] of Nike accompanied by her maid;[653] of Musaios and Amaryllis, with a relative or maid standing beside them;[654] of a bearded man, Aurelius Eutyches;[655] of Aphthonetos, who is flanked by two bulls;[656] and of a man and wife, the former holding a bunch of grapes and a pruning-knife.[657] There is a small number of stelai of Roman soldiers, who are also shown strictly frontal and accompanied by Latin inscriptions.[658] All of these, from Olympias onwards, are standing figures. A quite exceptional piece is the stele of Artemidoros, which has the usual pediment, architrave, and flanking pilasters, but displays in the *aedicula* a narrative hunting scene, in which the dead youth, with his dog beside him, lunges to the right to despatch a boar—all in a landscape setting of trees and rocks.[659]

Free-standing Roman stelai of the four-sided type are large square or rectangular blocks, richly carved with figure scenes on at least one side, often on three sides, and sometimes described as funerary 'pillars'. They are found in their least elaborate form at Aquileia, where the figure-work is confined to a panel, framed by simple mouldings, on one side only. Instances in the Aquileia Museum are the stelai of Lucius Arrius Macer, whose freedwoman, Arria Trophime, is shown standing to the front, but looking back towards the spectator's right, on a ledge; that of Maia Severa, who is seated to the right in a high-backed chair, with her feet on a footstool, her mirror in her left hand, and her pet bird, which she caresses with her right hand, on her lap;[660] and that of another freedwoman, Julia Donace, who stands on a pedestal and displays an open fan. But the most imposing pieces are provincial, from the Treviran region, where they represent the expensive sepulchral monuments, worked in local stone, of wealthy town-dwellers and of the proprietors of large estates in the countryside. In the Rheinisches Landesmuseum at Trier parts of such monuments, dating from the second and third centuries, have been reconstructed from fragments built into a late-Roman fort at Neumagen in the Mosel valley.[661] These carry portraits of the dead and scenes from daily life in relief—a school scene, a toilet scene, and business scenes of various kinds; and some have heavy cornices above the figured panels and richly ornamented angle pilasters. It is, indeed, possible that some of these pieces may once have belonged to tower-tombs such as that at Igel (*cf.* pp. 164, 165).

Two other groups of Treviran 'pillar' stelai are in modern Belgium, in the Musée Luxembourgeois at Arlon, the ancient Orolaunum, and in the underground museum on the site of the Celtic *oppidum* at Buzenol-Mountauban, near Virton. Of the Arlon stelai from the cemetery of the Roman town some are only fragmentary, while of others whole blocks, with carved reliefs on three of their sides, survive.[662] These reliefs are either full-length frontal figures of the dead occupying a complete panel on one, the principal, face, or a symbolic figure filling the field or two small scenes in superimposed tiers depicting episodes from daily life—business transactions, agricultural operations, travel and transport, and the like. For example, the 'Pilier du Drapier' displays on the front the tall, slender figures of a woman in the centre, grasping a flask, and of two men, one on either side of her, holding tablets by a string and a bag respectively. On the left-hand face, above, there is a shop scene, with a soldier-customer fingering fastidiously a piece of cloth, below, an accountancy scene; and on the right-hand face, above, a man drives a one-horse cart towards the right, while below another man leads a two-horse cart through a city gate.[663] On the front of the 'Pilier du Cultivateur', presumably a market-gardener domiciled in town, a man and wife stand side by side, he with a pruning-knife and she with a scroll and box. On the left-hand side, above, three men gather fruit into as many baskets, while two men dig and hoe respectively below; and on the right-hand side, above, a man drives a cart towards the left, perhaps the transport of garden produce, below, two more men gather more fruit into baskets.[664] On other stelai the portraits of the dead are combined, not with realistic episodes, but with figures that symbolize either the qualities on which the claims of the deceased to a happy hereafter rested or the joys of paradise. For instance, the block inscribed with the name of Attianus has on the front a woman and two men, one with a scroll, the other with tablets: on the right-hand side stands a 'philosophic' figure with cloak, scroll, knotted staff, and a box of scrolls beside him and on the left-hand side a female figure that could well be intended for a Muse.[665] Another large block, the 'Stèle au Satyre', shows two married couples on its main face and a dancing Satyr and a dancing Maenad on the left-hand and right-hand sides respectively.[666] Either a pyramidal or pedimental feature may once have crowned 'pillars' of this type. (*Pl.* 80)

The carved stones built into the late-Roman fort inside the fortifications of the *oppidum* of Buzenol-Montauban include no complete four-sided blocks; but the size, shape, and character of the sculptured slabs leave little room for doubt that they are parts of 'pillar' stelai of the Neumagen and Arlon type.[667] But while providing little detailed evidence for the structure of their monuments, these slabs are outstanding for the very high quality of their carving, which is as good as, if not better than, that of the Neumagen reliefs and superior to that of most of the Arlon stones. The subjects comprise portrait figures of the dead, the famous *vallus* (reaping machine) scene, business and rent-paying scenes, and the very sensitively rendered head of an elderly and weary peasant returning from a day's work in the fields. The landowners who commissioned these stelai could obviously afford the services of the best available sculptors in the area.

The free-standing round or columnar stelai appear to have been a speciality of northern Italy in early-imperial times. Of the three pieces of this type in the Museo Archeologico (Cittadella) at Bergamo, for example, two stones show a pair of fish-tailed personages holding up between them a shell above a *bucranium*: they are flanked by two mourning Atys figures; and above is a frieze of arms. The third piece carries on its front a concave, pedimented *aedicula* containing the busts of a husband and wife, while a spreading vine is worked in low relief on the column's back and sides.[668]

Another local speciality, widespread in northern Gaul, is the house-stelai, whose interest lies in their architectural character: they appear to be derived from huts, being ovoid or rectangular, in the latter case, topped by gabled roofs.[669]

A strange form of gravestone, peculiar, so it seems, to Roman sites in modern Portugal, is the wine barrel lying on its side on a low base, generally with its hoops, and sometimes with rows of wineskins, rendered in relief on its curving surface and a panel reserved for the funerary inscription in a central space between the groups of hoops. The Evora (Ebora) Museum has one, the Conimbriga Museum, near Coimbra, one (without hoops), the Beja (Pax Julia) Museum as many as thirteen and fragments of a number of others; and there is a particularly well preserved example from Algarve in the National Archaeological Museum at Belém on the outskirts of Lisbon.[670] Many more must still exist or have existed. It would appear to be improbable that all the dead persons above whose remains these objects stood had been in the wine trade. The piece at Belém is, in fact, inscribed with the name of a woman who died at the age of twenty-five. These barrels must be symbols of other-world potations or of the wine of new life beyond the grave. Whether they stood directly on the ground or were mounted on pedestals is not known. At any rate they provide a very unusual type of free-standing stelai. (*Pl.* 81)

## (C) ASH-CONTAINERS AND FUNERARY ALTARS OF THE WELL-TO-DO

Whereas the burnt bones and ashes from cremations of the relatively poor were placed in cheap earthenware pots or in glass vessels or jars or, at the best, in plain lead canisters,[670a] the remains of the cremated well-to-do—more often of middle-class persons of slave or freedman origin than of members of the upper strata of society—were housed in containers of a more expensive kind (*cf.* p. 50). And it is with these 'show' articles of sepulchral furniture, mainly worked in marble, sometimes in stone, and occasionally in alabaster and meant to be admired for their shape or colour or elaborate carving, that we are here concerned.[671] Of the altar-shaped pieces, the largest objects of this class, not all are receptacles, provided, that is, with recesses for ashes or for vessels holding ashes (termed by Altmann 'Aschenaltäre'), but served as commemorative *cippi* or bases on which libations could be poured (termed by Altmann 'Grabaltäre'). 'Grabaltäre' range in height from 1 to 1·20 metres: 'Aschenaltäre' can often be as low as 0·80 to 0·70 metres. But all, whether of the larger or of the smaller variety, whether true receptacles or not, display the same types of structural form and the same iconographic repertory; and all are to be distinguished from the great monumental altar-tombs that stood in the open, as, for instance, at Aquileia (*cf.* pp. 79–82) and at Pompeii (*cf.* pp. 123–5).

The smallest of these costly receptacles are those in the form of vessels of various types. In the first-century AD Tomb of the Platorini, found in 1880 in Trastevere, between the Ponte Sisto and the Aurelian Wall, there came to light a goblet-shaped marble urn, with a low foot, two small unpierced handles resembling ears, and a conical lid topped by a knob: it has no decoration—only the inscription 'Minatiae Pollae'.[672] From niches in the west wall of the Tomb of the Aelii in the Vatican necropolis come two exquisitely shaped ash-containers of honey-coloured alabaster.[673] One is a chalice, with a widely spreading mouth, a slender foot, and two handles set low on the body of the vase: the second is a flagon (*oenochoe*), with a single ribbed handle that is foliate-shaped at the top and meets the body of the vase below in a Medusa-head of superb workmanship. A goblet-shaped two-handled urn of porphyry, with a wide mouth, a low foot, and a conical lid, was found in London.[674]

Likewise intended for insertion in niches in the walls of *columbaria* (*cf.* pp. 113–16) and house-tombs (*cf.* pp. 132–43) are the ash-chests or *cineraria* of different shapes—polygonal, round, and rectangular, the last being normally wider than they are high. The best-known polygonal example is the marble octagonal *cinerarium* of Decimus Lucilius Felix in the Capitoline Museum, with a conical lid topped by a pine-cone, a frieze of masks and sprays of olive and ivy round the top, and the figures of seven dancing Cupids, three of whom are playing on mucical instruments, in the main field of the vessel's wall, one on each of seven of the eight facets.[675] A circular marble piece in the Ny-Carlsberg Museum in Copenhagen, dedicated by Aegrilia Probiana to her husband Gaius Licinius Licinianus, also has a conical lid; and its decoration consists of heavy fruit- and leaf-garlands supported on the shoulders of Cupids: one garland has above it the inscription panel and below it small busts of the married pair.[676]

Three round *cineraria*, one of marble and two of stone, appear to counterfeit wicker baskets. The marble example, in the Vatican (Galleria Lapidaria), has a domed lid and imitation basket-work vertical 'flutes' on lid and wall and horizontal bands of plaiting girdling the top, centre, and bottom of the wall.[677] The two stone pieces are in the Archaeological Museum at Aquileia. One has a flat lid on which sprawls a large dog, keeping guard over all that remains of its master, and bands of plait-work round the wall, on the front of which is an ansate inscription die uninscribed.[678] The other also has a flat lid and bands of plaiting at the top and bottom of the wall, on which are a small uninscribed inscription die and a lively funerary banquet scene involving seven persons. The narrow criss-cross bands in the background behind the figures may be intended to represent strips of wickerwork.[679] Why *cineraria* should take the form of wicker baskets is not immediately obvious. Possibly the baskets are *panaria* symbolizing provisions for the journey to the next world or after-life banquets. Two extremely elaborate circular marble ash-chests came to light in the Tomb of the Platorini. Both have conical lids topped by knobs and carved with oak-leaves in one case and with vine-leaves in the other, while the walls are loaded with heavy fruit-garlands slung between *bucrania* and with birds and fluttering *taeniae* in the intervening spaces.[680]

Of the rectangular *cineraria* some are in the form of houses or temples, with gabled roofs and architectural elements worked in relief on their walls. A piece in the Museo Nazionale Romano from the Tomb of the Platorini, 0·38 metres high, has a very low gabled roof, terminating at the sides in altar-like 'bolsters': each wall carries a couple of blind arches between flat pilasters.[681] Another piece, in the Vatican, has a high-pitched, tiled roof and on each wall a pair of panelled false doors, each surmounted by a pediment and divided from its neighbour by a flat, fluted pilaster: in the centre of each wall a snake wriggles upwards.[682] The doors are presumably tomb-doors, while the snakes could symbolize the dead.

The great majority of rectangular *cineraria* are, however, what might be described as casket-shaped, with gabled lids and an average height of 0·40 to 0·60 metres. Two examples with particularly rich and elaborate sculpture come from the Tomb of the Platorini.[683] These have low-pitched gabled lids with carved *tympana* and terminating at the sides in 'bolsters', while the main surfaces of their walls are filled with heavy swags of fruit slung between *bucrania* and in one case flanked by dangling woollen fillets: birds and insects occupy such spaces as are left. But the commonest type, which has a more steeply gabled lid with palmettes or 'bolster'-ends flanking the carved *tympanum*, carries on the front a centrally placed inscription die, the top of which is flush with the upper edge of the casket, while a heavy garland, slung between Ammon heads or rams' heads or Cupids' shoulders, encircles its bottom and sides: birds fill the crescent-shaped space between the swag and the inscription die and in the bottom corners are birds, masks, human busts, and so forth. Examples are the *cineraria* of Tiberius Claudius Argyrus on the Louvre;[684] of Marcus Caetennius Tertius in the First Tomb of the Caetennii in the Vatican necropolis;[685] of Nicanor, once in trade in Rome;[686] and of Lucius Cacus Hilarus in the Lateran collection.[687] On the front of a *cinerarium* in the same collection, that of Cacia Daphne, the inscription die is flanked by two large tripods, while beneath it two griffins are seated.[688] Yet another piece in the Lateran collection is unusual in that below the inscription die, in the centre, there is a large chalice from which sprays of ivy spread into every corner of the field, figure motifs being completely absent.[689] Still more exceptional is a stone piece in Vienna which has on its front, on a kind of low *podium*, a group of Bacchus and Ariadne between flat pilasters carved with running vine-scrolls: on each of the small sides is a slave at work, one with a wine jar, and on the back two men seated at a game of dice.[690] These scenes would appear to combine allusions to the Bacchic paradise and to the chances of

74, 75 *Above*, fragment of a marble Jewish sarcophagus from the Rondanini catacomb, Rome, showing a mixture of motifs—Jewish (menorah) and pagan (Victories, Seasons, grape-treading *putti*) (p. 238). *Below*, a painting in the new *Via Latina* catacomb: Hercules slays the Hydra (p. 244).

76–8 *Above*, a marble Antonine tomb relief at Athens with busts in the Roman republican tradition (p. 246). *Below*, two marble stelai at Nice, each in the form of a tomb door (p. 247).

79 A marble stele showing a young woman with Trajanic coiffure standing in an arched niche. She appears in the guise of Venus Victrix, largely nude, leaning on a pillar at her left, and holding a palm-branch, while a dove is on the ground beside her. She lifts her right hand, palm outwards, in greeting. The inscription die under her feet is blank (p. 249).

80, 81 *Left*, the principal relief on a stone 'pillar-stele' at Arlon, showing the graceful, full-length figures of two married couples (p. 252). *Below*, the gravestone of a young woman, Eppatricia, in the form of a wine-barrel adorned with hoops and wine-skins—a type of monument apparently peculiar to Roman sites in what is now Portugal (p. 253).

2, 83 *Above*, *left*, the elaborately carved marble
ınerary altar of the freedman Amemptus
›. 266); *right*, the marble funerary *cippus* in
ıe First Tomb of the Caetennii (F) in the St
eter's necropolis (pp. 266–7).

4 The marble effigy of a half-draped lady with Flavian coiffure on her
ınerary couch (p. 269).

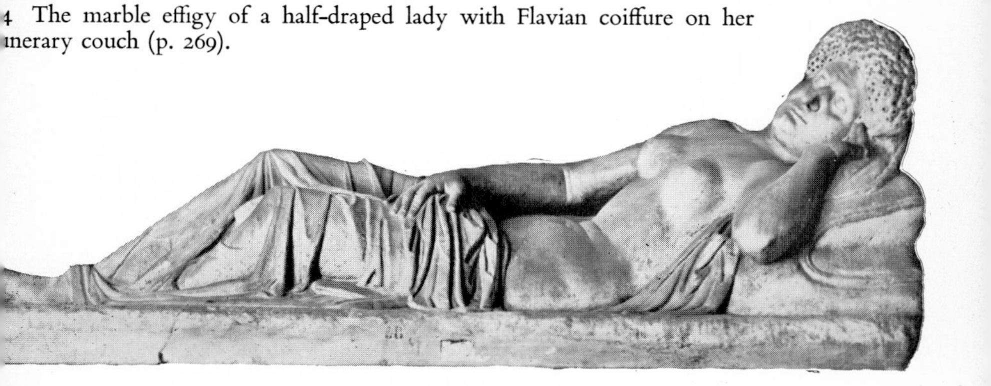

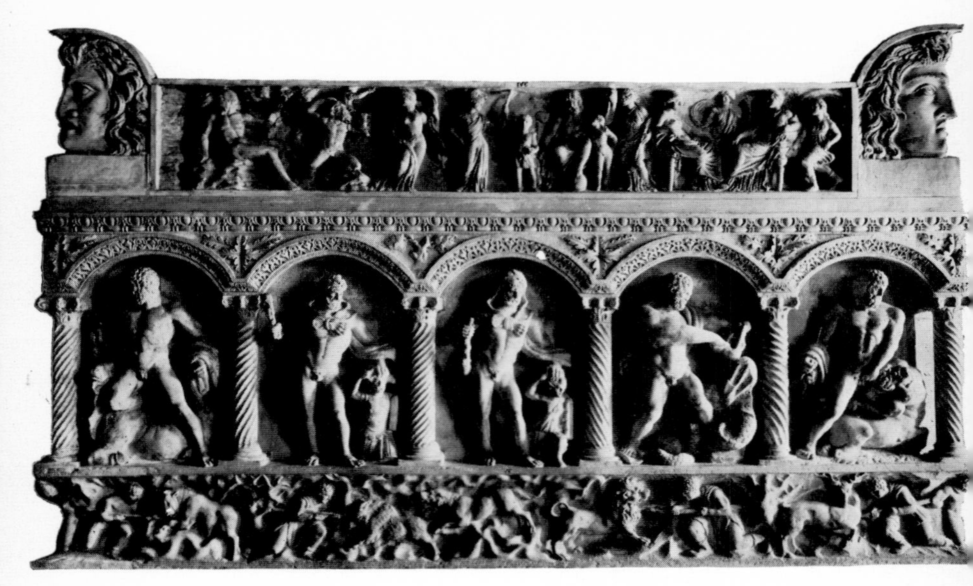

85, 86 *Above*, a marble sarcophagus with colonnettes forming a series of niches, in each of which a Labour of Hercules is carved in high relief (*cf.* pp. 272–3). *Below*, a marble sarcophagus from Sidamara in Asia Minor showing statuesque figures of the deceased (centre), the Dioscuri (at the ends), etc. (*cf.* pp. 272–3).

87 *Above*, a marble early-third-century sarcophagus in Tomb Φ (Marcii) in the St Peter's necropolis. The three figure-groups—Bacchus drunk and supported by a Satyr (centre), a pipe-playing Maenad (left), a dancing Satyr holding the baby Bacchus (right)—are separated by two panels of curved fluting (*cf.* p. 271).

88, 89 Two lead sarcophagi from Syria decorated with small motifs in relief —floral scrolls, human figures, colonnettes, garlands, etc. (pp. 275–6).

90–2 *Left*, a stone funerary group, sculptured in the round, from Cologne. It depicts Hercules (whose head is restored) wrestling with the lion, a symbol of victory over death and evil (p. 279). *Below*, two views of the stone sarcophagus of a wealthy lady from Simpelveld. The interior is carved with the effigy of the deceased lying on her funerary couch and surrounded by all the amenities of her home—stove or bath-house, furniture, large vessels of metal or glass (p. 281).

mortal life. Two pieces, one in the Louvre, the other in the Villa Pacca in Rome, have figure scenes filling the entire front, on the first, a group of musicians:[691] on the second, Meleager's boar-hunt.[692] Most peculiar, perhaps, of all is a *cinerarium* from the Haterii monument in Rome, which carries in the upper corners of the face the heads of two bulls munching bunches of grapes, while the rest of the field is filled with water, falling from a mussel-shell just below the upper edge, in which fish, water-birds, and dolphins are swimming and tumbling.[693] Such motifs could symbolize afterlife refreshment.

The forms and the decorative motifs of the funerary altars, which stood in the interiors of tombs, both those containing ashes and those that were solid bases, have been described and analysed in detail by Altmann. Most are crowned with either rounded or gabled pediments flanked by 'bolsters'. It is noteworthy that some of the most austere pieces have come to light in the upper-class Tombs of the Calpurnii Pisones and Volusii, of which the former is also known as the Licinian Tomb. Of these some have nothing on the main face but the inscription, such ornament as there is being confined to a rounded or gabled pediment or to a narrow frieze running between angle pilasters above the inscription and separated from the pediment by a heavy cornice.[694] Other altars from the same tombs are more elaborate, with heavy laurel-wreaths or fruit-swags suspended from Ammon heads or from *bucrania* and framing the inscription on the front and various objects on the sides;[695] and it was ornament of this and other exuberant types that appealed more strongly to the rather showy taste of wealthy persons of slave or freedman extraction. Examples of altars with these laurel-wreaths and fruit-swags slung between *bucrania*, rams' heads, and Ammon heads are catalogued and reproduced in Altmann's Chapters VI to VIII. Many of them are crammed with subsidiary motifs—eagles or Sphinxes at the bottom corners, Medusa-masks or sea-monsters above the garlands, birds, sea monsters, and figure groups of various kinds below them.[696] The garlands are doubtless translations into marble of actual garlands offered to the dead; and many of the subsidiary motifs have a funerary or other-worldly significance, while others may be purely decorative. On some altars the front is flanked by palm trees, as in the case of a Vatican piece, where backed against each tree-trunk is a Victory holding one of the handles of a tomb door that stands ajar below the inscription.[697] Another Vatican altar has again flanking palms and between them, above the inscription, in a deep recess, the *imago* of Cornelia Glyce with Flavian hair-style.[698] One of the finest and most famous of all Roman funerary altars is that of Amemptus, a freedman of the empress Livia, in the Louvre.[699] On the front there are flaming torches at the sides and the inscription die is completely framed by garlands of leaves and fruit, with a mask above it and a spread eagle perched on one of the swags beneath it. Below that swag are the dainty figures of a Centaur and Centauress making music, each with a Cupid, similarly employed, on its back. (*Pl.* 82)

Altars on which the flanking features are pilasters with straight flutes or spirally fluted colonnettes are described in Altmann's Chapter XII. Some of these are simple in character, with only an inscription on the front. On others figure scenes are introduced. For instance, three pieces show below the inscription a man and wife taking leave of one another at the tomb door.[700] On another piece, in the Museo Nazionale Romano, the field between the spiral colonnettes is equally divided between the inscription die, below, and and a scene of the Rape of Persephone, above:[701] and on yet another altar in the same collection, similarly divided, but with garlands hanging vertically on the inner sides of the colonnettes, is depicted below the text the story of Daedalus and Pasiphae: it would seem that the dead man, Gaius Volcacius Artemidorus, had been a carver in wood or a sculptor.[702]

An attractive, and again less exuberantly ornamented, type of altar, described and illustrated in Altmann's Chapter XI, is that on which the main element on the front is the inscription framed on all four sides by a border filled with running floral scrolls worked in low relief. Most of these are *cippi* and many of them have laurel trees, framed or unframed, on their lateral faces, presumably signifying other-world fertility. A particularly fine example, with a delicately carved, rounded pediment, dedicated to Marcus Caetennius Antigonus and Tullia Secunda, stands in the First Tomb of the Caetennii in the Vatican necropolis.[703] More ambitious is the *cippus* in the Louvre of Julia Victorina, who died at the age of eleven years five months, and whose bust, in high relief with a crescent on her head, occupies the larger part of the framed field and crowds the inscription into the space that is left below it. On the back, also within a frame of floral scrolls, is the radiate bust of an unnamed woman of mature years, perhaps a relative; and on each of the lateral faces is an unframed olive tree. Crescent and rays betoken the lunar and solar apotheosis of the dead.[704] (*Pl.* 83)

A *cippus* in the Ducal Palace at Urbino is of special interest for its material, red, instead of the usual white, marble, for the layout of its decoration, and for the content of its iconography.[705] Within a simple moulded frame, without flanking colonnettes or other lateral features, are three superimposed panels, as on many stelai (*cf.* pp. 247, 248). The inscription in the central panel records that the piece commemorates an imperial freedman, most probably of Domitian, one Titus Flavius Abascantus, a civil servant *a cognitionibus* (assistant to the emperor in the exercise of his personal jurisdiction). The top panel depicts the funerary banquet of the dead; and in the bottom one appears the famous charioteer Scorpus, driving a *quadriga* towards the right, his name and the names of his victorious horses being inscribed in small characters along the lower edge of the inscription die. This scene can only be explained as a symbol of Abascantus' triumph over death.

A final series of funerary altars is that in which subsidiary ornament is either absent or very much toned down and all the interest is concentrated on the portraiture of the dead—reclining at the sepulchral banquet, seated or standing as a solitary figure, or in bust form. A piece in the Vatican shows a woman, Attia Agele, reclining for the feast with drinking vessels on a table beside her.[706] Another Vatican altar presents Publius Vitellius Sucessus similarly reclining, with his wife, Vitellia, seated at his feet and a palm tree and a horse, for the ride to the afterlife, behind him: on the pediment between the 'bolsters' are busts of the pair.[707] An altar from the Tomb of the Volusii shows a seated male figure filling the entire field on the front;[708] and the well-known altar-shaped monument in the Palazzo dei Conservatori of the eleven-year-old poet, Quintus Sulpicius, has a full-length figure of the boy standing in a deep, arched niche above a panel on which his prize-poem is inscribed.[709] Other pieces display only busts, singly or in pairs, and carry on, like stelai of certain types (*cf.* pp. 247, 248), through the first century of our era the ancient line of republican *imagines*.[710]

### (D) FUNERARY COUCHES WITH EFFIGIES OF THE DEAD

During the first century AD, when cremation was still the normal rite in Rome, and the practice of setting up elaborately carved ash-receptacles and commemorative altars was still in vogue among the well-to-do, there was evolved another, but rarer, form of marble monument, which seems to have survived, sporadically at least, into the second and third centuries. This form was in part derived from the Etruscan tradition of 'gisants' figures on the lids of sarcophagi (*cf.* p. 14); but the Roman objects that represent it are not themselves sarcophagus lids, as they have often been termed, but independent couches (*klinai*) on which the effigies of the dead lie recumbent on their backs or on their sides or propped on pillows. No first-century example, so far as the present writer is aware, has yet been found resting on the trough of a sarcophagus; but the short turned or plain legs of these couches, now mostly lost, would have rested on the ground or on a platform in the tomb. Couches of this type are, of course, extremely familiar from reliefs with renderings of the funerary banquet, where the 'dead' are very much 'alive'. A Flavian relief in the Museo Capitolino shows a leave-taking scene, with a young man reclining, still alive and alert, on a similar couch and holding his scroll of destiny, while an elderly woman, probably his mother, sits beside him with her right arm round his shoulders.[711] Other reliefs of the same period present the effigy of the deceased resting on the couch in repose. For example, on the relief from the Haterii monument with the large temple-tomb (*cf.* pp. 81, 132) there is, above the temple-tomb's gabled roof, on a kind of shelf upheld by eagles with festoons slung around their necks, a scene depicting what would seem to be another tomb's interior. To the right is a niche, in which the naked figure of Venus stands, flanked, on either side, by two colonnettes, in their turn flanking a *candelabrum*, and surmounted by an entablature carrying portrait-busts. In the centre on a couch backed by curtains lies the image of a woman propped against a pillow, while her right hand rests on the back-feathers of a bird that perches on her knee. Below the couch three children are playing on the ground and an old woman tends a flaming altar. On the left side of the picture is a heavily built flaming *candelabrum*.[712] Another relief in the Lateran collection, which might once have been inset in a wall of the Tomb of the Volusii, in which it came to light, shows in a deep rectangular recess the effigy of Ulpia Epigone, half-draped and with Flavian coiffure, lying tipped up on her left side on a couch with elegantly turned legs: she supports her head, which rests on a pillow, on her left hand, beneath her feet is a small wicker basket, and from behind her left forearm emerge the head and forepaws of a tiny lap-dog.[713]

The independent couches generally portray the sleep of death with the limbs of the effigy, which is worked virtually in the round, relaxed as in slumber, although usually the eyes are open. One of the earliest of these pieces, in the Museo Nazionale Romano, shows the figure of a Julio-Claudian boy with a snake beside him.[714] A couch in the Vatican has the half-draped figure of a woman coiffured in the Flavian style.[715] Two more couches with the effigies of boys must be well post-first-century in date, since the irises and pupils of the eyes are rendered: one of these, in the Museo Capitolino, holds poppies and has his little dog beside him,[716] the other, in the Lateran collection, grasps a wreath.[717] Another couch in the Vatican, with the legs preserved, bears the figure of a woman with the hair-style of Faustina I.[718] In the Palazzo Farnese in Rome there is a *kline* on which a man and wife repose, the latter, who has Julia Domna's coiffure, with a wreath, the former with the attributes of Hercules—cup, lion's skin, quiver, and club—betokening apotheosis;[719] and the cup held by another, more 'alive', third-century man on a couch in the Museo Nazionale Romano may be meant to indicate that he too has attained the hero's reward of immortality.[720] Finally, there is the effigy of a priest of Cybele, again of third-century date, lying on a couch, which does not seem to have been the lid of a sarcophagus, from one of the Isola Sacra tombs (*cf.* p. 138).[721] (*Pl.* 84)

## (E) DECORATED SARCOPHAGI

Just as the cheap earthenware and glass vessels and the plain leaden canisters that received the ashes of the poorer classes of society had their expensive counterparts in the marble and alabaster urns and carved ash-chests and funerary altars of the rich; so the plain, purely functional, wooden, stone, lead, and terracotta coffins used for the inhumation burials of the less well-off were counterbalanced by the marble, stone, and lead sarcophagi adorned with decoration of varying levels of artistry and elaboration, in which better-off persons and the really wealthy could afford to lay the bodies of their dead to rest (*cf.* p. 49). And again it is these 'show' sarcophagi, made both to gratify the departed and, in the case of those of stone and marble, to impress the living beholders, that play an important part in the study of sepulchral furniture.

Some of the very large and heavily lidded pieces of the 'Greek' or eastern free-standing types, carved on all four sides, may have stood in the open air along roadsides or within the walls of funerary precincts. But the great majority of stone and marble sarcophagi, particularly those of the 'Roman' or western types, with uncarved backs, were designed to be placed in tombs up against the walls or in niches or, in the case of those with ornament on every face, well out from the walls on the floor of the chamber where they could be walked round and the backs as well as their fronts and sides appreciated. Most of the provenances of sarcophagi, when they are recorded, are, in fact, the interiors of tombs, where they came to light either singly or in groups. Representative examples of the latter are the trio in the Lateran collection, which was found in a tomb with Hadrianic brick-stamps near the *Porta Viminalis* in Rome;[722] the three placed each in an arched recess in the upper part of the walls of the Tomb of the Egyptians in the Vatican necropolis;[723] and the ten discovered in 1885 in two subterranean burial chambers in the private cemetery of the Calpurnii Pisones (Licinian Tomb), of which one was undecorated and destroyed shortly after the excavation, two are in the Museo Nazionale Romano, and the remaining seven are in the Walters Art Gallery in Baltimore.[724] The pieces belonging to the last group range in date from the early-second to the early-third century AD, continuing the series of richly ornamented objects from the site represented in the first century by the sepulchral altars (*cf.* pp. 253, 254, 265–8).

The style, technique, and composition of the designs, figure scenes, and portraits carved on the marble sarcophagi are properly part of the study of Roman art.[725] This is, of course, also the case to some extent with the built-in grave reliefs and free-standing stelai, with the ash-chests and funerary altars, and with the effigies on independent couches. But these have not the same intrinsic interest to the art-historian in that they do not illustrate continuously, as the sarcophagi do, the whole unbroken evolution of pictorial relief-work from the early-second century to the period of the early Christian Empire of the fourth, fifth, and sixth centuries. That development is, in fact, first and foremost an artistic question. The content, on the other hand, of these sarcophagus reliefs has obviously an important bearing on funerary practice and afterlife ideas; and this content, together with the main structural features of the objects themselves, will now be briefly analysed.

The 'Roman' or western pieces, carved on the front and sides but normally left unworked behind, have a lid that is either flat or slopes up slightly from the back towards the front, where it is edged by a horizontal carved panel standing upright, running the whole length of the front, and generally terminating in a mask at either end. Throughout the second century troughs were rectangular; but in the third century an alternative form with rounded ends came into vogue. On all second-, and on a large number of third-, century pieces the design on the front is continuous; but in the third century there were introduced rectangular troughs with two fluted panels separating a central from two lateral figured panels. The subject-matter of these western sarcophagus reliefs falls into two main types. One type consists on the front of two or three garlands of fruit, leaves, and flowers slung from the shoulders of three or four standing figures of Cupids, for the most part, but sometimes of Satyrs, Nymphs, or Victories. These swags represent, as on the ash-chests and altars, the actual garlands offered to the dead on festivals and anniversaries, while the supporting figures symbolize aspects of the after-life. The second type of subject comprises narrative scenes drawn from mythology or from the public and private life of the deceased, the former serving as allegories of death and the life beyond the grave, the latter as reminders of the cultural, business, and other professional tasks and activities of this world as a form of preparation for the next. The carving on the lid has normally a general, that on the short sides a closer, connection with the subject on the front.[726] (*Pls.* 85, 87)

Some third-century western sarcophagi are equipped with lids on which the figures of the dead recline on couches—a feature that is found on a number of the 'Greek' or eastern pieces of the so-called Attic class made in workshops on the Greek mainland.[727] Other Attic pieces have heavy gabled, roof-like lids. A few are garland-sarcophagi: some have rows of busts or figures of the dead on their troughs; but most bear scenes or groups of mythological content. All are carved on all four sides, as are also the sarcophagi of the second main eastern class known as Asiatic from the fact that their Asiatic origin is attested by the large number of examples found on Anatolian sites. The lid when preserved generally represents a couch on which the departed is shown either lying flat on his or her back or reclining with head and shoulders upright. The trough is an elaborate architectural structure resembling an actual tomb, often with a door on one of the short sides; and each of the four faces has a series of *aediculae* with rounded or gabled tops and flanking colonnettes and each containing, worked in very high relief, in fact, practically in the round, the figure either of the dead or of one of his or her relatives or of a god or mythological personage appropriate to a funerary context.[728] (*Pl.* 86)

It is these products of Greek and Asiatic workshops that provide most of the evidence for sarcophagi as objects of commerce in the

Roman world. Of the Attic pieces found in the West and in east-Mediterranean lands outside Greece itself some were clearly prepared only in their early stages in Attic workshops and were shipped abroad to foreign markets with their decoration on all four sides just roughly blocked out, probably along with Attic craftsmen to complete their carving at their places of destination, on the front alone in the West, where they would not generally have been free-standing. Other Attic pieces of non-Greek provenance would have been worked on the spot *ab initio* partly by immigrant craftsmen and partly by their local pupils and imitators. On the other hand, the Asiatic sarcophagi that have come to light in Italy are mostly worked on all four sides and must have been completely finished before they left the Anatolian workshops. Of these imports the most imposing is the great piece found near Melfi with a woman lying on her back on its lid and sporting the hair-style of about 170.[729]

Among the local Roman imitations of the columned Asiatic imports is a most unusual sarcophagus found at Velletri, which departs quite freely from its models in that it has a gabled, not a *kline*, lid and two tiers of small, interrelated figure scenes, instead of one zone of large, isolated statuesque figures.[730]

Some of the artistically very best carved marble sarcophagi, whether 'Roman' or 'Greek', may well have been specially commissioned by or for the persons whose bodies they were destined to receive. But the vast majority were workshop pieces, kept in stock and selected by customers as need arose. This is well attested by the fact that portrait-busts of the deceased and the heads of reclining figures representing the dead or the head of the protagonist in a mythological or 'daily-life' scene, with whom the occupant of the sarcophagus was assimilated or equated, are often found in a merely blocked-out stage. It is clear that in such cases the last-minute completion in the workshop of the head with features and hair resembling those of the recently departed was for some reason never carried out. There are also some instances of effigies on lids where the whole figure, not the head alone, is unfinished.

Structurally the early-Christian sarcophagi of the third, fourth, fifth, and sixth centuries, chiefly produced in Roman, north-Italian, and south-Gaulish workshops, were to a large extent modelled on their pagan precursors and contemporary counterparts.[731] The commonest form has on the front a continuous frieze of symbolic figures or of biblical scenes or one composed of a group showing Christ with Apostles on either side of Him; but the introduction of two superimposed friezes, mainly of biblical scenes, was a Christian speciality, apart from a few rare pagan examples (see above). So was the occasional appearance of columned sarcophagi, ultimately based on pagan Asiatic prototypes, with two tiers of figures or groups in juxtaposed *aediculae*,[732] although the pieces with a single columned zone are far more frequent. The use of fluted areas separating figured panels is also found on Christian pieces. Peculiar to the early Christians are the so-called 'city-gate' sarcophagi, on which biblical and other scenes are enacted against a backdrop of elaborate architectural elements. Many of the pieces of Roman provenance come from catacombs. Of the fifth- and sixth-century pieces at Ravenna some have barrel-vaulted, others heavy gabled, lids and the great majority are carved on all four sides.

Of the decorated sarcophagi, mostly of stone, much more rarely of marble, that were made in the workshops of the northern provinces, those from Danubian countries bear a close resemblance to pieces of the Attic class with their heavy lids in the form of tiled, gabled roofs. Some of these, again like their Attic models, have garlands on all four sides and figured pediments and *acroteria*.[733] The Ghica sarcophagus in Budapest has portraits of four dead persons in *aediculae* on its front, music-making Cupids on its short sides and back, and corner figures of Victories.[734] Gable-lidded pieces from Alisca, Sirmium, Zagreb, and Timissoara carry figured and floral panels, portrait-busts, and abstract motifs.[735] An exceptional sandstone sarcophagus at Cologne, that of Gaius Severinus Vitealis, has four panels carved with figure groups—two dancers, Hercules and Hesione, Apollo and Hercules with the Delphic tripod, Theseus and the Minotaur.[736] A simpler provincial type is that which bears on the front a laterally spreading, ansate inscription die upheld on either side by a Cupid.

Examples are the sandstone sarcophagus at Cologne made by Desideratus for himself, his wife, Verecundina Placida, and their son, Verecundineius Desideratus, with a heavy gabled lid, on the front of which are busts of father, mother, and child at the centre and two other busts at the corners;[737] that of Traiana Herodiana at Königsweiler, made for her by her husband Arturius Seneca, similarly lidded, with busts of the pair at the centre and two other busts at the corners;[738] and that of Julia Victorina and her son, Constantius, at York, worked in local stone and made for them by Julia's husband, Septimius Lupianus, where the carving of the Cupids is particularly good and the lid is slightly gabled.[739] Two other stone British pieces have only *peltae* flanking the inscription die;[740] and a fourth coffin of British stone has at the centre of the front a portrait-bust in a roundel, the rest of the field being fluted, a basket of fruit on each short side, and a foliate pattern on the gabled lid.[741]

There can be no doubt at all, as has been already said (*cf.* p. 272), that all the decorated marble and stone sarcophagi described above were meant to be admired and meditated on by passers-by, if ranged along roadsides, or by relatives and friends, if placed in tombs or in sepulchral precincts. Many bear inscriptions that were obviously intended to be read. The decorated lead sarcophagi never, with some very rare exceptions, carry texts. Moreover, many of them were hidden away from human sight—either encased in plain outer coffins of wood or stone or, in east-Mediterranean lands, lowered into rock-cut cavities in the floors of tombs and covered over with slabs of stone or placed in serried rows on the floors of sepulchral chambers or, in the case of one British piece, concealed beneath the earthen mound of a tumulus. The ornamental motifs on the flat or slightly curved lids and on all four sides of sarcophagi of this class must, then, have mainly been designed to please the dead, whose souls, while located in paradise, were yet believed to inhabit, in some sense, or at least to visit from time to time, the places where their bodies reposed.

Decorated lead sarcophagi are found in the West principally in Britain, where supplies of lead were plentiful,[742] in Gaul,[743] and in Roman Germany;[744] and, above all, in the East, in Syria and

Palestine, where the lead must have been imported, but where this form of art flourished more prolifically than elsewhere in the Roman world.[745] They are sand-cast, matrices of wet sand having been first prepared for the lead sheets that composed the coffin's bottom, lid, and sides. The ornament, which is on a small scale and very repetitive, was almost certainly produced by a series of positive stamps, most probably carved in wood in relief on separate plaques or blocks for individual figures and motifs and on long strips in the case of borders of running scrolls or garlands, while carved wooden rods would have served as stamps for the cable and bead-and-reel lines in edgings and in geometric patterns, particularly in the networks of criss-cross lines that are a favourite decorative feature. These stamps would have been pressed face-downwards into the wet sand matrix so as to imprint in it sharp negative impressions arranged according to a preconceived scheme selected by the craftsman from his copy-book. The stamps having made their impressions were then removed; and when the molten lead was poured on to the matrix the negatives left in the sand produced positive figures and patterns standing out in relief on the surface of the sheet. In the eastern areas the lead sarcophagi are almost exclusively rectangular, with the ends of equal length and the centripetal designs on the lid viewable from all sides. But in Britain there is also a tapering variety, with the longer end at the head and the main axis of the lid's design set lengthwise, as though to be viewed by a spectator standing at the foot. An interesting instance of this is the sarcophagus of a child found as a secondary burial in the tumulus at Holborough in Kent (*cf.* pp. 181, 182).[746]

A common motif on the British pieces is a large scallop-shell (*pecten*). This may well allude to the soul's journey across the ocean to the Blessed Isles, as would also the smaller cockle-shell variety (*carden*) found on eastern sarcophagi, where real shells seem to have been used as stamps. Virtually all the motifs employed for the decoration of the lead sarcophagi, both eastern and western, have in fact, a place in the standard iconographic repertory of Roman-age funerary art. To take a few examples—one of the German pieces has a repeating hunting scene;[747] a British fragment shows a racing *biga*;[748] Minerva as conqueress of death appears both in Britain and in Syria and Palestine;[749] the Bacchic content of the Holborough lid design is matched by Bacchic figures on many eastern pieces. Cupids, Psyches, Sphinxes, Medusa-heads, lions, and dolphins abound. There are also numerous rosettes, garlands, running floral scrolls, and leaf-sprays, symbols of afterlife fruitfulness. Two eastern sarcophagi show a rarer sepulchral motif, the famous group of the Three Graces,[750] who may symbolize, as do the Muses in funerary contexts, culture and the arts as a road to immortality. This motif is also found on a few fluted marble pieces, where the Graces sometimes hold corn-ears as emblems of fertility.[751] (*Pls.* 88, 89)

## (F) OTHER SCULPTURES

The Weiden bei Köln hypogeum has already furnished an important instance of the practice of placing in interiors of tombs portrait-busts of the deceased (*cf.* p. 215). Another example of it is the Licinian Tomb in Rome, where sixteen marble portraits came to light, ranging in date from the mid-first to the late-second century AD.[752] One of the interesting features of this collection is that it includes, besides likenesses of members of the family, those of distinguished persons with whom it had some connection. There are portraits of Livia and of both the Elder and the Young Agrippina and one of Pompeius Magnus. The last piece is clearly a posthumous likeness and may well be of Julio-Claudian date, in view of the fact that Marcus Licinius Crassus Frugi, consul in AD 27, gave one of his sons the name of Gnaeus Pompeius Magnus, to mark his descent from Pompey through his mother. That portrait-busts of the dead were sometimes set in niches on the walls of a temple-tomb's exterior would seem to be suggested by the Haterii Tomb relief discussed in Chapter V (*cf.* p. 132). Tomb portraits in the round sometimes take the form of full-length statues.[753]

Funerary sculptures in the round of another type would appear to have been erected in the open, either on lofty *podia* by road-sides or within sepulchral precincts or as part of the adornment of a precinct wall. Particularly favoured in the Celtic provinces of Gaul and Britain is the neckless head of a deity, with the chin resting directly on a plinth which could well have once been the crowning feature of a tall base. Examples are the large female head, worked in native stone and style, perhaps of some goddess of the Celtic underworld, from Towcester in Northamptonshire, now in the British Museum;[754] and the head of Hercules from Mouriès (Bouches du Rhône), now serving as a fountain decoration in the Château de Servane.[755] A group of large theatre masks at Vienne might have had the same function.[756] Large-scale figures of animals on high bases are, of course, among the best-known fourth-century BC monuments in the Kerameikos cemetery on the outskirts of ancient Athens, where lions, bulls and dogs are represented.[757] But it would appear to be improbable that classical Greek works of this kind directly influenced their Roman-age successors. These do, at any rate, play a quite distinctive role in provincial funerary art. In the Danubian lands lions are plentiful, sometimes with the remnants of a victim between their fore-paws—symbols of the ravening power of death.[758] Lions, boars, and bears, also often devouring their prey, are found in Roman Germany.[759] Similar lions that have come to light in Britain are those in the Guildhall Museum, which had been reused as a building stone in one of the fourth-century bastions on Londinium's city-wall,[760] and in the Cambridge Museum of Archaeology and Ethnology, discovered in the Roman and Anglo-Saxon cemetery in the grounds of Girton College, where it would have faced the Roman road between Cambridge and Godmanchester.[761]

Three sepulchral Sphinxes worked somewhat crudely in the round, two of them guarding human heads between their paws, were found at Alba Julia in Dacia.[762] But by far the most attractive and skilfully sculptured funerary Sphinx is the well-known winged and seated creature from one of the Camulodunum (Colchester) cemeteries.[763] Carved in British stone, this is among the best surviving sculptures that were executed in the northern provinces. Between her forepaws is the male portrait-head of an elderly, clean-shaven man, with sketchily rendered hair, furrowed brow, plain eyes, and fleshy cheeks—a head, in fact, of Flavian or early-Trajanic date. No less good artistically are two mythological tomb-groups, carved in limestone, from Cologne, that must have been reared on bases, one of Hercules wrestling with the lion, the other of Ganymede watering the eagle, both of them motifs appropriate to a funerary context.[764] (*Pl.* 90)

Two figures in the round of Sphinxes have been restored as perched on the top of the circular wall in which is inset the famous stele of Dexileos in the Kerameikos cemetery;[765] and the pair of lions poised on the low balustrade surrounding the Augustan base-and-'canopy' tomb at Aquileia has been already noted (*cf.* p. 126). Two Romano-British lions, each devouring its prey, stand on sections of curved coping that are likely to have topped the precinct walls of tombs. One of these is the famous Corbridge lion, reconditioned at a later stage as a fountain group and cut to accommodate a leaden water pipe;[766] the second lion comes from a Roman cemetery site in the southern suburbs of Chester.[767] Certainly sepulchral, since it bears below it the inscription *D*(*is*) *M*(*anibus*) *C*(*onsecratum*) *E*(*st*), is the young male head with wind-blown hair on a corner stone from Roman York, which may well have been one of four heads, probably of Winds, which marked the four angles of a tomb balustrade.[768]

That Roman tombs could be furnished with high-backed chairs and couches for the use of the souls of the dead when attending commemorative meals has been proved by the Weiden bei Köln discovery (*cf.* pp. 214, 215). A carved limestone table leg, with a leaf-sheath round the 'knee' and a claw foot, found in a cemetery area at York, could also have been an article of funerary furniture serving for feasts or for offerings to the departed.[769] Other furnishings that the dead required in the tomb were candlesticks and *candelabra* either to illuminate the darkness of death or to symbolize the *lux perpetua* of paradise. The two painted candlesticks in the hypogeum at Silistria, holding lighted candles and equipped with feet in the form of animal claws (*cf.* p. 217), may very well represent real candlesticks, probably of bronze, that once stood in the chamber; and there can be little doubt that the elaborate flaming *candelabrum* in the tomb-interior scene on one of the Haterii reliefs (*cf.* p. 269) is a two dimensional rendering of an actual object in stone or marble. We have also noted an inscription in which provision is made for the lighting of lamps at a grave on specified occasions (*cf.* p. 63 and Note 259). Again, there are the instances of ash-chests and sepulchral altars, catalogued by Altmann,[770] on which torches and *candelabra*, sometimes in the form of palm trees, occur at the corners (*cf.* p. 266). In the Ashmolean Museum, Oxford, are three tall marble pilasters from the neighbourhood of Smyrna, each with relief work in a vertical recessed panel on the front, and it seems not unlikely that they came from some richly furnished tomb. One has a scroll of vine leaves that could be an emblem of afterlife fertility. But the other two show very elaborately adorned *candelabra*, of which the upper part of one takes the form of a palm tree, while the other has, below, a three-sided element decorated with figures in relief and resting on Sphinxes, and, above, figures of swans and a basket-like feature crowned with a calyx of foliage, which may once have held the receptacle, now broken off, for the lamp.[771] These, like the painted candlesticks at Silistria, might be substitutes for, or renderings of, real *candelabra*.

As regards the actual objects of this type that have descended to us from antiquity, it has been suggested that the six ancient marble *candelabra*, which were once in the imperial mausoleum that is now the church of Santa Costanza in Rome, were funerary *candelabra* belonging to the burial place of Constantine's daughters.[772] One of them is lost, one is now in the church of Sant' Agnese, and four are in the Vatican. The sepulchral use of the many marble *candelabrum* fragments that are now to be seen in the museums of Rome and elsewhere cannot be proved. But Roman Britain has produced what can hardly be other than the remnant of a stone funerary *candelabrum*, found in one of the cemetery sites of Roman York.[773] The piece is part of a vertical shaft carved in the round and has large dowel holes at top and bottom, indicating that it formed the central portion of a larger object. The ornament consists of one complete, and one very fragmentary, Cupid clambering up the side of an hour-glass-shaped basket, above which are four human heads alternating with four now headless seated creatures, probably Sphinxes. All of these motifs fit well into a funerary context; and this fact, combined with the find-spot, leaves little room for doubt that we have here the relic of a monumental lampstand, possibly from 13 to 16 feet high, from the tomb of a wealthy provincial who employed a local carver with access to a copy-book from the Mediterranean world.

It is possible that some Roman tombs contained renderings of articles of furniture of other kinds for the use of the souls of the deceased. This thought reminds us of the unique Simpelveld sarcophagus at Leiden.[774] There, carved on the interior of its walls, and so hidden, once the burial had taken place, from all living sight, is the dead lady reclining in effigy on her funerary couch and surrounded by all her this-worldly goods. We see, amongst other things, her high-backed chair, her stove or bath house, her sideboards, on which large glass or metal vessels are displayed, her cupboards and cabinets, her clothes-chest, and her three-legged dining-room table. The whole of this 'Dutch interior' was most probably designed to make the dead feel 'at home' in her final resting-place by reproducing in detail the contents of the house of which she was once the wealthy mistress. We have no evidence that any tomb was in actuality so elaborately equipped with objects carved in the round. But stone imitations of some at least of these desirable domestic comforts, additional to tables, chairs, and couches, may have been provided in tombs that are now destroyed or that still await discovery. (*Pls.* 91, 92)

# NOTES

## CHAPTER I

1 E.g. Tomb of the Leopards, Tarquinia: R. Bartoccini, *Les peintures étrusques de Tarquinia*, 1955, pls. 9, 10; P. J. Riis, *An Introduction to Etruscan Art*, 1953, pl. 53; F. Poulsen, *Etruscan Tomb Painting*, 1922, fig. 24; Tomb of the Lionesses, Tarquinia: Bartocinni, *op. cit.*, pl. 4; Tomb of the Bigae, Tarquinia: Poulsen, *op. cit.*, fig. 23

2 E.g. Tomb of Hunting and Fishing, Tarquinia: Bartoccini, *op. cit.*, pls. 5, 6; Riis, *op. cit.*, pl. 51; L. Banti, *Die Welt der Etrusker*, 1960, colour-plate II; H. H. Scullard, *The Etruscan Cities and Rome*, 1967, pl. 9

3 E.g. Tomb of the Augurs, Tarquinia: Poulsen, *op. cit.*, fig. 4

4 E.g. Tomb of the Inscriptions, Tarquinia: *ibid.*, figs. 7, 8; Tomb of the Dying or Dead Man ('Morente' or 'Morto'), Tarquinia: *ibid.*, fig. 18

5 E.g. Tomb of the Inscriptions, Tarquinia: *ibid.*, fig. 8; Tomb of the Triclinium, Tarquinia: *ibid.*, fig. 10; Bartoccini, *op. cit.*, pls. 13–15; Tomb of the Bigae, Tarquinia: Poulsen, *op. cit.*, fig. 15

6 E.g. Tomb of the Lionesses, Tarquinia: Bartoccini, pl. 3; Tomb of the Triclinium, Tarquinia: *ibid.*, pl. 12; Tomb of the Leopards, Tarquinia: Banti, *op. cit.*, pl. 64 (below); Scullard, *op. cit.*, pl. 16

7 See Note 1 and the Golini Tomb, Orvieto: Poulsen, *op. cit.*, fig. 31; terracotta funerary group of husband and wife reclining side by side on a funerary couch, from Caere, Villa Giulia, Rome: Riis, *op. cit.*, pl. 30, (fig. 45); Scullard, *op. cit.*, pl. 31

8 Tomb of the Shields, Tarquinia: Poulsen, *op. cit.*, figs. 26, 27; Bartoccini, *op. cit.*, pls. 22, 23

9 E.g. marble ash-chest in the Tomb of the Volumnii, near Perugia: Riis, *op. cit.*, pl. 72; terracotta ash-chest from Volterra, Volterra Museum: *ibid.*, pl. 74 (fig. 108)

10 British Museum: R. Herbig, *Götter und Dämonen der Etrusker*, 1965, pl. 25

11 From Chianciano, Archaeological Museum, Florence: *ibid.*, pl. 28, fig. 1

12 From Chiusi, Perugia Museum: *ibid.*, pl. 29, fig. 1

13 E.g. alabaster ash-chest, Vatican Museum: *ibid.*, pl. 28, fig. 2; alabaster ash-chest, from Sarteano, Sienna Museum: *ibid.*, pl. 29, fig. 2

14 E.g. Tomb of Orcus, Tarquinia: *ibid.*, pl. 36; Poulsen, *op. cit.*, fig. 35; Bartocinni, *op. cit.*, pl. 19; François Tomb, Vulci, Museo Torlonia, Rome:

Herbig, *op. cit.* pl. 39; Tomb of the Typhon, Tarquinia: Poulsen, *op. cit.*, fig. 45

15 Herbig, *op. cit.*, p. 19; Poulsen, *op. cit.*, p. 59

16 E.g. Tomb of Orcus, Tarquinia; Tomb of the Typhon, Tarquinia; François Tomb, Vulci

17 R. Herbig, *Die Jüngeretruskischen Steinsarkophage*, 1952

18 E. Brunn, G. Körte, *I rilievi dell' urne etrusche*, 1870, 1890–6, 1916

19 Poulsen, *op. cit.*, p. 59

20 Scullard, *op. cit.*, pl. 17. Cf. *ibid.*, pl. 50 for a sarcophagus lid on which a husband and wife embrace in the sleep of death

21 E.g. RF skyphos: Museum of Fine Arts, Boston (Mass.): Herbig, *Götter, etc.*, pl. 32, fig. 2; RF volute-krater: Bibliothèque Nationale, Paris: *ibid.*, pl. 34

22 E.g. fourth-century BC bronze mirror: Hermitage, Leningrad: *ibid.*, pp. 26–27, fig. 9; stone sarcophagus from Tarquinia: Tarquinia Museum: *ibid.*, pl. 30, fig. 2; ash chests in the Tomb of the Volumnii: see p. 24.

23 E.g. Tomb of Orcus, Tarquinia: Hades and Persphone seated in judgment: *ibid.*, pl. 37; Poulsen, *op. cit.*, fig. 37

24 From Tarquinia: Archaeological Museum, Florence: Herbig, *op. cit.*, pl. 30, fig. 1

25 B. Nogara, *Gli etruschi e la loro civiltà*, 1933, pp. 246–9; Herbig, *Die Jüngeretruskischen Steinsarkophage*, 1952, pp. 96–8

26 Nogara, *op. cit.*, p. 241, fig. 130; Herbig, *Die Götter, etc.*, pl. 24; G. Q. Giglioli, *L'arte etrusca*, 1935, pls. 60–3; Scullard, *op. cit.*, pl. 73

27 Nogara, *op. cit.*, pp. 274–5. figs. 148–9; Riis, *op. cit.*, pl. 12; Giglioli, *op. cit.*, pls. 3; 4, fig 4; Scullard, *op. cit.*, pl. 2

28 Herbig, *op. cit.*, pls. 26–7

29 Giglioli, *op. cit.*, pl. 336; Scullard, *op. cit.*, p. 81, fig. 5

30 See Note 18 and Scullard, *op. cit.*, pls. 69 (Tomb of the Atian family at Volterra), 70, 72

31 Giglioli, *op. cit.*, pl. 338, fig. 2: Caere, Tomb of the Sarcophagi

32 *Ibid.*, pls. 340–3; Scullard, *op. cit.*, pl. 26

33 Gigioli, *op. cit.*, pl. 339, fig. 2

34 Nogara, *op. cit.*, p. 235, fig. 126; Poulsen, *op. cit.*, fig. 9

35 For this gesture, *cf.* the painting in the Tomb of the Augurs, Tarquinia: *ibid.*, fig. 3; Bartoccini, *op. cit.*, pl. 2

36 Giglioli, *op. cit.*, pl. 74, fig. 1. For a death-bed scene in relief on an archaic sarcophagus from Clusium, see Scullard, *op. cit.*, pl. 74

37 For the Funeral Way for these processions at Caere, see Scullard, *op. cit.*, pl. 23

38 Herbig, *Die Jüngeretruskischen Steinsarkophage*, pls. 40, b, c, d; 41, b; 42, a; 55–7, a; 70, b; 74, c; Nogara, *op. cit.*, p. 231, fig. 122; p. 232, fig. 124; p. 233, fig. 125

39 Poulsen; *op. cit.*, figs. 45–7

40 Herbig, *op. cit.*, pls. 43, d; 70, b; 74, b; 80, a; Nogara, *op. cit.*, p. 240, fig. 129; Scullard, *op. cit.*, pl. 102. For numerous illustrations of scenes of this type, see R. Lambrechts, *Essai sur les magistratures des républiques étrusques*, 1959

41 E.g. Poulsen, *op. cit.*, figs. 7, 8, 12 (Tomb of the Inscriptions, Tarquinia); for the nail-studded doors, *cf.* the Tomb of the Augurs, Tarquinia, where a precisely similar door is flanked by two mourners: *ibid.*, fig. 3

42 *Ibid.*, fig. 13; Bartoccini, *op. cit.*, pl. 3

43 Nogara, *op. cit.*, p. 268

44 *Ibid.*, pp. 268, 270

45 For pre-Etruscan Bronze Age and Iron Age 'pozzo' and 'fossa' burials, and for the distinction between Villanovan burials in Etruria and Etruscan practice, see Scullard, *op. cit.*, pp. 20, 21, 26, 42, 48–9

46 Nogara, *op. cit.*, pp. 269–71, fig. 147; p. 315, fig. 179; Riis, *op. cit.*, pl. 11, fig. 14

47 *Monumenti Antichi* (Accademia Nazionale dei Lincei), xlii, 1955, cols. 201–1048, pls. 1, 2, 7, 8, 10, 11, 12; M. Pallottino, *La necropoli di Cerveteri* (*Itinerari dei Musei e Monumenti d'Italia*, No. 70), 1939, pp. 9–12 and plan on back of cover; Scullard, *op. cit.*, pls. 21, 24

48 *Monumenti Antichi*, xlii, 1955, figs. 100–3

49 *Ibid.*, figs. 1, 2, 16

50 *Ibid.*, figs. 98, 132

51 *Ibid.*, figs. 210–12b

52 R. Meiggs, *Roman Ostia*, 1960, frontispiece

53 *Monumenti Antichi*, xxxvi, 1937, cols. 13–594, pls. 1–6; P. Romanelli, *Tarquinia: la necropoli e il museo* (*Itinerari dei Musei e Monumenti d'Italia*, No. 75), 1959

54 F. Messerschmidt, *Necropolen von Vulci*, 1930, Beilage 1

55 *Ibid.*, Beilagen 3, 4

56 Banti, *op. cit.*, pl. 5; *Studi Etruschi*, iv, 1930, pp. 58–68, fig. 39

57 *Studi Etruschi*, viii, 1934, pp. 59–75, pl. 25. *Cf.* the vault of the seventh century chamber-tomb, La Montagnola, found at Quinto Fiorentino in 1959: Scullard, *op. cit.*, pl. 85

58 Nogara, *op. cit.*, p. 263, fig. 144; Banti, *op. cit.*, pl. 6 (above)

59 Scullard, *op. cit.*, pl. 54; Nogara, *op. cit.*, p. 261, fig. 143

60 *Ibid.*, p. 305, fig. 170

61 Scullard, *op. cit.*, pl. 64; Banti, *op. cit.*, pl. 8 (above)

62 *Ibid.*, pl. 7

63 *Journal of Roman Studies*, xv, 1925, pp. 1–59, figs. 13, 34, 35, 40; xvii, 1927, pp. 59–96; Scullard, *op. cit.*, pls. 19, 20

64 *Mitteilungen des Deutschen Archäologischen Instituts: Römische Abteilung*, lvii, 1942, pp. 122–235

# CHAPTER II

65 E.g. E. Strong, *Apotheosis and After Life*, 1915; F. Cumont, *Recherches sur le symbolisme funéraire des Romains*, 1942; *Lux Perpetua*, 1949; I. A. Richmond, *Archaeology and the After-Life in Pagan and Christian Imagery*, 1950; J. M. C. Toynbee and J. B. Ward Perkins, *The Shrine of St Peter and the Vatican Excavations*, 1956, pp. 109–17

66 E.g. Cicero, *Tusc.* i, 12, 27: 'itaque unum illud erat insitum priscis illis, quos cascos appellat Ennius, esse in morte sensum neque excessu vitae sic deleri hominem ut funditus interiret'

67 *CIL* xi, 856: 'We are mortals, not immortals'

68 F. Bücheler, *Carmina Latina Epigraphica*, i, 1895, no. 420: 'When life ends, all things perish and turn to nothing'

69 *Ibid.*, ii, 1897, no. 1495: 'We are and were nothing. Look, reader, how swiftly we mortals pass from nothing to nothing'

70 'I was not, I was, I am not, I don't care'

71 G. Kaibel, *Epigrammata graeca e lapidibus collecta*, 1878, no. 646. *Cf.* H. Dessau, *Inscriptiones Latinae Selectae*, 8156

72 46: 'si quis piorum manibus locus, si, ut sapientibus placet, non cum corpore extinguuntur magnae animae'

73 499–500: 'nam me Acheruntem recipere Orcus noluit, quia praemature vita careo'

74 *Capitivi* 998–9: 'vidi ego multa saepe picta, quae Acherunti fierent cruciamenta'

75 Cicero *De leg.* ii, 9, 22: 'deorum manium iura sancta sunto. suos leto datos divos habento; sumptum in ollos luctumque minuunto'

76 *Capt.* 598: 'larvae stimulant virum'; *Cas.* 592: 'amator . . . qui me atque uxorem ludificatust, larva'; *Am.* 777: 'haec quidem edepol lavarum plenast'

77 Cicero, *Pis.* 7, 16: 'coniuratorum manes mortuorum'; Livy, iii, 58, 11: 'manes Verginiae'; Virgil, *Aen.* vi, 743: 'quisque suos patimur manes'

78 *S.S.* iii, 6 = *Rep.* vi, 16: 'ea vita est in caelum et in hunc coetum eorum, qui iam vixerunt et corpore laxati illum incolunt locum, quem vides (erat autem is splendidissimo candore inter flammas circus elucens), quem vos, ut a Graiis accepistis, orbem lacteum nuncupatis'. ('Such a life is the road to heaven, to the company of those whose earthly life is done and who are freed from the body and live in that place which you see (it was the circle that blazed with the most brilliant light among the fires) and which you, borrowing a Greek term, call the Milky Way')

79 *Ibid.* i, 4 = vi, 10: 'Africanus se ostendit ea forma, quae mihi ex imagine

eius quam ex ipso erat notior.' *Cf.* Propertius, iv, 7: 'sunt aliquid manes: letum non omnia finit . . . Cynthia namque meo visa est incumbere fulcro . . . eosdem habuit secum quibus est elata capillis, eosdem oculos'

80 Propertius, iv, 11: see especially the concluding lines 99–102:

> *causa perorata est. flentes me surgite, testes,*
> *dum pretium vitae grata rependit humus.*
> *moribus et caelum patuit: sim digna merendo,*
> *cuius honoratis ossa vehantur avis.*

('The case for my defence is done. Rise up, my witnesses, who weep for me, while kindly Earth requites my life's deserts. Even heaven has unbarred its gates to virtue. May I be found worthy that my bones be borne to join my honoured ancestors')

81 E.g. *CIL* v, 1, 3415: 'nunc labor omnis [abest durus] curaeque molestae'; viii, 1, 2401: 'qui post tantum onus multos crebrosque labores/nunc silet et tacito contentus sede quiescit'; ix, 60: 'hic meas deposui curas omnesque labores'

82 See, for instance, Cumont, *Lux Perpetua*, p. 73, n. 7

83 *Ibid.*, p. 29ff

84 E.g. Toynbee and Ward Perkins, *op. cit.*, pl. 12: stucco relief in the Tomb of the Valerii under St Peter's, Rome

85 *CIL* vi, 4, 29609. 'I am ash, ash is earth, earth is a goddess, therefore I am not dead'

86 *CIL* ix, 3184

87 As is inferred by Richmond, *op. cit.*, pp. 25–8

88 E.g. Cumont, *Lux Perpetua*, pl. 1: Simpelveld sarcophagus at Leiden; Toynbee and Ward Perkins, *op. cit.*, pl. 15: stucco relief in the Tomb of the Valerii under St Peter's, Rome

89 Cumont, *Recherches, etc.* Chapter I

90 *Ibid.*, Chapters II and III

91 E.g. Cumont, *Recherches, etc.*, pl. 12: sarcophagus in the Vatican; pl. 29: sarcophagi at Naples and in the Lateran collection; p. 169, fig. 32: grave relief from Carnuntum; G. Pesce, *Sarcofagi romani di Sardegna*, 1957, figs. 4 and 5: sarcophagus in Cagliari Museum; Toynbee and Ward Perkins, *op. cit.*, pl. 13: stucco relief of Oceanus in the Tomb of the Valerii under St Peter's, Rome; pls. 28 and 29: sarcophagi from under St Peter's, Rome

92 For Dionysiac themes, see, for example, K. Lehmann-Hartleben and E. C. Olsen, *Dionysiac Sarcophagi in Baltimore*, 1942, figs. 1, 7–10, 30, 39, 40, 42, 44; R. Turean, *Les sarcophages romains à représentations dionysiaques*, 1966

93 E.g. Lehmann-Hartleben and Olsen, *op. cit.*, fig. 27

94 E.g. Cumont, *op. cit.*, p. 345, fig. 76: painting from a tomb on the *Via Triumphalis*, near Rome: Mercury conducts a chariot, drawn by doves, in

which Cupid carries the soul of the child Octavia Paulina to paradise, represented as a garden where children, accompanied by a miniature Minerva, as conqueress of death, are gathering crimson roses

95 Examples in sculpture and painting of the other subjects here listed will be found illustrated in the books cited in Note 65. A further interesting example of such symbolic scenes is the sarcophagus in the Museo Nazionale Romano, of Julius Achilleus, who was no farmer, but an official of the *Ludus Magnus* (gladiatorial school) and a civil servant; yet the carving shows an elaborate farm scene that can only be explained as an allusion to the pastoral paradise (*Archäologischer Anzeiger*, 1940, cols. 449–50, figs. 21, 22: third century AD)

96 *De leg.* ii, 22, 56

97 *Hist. Nat.* vii, 187: 'ipsum cremare, apud Romanos non fuit veteris instituti: terra condebantur'

98 E. Nash, *Pictorial Dictionary of Ancient Rome*, ii, 1962, pp. 306–7; H. H. Scullard, *The Etruscan Cities and Rome*, 1967, pl. 105

99 Cicero, *De leg.* ii, 23, 58: 'hominem mortuum in urbe ne sepelito neve urito'

100 iii, 890–3

101 *Loc. cit.*

102 *Loc. cit.*, Note 96

103 J. E. Sandys and S. G. Campbell, *Latin Epigraphy*, 1927, fig. 1 and pp. 65–9

104 *Ann.* xvi, 6

105 J. M. C. Toynbee, *The Hadrianic School*, 1934, p. 161ff

106 A. D. Nock, 'Cremation and Burial in the Roman Empire' (*Harvard Theological Review*, xxv, 1932, p. 321ff)

107 *Ibid.*, p. 333, n. 61. *Cf.* also the Simpelveld sarcophagus at Leiden, in which were found cremated human relics (*Académie des Inscriptions et Belles-Lettres: Comptes rendus*, 1931, p. 351ff). The primary burial in a Roman barrow erected in the early-third century AD at Holborough, Snodland, in Kent consisted of a long, narrow, shallow wooden coffin containing the calcined bones of a man (*Archaeologia Cantiana*, lxviii, 1954, pp. 11, 52, 57)

108 See Note 104. *Cf.* Cicero, *Tusc.* i, 45, 108: 'condiunt Aegyptii mortuos et eos servant domi, Persae etiam cera circumlitos condunt, ut quam maxime permeant diuturna corpora'

109 *Illustrated London News*, 22 February 1964, p. 269; *Rivista di Studi Classici*, xii, 1964, pp. 264–80, figs. 1–5

110 For the embalmment of the body of Priscilla, wife of Domitian's Secretary of State, Abascantus, see Statius, *Silvae* v, i, 228–30: 'nil longior aetas/ carpere, nil aevi poterunt vitiare labores /sic cautum membris, tantas venerabile marmor/spirat opes'

111 L. Dérobert and H. Reichlen, *Les momies: le culte des morts dans le monde sauvage et civilisé*, n.d., p. 129. I owe this reference and the references that follow, to the kindness of Professor John Harris, formerly of the Department of Egyptian Antiquities, Ashmolean Museum, Oxford

112 W. Wessetsky, *Die ägyptische Kulte zur Römeszeit in Ungarn*, 1961, pp. 10f; *Orientalia* xxxxvi, 1967, p. 220, nn. 5, 6; xxxvii, 1968, p. 132, n. 10

113 T. J. Pettigrew, *History of Egyptian Mummies*, 1834, pp. 253–4; Dérobert and Reichlen, *op. cit.*, pl. 55

## CHAPTER III

114 For a very detailed, but obviously out-of-date, account of Roman funerary rites in their widest sense, based mainly on literary and epigraphic evidence, with references that are by no means always correctly given, see C. Daremberg and E. Saglio, *Dictionnaire des antiquités grecques et romaines*, 1896, s.v. *funus*, pp. 1386–1409. Slightly more up-to-date is H. Blümner, *Die römischen Privataltertümer*, 1911, pp. 482–511

115 For such a death-bed scene, see a relief in the Lapidario Maffeiano at Verona (unpublished, apart from a very poor and inaccurate drawing in S. Maffei, *Museum Veronese*, 1749, pl. 7, fig. 4). The dying person lies propped up on a couch. On the couch, at the dying person's feet, a man is seated. At the head of the couch a man is seated on a stool, with a mourning woman seated to the right of him. Another man is seated at the foot of the couch. To the left of him stands a man with legs crossed and to the left again stands a woman(?) holding a basin(?)

116 E.g. Seneca, *Ad Marciam* 3, 2: 'non licuerat matri ultima filii oscula . . . haurire'

117 E.g. Virgil, *Aen.* iv, 684–5: 'et, extremas si quis super halitus errat, ore legam'

118 E.g. Virgil, *Aen.* ix, 486–7: 'nec te, tua funera, mater/produxi pressive oculos.' *Cf.* Pliny, *Nat. Hist.* xi, 150

119 Servius on Virgil, *Aen.* vi, 218: 'Plinius in naturali historia dicit hanc esse causam ut mortui et calida abluantur et per intervalla conclamentur, quod solet plerumque vitalis spiritus exclusus putari et homines fallere. denique refert quemdam superpositum pyrae abhibitis ignibus erectum esse nec potuisse liberari.' *Cf.* Lucan ii, 21–3: 'sic funere primo/ . . . cum corpora nondum/conclamata iacent.' The purpose of this custom may, then, have been to ascertain that death had really taken place. A relic of it survives today at a papal death-bed, when the dead pope is tapped three times on the brow and called three times by his baptismal name.

A relief, probably from the front of a sarcophagus, found in Paris and now in the Musée de Cluny, and a similar relief in the Louvre depict the situation after death has taken place. The Cluny relief (Daremberg and Saglio, *op. cit.*, p. 1386, fig. 3357; E. Espérandieu, *Recueil général des bas-reliefs, statues et bustes de la Gaule romaine*, iv, 1911, p. 241, no. 3170, with photograph) shows a young girl lying dead on a couch with her feet crossed. At the head of the couch her father is seated mourning, his right knee clasped by his hands. At the foot of the couch is seated her mother, mourning, with her head on her hand and a girl standing on either side of her, the girl on the right covering her face with both hands. Behind the couch stand two girls, one stretching out her hand towards the dead girl on the couch. All five women have loose, dishevelled hair. Two young men stand near the head of the couch. On the Louvre relief (S. Reinach, *Répertoire de la statuaire*, i, 1897, p. 48: scene on the right, in the top register) a young boy or girl is lying dead on a couch. The father and mother are seated mourning at the head and foot of the couch respectively. There are five other male mourners standing and four other female mourners standing, three of them behind the couch

120 E.g. Ovid, *Pont.* ii, 2.45: 'iam prope depositus, certe iam frigidus.' According to Blümner (*op. cit.*, p. 482, n. 8) this was done before death took place

121 E.g. Virgil, *Aen.* vi, 219: 'corpusque lavant frigentis et unguunt'

122 E.g. Martial, *Epigr.* ix, 57, 8: 'nec pallens toga mortui tribulis.' Juvenal, iii, 171–2: 'pars magna Italiae est, si verum admittimus, in qua/nemo togam sumit nisi mortuus'

123 E.g. Cicero, *De leg.* ii, 24, 60: 'illa iam significatio est laudis ornamenta ad mortuos pertinere, quod coronam virtute partam et ei, qui peperisset, et eius parenti sine fraude esse lex impositam iubet'

124 E.g. Juvenal, iii, 267: 'nec habet quam porrigat ore trientem.' This is confirmed by numerous discoveries in graves

125 Scriptores Historiae Augustae, *Antoninus Pius* 5, 1: 'sed Hadriano apud Baias mortuo reliquias eius Roman pervexit sancte ac reverente atque in hortis Domitiae collocavit'

126 E.g. Persius, iii, 103–5: 'tandemque beatulus alto/compositus lecto crassisque lutatus amomis/in portam rigidas calces extendit.' Some rich people may have been also embalmed before the lying-in-state and masks may have been placed over their faces

127 O. Benndorf and R. Schöne, *Die antiken Bildwerke des lateranensischen Museums*, 1867, pp. 221–4, no. 348; D. E. Strong, *Roman Imperial Sculpture*, 1961, pl. 66; *Atti della Accademia Nazionale dei Lincei: Memorie* (Classe di Scienze morali, etc.), ser. 8, xiii, 1968, pl. 6, fig. 12 (after p. 482); Anderson photo no. 24116 Roma

128 E.g. Varro, *De ling. lat.* vii, 70: 'praefica dicta, ut Aurelius scribit, mulier de lucro quae conduceretur quae ante domum mortui laudes eius caneret'

129 E.g. Servius on Virgil, *Aen.* vi, 218: 'servabantur cadavera septem diebus.' Members of the lower classes were, however, sometimes burnt or buried

on the day following that of their death: e.g. Cicero, *Pro Cluentio* 9, 27: 'puer . . . ante noctem mortuus et postridie, antequam luceret, combustus est'

130 E.g. Seneca, *De benef.* vi, 38. The name of the *libitinarii* comes from that of the goddess of the dead, Libitina, in whose temple death-registers were kept

131 E.g. Martial, *Epigr.* x, 97, 3

132 E.g. Suetonius, *Domit.* 17: 'cadaver eius populari sandapila per vespillones exportatum', Martial, *Epigr.* ii, 81: 'laxior hexaphoris tua sit lectica licebit:/ cum tamen haec tua sit, Zoile, sandapila est'

133 E.g. Martial, *Epigr.* iii, 93, 26

134 A term found in late Latin inscriptions to denote catacomb diggers: e.g. *CIL* vi, 7543

135 See Note 130

136 Varro, *De ling. lat.* v. 160; vii, 42: 'a praecone . . . in funeribus indictivis'

137 E.g. Cicero, *Pro Cluentio* 71, 201: 'mater exequias illius funeris prosecuta'

138 E.g. Servius on Virgil, *Aen.* vi, 224: 'facem de fune, ut Varro dicit. unde et funus dictum est. per noctem autem urebantur: unde et permansit ut mortuos faces antecedant'

139 Varro, *De ling. lat.* v. 166: 'ubi lectus mortui fertur, dicebant feretrum nostri'

140 Persius iii, 105–6: 'at illum/hesterni capite induto subiere Quirites'

141 E.g. Martial, *Epigr.* viii, 75, 9: 'quattuor inscripti portabant vile cadaver'

142 E. Strong, *Apotheosis and After Life*, 1915, pp. 175–9, pl. 23; F. Cumont, *Recherches sur le symbolisme funéraire des Romains*, 1941, p. 239, pl. 19; Alinari photo no. 26101 Aquila; R. Bianchi Bandinelli, etc. *Sculture municipali dell'area sabellica fra l'età di Cesare e quella di Nerone* (*Studi Miscellanei* 10, 1966), pp. 23–9, pls. 5–10

143 *CIL* ix, 4454, 4458–60, 4465, 4467, 4471. On the other hand, the short and skimpy toga worn by most of the men on the relief suggests a date for it in the middle of the first century BC

144 *Cf.* Suetonius, *Iul.* 84

145 *Cf.* Seneca, *Apoloc.* 12

146 *Ibid.*

147 vi. 53

148 This was the *laudatio* (e.g. Cicero, *Pro Milone* 13, 33) or *contio funebris* (Cicero, *De oratore* ii, 84). For *laudes* chanted in front of the dead person's house by hired *praefices*, see Note 128

149 *Nat. Hist.* xxxv, 6

150 Suetonius, *Vesp.* 19

151 A. N. Zadoks-Josephus Jitta, *Ancestral Portraiture in Rome*, 1932, pls. 4, 5

152 *Ibid.*, pl. 6, a, b

153 ii, 32: AD 16

154 iii, 5: 9 BC
155 iii, 76: AD 22
156 iv, 9: AD 23: 'funus imaginum pompa maxime inlustre fuit'
157 See Chapter II, Note 99
158 Cicero, *De leg.* ii, 23, 58. Gaius Julius Celsus Polemaeanus, founder of the public library of Ephesus, was buried in it in a fine marble sarcophagus: F. Miltner, *Ephesus*, 1958, pp. 55, 56
159 E.g. Trajan, whose ashes were placed in a funerary chamber in the base of his Column near the centre of Rome: Dio Cassius, lxviii, 16; lxix, 2
160 E.g. Sulla: Plutarch, *Sulla* 38; Hirtius and Pansa: Livy, *Epit.* 119; Agrippa: Dio Cassius, liv, 28
161 *De ling lat.* v. 25
162 E.g. the Treviran landowners of modern Belgium: see Chapter VII (B)
163 Cicero, *De leg.*, ii, 22, 55
164 E.g. *Eburacum* (Royal Commission on Historical Monuments: England), 1962, pl. 27 (below)
165 *Ibid.*, p. 79
166 *Ibid.*, pp. 67, 68, 79–85, 100, 106. A notable instance is that of the body of a woman with a child between her legs: *ibid.* p. 108, pl. 33. (See p. 320)
167 E.g. York: *Eburacum*, p. 107; Chichester, Sussex, St Pancras Roman cemetery: unpublished information from Mr Alec Down
168 *Illustrated London News*, 21 September 1968, p. 27. For instances of coins found in cinerary urns, see G. Calza, *La necropoli del Porto di Roma nell'Isola Sacra*, 1940, p. 53 and pp. 119, 124 below
169 Julius Paulus, in Festus, p. 32: 'bustum proprie dicitur locus in quo mortuus est combustus et sepultus . . . ubi vero combustus est tantummodo, alibi vero est sepultus, is locus ab urendo ustrina vocatur'
170 Martial, *Epigr.* viii, 44, 14; x, 97, 1
171 Pliny, *Nat. Hist.* xi, 150: '(oculos) in rogo patefacere'
172 Pliny, *Epist.* iv, 2: 'habebat puer mannulos multos et iunctes et solutos, habebat canes maiores minoresque, habebat luscinias, psittacos, merulas: omnes Regulus circa rogum trucidavit'
173 E.g. Statius, *Silv.* ii, 6, 90–1: 'tibi Setia canos/restinxit cineres'
174 E.g. Virgil, *Aen.* vi, 228: 'ossaque lecta cado texit Corynaeus aeno'
175 A Flavian cremation burial, found in 1966 on the site of the Central Criminal Court Extension in London, consisted of burnt human bones placed within a globular amphora, which lay on its side at the bottom of a shallow pit. The neck of the amphora had been broken off prior to burial and its entrance closed by a brick tile set on edge, against which three pottery lids had been placed: *Transactions of the London and Middlesex Archaeological Society*, xx, part 2, 1969, pp. 4–6, fig. 3
176 Cicero, *De leg.* ii, 22, 57: 'nec tamen eorum ante sepulchrum est quam iusta facta et porcus caesus est.' For the view that the formula *sub ascia* (or *ab ascia*

or *ad asciam*) *dedicare*, particularly widespread in the funerary inscriptions of Gaul, denotes, through the symbol of this workman's tool, the solemn act of laying the foundation of a legally established tomb-structure, see J. J. Hatt, *La tombe gallo-romaine*, 1951, pp. 85–107. For further discussion of the formula, see F. de Visscher, *Le droit des tombeaux romains*, 1963, pp. 277–94

177 Festus, p. 3: 'funus prosecuti redeuntes ignem supergradiebantur aqua aspersi: quod purgationis genus vocabant suffitionem'

178 Cicero, *De leg.* ii, 22, 55: 'nec vero tam denicales, quae a nece appellatae sunt, quia residentur mortuis, quam ceterorum caelestium quieti dies feriae nominarentur'

179 For references, see Pauly–Wissowa, *Realencyclopädie* s.v. *silicernium*

180 Tacitus, *Ann.* vi, 5; Petronius, *Satyricon* 65. For the periods of mourning beyond these nine days, to be observed by men and women for various categories of dead persons, see Blümner, *op. cit.*, pp. 310–11

181 E.g. Tibullus, i, 5, 53: 'ipsa fame stimulante furens herbasque sepulcris/ quaerit et a saevis ossa relicta lupis'

182 Cicero, *De leg.* ii, 22, 55: 'quod genus sacrificii Lari vervecibus fiat'

183 J. M. C. Toynbee and J. B. Ward Perkins, *The Shrine of St Peter and the Vatican Excavations*, 1956, p. 61, n. 30

184 *Ibid.*, pp. 118–19, n. 2, xviii

185 *Ibid.*, pp. 145–6 and fig. 13

186 *Notizie degli Scavi di Antichità*, 1913, pp. 272–3, fig. 15; *Antiquaries Journal*, ix, 1929, pp. 4–6, fig. 5

187 *Notizie degli Scavi di Antichità*, 1921, pp. 191–5, fig. 8; *Antiquaries Journal*, ix, 1929, p. 4 and pl. 1, fig. 2. For examples of this practice in the cemeteries of Pompeii, see H. Mau–F. W. Kelsey, *Pompeii, its Life and Art*, 1899, pp. 417, 421–2, 427

188 *Antiquaries Journal*, ix, 1929, pp. 4, 5, fig. 4

189 *Ibid.*, pp. 1–3, fig. 3 and pl. 1, fig. 1. For further examples, see R. Cagnat and U. Chapot, *Manuel d'archéologie romaine*, i, 1916, pp. 340–1; *Festschrift August Oxé*, 1938, pp. 197–204

190 W. Whiting, W. Hawley, and T. May, *Report on the Excavation of the Roman Cemetery at Ospringe, Kent*, 1931, pl. 56

191 *Journal of Roman Studies*, xlix, 1959, pp. 132–3, figs. 24, 25, pl. 18, figs. 1–3

192 J. M. C. Toynbee, *Art in Britain under the Romans*, 1964, pp. 419–20, pl. 96

193 *Antiquaries Journal*, xxviii, 1948, pp. 173–4, pl. 25, a

194 Toynbee, *op. cit.*, p. 81; Whiting, etc., *op. cit.*, pl. 55; *Bonner Jahrbücher*, cxvi, 1907, p. 155, no. 81, pl. 3, fig. 8 (wrongly described as Mars)

195 Toynbee and Ward Perkins, *op. cit.*, p. 84 and pl. 15

196 Virgil, *Aen.* vi, 505–6: 'tunc egomet tumulum Rhoeteo litore inanem/ constitui et magna manes ter voce vocavi'

197 *Germania Romana*, ed. 2, iii, 1926, p. 28, pl. 1, fig. 3; H. Dessau, *Inscriptiones Latinae Selectae*, 2244. The inscription reads: M(arco) Caelio

T(iti) f(ilio) (tribu) Lem(onia) (domo) Bon(onia) o(ptioni) [a mistake for 'centurioni'?] leg(ionis) XIIX ann(orum) LIII s(emissis) [ce]cidit bello Variano ossa [i]nferre licebit P(ublius) Caelius T(iti) f(ilius) (tribu) Lem (onia) frater fecit.' Under the left-hand bust is 'M(arcus) Caelius M(arci) l(ibertus)'; under the right-hand bust is 'M(arcus) Caelius M(arci) l(ibertus) Thiaminus.' For the view that this need not be a cenotaph, see *Answahlkatalog des Rheinisches Landesmuseums*, Bonn, 1963, p. 34

198 Suetonius, *Claud.* 1: 'exercitus honorarium ei tumulum excitavit'; Dio Cassius, lv, 2: τιμὰς ... κενοταφίου τε πρὸς αὐτῷ τῷ 'Ρήνῳ λαβών. For the possibility that the τρόπαια of St Peter and St Paul, on the Vatican Hill and *Via Ostiensis* respectively, marked cenotaphs or memorial shrines, not graves, see Toynbee and Ward Perkins, *op. cit.* pp. 128–9, 154–8

199 E.g. Cicero, *De leg.*, ii, 23, 59; 24, 60; Ovid, *Fasti* vi, 663–4: 'adde quod aedilis, pompam qui funeris irent,/artifices solos iusserat esse decem'

200 See Daremberg and Saglio, *loc. cit.*, p. 1402, for references to the legal texts

201 See *ibid.*, p. 1404, for references to the legal texts.

202 J. P. Waltzing, *Étude historique sur les corporations professionelles chez les Romains*, 1895–1900; C. Kornemann, s.v. *collegium* in Pauly-Wissowa, *op. cit.*; Dessau, *op. cit.*, ii, 2, ch. 15; iii, 2, pp. 710–25

203 E.g. Dessau, *op. cit.*, 7212: AD 136: 'quib[us coire co]nvenire collegiumq(ue) habere liceat. qui stipem menstruam conferre volen[t in fun]era in it collegium coeant neq(ue) sub specie eius collegi nisi semel in mense c[oeant co]nferendi causa unde defuncti sepeliantur'. For burial clubs in Gaul, mainly in the south, see Hatt, *op. cit.*, pp. 77–83

204 Dessau, *op. cit.*, 7212

205 E.g. *CIL* vi, 5961, 9320, 10415

206 E.g. *CIL* vi, 4421, 5818, 21415

207 E.g. Livy, xxvii, 2, 9: 'congestos in unum locum (Romani) cremavere suos'

208 E.g. those who fell in the *clades Variana* in the Teutoberger Forest: Tacitus, *Ann.* i, 62; Suetonius, *Gaius* 3. *Cf.* Note 197

209 Vegetius, *Epitome rei militaris* ii, 20: 'addebatur etiam saccus undecimus, in quem tota legio particulam aliquam conferabat, sepulturae scilicet causa, ut si quis ex contubernalibus defecisset, de illo undecimo sacco as sepulturam ipsius promeretur expensa'

210 E.g. Livy, xxv, 17, 5; Tacitus, *Ann.* ii, 7

211 E.g. Cicero, *Philip.* ix, 7

212 Cicero, *De leg.* ii, 24, 62: 'honoratorum virorum laudes in contione memorentur easque etiam cantus ad tibicinem prosequatur, cui nomen neniae'

213 E.g. the Numidian prince Syphax: Livy, xxx, 45, 4: 'conspecta tamen mors eius fuit quia publico funere elatus est'

214 Appian, *De bell. civ.* i, 105–6

215 E.g. *CIL* viii, 15880: Licinius Paternus of Sicca in Numidia

216 E.g. *CIL* x, 1784: Gavia Marciana of Puteoli

217 E.g. *CIL* xiv, 413: Lucius Cacius Reburrus of Ostia: 'L(ucius) Kacius Reburrus h(onore) u(sus) funeris [publici] impensam remisit'

218 Livy, *Epit.* 16: 'Decimus Iunius Brutus munus gladiatorium in honorem defuncti patris primus edidit'; Valerius Maximus, ii, 4, 7: 'nam gladiatorium munus primum Romae datum est in foro boario App. Claudio Q. Fulvio consulibus. dederunt Marcus et Decimus filii Bruti [Perae] funebri memoria patris cineres honorando'

219 Livy, xxiii, 30, 15: 'et Marco Aemilio Lepido, qui bis consul augurque fuerat, filii tres, Lucius, Marcus, Quintus, ludos funebres per triduum et gladiatorum paria duo et viginti in foro dederunt'

220 Livy, xxxi, 50, 4: 'et ludi funebres eo anno per quadriduum in foro mortis causa Marci Valerii Laevini a Publio et Marco filiis eius facti et munus gladiatorium datum ab iis; paria quinque et viginti pugnarunt'

221 Livy, xxxix, 46, 2: 'Publii Licinii funeris causa visceratio data et gladiatores centum viginti pugnaverunt et ludi funebres per triduum facti'

222 Livy, xli, 28, 11: 'munus gladiatorum eo anno aliquot parva alia data; unum ante cetera insigne fuit T. Flaminini quod mortis causa patris sui cum visceratione epuloque et ludis scaenicis quadriduum dedit. magni tamen muneris ea summa fuit, ut per triduum quattuor et septuaginta homines pugnarint'

223 Dio Cassius, xlviii, 33: *Σφαῖρον ὁ Καῖσαρ παιδαγωγόν τε καὶ ἐξελεύθερον αὐτοῦ γενόμενον δημοσίᾳ ἔθαψε*

224 Tacitus, *Ann.* vi, 11: 'publico funere ex decreto senatus celebratus est'

225 *Ibid.*, iv, 15: 'ita quamquam novo homini censorium funus, effigiem apud forum Augusti publica pecunia patres decrevere.' *Cf.* iii, 48 (AD 21): 'ut mors Sulpicii Quirini publicis exequiis frequenturetur petivit (*sc.* Tiberius) a senatu'

226 *Ibid.*, vi, 27: 'mors Aelii Lamiae funere censorio celebrata'

227 Tacitus, *Hist.* iv, 47: 'funusque censorium Flavio Sabino ductum.' It seems probable that Virginius Rufus, who died under Nerva in AD 97, was accorded a public funeral: Pliny, *Epist.* ii, 1: 'huius viri exequiae magnum ornamentum principi . . . laudatus est a consule Cornelio Tacito'

228 Tacitus, *Ann.* xiii, 2: 'decreti et a senatu . . . Claudio censorium funus et mox consecratio'

229 Scriptores Historiae Augustae, *Severus* 7: 'funus deinde censorium Pertinacis imagini duxit'

230 Tacitus, *Ann.* iii, 5; Suetonius, *Tib.* 7; Dio Cassius, lv, 52

231 Tacitus, *Ann.* iii, 4, 5, From *Ann.* ii, 82 we learn that a *iustitium* (closure of the lawcourts) was decreed when the news of Germanicus' death reached Rome. *Cf.* Suetonius, *Gaius* 5

232 Tacitus, *Ann.* iv, 9

233 Scriptores Historiae Augustae, *Verus* 6.

234 Dio Cassius, xlvii, 17: *τῆς Ἀττίας τῆς τοῦ Καίσαρος μητρὸς . . . δημοσίᾳ ταφῇ τιμηθείσης*

235 *Ibid.*, lviii, 2: *οὐ μὴν οὐδὲ ἐς τιμὴν ἄλλο τι αὐτῇ πλήν δημοσίας ἐκφορᾶς*

236 Tacitus, *Ann.* xvi, 6: 'ductae tamen publicae exequiae'

237 Dio Cassius, lviii, 28; lix, 3; Suetonius, *Tib.* 75: 'corpus . . . Roman per milites deportatum est crematumque publico funere'

238 Dio Cassius, lxi, 35: *ἔτυχε δὲ καὶ τῆς ταφῆς καὶ τῶν ἄλλων ὅσων ὁ Αὔγουστος*; Tacitus, *Ann.* xii, 69: 'funeris solemne perinde ac divo Augusto celebratur;' xiii, 3; Suetonius, *Claud.* 45: 'funeratus est solemni principum pompa'

239 *Vesp.* 19

240 Scriptores Historiae Augustae, *Marcus Antoninus Philosophus*, 7: 'Hadriani autem sepulcro corpus patris intulerunt magnifico exequiarum officio, mox iustitio secuto publice quoque funeris expeditus est ordo. et laudavere uterque pro rostris patrem'

241 Appian, *De bell. civ.* ii, 147; Suetonius, *Iul.* 84; Dio Cassius, xliv, 35–51

242 Tacitus, *Ann.* i, 8, 16, 50; Suetonius, *Aug.* 100; Dio Cassius, lvi, 31, 34

243 Scriptores Historiae Augustae, *Severus*, 24; Herodian, iv, 2

244 H. Mattingly, *Coins of the Roman Empire in the British Museum*, iii, 1936, pp. clii, clxxxvi, 364, n.*, 549, n.*, pl. 101, 9. Aelius Verus was never actually consecrated

245 *Ibid.*, iv, 1940, p. 231, no. 1429, pl. 34, 10: Æ

246 *Ibid.*, pp. 393–4, nos. 55, 56, 58, 61, pl. 54, 12–15: AV, AR; p. 525, no. 872, pl. 71, 8: Æ; p. 528, no. 892, pl. 72, 10: Æ

247 *Ibid.*, p. 612, no. 1360, pl. 81, 7; Æ

248 *Ibid.*, p. 487, no. 699, pl. 67, 12: Æ; p. 488, no. 703, pl. 67, 14: Æ

249 *Ibid.*, p. 693, nos. 26, 27, pl. 91, 14, 15: AV, Æ;p. 764, nos. 399, 400, pl. 101, 10, 11: Æ

250 *Ibid.*, v, 1950, p. 120, no. 480, pl. 20, 9

251 *Ibid.*, p. 424, nos. 26, 27, pl. 65, 17, 18: AV, AR; p. 428, no. 50, pl. 66, 7: Æ

252 *Ibid.*, vi, 1962, p. 136, no. 218, pl. 8: Æ

253 E.g. Dessau, *op. cit.*, 7213, 7258, 8369, 8370, 8371, 8372, 8373, 8374; *CIL* iii, 703, 754; v, 2072; xii, 4015

254 *CIL* xiii, 5708. (See p. 320)

255 E.g. *CIL* v, 2090, 2176, 2315, 4015, 4017, 4448: in the last inscription a husband is recorded as giving a sum of money to the *collegium fabrorum* on behalf of his deceased wife and son 'ut ex usuris quodannis profusion(em) faciant et rosas ponant'

256 *Epit.* xxxi: 'sparge mero cineres bene olentis et unguine nardi,/hospes, et adde rosis balsama puniceis./perpetuum mihi ver agit inlacrimabilis urna/et commutavi saecula, non obii'

257 Toynbee and Ward Perkins, *op. cit.*, pp. 76–80
258 Pauly-Wissowa, *op. cit.*, s.v. *Rosalia*
259 E.g. Dessau, *op. cit.*, 8366: 'et praeterea omnib(us) k(alendis) nonis idibus suis quib(us) mensib(us) lucerna lucens sibi ponatur incenso inposito'
260 See Note 253
261 *Fasti* ii, 533–570
262 *De ling. lat.* vi, 13: 'feralia ab inferis et ferendo, quod ferunt tum epulas ad sepulcrum quibus ius est parentare'
263 Ovid, *Fasti* v, 419–493. Ovid's assertion that the object of this ritual was the *Manes Paterni* must be wrong

## CHAPTER IV

264 There is an excellent sectional map of the Via Appia Antica, with the tombs marked in, in the Touring Club Italiano volume *Roma e Dintorni*
265 R. C. Carrington, *Pompeii*, 1936, pp. 162–3; A Maiuri, *Pompeii* (Guide-Books to the Museums and Monuments of Italy, No. 3), 1956, pp. 87–90, fig. 14
266 J. J. Wilkes, *Dalmatia*, 1969, p. 359, fig. 15, pp. 412–13
267 *Sat.* i, 8, 12–13: 'This pillar marked an area of 1000 feet in frontage, 300 feet in depth: the tomb was not to pass to his heir'
268 Petronius, *Satyricon* 71
269 Isola Sacra: H. Thylander, *Inscriptions du Port d'Ostie*, 1952, no. A 19 (time of Hadrian): 'D(is) M(anibus) M(arcus) Antonius Vitalis et M(arcus) Antonius M(arci) filius Verus fecerunt sib(i) et suis libertis libertabusque posterisqu⟨a⟩e eorum quodsi quis in hoc munimentum (=monumentum) vel intra maceriam quam (=aliquam) eius post excessum M(arci) Antoni Vitalis vendere vel donare aliove genere abalienare volet aut corpus ossave alienigeri nominis quam titulo s(upra) s(cripto) continetur intulerit tunc poenae no[min]e in singula corpora cultoribus Larum Portus [Aug(u)]sti HS III M N h(oc) m(onumentum) h(eredem) e(xterum) [n(on)] s(equetur)'
270 Ostia: *CIL* xiv, 850: 'L(ucius) Cocceius Adiutor fecit sibi idem denuntiat ne quis velit in parte sinisteriore intrantibus neque commurere (=comburere) neq(ue) obruere cadaver sin autem dabit reip(ublicae) Ostiensium HS L M N delator quartas accipiet'
271 H. Dessau, *Inscriptiones Latinae Selectae*, 7602
272 *Ibid.*, 8174
273 *Cf.* Thylander, *op. cit.*, no. A245 (end of third century): 'D(is) M(anibus) Terentius Lucifer et Terenteae Kallotyceni et filis suis fecit siquit in (a)eo

sarcofago inferet corpus sibe (=sive) ossa inferet aerario Saturni S XXX M N' (=30,000 sesterces)

274 E.g. London: R. Merrifield, *The Roman City of London*, 1965, p. 112; Chester: R. P. Wright and I. A. Richmond, *The Roman Inscribed and Sculptured Stones in the Grosvenor Museum, Chester*, 1955, pp. 4–5; Neumagen, on the Mosel: W. von Massow, *Die Grabmäler von Neumagen*, 1932; Buzenol-Montauban: M. E. Marien, *Les monuments funéraires de Buzenol*, 1948; *Fasti Archaeologici*, xiii, 1960, nos. 4967–70, 5159, figs. 91, 93–4; xiv, 1962, nos. 5104, 5187: these tombstones would appear to have been filched from family tombs put up on lands privately owned by the local country gentry

275 R. Meiggs, *Roman Ostia*, 1960, p. 143

276 Dessau, *op. cit.*, 8184: 'Dis Man(ibus) C(aius) Tullius Hesper aram fecit sibi ubi ossa sua coiciantur qua(e) si quis violaverit aut inde exemerit opto ei ut cum dolore corporis longo tempore vivat et cum mortuus fuerit inferi eum non recipiant'. For *violatio sepulchri* in general and the legal aspects of tomb-ownership, see F. de Visscher, *Le droit des tombeaux romains*, 1963; J. A. Crook, *Law and Life of Rome*, 1967, pp. 133–8. For the Nazareth *Diatagma* in particular, see de Visscher, *op. cit.*, pp. 161–95; *Journal of Roman Studies*, xxii, 1932, pp. 184–97; A. Momigliano, *Claudius* ed. 2, 1961, pp. 100–1, 133–4

277 G. Calza, *La necropoli del Porto di Roma nell' Isola Sacra*, 1940, pp. 359–61

278 Thylander, *op. cit.*, no. A 124: 'D(is) M(anibus) C(aius) Galgestius Helius loco puro empto a Valeria Trophime fecit sibi et suis aediculam iunctam parieti intrantibus parte dextra in qua sunt ollae n(umero) XIIII praeter eam ollam quam donavit Trophime Galgestio Vitali ex quib(us) ol(lis) I Pompon(io) Chrysopoli d(onum) d(ed)i(t)'

279 *Ibid.*, no. A 251: 'Dis Manibus Trophimus Caes(aris) n(ostri) ser(vus) et Claudia Tyche sibi et Claudiae Saturninae filiae pientissimae quae vixit ann(is) XV mensibus VI dieb(us) XIII et libertis libertabus posterisque eorum comparato loco a Valeria Trophime p(ro) p(arte) IIII huius monumenti'

280 *Ibid.*, no. A 96: 'D(is) M(anibus) Euhodus Caes(aris) n(ostri) ser(vus) et Vennonia Apphis loco empto a Valeria Trophime fecerunt sibi et libertis libertabusque posterisque eorum'

281 *CIL* xiv Suppl. 4761: 'M(anius) Acilius M(anii) f(ilius) Vot(uria) (tribu) Marianus sibi et Ausciae M(anii) l(ibertae) Eucheni contub(e)rnali suae libertis libertabus suis posterisque eorum omnibus in fr(onte) p(edes) XXVIII hoc monumentum commu(ne) est cum Cognita Optata.' 'Cognit [a] Optat[a] sibi et s[uis] libertis libe[rtabus] posteri[sque] eorum om[nibus] in ag(ro) p(edes) . . . hoc monumen[tum commune] est cum M(anio) Acili[o Mariano]'

282 *Ibid.*, 5176=Thylander, *op. cit.*, no. A 253: 'M(arcus) Ulpius Artemidorus

fecit M(arco) Ulpio Hilaro patri et Atriae Fortunatae co(n)iugi libertis libertabusq(ue) posterisq(ue) eorum. Atria Fortunata P(ublio) Afranio Callisto co(n)iugi concessit ex portione sua parte dimidia libertis libertabusq(ue) eius.' 'L(ucius) Domitius Callistion et Domitia Eutychia p(ro) p(arte) dimidia recepti in soc(c)ietate(m) ab Ulpio Artemidoro fecerunt sibi et Domitis Callisto Plotinae Baeticae filis et libertis libertabusq(ue) posterisq(ue) eorum'

283 Calza, *op. cit.*, pp. 330–4 and pl. 3

284 Thylander, *op. cit.*, no. A 83: 'D(is) M(anibus) M(arcus) Cocceius Daphnus fecit sibi et suis et libertis libertabusque posterisque eorum et M(arco) Antonio Agathiae et suis et libertis libertabusque posterisque eorum et M(arco) Ulpio Domito et suis et libertis libertabusque posterisque eorum per fronte pedes XL in agro pedes XL'

285 *Ibid.*, no. A 16: 'D(is) M(anibus) M(arcus) Antonius Agathias aediculam puram ex sepulchro M(arci) Coccei Daphni cuius heres est facta divisione inter se et coheredes suos adiecto de suo pariete medio et ostio libero facto fecit sibi et libertis libertabusque posterisque eorum'

286 J. M. C. Toynbee and J. B. Ward Perkins, *The Shrine of St Peter and the Vatican Excavations*, 1956, pp. 118–19, n. 2, xvi: 'D(is) M(anibus) M(arcus) Aebutius Charito fecit sibi et libertis libertabusque suis posterisque eorum D(is) M(anibus) C(ai) Clodi Romani q(ui) vix(it) a(nnis) XIX m(ense) I d(iebus) XXI L(ucius) Volusius Sucessus et Volusia Megiste filio dulcissimo emerunt in parte dimidia et sibi posterisq(ue) suis lib(ertis) lib(ertabus)q(ue) p(osterisque) eorum h(uic) m(onumento) d(olus) m(alus) a(besto)'

287 *CIL* xiv, 1051: 'Flavia Marcellina conditivom f(ecit) Flaviae Hilaritati sorori b(ene) m(erenti) concesso loco intrantibus in parte dexteriore a Plotio Hermete et Valeria Saturnina'

288 *Ibid.*, 705: 'L(ucio) Kacio Volusiano qui vixit annis XVIIII mens(e) I dieb(us) XXVI Primitivianus et Volusia parentes fecerunt loco concesso a Gabinio Adiecto amico optimo'

289 Toynbee and Ward Perkins, *op. cit.*, pp. 118–19, n. 2, i: 'D(is) M(anibus) Tullia ⟨e⟩ Secunda filia ⟨e⟩ hic sita est Passullenae Secundinae mater; cessit'

290 *Ibid.*, n. 2, xiv: 'D(is M(anibus) Tito Pompeio T(iti) f(ilio) Successo iun(iori) qui vixit annis decemnovem me(n)sibus duobus die uno filio carissimo dulcissimo T(itus) Pompeius Succ(essus) pater cui locum obt(ulerunt) Valerii Philumenus et Galatia amico benemerenti'

291 G. Brusin, *Nuovi monumenti sepolcrali di Aquileia*, 1941

292 S. Aurigemma, 'Il monumento dei Concordii presso Boretto' (*Rivista del R. Istituto d'Archeologia e Storia dell' Arte*, iii, 1931–2, pp. 268–98, pls. 1–3)

293 E. Strong, *La scultura romana*, i, 1923, p. 130, fig. 83; *Atti della Accademia Nazionale dei Lincei: Memorie* (Classe di Scienze morali, etc.), ser. 8, xiii, 1968, pls. 8, 9. (after p. 482). The men operating a huge wheel and ropes

with pulleys would appear to be erecting an obelisk in front of the mausoleum; Anderson photo no. 1875b Roma

294 Calza, *op. cit.*; for the name Isola Sacra, see pp. 18–21; for the general topography and plan of the excavated portion, see pls. 2, 3

295 From the immense literature that has gathered round these excavations three items dealing with the cemetery as a whole may be cited here: B. M. Apollonj-Ghetti, A. Ferrua, S.J., E. Josi, E. Kirschbaum, S.J., *Esplorazioni sotto la confessione di San Pietro in Vaticano eseguite negli anni 1940–1949*, 1951; Toynbee and Ward Perkins, *op. cit.*, 1956; E. Kirschbaum, S.J., *The Tombs of St. Peter and St Paul*, 1959

296 F. Castignoli, 'Il circo di Nerone in Vaticano' (*Pontificia Accademia Romana di archeologia: Rendiconti*, ser. 3, xxxii, 1960, pp. 97–122)

297 R. F. Jessup, 'Walled Cemeteries in Roman Britain' (*Journal of the British Archaeological Association*, ser. 3, xxii, 1959, pp. 11–32)

298 *Ibid.*, pp. 22–3, pl. 6, fig. 1; *St Albans and Hertfordshire Architectural and Archaeological Society Transactions*, n.s., v, 1938, pp. 108–14

299 Jessup, *op. cit.*, pp. 29–30, fig. 2.

300 *Ibid.*, op. cit., pp. 15–16, pl. 2, fig. 2

301 *Archaeologia Aeliana*, ser. 4, xxxix, 1961, pp. 37–61

302 Jessup, *op. cit.*, pp. 14–15, 26–7, fig. 1

303 *Ibid.*, pp. 21–22; *Archaeological Journal*, ci, 1944 (1946), pp. 68–90

304 Jessup, *op. cit.*, pp. 31–2, fig. 3

305 Petronius, *Satyricon* 71: 'omne genus enim poma volo sint circa cineres meos et vinearum largiter.' It is possible that a funerary garden is alluded to in Martial, *Epigr.* i, 114: 'hos tibi vicinos, Faustine, Telesphorus hortos/ Faenius et breve rus udaque prata tenet./condidit hic natae cineres'

306 P. Grimal, *Les jardins romains*, 1943, *passim*

307 *Cf.* Servius on Virgil, *Aen.* v, 760: 'nemora aptabant sepulcris ut in amoenitate animae forent post vitam' (the last seven words are not in all MSS)

308 xvii, 1, 10

309 *Berliner griechische Urkunden*, iv, 1912, 1120

310 *Journal of Roman Studies*, xlviii, 1958, pp. 117–29; lii, 1962, pp. 156–9; P. Stein, 'Some Reflections on *jus sepulchri*' (*Studi in onore di Biondo Biondi*, ii, 1965, pp. 113–22). See also de Visscher, *op. cit.* (Note 276), pp. 197–224

311 J. R. S. Sterrett, 'The Wolfe Expedition to Asia Minor' (*Papers of the American School of Classical Studies at Athens*, iii, 1888, p. 424, no. 621)

312 *Bullettino della Commissione Archeologica Comunale di Roma*, lxi, 1933 pp. 211–15

313 *CIL* vi, 10675 (Rome)

314 *Ibid.*, 13040

315 *Ibid.*, 13244/5

316 *Ibid.*, 21020

317 *Ibid.*, 29135. *Cf.* also 2469, 3554, 19039, 25250

318 *CIL* x, 2066 (Puteoli)

319 *CIL* vi, 2259 (Rome)

320 E.g. *CIL* iii, 2397 (Salonae); vi, 15593 (Rome), 15640, 17992, 29961; ix. 1938 (Beneventum); xiii, 1072: 'hortus maior' (Saintes). Also at Salonae, on the north side of the road running from the west city gate, is a walled cemetery area enclosed by a massive masonry wall and containing blocks about 4 metres long, within each of which family burial plots are defined by dividing walls (Wilkes, *op. cit.* pp. 360–1, fig. 16): a tomb inscription (*CIL* iii, 2207) suggets that the whole of this area bore the name of 'hortus Metrodori'

321 E.g. *CIL* ii, 3960 (Hispania Tarraconensis); v, 2176 (Altinum, Cisalpine Gaul), 7454 (Vardagate, Cisalpine Gaul); xiv, 396: 'siccanum totum hortorum' (Ostia)

322 E.g. *CIL* vi, 1600 (Rome), 9681, 10876, 22518: 'hortulus religiosus', 26942, 29322, 29964; xiv, 2139 (Ostia)

323 E.g. *CIL* vi, 26942: 'hortulu(m) maceria clus(um)' (Rome); 10876: 'hortulum maceria cintum'; 15640: 'monumentum . . . maceria clusum cum horto'; 22518: 'hic locus cum hortulo suo religioso et aedificiolis suis muro cinctus'; 29322: 'maceria sacrata cum hortulo suo'; 29961: 'locus maceria clusus sive is hortus est'; 29964: 'hortulum maceria cinctum'; xiv, 2139: 'hortulus sive pomarium quod est maceria cinctum.' *Cf. Papers of the British School at Rome*, xxxiv, 1966, pp. 58–60, n. 4

324 E.g. *CIL* ix, 1938 (Beneventum)

325 E.g. *CIL* vi, 1600 (Rome), 9681, 29964. *Cf. PBSR* xxxiv, 1966, pp. 58–90, no. 4: 'tabernas cum pergulis' (=vine-arbours?)

326 E.g. *CIL* vi, 15593 (Rome)

327 E.g. *CIL*, vi, 10876: 'dieta membrorum V' (Rome). *Cf. PBSR*, xxxiv, 1966, pp. 58–60, n. 4

328 E.g. *CIL* xi, 3895 (Capena)

329 E.g. *ibid.*

330 E.g. *CIL* vi, 15640 (Rome)

331 E.g. *CIL* vi, 29959 (Rome); xi, 3895 (Capena)

332 E.g. *CIL* vi, 26942 (Rome); xi, 3895 (Capena)

333 E.g. *CIL* iii, 2279 (Salonae); xi, 3895 (Capena); xiv, 396 (Ostia)

334 E.g. *CIL* xi, 3895 (Capena)

335 E.g. *CIL* vi, 15593 (Rome), 29959. *Cf.* a Boeotian inscription of the second century AD: Γάλλατις Πυθίωνος ἑ[α]υτῷ καὶ τῇ γυναικὶ καὶ τοῖς τέκνοι[ς μ]ου . . . σὺν τῷ φρέ[ατι] καὶ κήπῳ: *IG* vii, 3453

336 E.g. *CIL* xiii, 5708 (Andematunnum=civitas Lingonum=Langres: cf. pp. 62, 63)

337 E.g. *CIL* vi, 29964 (Rome)

338 *CIL* vi, 15526 (Rome). *Cf. PBSR*, xxxiv, 1966, pp. 58–60, no. 4

339 E.g. *CIL* x, 3594 (Puteoli); xiii, 5708 (Langres: the testator directs, in 'this lengthy will', 'that the *pomaria* should be tended by three gardeners (*tres topiarii*) and their apprentices (*discentes eorum*)); xiv, 2139 (Ostia)

340 *CIL* vi, 10237: 'vitium pomorumq(ue) et florum viridumque omnium generum seminibus ea loca . . . adornaverunt' (Rome)

341 *CIL* xii, 3637: 'mausoleum excoluit et ut esset fru[giferum feci]t positis arboribus vitibus rosariis' (Nîmes)

342 *CIL* xiii, 2494: 'aediclam cum vinea et muris' (Géligneux, Ain)

343 *CIL* xiii, 2465: '[ad Pa]rentalia celebranda vineae arepenn . . .' (Briord, Ain)

344 *CIL* v, 2176: 'hortos cum aedificio huic sepult[ur]a[e] iunctos vivos donabit ut ex reditu eor(um) largius rosae et esc(a)e patrono suo et quandoque sibi ponerentur' (Altinum, Cisalpine Gaul). In this case *aedificium* clearly refers, not to the actual tomb, but to some subsidiary building: *cf. aedificiola* in *CIL* vi, 22518 (Note 322)

345 *CIL* v, 7454: 'ex horum hortorum reditu natale meo per (=fer(ant)?) rosam in perpetuo hos hortos neque dividi volo neq(ue) abalienari' (Vardagate, Cisalpine Gaul). Cf. the Mousa inscription (p. 96)

346 *CIL* xii, 1657: 'D(is) M(anibus) liberorum ac coniugibus Publici Calisti et ipsius consecratu[m] cum bese vineae arep(ennis) ex cuius reditu omni[bus] annis prolibari volo ne minus XV v(ini) se(xtariis)' (Die)

347 C, Huelsen, 'Piante iconografiche incise in marmo' (*Mitteilungen des Deutschen Archäologischen Instituts: Römische Abteilung*, v, 1890, pp. 46–63)

348 *Ibid.*, pl. 3: the inscription reads: 'Claudia Octaviae divi Claudi f(iliae) lib(erta) Peloris et Ti(berius) Claudius Aug(usti) lib(ertus) Eutychus proc(urator) Augustor(um) sororibus et lib(ertis) libertabusq(ue) posterisq(ue) eorum'; Grimal, *op. cit.*, p. 80, fig. 2 (part only)

349 Huelsen, *op. cit.*, p. 53, fig. 4; p. 56, fig. 5; Grimal, *op. cit.*, p. 341, fig. 28

350 R. P. Wright and I. A. Richmond, *Catalogue of the Roman Inscribed and Sculptured Stones in the Grosvenor Museum, Chester*, 1955, p. 40, no. 92, pl. 26

## CHAPTER V

351 G. Calza, *La necropoli del Porto di Roma nell' Isola Sacra*, 1940, pp. 44, 54, 80 and figs. 9, 10

352 *Germania Romana*, ed. 2. ii, 1924, pls. 36, fig. 4 (Trier), 37, fig. 4 (Bingen)

353 T. May, *Catalogue of the Roman Pottery in the Colchester and Essex Museum*, 1930, pls. 80, no. 42 (red bricks: AD 55–100); 85, no. 80 (flanged roofing tiles: AD 100–150); 90, no. 13 (red bricks: AD *c.* 117–38); 90, no. 14 (flanged roofing tiles: AD 150–200)

354 J. M. C. Toynbee and J. B. Ward Perkins, *The Shrine of St Peter and the Vatican Excavations*, 1956, p. 143, fig. 12

355 *Eburacum* (Royal Commission on Historical Monuments, England), 1962, pl. 28 (above)
356 *Germania Romana*, ed. 2, ii, 1924, pl. 37, fig. 2
357 *Eburacum*, pl. 28 (below). See also L. P. Wenham, *The Romano-British Cemetery at Trentholme Drive, York*, 1968
358 Calza, *op. cit.*, pp. 55, 80 and fig. 10
359 *Eburacum*, pl. 27 (above)
360 Calza, *op. cit.*, pp. 53, 54 and fig. 13
361 E.g. *ibid.*, pp. 78, 366, no. 99 and fig. 29
362 *Ibid.*, p. 314, no. 51 *bis*
363 *Ibid.*, pp. 285, 286, no. 1
364 *Ibid.*, pp. 44, 314, no. 51 and fig. 9
365 *Ibid.*, p. 317, no. 56 and fig. 30
366 *Eburacum*, p. 74
367 *Ibid.*, pp. 79, 80
368 *Ibid.*, pp. 95, 96 and fig. 72
369 *Germania Romana*, ed. 2, ii, 1924, pl. 37, fig. 3
370 T. Ashby, *A Topographical Dictionary of Ancient Rome*, 1929, pp. 484–6; G. Lugli, *I monumenti antichi di Roma e suburbio*, i, 1931, pp. 432–9; E. Nash, *Pictorial Dictionary of Ancient Rome*, ii, 1962, pp. 352–6 (where a full bibliography will be found)
371 Lugli, *op. cit.*, pl. 7 opp. p. 432
372 *Ibid.*, p. 437
373 *Ibid.*, p. 438
374 Nash, *op. cit.*, p. 355, fig. 1131
375 Lugli, *op. cit.*, pp. 446–57; Nash, *op. cit.*, pp. 333–9
376 Nash, *op. cit.*, figs. 1103–5
377 *Ibid.*, figs. 1106–7
378 *Ibid.*, figs. 1108–10
379 Ashby, *op. cit.*, p. 482; Lugli, *op. cit.*, pp. 439–46; Nash, *op. cit.*, pp. 346–8
380 Lugli, *op. cit.*, iii, 1938 pp. 431–3; Nash, *op. cit.*, pp. 324–6. For a completely subterranean *columbarium* near Lake Fusaro, see A. De Franciscis and R. Pane, *Mausolei romani in Campania*, 1957, pp. 69, 73, figs. 49, 50
381 R. Meiggs, *Roman Ostia*, 1960, p. 457
382 *Ibid.*, pp. 457–8, fig. 31 and pl. 32, a
383 *Ibid.*, pp. 458–9, fig. 32 and pl. 32, b. For the interior of such an Ostian *columbarium*, with rows of niches in the walls, in the cemetery outside the *Porta Romana*, see F. M. Squarciapino, *Scavi di Ostia iii: Le necropoli i*, 1958, pl. 1, fig. 2 = Tomb 18 on the *Via Ostiensis*
384 *Notizie degli Scavi*, 1917, pp. 174–9, figs. 1, 2; *Capitolium*, xviii, 1943, pp. 268–78, figs. 2–12; Nash, *op. cit.*, pp. 349–51; L. Crema, *L'architettura romana*, 1959, pp. 126–7, fig. 115
385 O. Vessberg, *Studien zur Kunstgeschichte der römischen Republik*, 1941,

pls. 25, fig. 2; 26, figs. 1–3; 30, figs. 1, 2; 31, figs. 1–3; 35, figs. 1, 2; 38–43, figs. 1, 2; *Opuscula Romana*. v, 1965, pp. 134–5, no. 24, pl. 13. For a slab in the Louvre with five busts, two of them women with Flavian coiffure, see W. Altmann, *Die römischen Grabaltäre der Kaiserzeit*, 1905, fig. 160

386 A. Mau–F. W. Kelsey, *Pompeii: its Life and Art*, 1899, part iv, pp. 397–428 is still one of the best and most accessible accounts in English of Pompeian tombs

387 *Ibid.*, plan v, no. 2 (N. side of street)

388 *Ibid.*, no. 23 (S. side of street), p. 417, fig. 235; Franciscis, Pane, *op. cit.*, p. 17, fig. 5

389 Mau-Kelsey, *op. cit.*, no. 21 (S. side of street)

390 *Ibid.*, no. 1 (S. side of street)

391 *Ibid.*, nos. 2, 4 (S. side of street), p. 401, fig. 226; Franciscis, Pane, *op. cit.*, p. 19, fig. 8

392 Mau-Kelsey, *op. cit.*, p. 422

393 *Ibid.*, no. 9 (N. side of street), p. 406, fig. 228; Franciscis, Pane, *op. cit.*, pp. 37, 39, figs. 23, 24

394 Mau-Kelsey, *op. cit.*, p. 417

395 *Ibid.*, no. 18 (S. side of street) and pl. 9; Franciscis, Pane, *op. cit.*, p. 30, figs. 15, 16. For a cylindrical tomb at the fifth milestone on the *Via Appia*, see Crema, *op. cit.*, p. 494, fig. 636 (after Canina). For Greek forerunners of the Roman cylindrical masonry tomb, see, for example, Cyrene: *Papers of the British School at Rome*, xxiii, 1955, pp. 11–14, pl. 4

396 A. De Franciscis, *Pompei*, 1968, fig. 98

397 Mau-Kelsey, *op. cit.*, no. 3 (S. side of street), p. 401, fig. 226

398 *Ibid.*, no. 1 (N. side of street)

399 *Ibid.*, nos. 16, 17, 20, 22, pp. 410–16, figs. 232, 233, pl. 9; Franciscis, Pane, *op. cit.*, pp. 30, 32, 33, figs. 4, 15, 18–20: *ibid.*, p. 31, fig. 17 is the altar-tomb of Marcus Alleius Luccius Libella: Mau-Kelsey no. 37 (N. Side of Street)

400 For an Italian tomb of the late-first century BC with a similar 'canopy' sheltering a statue, but with only three columns (Ionic) and an entablature and a pyramidal roof that are concave and three-sided, set on a circular base and enclosed by low walls, see the Tomb of the Curtii at Aquileia: Crema, *op. cit.*, p. 260, fig. 289

401 Mau–Kelsey, *op. cit.*, plan v, no. 4a (S. side of street), pp. 401, 403, figs. 226, 227; Franciscis, Pane, *op. cit.*, pp. 18, 19, 21, figs. 6–9, 11, 12

402 Mau–Kelsey, *op. cit.*, no. 6 (N. side of street), p. 406, fig. 228; Franciscis, Pane, *op. cit.*, p. 35, figs. 21, 22

403 The same guess may be made with regard to Tomb no. 6 east of the amphitheatre, whose rectangular base is ornamented with engaged columns: Mau–Kelsey, *op. cit.*, pp. 426, 427, fig. 238

404 *Ibid.* no. 38 (N. side of street), pp. 418, 419, pl. 9

405 Outside the Nocera Gate is what would seem to be a variant of this type of

Pompeian tomb. Here the square base is surmounted, not by a ring of columns, but by four pilasters at its corners, each composed of a cluster of half-columns, whose shafts are of alternating courses of brick and stone, while their Corinthian capitals and bases are of marble. Some kind of roof must have completed the 'canopy' (Franciscis, *op. cit.*, fig. 97). *Cf.* the mausoleum with high square base, four corner-pilasters and pyramidal roof at Assar in Commagene (Crema, *op. cit.*, p. 260, fig. 287) and the mausolea at Brad and Dana in northern Syria (*Syria*, xxvi, 1949, pls. 13, fig. 2; 14, fig. 1)

406 G. Brusin and V. de Grassi, *Il mausoleo di Aquileia*, 1956; Crema, *op. cit.*, p. 259, fig. 284

407 H. Schoppa, *Die Kunst der Römerzeit in Gallien, Germanien und Britannien*, 1957, pl. 7; M. Pobé and J. Roubier, *The Art of Roman Gaul*, 1961, pl. 76

408 Ashby, *op. cit.*, p. 477; Lugli, *op. cit.*, iii, 1938, pp. 262–4 and fig. 56; Nash, *op. cit.*, pp. 319–20

409 Lugli, *op. cit.*, ii, 1934, pp. 173, 174; iii, 1938, p. 340; Nash, *op. cit.*, pp. 327–8

410 Ashby, *op. cit.*, p. 478; Lugli, *op. cit.*, iii, pp. 612–15; Nash, *op. cit.*, pp. 321–3 (where a full bibliography will be found)

411 Ashby, *op. cit.*, p. 479; Lugli, *op. cit.*, iii, pp. 493–5; Nash, *op. cit.*, pp. 329–32

412 Crema, *op. cit.*, p. 494, fig. 636

413 G. V. Gentili, etc., *Sarsina: la città romana, il museo archeologico*, 1967, p. 65, pls. 4, 5, fig. 3; S. Aurigemma, *I monumenti della necropoli romana di Sarsina*, 1963, pp. 89–94, figs. 93–9

414 Franciscis, Pane, *op. cit.*, pp. 68–71, figs. 46–8

415 Crema, *op. cit.*, pp. 247, 252, figs. 273–4

416 Franciscis, Pane, *op. cit.*, pp. 76, 78, 80, 86, 87, 89, 91, 93, 95–7, figs. 65–73; Crema, *op. cit.*, pp. 327, 332, figs. 379–80, where the monument is dated to the Flavian period

417 W. B. Dinsmoor, *The Architecture of Ancient Greece*, ed. 3, 1950, p. 330, pl. 71 (above)

418 *Bollettino del Museo Civico di Padova*, xlv, 1956, pp. 52–4, figs. 12, a–g

419 Gentili, etc., *op. cit.*, pp. 35–6, pls. 2, 4; Aurigemma, *op. cit.*, pp. 65–86, figs. 84–97

420 Gentili, etc., *op. cit.*, pp. 53–5, pls. 4; 5, figs. 1, 2; 6; Aurigemma, *op. cit.*, pp. 23–61, figs. 15, 16, 56–62

421 Crema, *op. cit.*, p. 499, fig. 645

422 *Ibid.*, p. 499, fig. 647

423 *Boletin de la Real Academia de la Historia*, i, 1877, pp. 440–6, pl. opp. p. 440 (front view); R. M. Pidal, *Historia de España ii: España Romana*, 1935, pp. 649, 651, figs. 444–5 (side and back views); B. Taracena, etc., *Ars Hispaniae*, ii, 1947, pp. 53, 56, 56, fig. 34; F. J. Wiseman, *Roman Spain*, 1956, pl. opp. p. 73 (front view)

424 E. Strong, *Art in Ancient Rome*, i, 1929, p. 172, fig. 211

425 R. Bianchi Bandinelli, etc., *Sculture municipali dell'area sabellica tra l'età di Cesare e quella di Nerone*, (Studi Miscellani 10, 1966) pp. 59–60

426 *Notizie degli Scavi*, 1926, pp. 106–18, pl. 4, a, and fig. 11; P. Marconi, *Agrigento*, 1929, pp. 122–4, figs. 75–8; Crema, *op. cit.*, p. 128

427 Crema, *op. cit.*, p. 494, figs. 639, 640. The tomb may be that of Herodes Atticus

428 See Chapter IV, Note 293

429 E.g. F. van der Meer and C. Mohrmann, *Atlas of the Early Christian World*, 1958, figs. 167–9

430 E.g. A. Ferrua, *La nuova catacomba di Via Latina*, 1960, pls. 85, 98. A temple-tomb which is not rectangular, but triconch, in shape is that of Claudia Antonia Sabina at Sardis, dating from the middle of the second century AD. It has a tetrastyle porch and steps leading up to the funerary chamber (C. Morey, *Sardis: the Sarcophagus of Claudia Antonia Sabina*, 1924, pp. 4–5, figs. 1, 2; Crema, *op. cit.*, pp. 564–5, fig. 746; A. Frova, *L'arte di Roma e del mondo romano*, 1961, pp. 761–2, fig 649)

431 *Papers of the British School at Rome*, iv, 1907, pp. 56–72; Touring Club Italiano volume *Roma e Dintorni*

432 *Memoirs of the American Academy in Rome*, iv, 1924, pp. 69–72, pls. 20–24 (Valerii); pp. 73–8, pls. 25–35 (Pancratii); Frova, *op. cit.*, 1961, pp. 414–15, figs. 384 (Pancratii), 385 (Valerii)

433 Frova, *op. cit.*, p. 93, fig. 77

434 *Ibid.*, pp. 92, 93, fig. 76; Crema, *op. cit.*, pp. 493, 495–6, fig. 641; *Die Antike*, iv, 1928, pp. 284–5, fig. 16

435 *Notizie degli Scavi*, 1923, pp. 46–79, pls. 9–16; J. Carcopino, *De Pythagore aux Apôtres*, 1956, pl. 17

436 *Ibid.*, pls. 21, 23, 24

437 *Ibid.*, pl. 18

438 *Memoirs of the American Academy in Rome*, iv, 1924, pp. 64–8, pls. 18, 19

439 Carcopino, *op. cit.*, pl. 22

440 The principal sources for the accounts that follow are G. Calza, *op. cit.*; Toynbee and Ward Perkins, *op. cit.*, Both of these books are amply illustrated

441 See, for example, Calza, *op. cit.*, pls. 1 and 4 (in colour)

442 The most complete series of illustrations of these stuccoes will be found in M. Guarducci, *Cristo e San Pietro in uno documento precostantiniano della necropoli vaticana*, 1953

443 *American Journal of Archaeology*, lxx, 1966, pp. 171–3, pl. 46

444 Strabo, v, 3, 8; *Papers of the British School at Rome*, x, 1927, pp. 23–35, pls. 9–19; *Capitolium*, x, 1930, pp. 7–51 (off-print); Lugli, *op. cit.*, iii, 1938, pp. 194–212; Crema, *op. cit.*, pp. 243–4, 246, figs. 263–6; Frova, *op. cit.*, pp. 53, 55, fig. 43; Nash, *op. cit.*, ii, 1962, pp. 38–43

445 Suetonius, *Aug.* 100: 'id opus inter Flaminiam viam ripamque Tiberis sexto suo consulatu extruxerat'

446 Suetonius, *Gaius* 15

447 Suetonius, *Claud.* 45

448 Suetonius, *Gaius* 59

449 *Ann.* xvi, 6

450 Dio Cassius, lxxix, 24

451 *American Journal of Archaeology*, xlvi, 1942, pp. 325–400; Crema, *op. cit.*, pp. 244, 249, fig. 268

452 See Note 443

453 *La tecnica edilizia romana*, i, 1957, p. 306, n. 1

454 M. E. Blake, *Ancient Roman Construction in Italy from the Prehistoric Period to Augustus*, 1947, p. 170; R. Fellmann, *Das Grab des Lucius Munatius Plancus bei Gaëta*, 1956; Crema, *op. cit.*, pp. 244, 247, 249, figs. 267, 269; Frova, *op. cit.*, p. 52, fig. 42

455 Crema. *op. cit.*, pp. 244, 249, fig. 270

456 *CIL* xiv, 3606; *Papers of the British School at Rome*, iii, 1906, pl. 6, fig. 12; Blake, *op. cit.*, p. 171; Crema, *op. cit.*, pp. 250, 253, figs. 276, 279; Frova, *op. cit.*, pp. 54–5, fig. 44

457 P. Ducati, *L'arte in Roma*, 1938, pl. 55, fig. 1; Blake, *op. cit.*, p. 170; Crema, *op. cit.*, p. 248; Frova, *op. cit.*, p. 55

458 Franciscis, Pane, *op. cit.*, pp. 104, 108, 110, 111, 113, figs. 85, 87, 88

459 *Ibid.*, pp. 110, 111, fig. 86

460 *Die Antike*, iv, 1928, p. 286, fig. 17; Blake, *op. cit.*, p. 171; Crema, *op. cit.*, pp. 248–51, 253, fig. 275; Frova, *op. cit.*, p. 55

461 See Note 443

462 *CIL* vi, 1274; 'Caeciliae Q(uinti) Cretici F(iliae) Metallae Crassi'

463 Franciscis, Pane, *op. cit.*, pp. 62, 63, 65, 66, 68, figs. 40–3; Crema, *op. cit.*, pp. 327, 329, figs. 377, 378

464 Franciscis, Pane, *op. cit.*, pp. 72, 74, 76, 81–5, fig. 57–64; Crema, *op. cit.*, pp. 326, 487, fig. 624

465 Franciscis, Pane, *op. cit.*, pp. 72, 77, 79, figs. 53–6

466 Crema, *op. cit.*, pp. 484–5; Frova, *op. cit.*, p. 763, fig. 650

467 Scriptores Historiae Augustae, *Hadrianus* 19: 'fecit et sui nominis pontem et sepulchrum iuxta Tiberim et aedem Bonae Deae'; *Antoninus Pius*, 5: 'Hadriano apud Balas mortuo reliquias eius . . . in hortis Domitiae collocavit'; *Journal of Roman Studies*, xv, 1925, pp. 75–103, pls. 12, fig. 1, 13–18; Lugli, *op. cit.*, iii, 1938, pp. 693–708; Crema, *op. cit.*, pp. 484, 487, figs. 622–3; Frova, *op. cit.*, pp. 83–4, fig. 69; Nash, *op. cit.*, ii, 1962, pp. 44–8

468 Dio Cassius, lxxix, 9

469 Frova, *op. cit.*, p. 671; S. Gsell, *Les monuments antiques de l'Algérie*, ii, 1901, pp. 97, fig. 112

470 Crema, *op. cit.*, p. 325
471 Crema, *op. cit.*, pp. 563, 565, figs. 744–5
472 Franciscis, Pane, *op. cit.*, pp. 87, 88, 90, 92, 94, 97–9, 100–7, 109, figs. 74–84; Crema, *op. cit.*, pp. 326, 328, figs. 371–3
473 Crema, *op. cit.*, p. 637; Frova, *op. cit.*, pp. 671–2
474 Crema, *op. cit.*, pp. 633, 636–7, figs. 842–3; Frova, *op. cit.*, pp. 671–2, fig. 583
475 *Die Antike*, iv, 1928, p. 289, fig. 19; Crema, *op. cit.*, pp. 625, 627, figs. 827–8; Frova, *op. cit.*, p. 103, fig. 83
476 Crema, *op. cit.*, pp. 625, 627–8, fig. 829; Frova, *op. cit.*, p. 104
477 Crema, *op. cit.*, pp. 625–6, figs. 825–6; Frova, *op. cit.*, p. 104; Nash, *op. cit.*, ii, 1962, pp. 268–71
478 D. S. Robertson, *A Handbook of Greek and Roman Architecture*, ed. 2, 1943, pp. 255–7, 317, figs. 108, 135; Crema, *op. cit.*, pp. 624–6, fig. 824; Frova, *op. cit.*, pp. 107, 594–5, fig. 540. For small hexagonal and octagonal, tower-like mausolea in northern Africa, see Gsell, *op. cit.*, pp. 93–7, figs. 109–11
479 J. G. Davies, *The Origin and Development of Early Christian Church Architecture*, 1952, pl. 9; Crema, *op. cit.*, pp. 628, 630, figs. 832–3; Frova, *op. cit.*, p. 107; W. F. Volbach, *Early Christian Art*, 1961, pls. 122–7, pp. 335–6, figs. 14, 15
480 Crema, *op. cit.*, p. 628; Frova, *op. cit.*, pp. 104–5
481 Robertson, *op. cit.*, pp. 257–8, fig. 109, pl. 19, b; Frova, *op. cit.*, pp. 105–6, fig. 85; Volbach, *op. cit.*, pls. 29–35, pp. 318–19, figs. 13, 14
482 *Madrider Mitteilungen*, ii, 1961, pp. 119–82, figs. 1–10, pls. 13–56
483 *Ibid.*, pp. 142, 181, pl. 26
484 Crema, *op. cit.*, p. 629; Frova, *op. cit.*, p. 108; Volbach, *op. cit.*, pl. 154, p. 342

## CHAPTER VI

485 *Die Antike*, iv, 1928, pp. 276–7, fig. 7; P. Marconi, *Agrigento*, 1929, pp. 124–7, figs. 79, 80
486 H. Dragendorff and E. Krüger, *Das Grabmal von Igel*, 1924; *Germania Romana*, ed. 2, iii, 1926, pp. 49–51, pl. 34; H. Schoppa, *Die Kunst der Römerzeit in Gallien, Germanien und Britannien*, 1957, pl. 69
487 R. M. Pidal, *Historia de España*, ii, 1935, pp. 648–9, figs. 440–1; B. Taracena, etc., *Ars Hispaniae*, ii, 1947, pp. 56–7, fig. 37; F. J. Wiseman, *Roman Spain*, 1956, pp. 115–16
488 S. Gsell, *Les monuments antiques de L'Algérie*, ii, 1901, ch. xiii, pp. 39–99
489 *Ibid.*, p. 67 and pl. 77

490 *Ibid.*, pp. 70–1, fig. 96
491 *Ibid.*, pp. 72–3, fig. 97
492 *Ibid.*, pp. 87–8, fig. 107 and pl. 82
493 *Ibid.*, p. 75, pl. 79; pp. 76–7, fig. 99 and pl. 80; p. 77, fig. 100
494 *Ibid.*, pp. 81–2, fig. 105
495 *Ibid.*, pp. 77–8, fig. 101 and pl. 81
496 *Ibid.*, pp. 61–2, fig. 94
497 *Ibid.*, pp. 71–2, pl. 78 (above)
498 *Ibid.*, pp. 80–1, fig. 104 and pl. 78 (below)
499 *Ibid.*, pp. 65–7, fig. 95
500 L. Crema, *L'architettura romana*, 1959, pp. 500, 503, fig. 652
501 *Ibid.*, pp. 500, 503, fig. 653
502 Ed. M. Rostovtzeff, etc., *Excavations at Dura Europos: Preliminary Report on the Ninth Season of Work ii: the Necropolis* (N. P. Toll), 1946, pp. 140–50
503 *Ibid.*, pls. 23, 62, fig. 1
504 *Ibid.*, pls. 24, 63
505 *Ibid.*, pl. 65
506 *Ibid.*, pl. 25
507 Hoyningen-Heune and D. M. Robinson, *Baalbek/Palmyra*, 1946, pls. on pp. 106, 124–7; *Syria*, xxvi, 1949, pp. 87–116; J. Starky, *Palmyre*, 1952, pp. 116–18, pl. 7, fig. 2; A. Frova, *L'arte di Roma e del mondo romano*, 1961, p. 764, fig. 651; M. A. R. Colledge, *The Parthians*, 1967, pp. 112–14, pl. 26
508 *Syria*, xxvi, 1949, pl. 5, fig. 2
509 *Ibid.*, fig. 9
510 *Ibid.*, pl. 6, fig. 1
511 *Ibid.*, pl. 6, fig. 2
512 *Ibid.*, pl. 5, fig. 1
513 Frova, *op. cit.*, p. 764, fig. 651
514 *Syria*, xxvi, 1949, figs. 5 and 22
515 See Notes 503, 504, 506
516 *Ibid.*, fig. 22
517 *Syria*, xxvi, 1949, pp. 258–312
518 *Ibid.*, figs. 2, 3
519 *Ibid.*, fig. 7
520 *Ibid.*, pl. 13, fig. 1
521 *Ibid.*, pl. 14, fig. 2
522 Colledge, *op. cit.*, pp. 111–12, fig. 23
523 J. Klemenc, *Rimske Izkopanine v Šempetru*, 1961
524 'Quintus Ennius Liberalis et Ennia Oppidana fecit sibi et Kalendinae filiae annorum XVII et Vitulo filio annorum XXX': Klemenc, *op. cit.*, pls. 33–40
525 'Caio Spectatio Caii filio . . . Prisciano duumviro iure dicundo . . . Caius Spectatius Finitimus duumvir iure dicundo Claudiae Celeiae pater . . .

infelicissimus fecit—Caiae Septimiaae Caii filiae Iustae annorum LV uxori Spectatii Prisciani': Klemenc, *op. cit.*, pls. 11–32

526 'Caius Vindonus Successus aedilis Claudiae Celeiae fecit sibi et Iuliae Sexti filiae Ingenuae uxori fidelissimae annorum L': Klemenc, *op. cit.*, pls. 4–10

527 'Caius Spectatius Secundianus vivus sibi fecit et Tutoriae Avitae coniugi carissimae annorum LV et Caio Spectatio Cervae filio annorum XXVIII et Caio Rusticio Tutori nepoti annorum XII': Klemenc, *op. cit.*, pls. 42–45

528 'Spectatiae Serverinae annorm XXV—Rusticium Albinu filio (?)—Spectatius Avitus annorum LXXX—Aurelia Severina'

529 'Statutius Secundianus et Cerva coniunx filio Statutio Secundo obito annorum IIII': Klemenc, *op. cit.*, pls. 49, 50

530 (i) *Africa Italiana*, vi, 1935, pp. 61–78, figs. 1–33; (ii) D. E. L. Haynes, *The Antiquities of Tripolitania*, 1955, pp. 153–61, fig. 21, pls. 28–31; (iii) *Illustrated London News*, 22 January 1955, pp. 138–42, figs. 1–20; (iv) *Ibid.*, 29 January 1955, pp. 182–5, figs. 1–22

531 (i) figs. 1–3; (ii) pl. 28; (iv) fig. 1

532 (i) figs. 4, 5, (ii) pl. 29; (iv) figs. 2, 3

533 (i) figs. 6, 10–12; (iv) figs. 4–10

534 (ii) pl. 30; (iii) figs. 16–19; (iv) figs. 11–22

535 (i) fig. 14; (ii) fig. 21, d

536 (i) figs. 26, 27; (ii) fig. 21, a

537 (i) fig. 16; *cf.* fig. 15; (ii) fig. 21, b; *cf.* pl. 31

538 (i) figs. 17–19; (ii) fig. 21, c

539 L. Canina, *La prima parte della Via Appia*, ii, 1853, pls. 29–31, 46

540 For provincial Roman-age tumuli in general, see C. Fox in *The Archaeology of the Cambridge Region*, 1923, pp. 191–200 (Britain); G. C. Dunning and R. F. Jessup in *Antiquity*, x, 1936, pp. 37–53, pls. 1–3 (Britain); R. F. Jessup in (i) *Journal of the British Archaeological Association*, ser. 3, xxii, 1959, pp. 1–11; (ii) in *Collection Latomus*, lviii, 1962, pp. 853–67, pls. 177–8 (Britain); M. Amand (i) in *Analecta Archaeologica: Festschrift Fritz Fremersdorf*, 1960, pp. 69–81, pls. 18, 19 (Belgium); (ii) *Nos tumulus splendeurs impériales*, 1969 (Belgium); H. Koethe, in (i) *Germania*, xix, 1935, pp. 20–24 with fig. 1; (ii) *Trierer Zeitschrift*, xiv, 1939, pp. 113–53 (Treviran region); E. Ewig, in *Trierer Zeitschrift*, xxi, 1952, pp. 11–13 (Treviran region)

541 Fox, *op. cit.*, pp. 76–80; J. and C. Hawkes, *Prehistoric Britain*, 1947, pp. 57, 69, 82, 97–8

542 *Archaeological Journal*, lxxxvii, 1930, p. 217

543 Hawkes, *op. cit.*, p. 106

544 *Ibid.*, p. 110

545 C. F. C. Hawkes and M. R. Hull, *Camulodunum*, 1947, p. 13. *Cf.* the small Belgic 'barrow' at Hurstbourne Tarrant, near Andover: *Archaeological Journal*, lxxxvii, 1930, pp. 304–9

546 See Note 540

547 See Note 540 and F. Cumont in *Comment la Belgique fut romanisée*, 1919, pp. 88–9, fig. 60; A. Grenier in *Manuel d'archéologie gallo-romaine*, ii, 1934, pp. 214–15, fig. 73

548 See Note 540

549 (i) M. Hell in *Mitteilungen der Anthropologischen Gesellschaft in Wien*, lxiv, 1934, pp. 129–46; (ii) M. Amand in *Latomus*, xxiv, 1965, pp. 614–28; list of sites, discussion of chronology and distribution

550 A. M. Mansel in *Archäologischer Anzeiger*, lvi, 1941, cols. 119–87

551 *Antiquity*, x, 1936, pl. 1 opp. p. 40

552 *Ibid.*, pl. 2; *VCH Essex*, iii, 1963, pp. 39–43, pl. 4A. The western row of three tumuli was destroyed by agricultural operations in 1832, but not before they had been excavated

553 *Cf.* the large tumulus on Mersea Island (Mersea Mount) in Essex, 110 feet in diameter and 22½ feet high, which contained a masonry chamber of tile and mortar: *VCH Essex*, iii, 1963, pp. 159–60

554 *Richborough III*, 1932, pp. 5, 25–9, pls. 3, 45

555 *VCH Suffolk*, i, 1911, p. 315

556 *Archaeologia Cantiana*, lxviii, 1954, pp. 1–61

557 *Sussex Archaeological Collections*, xi, 1859, pp. 141–2

558 I. A. Richmond, *The Romans in Redesdale* (*History of Northumberland* xv), 1940, pp. 104–5, figs. 25, 26

559 R. G. Collingwood and I. A. Richmond, *The Archaeology of Roman Britain*, 1969, p. 173, fig. 58; *Journal of the British Archaeological Association*, ser. 3, xxii, 1959, pl. 6, fig. 1. The square foundation could have supported a burial rather than a statue or altar and the niche could have contained another burial

560 *Journal of Roman Studies*, xiv, 1924, pp. 235–7, fig. 32

561 *Journal of the British Archaeological Association*, ser. 3, xxii, 1959, pl. 5, fig. 2; Collingwood and Richmond, *op. cit.*, pp. 171–2, fig. 57, a; *Current Archaeology*, xiv, 1969, pp. 73–5: this re-excavation and consolidation of the tomb produced no sign of the entrance marked in the two plans quoted above

562 A. W. Clapham in *Archaeological Journal*, lxxix, 1922, pp. 93–9, pl. 1 opp. p. 93, fig. 1, no. 1; *VCH Essex*, iii, 1963, p. 159, pl. 24A

563 Canina, *op. cit.*, pls. 31, 32; Clapham, *op. cit.*, pp. 94–5, fig. 1, no. 2

564 *Ibid.*, pp. 94–5, fig. 1, nos. 3, 4, 5

565 *Wiltshire Archaeological and Natural History Magazine*, lix, 1964, pp. 68–85

566 See Notes 540 and 547

567 *Antiquity*, x, 1936, pls. 4, 5 (between pp. 40, 41)

568 See Note 540 Amand (i) and *L'Antiquité Classique*, xxiii, 1954, pl. 4 opp. p. 445

569 For a stone-walled tumulus, 24 metres in diameter, recently found at Bill in Luxembourg, of classical type and containing a stone altar and urns, coins

and pottery that date it to *c.* 200–20, see *Antiquity*, xliii, 1969, p. 259; *Hémecht (Revue d'Histoire Luxembourgeoise)*, xxi, 1969, pp. 317–32, pls. 1–15, figs. 1–3. Here there was no trace of a *dromos* or central burial-chamber; and the main burial seems to have been in the urn-recess of of the altar, which appears to have been incorporated in the ring of the retaining wall. There was probably a central pillar that supported an external crowning motif

570 *Trierer Zeitschrift*, xiv, 1939, pp. 133, 135–6, 142

571 See Note 540, Koethe (i)

572 *Germania*, xvi, 1932, pp. 286–8; *Trierer Zeitschrift*, xiv, 1939, p. 149, fig. 13 (reconstruction)

573 See Note 549 (i)

574 *Fasti Archaeologici*, xviii–xix, 1968, pp. 730–1, no. 11019, with plan D at end of volume

575 See Note 550

575a For a Roman military cremation burial under a cairn of large boulders, see *Transactions of the Dumfriesshire and Galloway Natural History and Antiquarian Society*, ser. 3, xlvi, 1969, pp. 104, 107

576 C. Watzinger, *Denkmäler Palästinas*, ii, 1935, pp. 63–5, 71–3, pl. 11, figs. 32, 33; *Illustrated London News*, 29 October 1938, p. 777, figs. 1–3; N. Avigad, 'The Rock-carved Façades of the Jerusalem Necropolis' (*Israel Exploration Journal*, i, 1950–1, pp. 96–106); L. H. Vincent and M. A. Steve, *Jérusalem de l'ancien testament*, i, 1954, pp. 331–42, figs. 89–92, pls. 72–80

577 *ILN*, p. 779, fig. 6; Vincent and Steve, *op. cit.*, pl. 76

578 Watzinger, *op. cit.*, pp. 65–6, pl. 27, fig. 62; *ILN*, p. 779, fig. 12; Vincent and Steve, *op. cit.*, pp. 346–61, figs. 97–101, pls. 87–97

579 For a restoration on these lines, see *ibid.*, pl. 97

580 E.g. Watzinger, *op. cit.*, pl. 29, figs. 67, 68

581 *Ibid.*, pp. 74–6, pl. 30, figs. 6, 69, 70

582 Among the most important and accessible studies are: G. Dalman, *Petra und seine Felsheiligtümer*, 1908; R. E. Brunnow and A. von Domaszewski, *Die Provincia Arabia*, 1909; G. Dalman, *Neue Petra Forschungen*, 1912; T. Wiegand, *Petra*, 1921; A. B. W. Kennedy, *Petra: its History and Monuments*, 1925; A. Kammerer, *Pétra et la Nabatène*, 1929; M. Rostovtzeff, *Caravan Cities*, ch. ii, 1932; G. Lankester Harding, *The Antiquities of Jordan*, ch. vi, 1959; G. R. H. Wright, 'The Khazne at Petra: a Review' (*Annual of the Department of Antiquities of Jordan*, vi and vii, 1962, pp. 24–54, pls. 11–14. The belief that these rock-cut façades are those of tombs is not incompatible with Strabo's record (xvi, 4, 26) of the (perhaps temporary) revival in his day at Petra of the local custom of exposing bodies of kings in the open immediately after death: *Palestine Exploration Quarterly*, ci, 1969, pp. 113–16

583 *CIL* iii (Egypt and Asia), p. 17, no. 87; *Prosopographia Imperii Romani*, ii, 1897, pp. 84–5, no. 300

584 This view was communicated to me orally by the late Ian Richmond

585 See Note 582, Wright, *op. cit.*, pp. 38, 39 and n. 91

586 Wright, *op. cit.*, pp. 37, 40

587 G. R. H. Wright, 'Structure of the Qasr Bint Far 'un' (*Palestine Exploration Quarterly*, xciii, 1961, pp. 8–37)

588 P. J. Parr in *Jaarbericht van het Vooraziatisch-Egyptisch Genootschap Ex Oriente Lux*, xix, 1965–6 (1967), pp. 555–7

589 See especially, G. Bendinelli in *Monumenti Antichi*, xxviii, 1922, cols. 289–520, pls. 1–17; J. Carcopino, *De Pythagore aux Apôtres*, 1956, part ii, pp. 83–221, pls. 2–15a

590 For their arrangement, see the diagram in Carcopino, *op. cit.*, p. 144, fig. 5

591 Bendinelli, *op. cit.*, cols. 381–2, fig. 38; Carcopino, *op. cit.*, pl. 5 (lower left-hand fig.). Carcopino erroneously states (p. 93) that this painting is on the staircase-landing between the upper and lower levels of the tomb

592 F. Fremersdorf, *Das Römergrab in Weiden bei Köln*, 1957

593 G. Q. Giglioli, *L'arte etrusca*, 1935, pl. 95, fig. 1

594 Fremersdorf, *op. cit.*, pl. 9. *Cf.* also two stelai from Rumania: W. O. Doppelfeld, *Römer in Rumänien*, 1969, pls. 87, 90

595 A. Frova, *Pittura romana in Bulgaria*, 1943; *L'arte di Roma e del mondo romano*, 1961, pp. 588–90, figs. 535–8

596 *Cf.* the casket held by three chains by one of the bride's attendants at the centre of the back of the body of Projecta's silver toilet-box from the Esquiline Treasure: O. M. Dalton, *Catalogue of Early Christian Antiquities in the British Museum*, 1901, p. 63, pl. 16 (lower fig.); also the domed casket with figures of the Muses, likewise suspended by three chains, from the same treasure: *ibid.*, pp. 64–6, pl. 19

597 Ed. M. I. Rostovtzeff, etc., *The Excavations at Dura-Europos: Preliminary Report on the Ninth Season of Work ii; the Necropolis* (N. P. Toll), 1946

598 *Corpus Inscriptionum Semiticarum*, ii, part. 3, 4171–5, pl. 31; J. Starky, *Palmyre*, 1952, pp. 120–1, fig. 10; *Annales Archéologiques de Syrie*, xi–xii, 1961–2, pp. 13–18, pls. 1–16 (colour photographs)

599 *Syria*, xvii, 1936, pp. 354–5

600 The painted decoration of the tomb as a whole would appear to have been carried out at the time of its construction, while the portraits in the *clypeae* were added later, during the third century: *Annales* (see Note 598) pp. 15, 16

601 *Berytus*, ii, 1935, pp. 57–119, pls. 22–45

602 *Berytus*, v, 1938, pp. 93–140, pls. 34–50

603 *Annales Archéologiques de Syrie*, ii, 1952, pp. 193–251, pls. 1–12, with plans and figures

604 *Syria*, xvii, 1936, pp. 229–66, pls. 16–52; xix, 1938, pp. 153–60

605 *Syria*, xxvii, 1950, pls. 11, 12; A. Frova, *L'arte di Roma e del mondo romano*, pp. 814, 816, fig. 698; M. A. R. Colledge, *The Parthians*, 1967, pl. 37

606 For Jewish catacombs in general, in Rome and elsewhere, see especially H. Leclercq, *Manuel d'archéologie chrétienne*, i, 1907, pp. 495–528; O. Marucchi, *Le catacombe romane*, 1933, pp. 675–81; E. R. Goodenough, *Jewish Symbols in the Greco-Roman Period*, ii, iii, 1953, pp. 4–69, figs. 702–873; H. J. Leon, *The Jews of Ancient Rome*, 1960, pp. 46–66, 195–228, pls. 6–15, 23–7

607 Goodenough, *op. cit.*, pp. 33, 34

608 *Dissertazioni della Pontificia Accademia Romana di Archeologia*, ser. 2, ii, 1884, plan opp. p. 499; Leclercq, *op. cit.*, p. 503, fig. 137

609 *Dissertazioni, etc.*, ser. 2, xii, 1915, pp. 215–318, pls. 9, 10

610 Leclercq, *op. cit.*, p. 498, fig. 136; Goodenough, op. cit., fig. 734

611 *Ibid.*, fig. 735

612 Goodenough, *op. cit.*, fig. 789

613 H. W. Beyer and H. Lietzmann, *Jüdische Denkmäler I: Die jüdische Katacombe der Villa Torlonia in Rom*, 1930

614 *Ibid.*, pl. 31

615 Leclercq, *op. cit.*, p. 506, fig. 138; *Goodenough, op. cit.*, fig. 850

616 Leclercq, *op. cit.*, p. 507, fig. 139

617 The most important modern work on the Christian Roman catacombs is P. Styger's monumental *Die römischen Katacomben*, 1933. Useful general accounts will be found in O. Marucchi, *Le catacombe romane*, 1933, pp. 97–665; in L. Hertling and E. Kirschbaum, *The Roman Catacombs and their Martyrs*, 1960; and in P. du Bourguet, *La peinture paléo-chrétienne*, 1965. J. Wilpert's *Die Malereien der Katakomben Roms*, 1903, still remains the standard work on catacomb painting, in so far, at any rate, as its illustrations are concerned

618 *Jahrbuch für Antike und Christentum*, iv, 1961, pp. 130–1

619 T. Klauser, *Die Cathedra im Totenkult der heidnischen und christlichen Antike*, 1927

620 Leclercq, *op. cit.*, p. 464, n. 14

621 J. Führer and V. Schultze, *Die altchristliche Grabstätten Siziliens* (*Jahrbuch des Deutschen Archaologischen Instituts*, Erganzungsheft vii, 1907); M. I. Finley, *Ancient Sicily*, 1968, pp. 172–4

622 *Rivista di Archeologia Cristiana*, xxx, 1954, pp. 7–60, with plan opp. p. 60; xxxi, 1955, pp. 7–50

623 Finley, *op. cit.*, p. 173, fig. 8. There are also extensive Christian catacombs (third to fifth century) at Sousse in Tunisia

624 A. Ferrua, *Le pitture della nuova catacomba di Via Latina*, 1960

## CHAPTER VII

625 *Cambridge Ancient History*, vol. iv of plates, 1934, pp. 52–3, a; O. Vessberg, *Studien zur Kunstgeschichte der römischen Republik*, 1941, p. 264, pl. 24, fig. 2

626 A. N. Zadoks-Josephus Jitta, *Ancestral Portraiture in Rome*, 1932, pl. 4, a

627 *Ibid.*, pl. 4, b, c

628 *Ibid.*, pl. 5, a, b

629 Athens National Museum Inv. No. 2808; National Museum picture postcard

630 Vessberg, *op. cit.*, p. 270, pl. 38, fig. 3. *Cf.* a third-century AD stele from Turnu Severin, Rumania, with the busts of a husband and wife in a niche which takes the form of an *aedicula* with flanking colonnettes and arched top: ed. O. Doppelfeld, *Römer in Rumänien*, 1969, pl. 88

630a For Gaulish free-standing stelai incorporating a niche for a cinerary urn, see ed. P. Gilbert, *Bordeaux, capital d'Aquitaine*, 1968, p. 50, pl. 19

631 E.g. Germany: *Germania Romana*, ed. 2, iii, 1926, pls. 20–4; Danubian lands: A. Schober, *Die römischen Grabsteine von Noricum und Pannonien*, 1923, figs. 3–23; F. Cumont, *Recherches sur le symbolisme funéraire des Romains*, 1942, p. 229, figs. 48–50; Spain: *ibid.*, p. 237, figs. 54–9

632 E.g. *ibid.*, pl. 44; *Germania Romana*, ed. 2, iii, 1926, pls. 6, 7, 8, 9, figs. 1, 3 (cavalry stelai); pl. 29, figs. 1–4; Schober, *op. cit.*, figs. 43–5

633 *Germania Romana*, ed. 2, iii, 1926, pl. 26; S. Ferri, *Arte romana sul Danubio*, 1933, figs. 182, 183

634 Musée Villa des Arènes, Nice: (a) Titus Annius Firmus: a *vexillum* in each of the two upper panels; (b) Epicadus Velox: a sword in one, a dagger in the other, of the two upper panels. *Cf.* the tomb door legionary stele of L. Fabius from Tilurium (early-first century AD): J. J. Wilkes, *Dalmatia*, 1969, pl. 13

635 Vessberg, *op. cit.*, p. 273, pl. 45, fig. 2

636 For tall stelai with two tiers of busts, two in each tier, see W. Altmann, *Die römischen Grabaltäre der Kaiserzeit*, 1905, fig. 163 (Ny-Carlsberg Museum, Copenhagen); H. Schoppa, *Die Kunst der Römerzeit in Gallien, Germanien und Britannien*, 1957, pl. 48 (Utrecht Museum). For other north-Italian stelai with three tiers of busts, see S. Ferri, *Arte romana sul Reno*, 1931, figs. 54, 57, 58 (Ravenna), fig. 81 (Bologna)

637 E.g. Schober, *op. cit.*, figs. 143–8, 152; ed. Doppelfeld, *op. cit.*, 94, 95, 102: the medallion on pl. 102 was probably free-standing and mounted on a pillar: *cf.* Schober, *op. cit.*, figs. 164–79

638 E.g. *Germania Romana*, ed. 2, iii, 1926, pls. 1, 2, 16, fig. 3 (two tiers of busts), 17, fig. 3, 18, fig. 6; Schober, *op. cit.*, figs. 85–119, 121–42; Cumont, *op.*

*cit.*, pl. 10; ed. Doppelfeld, *op. cit.*, pl. 92 (one tier of three busts in a niche); pl. 93 (two tiers of three busts each in an *aedicula*)

639 Cumont, *op. cit.*, p. 156, fig. 25; Schober, *op. cit.*, fig. 99

640 *Jahrbuch des Deutschen Archäologischen Instituts*, xx, 1905, pp. 47–96, 123–55, figs. 22, 23, 26

641 Vessberg, *op. cit.*, p. 265, pl. 27; p. 268, pl. 34, fig. 3

642 *Ibid.*, 273, pl. 45, fig. 1

643 Inv. No. 1948.4.231

644 E.g. *Germania Romana*, ed. 2, iii, 1926, pls. 3–5; Schober, *op. cit.*, figs. 69–72, 74–8, 80; J. M. C. Toynbee, *Art in Roman Britain*, 1963, pls. 90, 93; *Art in Britain under the Romans*, 1964, pls. 46, 48, 49

645 E.g. *Germania Romana*, ed. 2, iii, 1926, pl. 15, fig. 1 (stele of Blussus and his wife at Mainz); Schober, *op. cit.*, fig. 73; Toynbee, 1963, pls. 85, 86; F. Benoit, *Art et dieux de la Gaule*, 1969, fig. 181 (stele of man seated, wife standing from Weisenau)

646 A. Conze, *Die attischen Grabreliefs iv*; *Römische Periode*, 1922, pp. 29–110, nos. 1831–2153, pls. vol. xvi, 1911, 388–400; xvii, 1913, 401–25; xviii, 1914, 426–50; xix, 1922, 451–72

647 *Ibid.*, p. 35, no. 1856, pls. xvi, 393

648 *Ibid.*, p. 37, no. 1872, pls. xvi, 397

649 *Ibid.*, p. 70, no. 2010, pls. xviii, 443

650 *Ibid.*, pp. 92–93, no. 2096, pls. xix, 460

651 *Ibid.*, p. 31, no. 1837, pls. xvi, 389

652 *Ibid.*, p. 47, no. 1921, pls. xvii, 411

653 *Ibid.*, p. 50, no. 1934, pls. xvii, 416

654 *Ibid.*, p. 59, no. 1971, pls. xvii, 424

655 *Ibid.*, p. 77, no. 2042, pls. xviii, 444

656 *Ibid.*, p. 79, no. 2049, pls. xviii, 448

657 *Ibid.*, p. 89, no. 2085, pls. xix, 457

658 E.g. of Marcus Julius Sabinianus and of Quintus Statius Rufinus: *ibid.*, pp. 102–3, nos. 2124, 2127, pls. xix, 469

659 *Ibid.*, p. 80, no. 2052, pls. xviii, 449

660 G. Brusin, *Kleiner Führer durch Aquileia und Grado*, 1958, p. 100, fig. 57 (Maia Severa); S. Ferri, *Arte romana sul Danubio*, 1933, p. 409, figs. 572, 573 (Maia Severa and Julia Donace). For the square Aquileian altar-like pillar-tomb of Gaius Oetius Rixa, with a Cupid on each of the two side faces, the inscription on the front, and unusually elaborate architectural features—corner pilasters and spirally fluted colonnettes, a heavy cornice, and an imbricated cone between two 'bolsters' on top—see *Aquileia Nostra*, xxvi, 1955, cols. 17–28, figs. 3–7; *Antiquaries Journal*, xlix, 1969, pp. 127–8, pl. 30

661 *Germania Romana*, ed. 2, iii, 1926, pls. 36, figs. 2, 3; 37, fig. 1; 38, 39, figs. 1, 2; 40, 47, figs. 1, 2; W. von Massow, *Die Grabmäler von Neumagen*, 1932

662 M. E. Mariën, *L'art en Belgique: la sculpture d'époque romaine*, 1945, describes and illustrates most of the important pieces

663 *Ibid.*, pls. 26–8

664 *Ibid.*, pls. 9, 10 and Arlon Museum picture postcards

665 *Ibid.*, pl. 11

666 *Ibid.*, pls. 24, 25; Benoit, *op. cit.*, figs. 193, 200

667 M. E. Mariën, *Les monuments funéraires de Buzenol*, 1948; *Germania*, xxxvi, 1958, pp. 386–92, pls. 49, 50, and fig. 3: *Archaeologia Belgica*, xlii, 1958, pp. 17–53, pls. 1–35, plans A–C; *Académie des Inscriptions et Belles-Lettres: Comptes rendus*, 1959, pp. 20–44; *Latomus*, xviii, 1959, 1, pp. 77–109, pl. 16; 2, pp. 307–33, pls. 27–9; *Fasti Archaeologici*, xiii, 1960, nos. 4967–70, 5159, figs. 91, 93–4; *Analecta Archaeologica=Festschrift F. Fremersdorf*, 1960, pp. 141–4, pls. 36–9

668 *Cf.* the round 'Liburnian' type of stele, e.g. that of Rubria Maximilla with conical top in the Split museum: Wilkes, *op. cit.*, pl. 22

669 E. Linckenheld, *Les steles funéraires en forme de maison chez les Médiomatriques et en Gaule*, 1927; J. J. Hatt, *La tombe gallo-romaine*, 1951, pp. 7, 39, 42, 76, 84, 126, 178, 219–20

670 Museu Regional de Beja, n.d., fig. 30; Portuguese National Archaeological Museum, Lisbon (Belém) picture post-card

670a For rare examples of leaden canisters with sparse decoration, see *Royal Commission on Historical Monuments (England), London iii (Roman)*, 1928, pl. 56, figs. 1, 2; *Hommages à Marcel Renard*, iii, 1960, pl. 201

671 W. Altmann's *Die römischen Grabaltäre der Kaiserzeit*, 1905, is still the standard analysis of these objects, although new material has obviously come to light since, for instance, in the Vatican necropolis. The Isola Sacra necropolis has produced surprisingly few decorated marble ash-chests or funerary altars: G. Calza, *La necropoli del Porto di Roma nell'Isola Sacra*, 1940, pp. 218–21

672 Altmann, *op. cit.*, p. 46, fig. 33

673 J. M. C. Toynbee and J. B. Ward Perkins, *The Shrine of St Peter and the Vatican Excavations*, 1956, pp. 95–6; Vatican coloured picture postcards, ser. v, 12; ser. vi, 2

674 *Royal Commission on Historical Monuments (England), London iii (Roman)* 1928, pl. 59; R. Merrifield, *Roman London* 1969, p. 135, fig. 34(b)

675 Altmann, *op. cit.*, pp. 110–1, figs. 90, 91; ed. H. Stuart Jones, *Catalogue of the Sculptures of the Museo Capitolino*, 1912, p. 91, no. 10, pl. 26; J. M. C. Toynbee, *The Hadrianic School*, 1934, pp. 216–17, pl. 49, figs. 2, 3, *CIL* vi, 21577

676 *Ibid.*, pp. 218–19, pl. 49, fig. 5

677 Altmann, *op. cit.*, pp. 238–9, 253, fig. 198

678 G. Brusin, *Il R. Museo Archeologico di Aquileia*, 1936, fig. 42. *Cf.* the tomb finial in the form of a wicker basket, with a pine-apple emerging from its

lid, found at Apulum (Alba Julia), Rumania: ed. Doppelfeld, *op. cit.*, pl. 30

679 Brusin, *op. cit.*, p. 13 and figs. 32, 33

680 Altmann, *op. cit.*, pp. 46, 47, figs. 34, 35

681 *Ibid.*, *op. cit.*, p. 20, fig. 12

682 *Ibid.*, pp. 20–1, fig. 13

683 *Ibid.*, pp. 46–7, figs. 36, 37. Similar decoration occurs on a *cinerarium* in the Ny-Carlsberg Museum, Copenhagen: *ibid.*, pp. 63–5, fig. 58

684 *Ibid.*, p. 67, fig. 60

685 Toynbee and Ward Perkins, *op. cit.*, pl. 21

686 Altmann, *op. cit.*, p. 99, fig. 83

687 *Ibid.*, p. 109, fig. 89

688 *Ibid.*, p. 120, fig. 97

689 *Ibid.*, p. 124, fig. 99

690 *Ibid.*, p. 165, fig. 134

691 *Ibid.*, p. 251, fig. 197

692 *Ibid.*, p. 256, fig. 200

693 *Ibid.*, pp. 26–7, fig. 19

694 *Ibid.*, pp. 38–42, figs. 23, 25, 26, 28–30; pp. 52–3, figs. 43, 44

695 *Ibid.*, pp. 38, 41, figs. 22, 27; pp. 50–1, figs. 39–41

696 For a piece on which the garland on the front encircles, not an inscription, but the portrait-bust of the deceased, the former being relegated to the *podium* of the altar below, see the Flavian altar of Junia Procula in the Uffizi Gallery, Florence: E. Strong, *La scultura romana*, i, 1923, p. 125, fig. 79

697 Altmann, *op. cit.*, pp. 101–3, fig. 85

698 *Ibid.*, p. 122, fig. 98

699 *Ibid.*, pp. 116–17, pl. 1

700 *Ibid.*, pp. 154, 163, figs. 125, 126, 132

701 *Ibid.*, p. 158, fig. 129; Cumont, *op. cit.*, p. 96, fig. 14

702 *Revue Archéologique*, ser. 3, xxxiii, 1898, pp. 11–14, pl. 10 opp. p. 152

703 Toynbee and Ward Perkins, *op. cit.*, pl. 20

704 Cumont, *op. cit.*, pp. 243–4, pls. 21, 22. Another very fine altar carved on all four sides, of Julio-Claudian date and now in the Museo Nazionale Romano, shows scenes from the 'mystic marriage' of a man and wife: *Le Arti*, iv, 1941–2, pp. 163–9, pls. 51, 52, figs. 4–6; J. M. C. Toynbee, *The Art of the Romans*, 1965, pl. 58

705 Cumont, *op. cit.*, pp. 457–62, pl. 45

706 Altmann, *op. cit.*, p. 191, fig. 153

707 *Ibid.*, pp. 192–3, fig. 154

708 *Ibid.*, p. 56, fig. 48

709 *Ibid.*, p. 219, fig. 180

710 *Ibid.*, pp. 210–14, 216–18, figs. 168, 170–3, 175, 177, 178

711 *Ibid.*, p. 204, fig. 161; ed. Stuart Jones, *op. cit.*, pl. 23, no. 65. For a funerary banquet scene with an elaborate couch, see G. W. Goethert, 'Grabara des Q. Socconius Felix' (*Antike Plastik*, ix, 1969, pp. 79–86, fig. 1, pl. 50)

712 See Chapter IV, Note 293. *Cf.* the *cinerarium* of Lorania Cypare in the Louvre: Goethert, *op. cit.*, fig. 14, pl. 55

713 Altmann, *op. cit.*, p. 58, fig. 50; Strong, *op. cit.*, pl. 23

714 Cumont, *op. cit.*, pl. 41, fig. 3; Toynbee, *op. cit.*, pl. 56

715 Cumont, *op. cit.*, p. 401, fig. 80

716 *Ibid.*, pl. 41, fig. 4. This couch could indeed be the lid of the early-third-century sarcophagus on which it now rests, but there seems to be no proof that they originally belonged to one another

717 *Ibid.*, pl. 42, fig. 1

718 W. Amelung, *Die Sculpturen des Vatikanischen Museums*, ii, 1908, pl. 1, no. 1. A relief of the same period in the Museo Nazionale Romano (Aula VI, no. 115174) shows a married pair reclining on a *kline* flanked by Cupid and Psyche. For the attitude of the sleeping woman on the Vatican couch, *cf.* that of Licinia Chrysis depicted in relief on a *kline* on her 'Aschenaltar', also in the Vatican: Altmann, *op. cit.*, p. 168, fig. 137

719 Cumont, *op. cit.*, pl. 43, fig. 1

720 *Ibid.*, pl. 43, fig. 2

721 *Ibid.*, pl. 41, fig. 1

722 J. M. C. Toynbee, *The Hadrianic School*, 1934, p. 164, pls. 37, figs. 1, 2; 43, fig. 1

723 Toynbee and Ward Perkins, *op. cit.*, pp. 55–7, pl. 7. The two small sarcophagi now standing on the floor of this tomb were moved there by the excavators from the Tomb of the Tullii, where Constantine's builders appear to have placed them

724 K. Lehmann-Hartleben and E. C. Olsen, *Dionysiac Sarcophagi in Baltimore*, 1942

725 Brief general discussions of these subjects will be found in D. E. Strong, *Roman Imperial Sculpture*, 1961, pp. 46–50, 53–5, 65–71 and in J. M. C. Toynbee, *The Art of the Romans*, 1965, pp. 95–107

726 For a detailed discussion of the afterlife symbolism of the mythological sarcophagi, see J. Ferguson, *The Religions of the Roman Empire*, 1970, Ch. viii

727 For Attic *kline* sarcophagi in general, see *Jahrbuch des Deutschen Archäologischen Instituts*, xlv, 1930, pp. 116–89

728 For Asiatic sarcophagi in general, see C. R. Morey, *The Sarcophagus of Claudia Antonia Sabina and the Asiatic Sarcophagi* (= *Sardis*, v, i), 1924

729 *Ibid.*, figs. 39–41

730 B. Andreae, *Studien zur römischen Grabkunst*, 1963, pl. 1–29

731 For Christian sarcophagi in general, see J. Wilpert, *I sarcofagi cristiani antichi*, 1929–36; F. Gerke, *Die christichen Sarkophage der vorkonstantinischen*

*Zeit*, 1940; M. Lawrence, *The Sarcophagi of Ravenna*, 1945; T. Klauser, *Frühchristliche Sarkophage in Bild und Wort*, 1966

732 E.g. F. Gerke, *Der Sarkophag des Iunius Bassus*, 1936

733 E.g. S. Ferri, *Arte romana sul Danubio*, 1933, pp. 365–9, figs. 492–500

734 *Ibid.*, pp. 368, 370, fig. 501

735 *Ibid.*, pp. 243–51, figs. 295–307

736 *Bonner Jahrbücher*, 1845, pp. 94–100, pls. 3, 4; S. Ferri, *Arte romana sul Reno*, 1931, pp. 164, 255–8, figs. 164–7; pp. 284–7

737 F. Fremersdorf, *Die Denkmäler des römischen Köln*, ii, 1950, pl. 81

738 *Germania Romana*, ed. 2, iii, 1926, pl. 48, fig. 1

739 *Eburacum*, 1962, p. 130, no. 107, pls. 56, 59

740 York, Julia Fortunata, with gabled lid: *ibid.*, p. 130, no. 106, pl. 57; London: *Royal Commission on Historical Monuments (England)*, *London iii (Roman)*, 1928, pl. 57

741 *Ibid.*, pl. 57. The marble sarcophagus from Clapton, with the bust of a woman in the centre of the front, a pilaster at either corner, and fluted areas between, was almost certainly imported from the continent: *ibid.*, pl. 57

742 J. M. C. Toynbee, *Art in Britain under the Romans*, 1964, pp. 345–53

743 E.g. Saint Auban (Basses Alpes): F. Benoit, *L'art primitif méditerranéen de la vallée du Rhône*, 1945, pl. 4, fig. 2; Beauvais: *Revue Archéologique*, xv, 1858, pp. 475–7, pl. 343, figs. 1–3, 5, 6; Boulogne-sur-Mer: E. Espérandieu, *Receuil général des bas-reliefs, statues et bustes de la Gaule romaine*, v, 1913, no. 3969, fig. on p. 181

744 E.g. Peffingen: *Germania Romana*, ed. 2, v, 1930, pl. 18, fig. 6

745 See especially, *Quarterly of the Department of Antiquities of Palestine*, i, 1932, p. 36, pl. 29; ii, 1933, p. 185; iv, 1935, pp. 87–99, figs. 1–5, pls. 55–60; pp. 138–53, figs. 1–4; *Syria*, x, 1929, pp. 238–51, figs. 1–5, pls. 44–6; xv, 1934, pp. 337–50 with 5 figs., pls. 41–8; xvi, 1935, pp. 51–72 with 11 figs., pls. 12–18; *Journal of Hellenic Studies*, l, 1930, pp. 300–12, pl. 12; lii, 1932, pp. 262–3, pls. 11, 12; *Jahrbuch des Deutschen Archäologischen Instituts; Archäologischer Anzeiger*, xlvii, 1932, cols. 387–446, figs. 1–47; li, 1936, cols. 252, 255–81, figs. 1–22; *Berytus*, iii, 1936, pp. 51–75, figs. 1–3, pls. 9–16; v, 1938, pp. 27–46, figs. 1, 2, pls. 5–13; vi, 1939, pp. 27–61, fig. 2, pls. 5–17; *Mélanges de l'Université Saint-Joseph, Beyrouth*, xxi, 1937–8, pp. 203–12, fig. 1, pls. 52, 53

746 *Archaeologia Cantiana*, lxviii, 1954, pp. 19, 34–46, pls. 13, 14

747 See Note 744

748 *Antiquaries Journal*, xxxiii, 1953, pls. 72–4, fig. 1 and pl. 17

749 Britain: *Archaeologia*, xvii, 1814, pl. 25, fig. 2; Syria and Palestine: *Syria*, xxx, 1953, pl. 7, fig. 1; *Berytus*, vi, 1939–40, pl. 7, fig. 3; *Syria* xv, 1934, pl. 44, no. 11

750 *Syria*, xvi, 1935, p. 52, no. 27, pl. 13

751 *Journal of Roman Studies*, xxviii, 1938, pp. 60–4, pls. 6–8; *The Connoisseur*,

April, 1965, colour-plate on p. 218 and fig. 14 on p. 222 (Hever Castle, Kent)

752 *Journal of the Walters Art Gallery, Baltimore*, 1948, pp. 10–13

753 E.g. ed. O. Doppelfeld, *op. cit.*, pls. 76, 77, 79

754 J. M. C. Toynbee, *Art in Roman Britain*, 1963, pl. 52

755 Espérandieu, *op. cit.*, xii, 1947, pl. 17, no. 7888, 1, 2

756 *Ibid.*, i, 1907, pp. 276–7, nos. 396–8

757 E.g. A. Brueckner, *Der Friedhof am Eridanos*, 1909, figs. 45, 47–9; M. Collignon, *Les statuaires funéraires dans l'art grec*, 1911, figs. 147, 148, 154, 155, 158; J. Charbonneaux and E. Peters, *Greece in Photographs*, 1954, pls. 91, 92

758 S. Ferri, *Arte romana sul Danubio*, 1933, figs. 339–57

759 S. Ferri, *Arte romana sul Reno*, 1931, figs. 122–5; Fremersdorf, *op. cit.*, pl. 67

760 *Royal Commission on Historical Monuments (England), London, iii (Roman)*, 1928, pp. 102–3, fig. 26, pl. 11

761 E. J. Hollingworth and M. M. O'Reilly, *The Anglo-Saxon Cemetery at Girton College, Cambridge*, 1925, pp. 35–6, pl. 9. For other Romano-British lions that are likely to have been sepulchral in function, see J. M. C. Toynbee, *Art in Britain under the Romans*, 1964, pp. 114–15, n. 3 on p. 115

762 S. Ferri, *Arte romana sul Danubio*, 1933, figs. 368–9

763 Toynbee, *op. cit.*, pl. 29, a. For a very inferior Sphinx at York, see *Eburacum*, 1962, pl. 62, no. 120

764 Fremersdorf, *op. cit.*, pls. 68, 69

765 Brueckner, *op. cit.*, figs. 34, 35

766 Toynbee, *op. cit.*, p. 114, pl. 29, b

767 R. P. Wright and I. A. Richmond, *Catalogue of the Inscribed and Sculptured Stones in the Grosvenor Museum, Chester*, 1955, p. 55, no. 168, pl. 40

768 *Eburacum*, 1962, p. 132, no. 130, pl. 61

769 *Ibid.*, p. 133, no. 138, pl. 60

770 *Op. cit.*, p. 103, fig. 85, and Chapter X

771 *Journal of Roman Studies*, v, 1915, p. 158, fig. 40

772 *Ibid.*, p. 153

773 *Antiquaries Journal*, xxvi, 1946, pp. 1–10, pl. 1; *Eburacum*, 1962, p. 133, no. 137, pl. 60

774 Espérandieu, *op. cit.*, xi, 1938, pp. 107–9, no. 7795 with figs.; F. Cumont, *Lux Perpetua*, 1949, pl. 1. *Cf.* Notes 88 and 107

166 (continued) For other examples of surviving fragments of the textiles in which corpses were wrapped, see J. P. Wild, *Textile Manufacture in the Northern Roman Provinces*, 1970

254 (continued) (*Cf.* the will of Gaius Popilius Heracla inscribed above the door of Tomb A in the St Peter's necropolis: Toynbee and Ward Perkins, *op. cit.*, pp. 9, 10)

# SOURCES OF ILLUSTRATIONS

## PLATES

1, 2, Museo Villa Giulia; 3, 6, 9, 11, 12, 17, 20, 28, 32, 34, 36, 37, 38, 41, 42, 52, 66, 74, 84, Mansell-Alinari; 4, 5, Soprintendenza Antichità, Florence; 7, Leonard von Matt; 8, 18, 19, 27, 30, 33, 35, 39, 40, 43, 44, 49, 50, 51, Fototeca Unione; 10, Château de Versailles (S. et O.); 13, National Museum, Copenhagen; 14, National Museum of Wales, Cardiff; 15, 16, Ray Gardner (from coins in the British Museum); 22, 23, Colchester and Essex Museum; 24, R.C.H.M. (England), Crown Copyright Reserved; 25, L. P. Wenham; 26, 29, 45, 85, Deutschen Archäologischen Instituts, Rome; 46, 48, 87, Renato Sansaini, Rome; 47, Reverenda Fabbrica della Basilica di San Pietro, Rome; 53, 54, 55, Max Hirmer; 56, Mas, Barcelona; 57, Landesmuseum, Trier; 58, 60, Institut Français d'Archéologie, Beirut; 61, 62, Celeia Museum; 65, Lady Brogan; 67, Professor J. K. St. Joseph; 68, R. F. Jessup; 70, Ronald Sheridan; 75, Pontifico Instituto di Archeologia Sacra; 79, 88, 89, Trustees of the British Museum; 81, Professor D. Fernando de Almeida, Belém Museum; 86, Deutschen Archäologischen Instituts, Istanbul; 90, Rheinisches Bildarchiv, Cologne Museum; 91, 92, National Museum of Antiquities, Leiden; 31, 63, 64, 76, 77, 78, 80, 82, 83, Thames and Hudson Archives; 21, 59, 69, 71, 72, 73, from photographs supplied by the author.

## FIGURES

1, after Messerschmidt; 2, after Brusin; 3, 4, after Toynbee and Ward Perkins; 5, after *JBAA*; 6, after *Arch. Ael.*; 7, 8, after *Mitt. Deutsch. Arch. Inst.; Röm. Abt.;* 9, after Nash; 10, after Meiggs; 11, after Mau-Kelsey; 12, 13, after Calza; 14, after *Capitolium*; 15, after *Madrider Mitt.*; 16, 23, 24, 25, after Rostovtzeff; 17, after *Hémecht*; 18, after *Fasti Arch.*; 19, 20, after *Mon. Antichi*; 21, after Fremersdorf; 22, after Frova; 26, after *Berytus*; 27, after *Ann. Arch. de Syria*; 28, after *Syria*; 29, after Führer-Schultze; 30, after Ferrua.

# INDEX